Tegami Bachi
LETTER · BEE

VOLUME 8

LIGHT·SHINING·UPON·DARKNESS

STORY AND ART BY
HIROYUKI ASADA

This is a country known as Amberground, where night never ends.

Its capital, Akatsuki, is illuminated by a man-made sun. The farther one strays from the capital, the weaker the light. The Yuusari region is cast in twilight; the Yodaka region survives only on pale moonlight.

Letter Bee Gauche Suede and young Lag Seeing meet in the Yodaka region—a postal worker and the "letter" he must deliver. In their short time together, they form a fast friendship, but when the journey ends, each departs down his own path. Gauche longs to become Head Bee, while Lag himself wants to be a Letter Bee, like Gauche.

After his interview, Lag learns from Zazie, the observer for his test, that Gauche is no longer a Letter Bee. Lag seeks out Sylvette, Gauche's sister, only to discover that Gauche was dismissed from his post and vanished.

After a difficult search, Lag discovers that Gauche has lost his *heart* and become a marauder named Noir, working for the rebel organization Reverse. Lag's only hope for saving Gauche is a Shindan called Letter Bullet, which may awaken his lost memories. In the town of Lament, Lag and his fellow Letter Bees stumble upon a Reverse hideout...

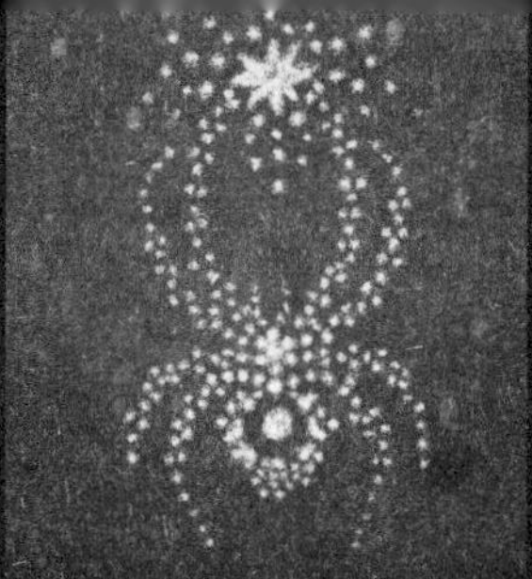

Before this manga launched, I had several possible titles in mind. I did a search on the Internet and found that one title brought up no matches. There was not a single instance of this phrase used anywhere in the world. No stories.

"Letter Bee."

Now that this series has reached volume 8, "Letter Bee" appears all over the Internet. I am grateful.

–Hiroyuki Asada, 2009

Hiroyuki Asada made his debut in *Monthly Shonen Jump* in 1986. He's best known for his basketball manga *I'll*. He's a contributor to artist Range Murata's quarterly manga anthology *Robot*. *Tegami Bachi: Letter Bee* is his most recent series.

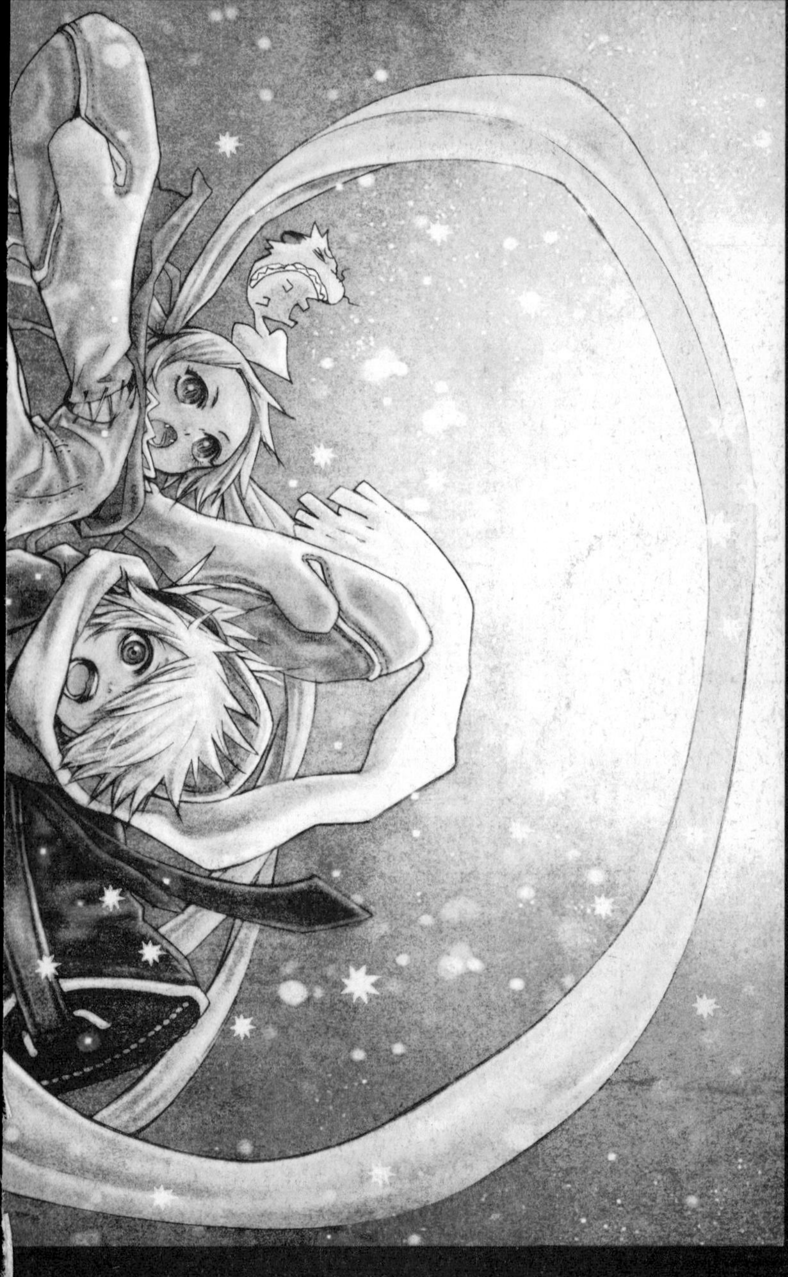

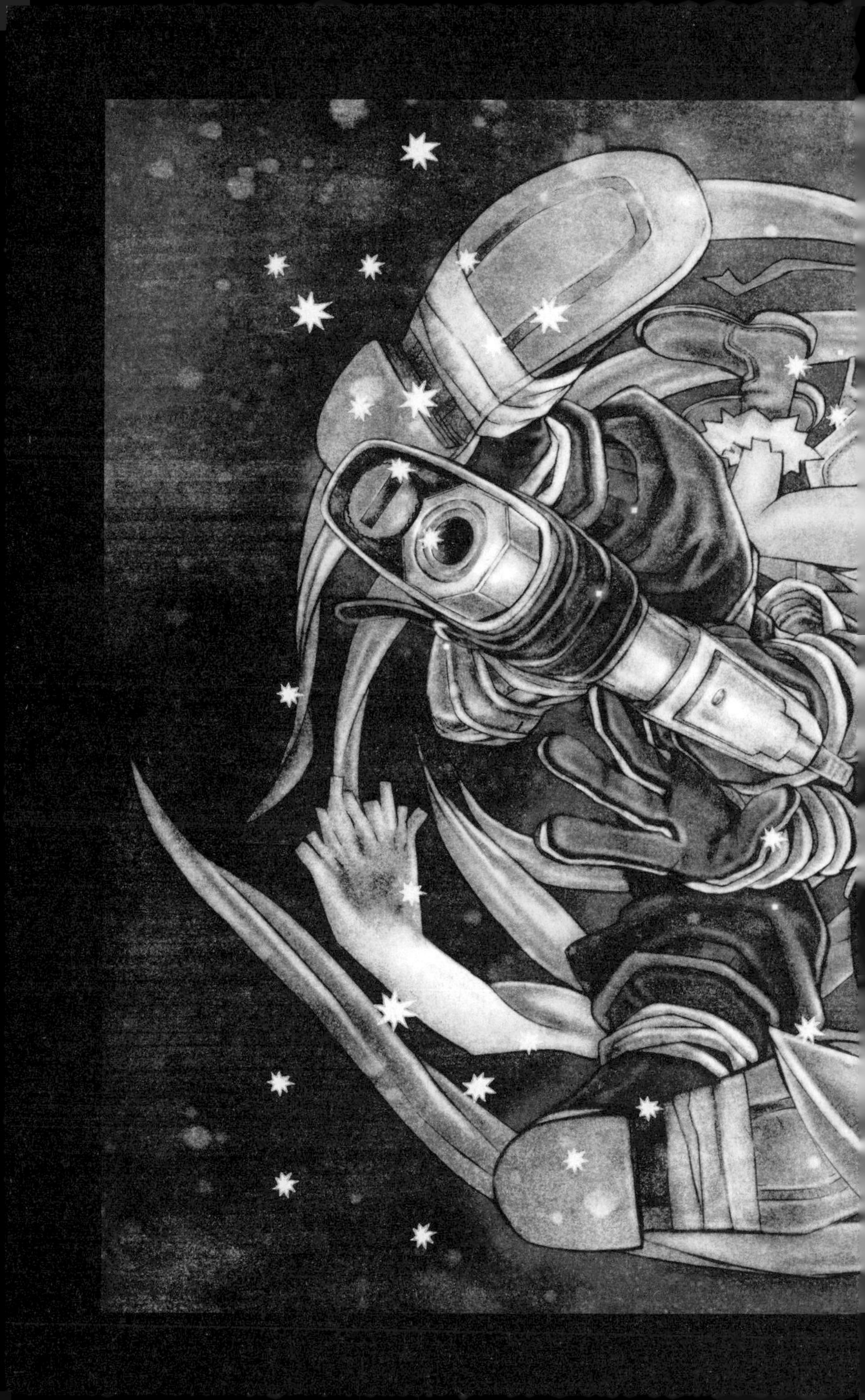

TEEN GRAPHIC
Tegami Bachi
v.8

3 1712 01392 6822

Volume 8

SHONEN JUMP Manga Edition

Story and Art by Hiroyuki Asada

English Adaptation/Rich Amtower
Translation/JN Productions
Touch-up & Lettering/Annaliese Christman
Design/Amy Martin
Editor/Shaenon K. Garrity

TEGAMIBACHI © 2006 by Hiroyuki Asada. All rights reserved.
First published in Japan in 2006 by SHUEISHA Inc., Tokyo. English
translation rights arranged by SHUEISHA Inc.

The rights of the author(s) of the work(s) in this publication to be so
identified have been asserted in accordance with the Copyright, Designs
and Patents Act 1988. A CIP catalogue record for this book is available
from the British Library.

Printed in the U.S.A.

Published by VIZ Media, LLC
P.O. Box 77010
San Francisco, CA 94107

10 9 8 7 6 5 4 3 2 1
First printing, February 2012

www.viz.com

THE WORLD'S
MOST POPULAR MANGA
SHONEN JUMP
www.shonenjump.com

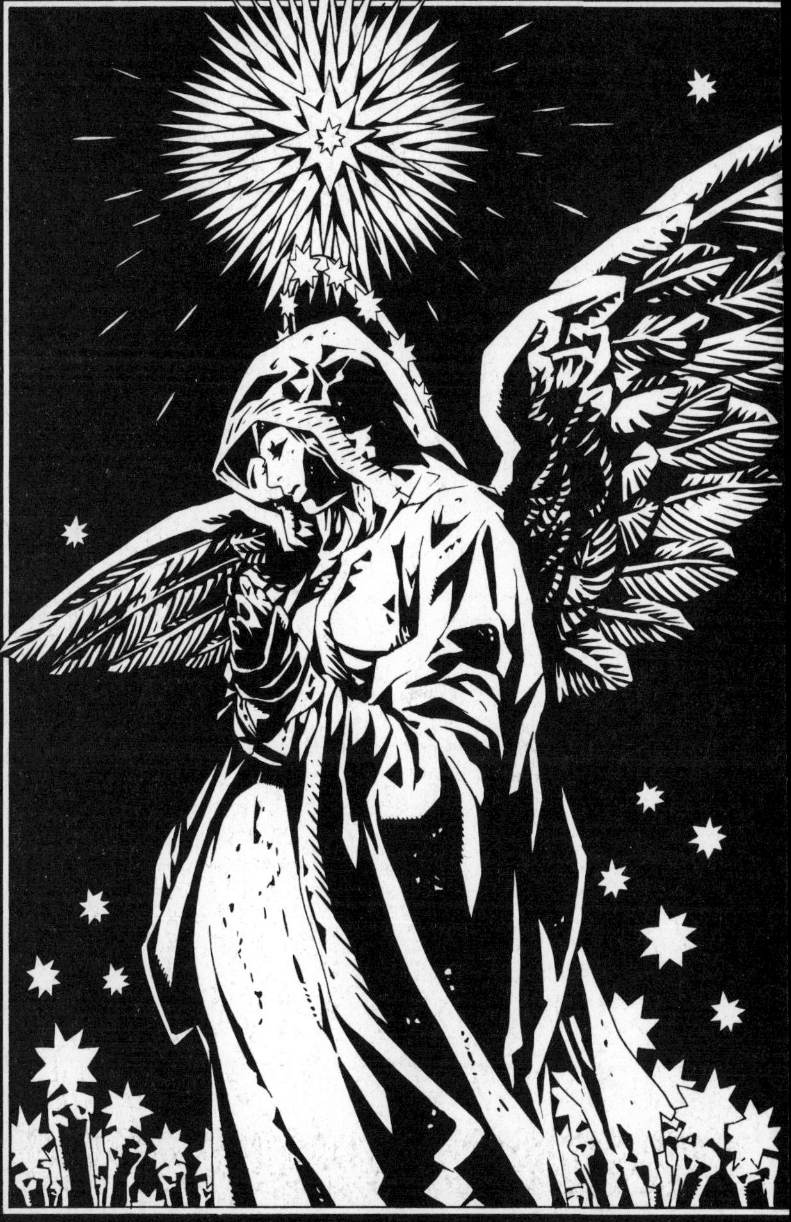

List of Characters

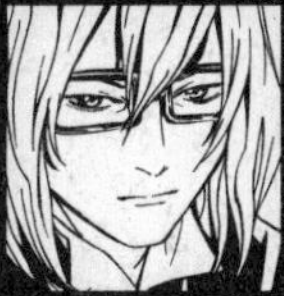

LARGO LLOYD
Beehive Director

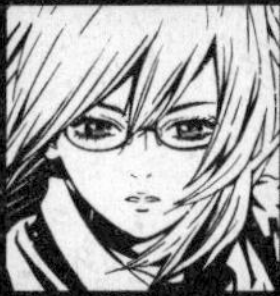

ARIA LINK
Beehive Assistant Director

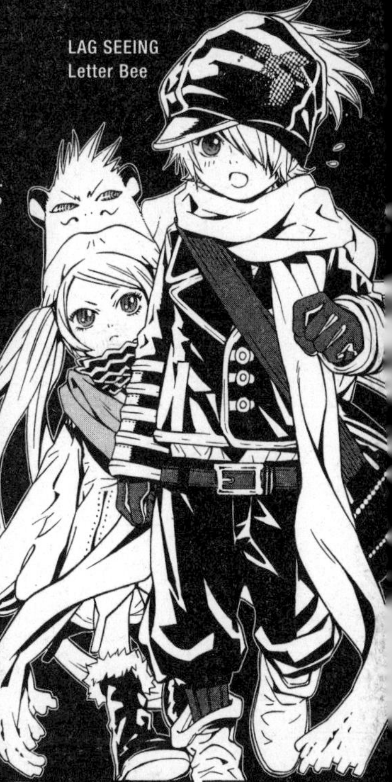

LAG SEEING
Letter Bee

STEAK
Niche's... live bait?

NICHE
Lag's Dingo

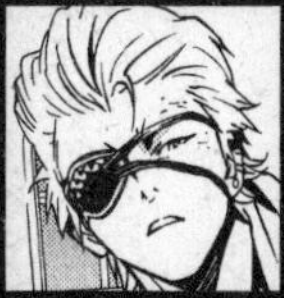

DR. THUNDERLAND, JR.
Member of the AG Biological Science Advisory Board, Third Division and head doctor at the Beehive

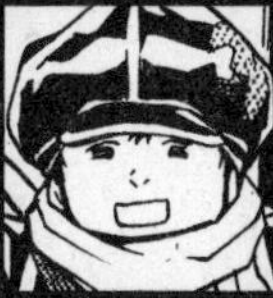

CONNOR KLUFF
Letter Bee

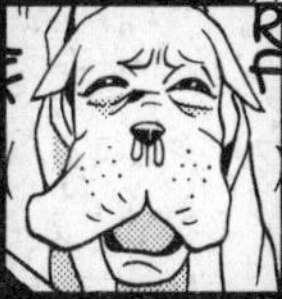

GUS
Connor's Dingo

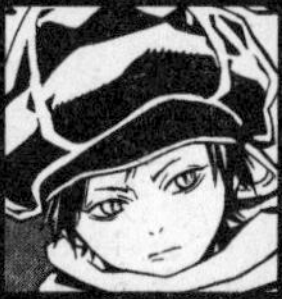

ZAZIE
Letter Bee

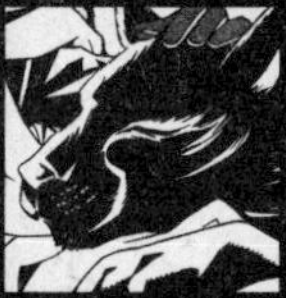

WASIOLKA
Zazie's Dingo

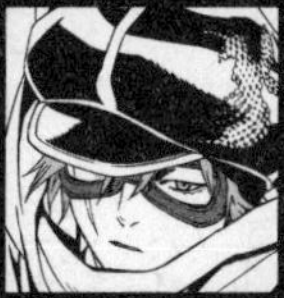

JIGGY PEPPER
Express Delivery Letter Bee

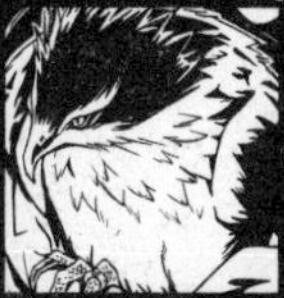

HARRY
Jiggy's Dingo

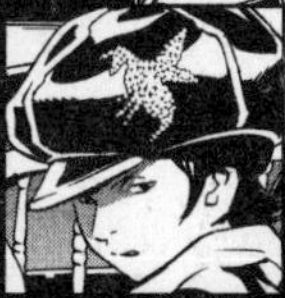

MOC SULLIVAN
Letter Bee

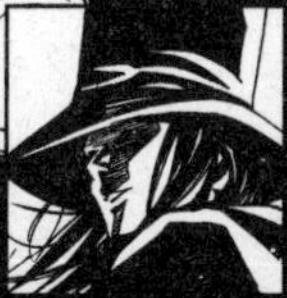

THE MAN WHO COULD NOT BECOME SPIRIT
The ringleader of Reverse

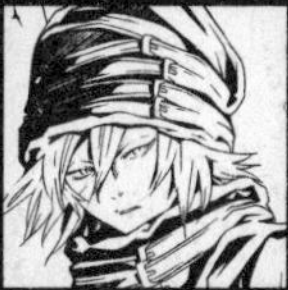

NOIR (FORMERLY GAUCHE SUEDE)
Marauder for Reverse and an ex–Letter Bee

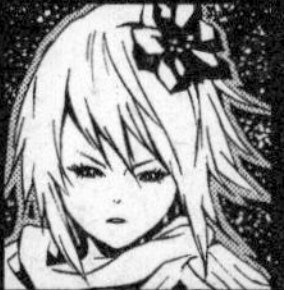

RODA
Noir's Dingo

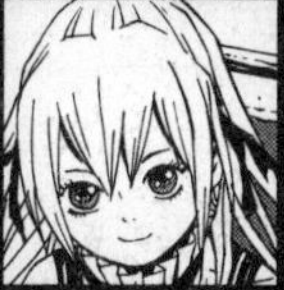

SYLVETTE SUEDE
Gauche's Sister

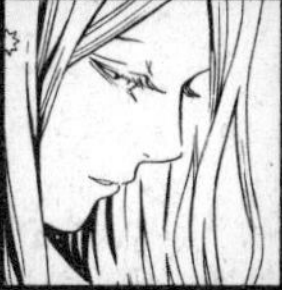

ANNE SEEING
Lag's Mother (Missing)

Tegami Bachi

LETTER • BEE

VOLUME 8

LIGHT SHINING UPON DARKNESS

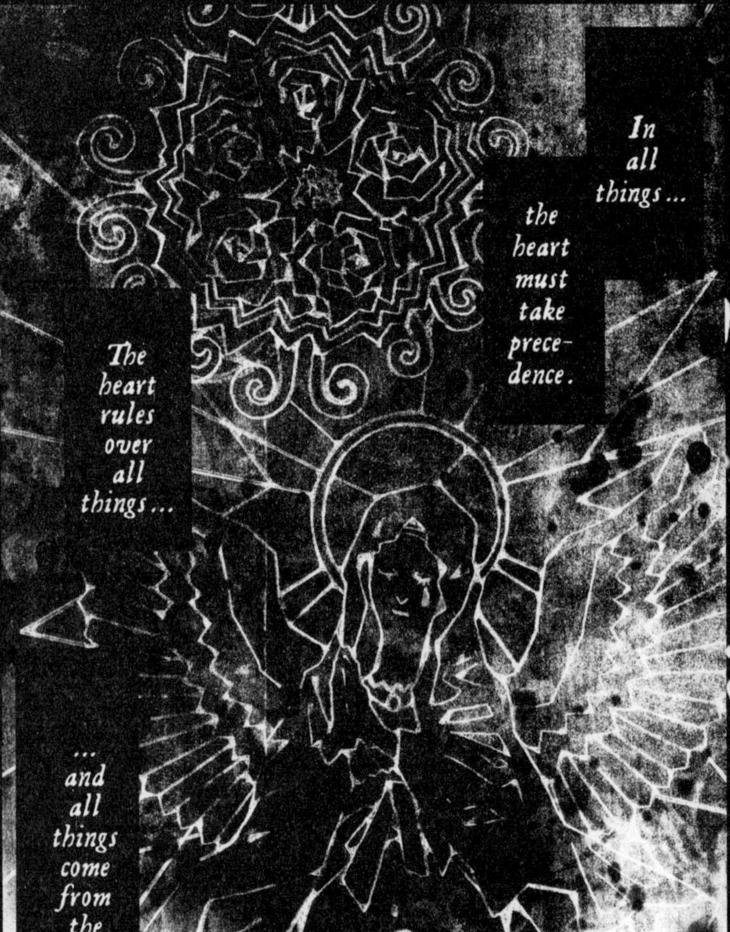
In all things... the heart must take precedence.
The heart rules over all things...
...and all things come from the heart.

–THE SCRIPTURES OF AMBERGROUND, 1st verse

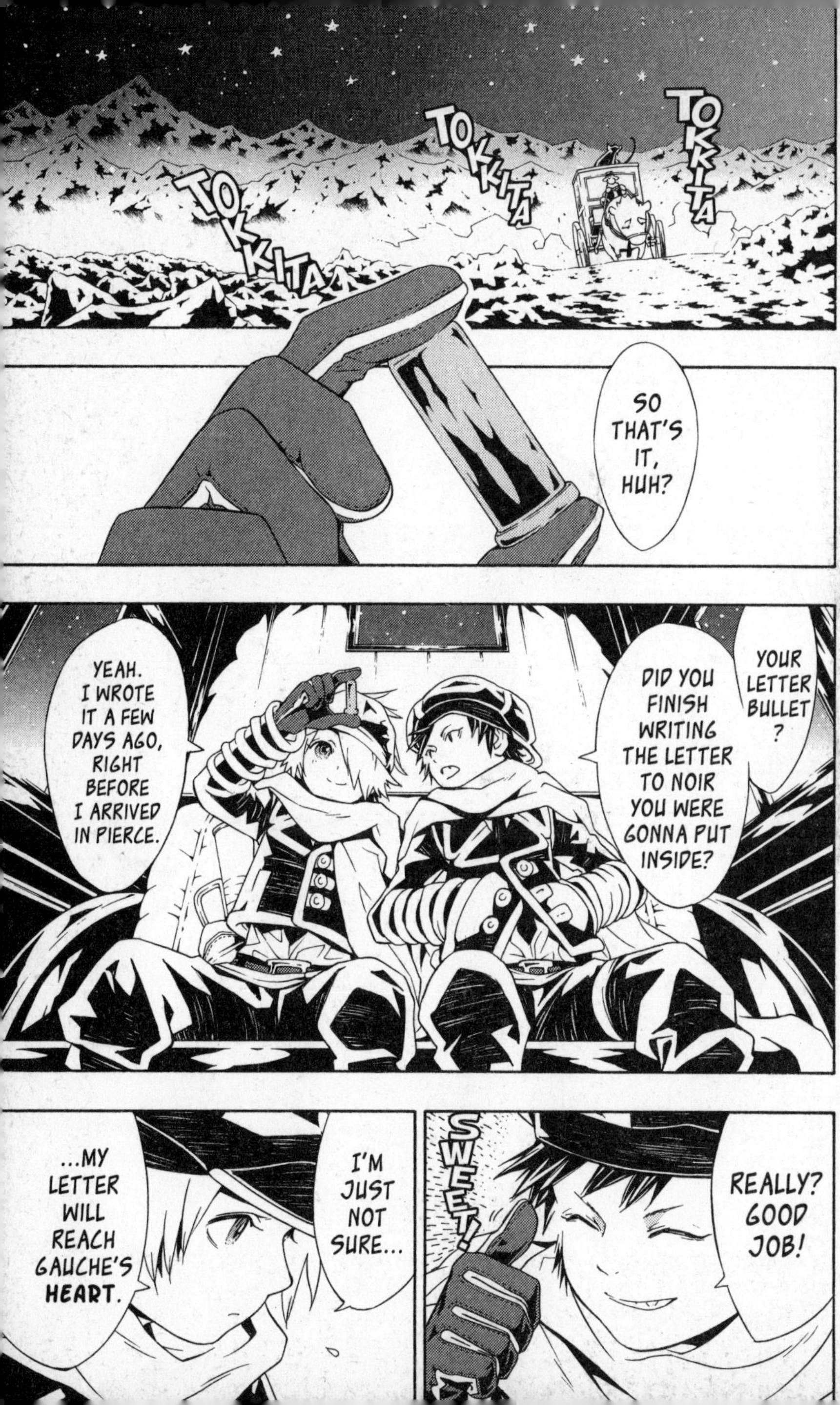
TOKKITA
TOKKITA
TOKKITA
SO THAT'S IT, HUH?
YOUR LETTER BULLET?
DID YOU FINISH WRITING THE LETTER TO NOIR YOU WERE GONNA PUT INSIDE?
YEAH. I WROTE IT A FEW DAYS AGO, RIGHT BEFORE I ARRIVED IN PIERCE.
REALLY? GOOD JOB!
SWEET!
I'M JUST NOT SURE...
...MY LETTER WILL REACH GAUCHE'S **HEART**.

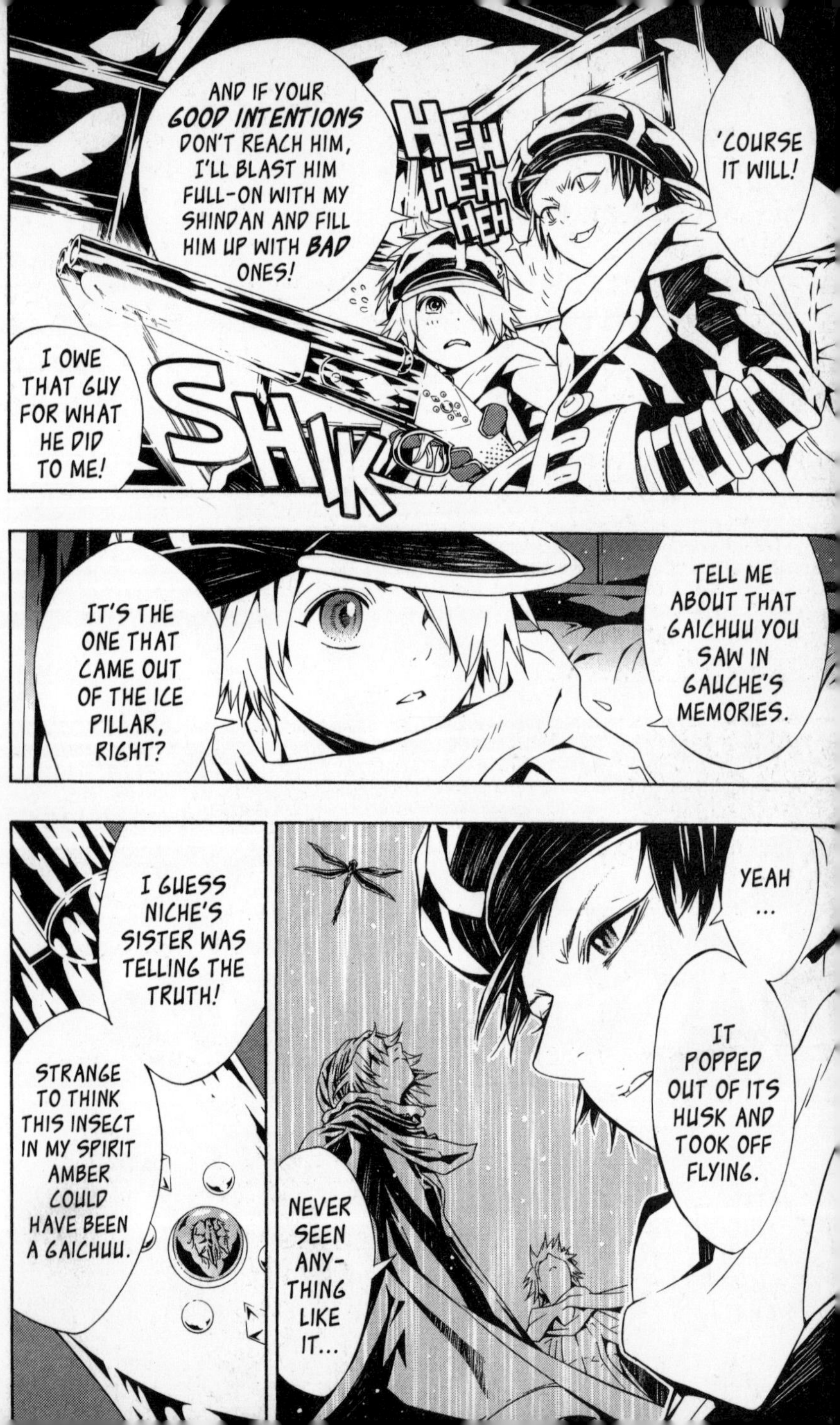
'COURSE IT WILL!
HEH HEH HEH
AND IF YOUR GOOD INTENTIONS DON'T REACH HIM, I'LL BLAST HIM FULL-ON WITH MY SHINDAN AND FILL HIM UP WITH BAD ONES!
I OWE THAT GUY FOR WHAT HE DID TO ME!
SHIK
TELL ME ABOUT THAT GAICHUU YOU SAW IN GAUCHE'S MEMORIES.
IT'S THE ONE THAT CAME OUT OF THE ICE PILLAR, RIGHT?
YEAH ...
IT POPPED OUT OF ITS HUSK AND TOOK OFF FLYING.
NEVER SEEN ANY-THING LIKE IT...
I GUESS NICHE'S SISTER WAS TELLING THE TRUTH!
STRANGE TO THINK THIS INSECT IN MY SPIRIT AMBER COULD HAVE BEEN A GAICHUU.

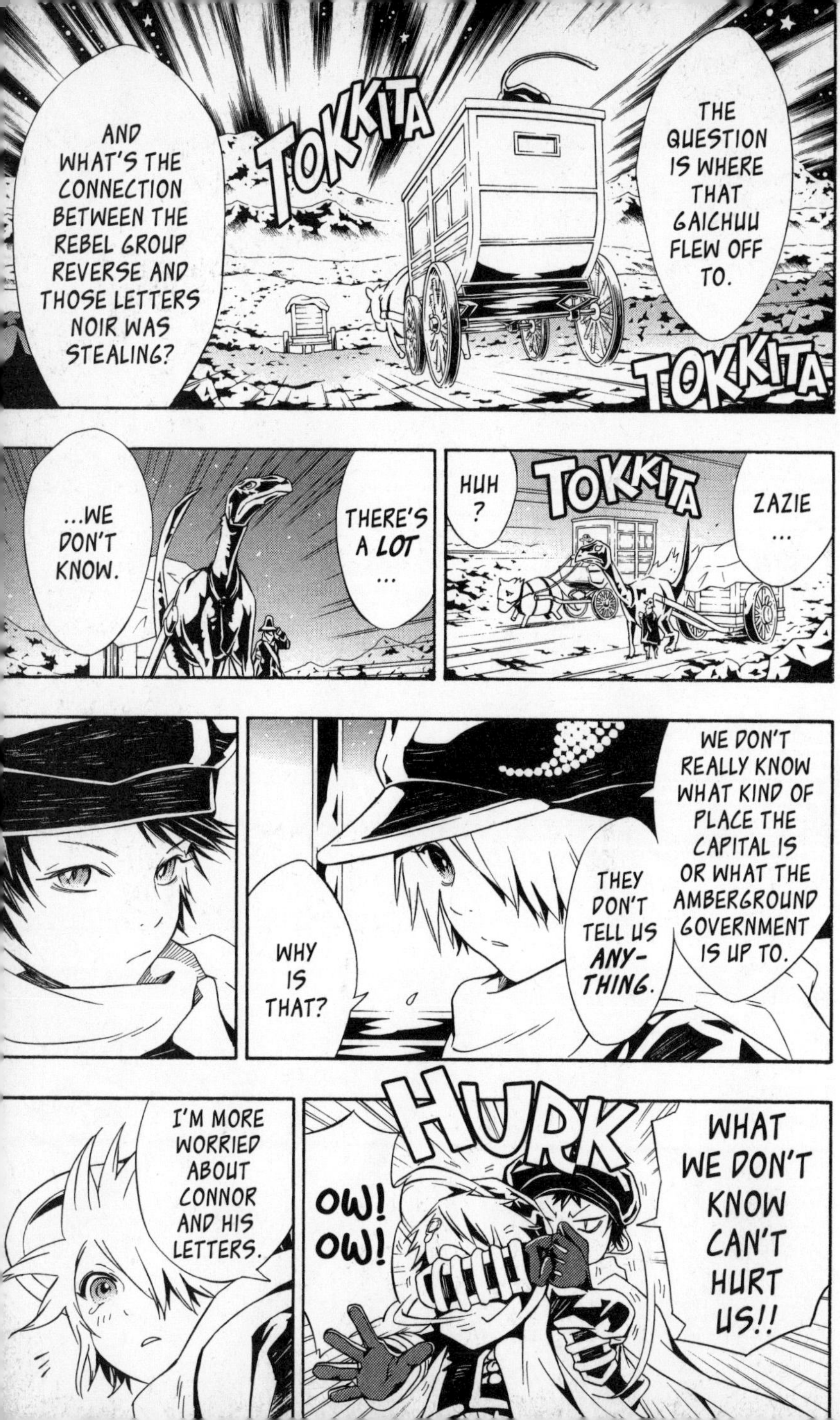
THE QUESTION IS WHERE THAT GAICHUU FLEW OFF TO.
TOKKITA
AND WHAT'S THE CONNECTION BETWEEN THE REBEL GROUP REVERSE AND THOSE LETTERS NOIR WAS STEALING?
TOKKITA
ZAZIE ...
TOKKITA
HUH ?
THERE'S A *LOT* ...
...WE DON'T KNOW.
WE DON'T REALLY KNOW WHAT KIND OF PLACE THE CAPITAL IS OR WHAT THE AMBERGROUND GOVERNMENT IS UP TO.
THEY DON'T TELL US *ANY-THING*.
WHY IS THAT?
WHAT WE DON'T KNOW CAN'T HURT US!!
HURK
OW! OW!
I'M MORE WORRIED ABOUT CONNOR AND HIS LETTERS.

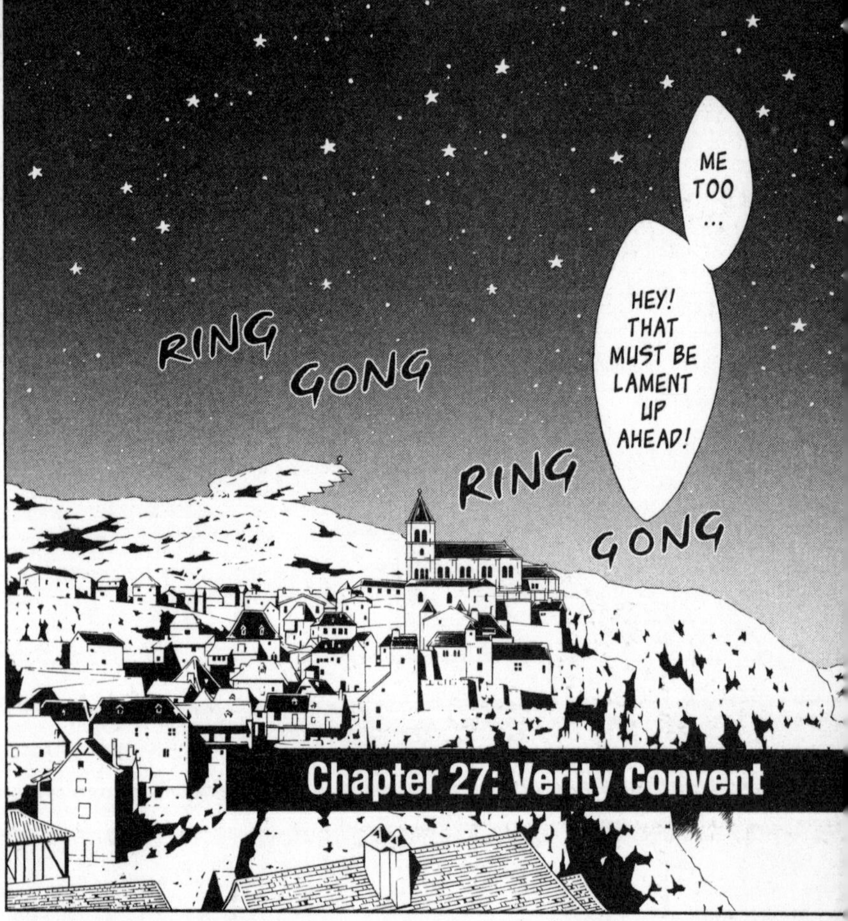
ME TOO...
HEY! THAT MUST BE LAMENT UP AHEAD!
RING
GONG
RING
GONG
Chapter 27: Verity Convent

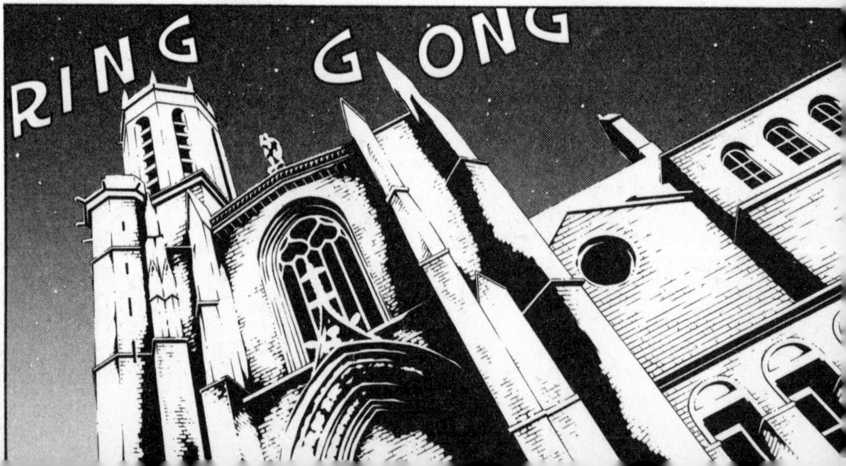
RING
GONG

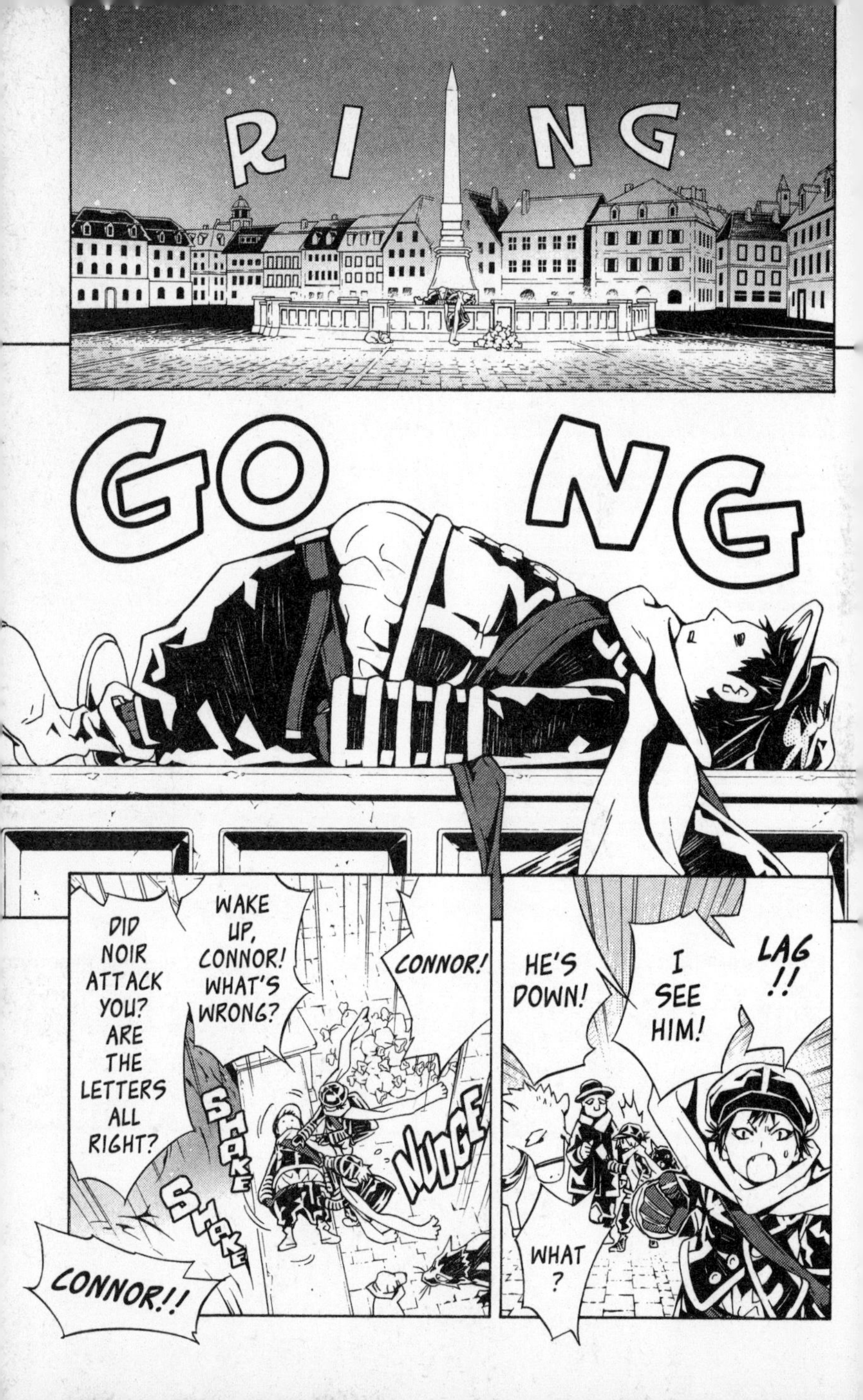
RING
GONG
LAG!!
I SEE HIM!
HE'S DOWN!
WHAT?
CONNOR!
WAKE UP, CONNOR! WHAT'S WRONG?
DID NOIR ATTACK YOU? ARE THE LETTERS ALL RIGHT?
NUDGE
SHAKE
SHAKE
CONNOR!!

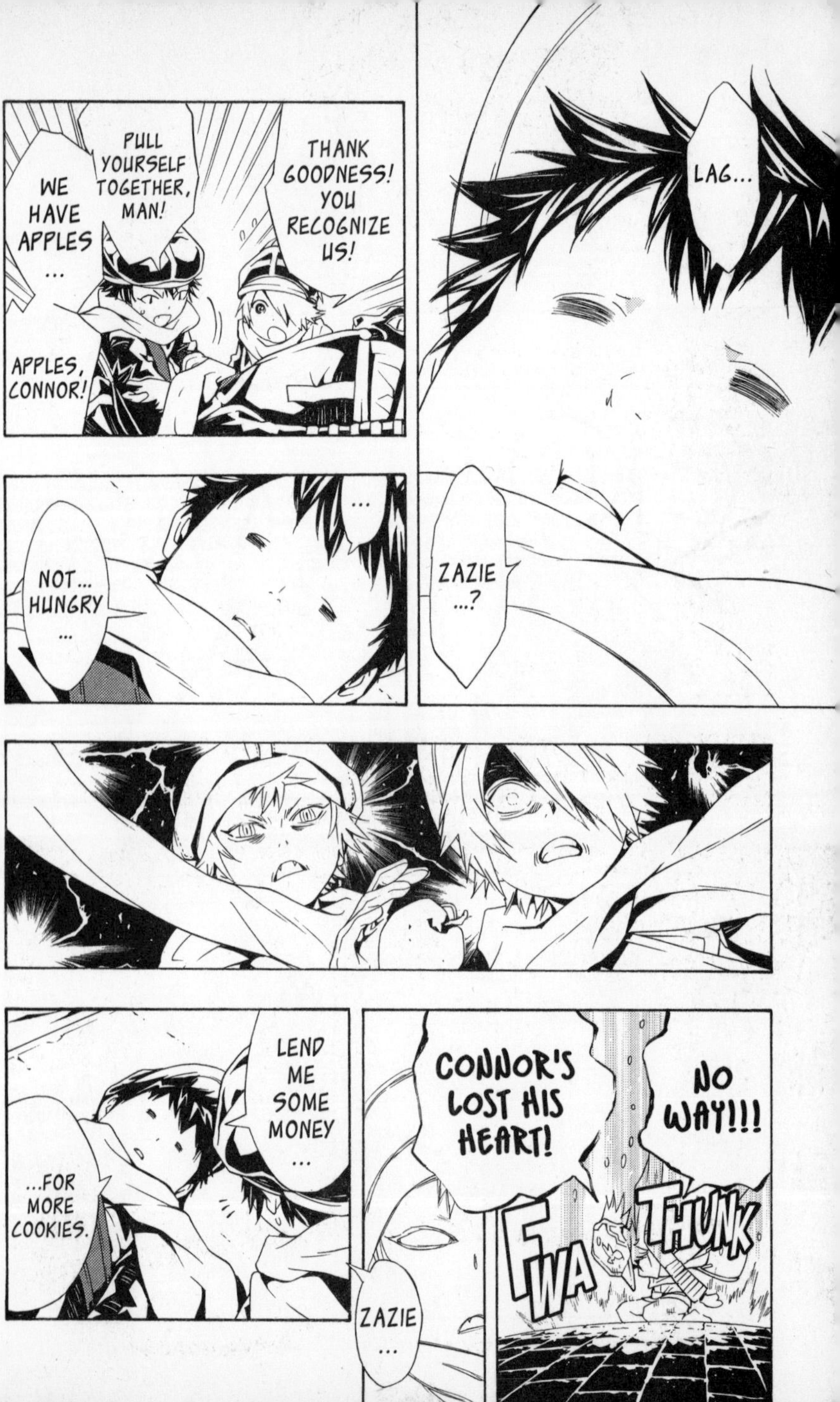
LAG...
ZAZIE ...?
THANK GOODNESS! YOU RECOGNIZE US!
PULL YOURSELF TOGETHER, MAN!
WE HAVE APPLES ...
APPLES, CONNOR!
...
NOT... HUNGRY ...
NO WAY!!!
CONNOR'S LOST HIS HEART!
FWA THUNK
ZAZIE ...
LEND ME SOME MONEY ...
...FOR MORE COOKIES.

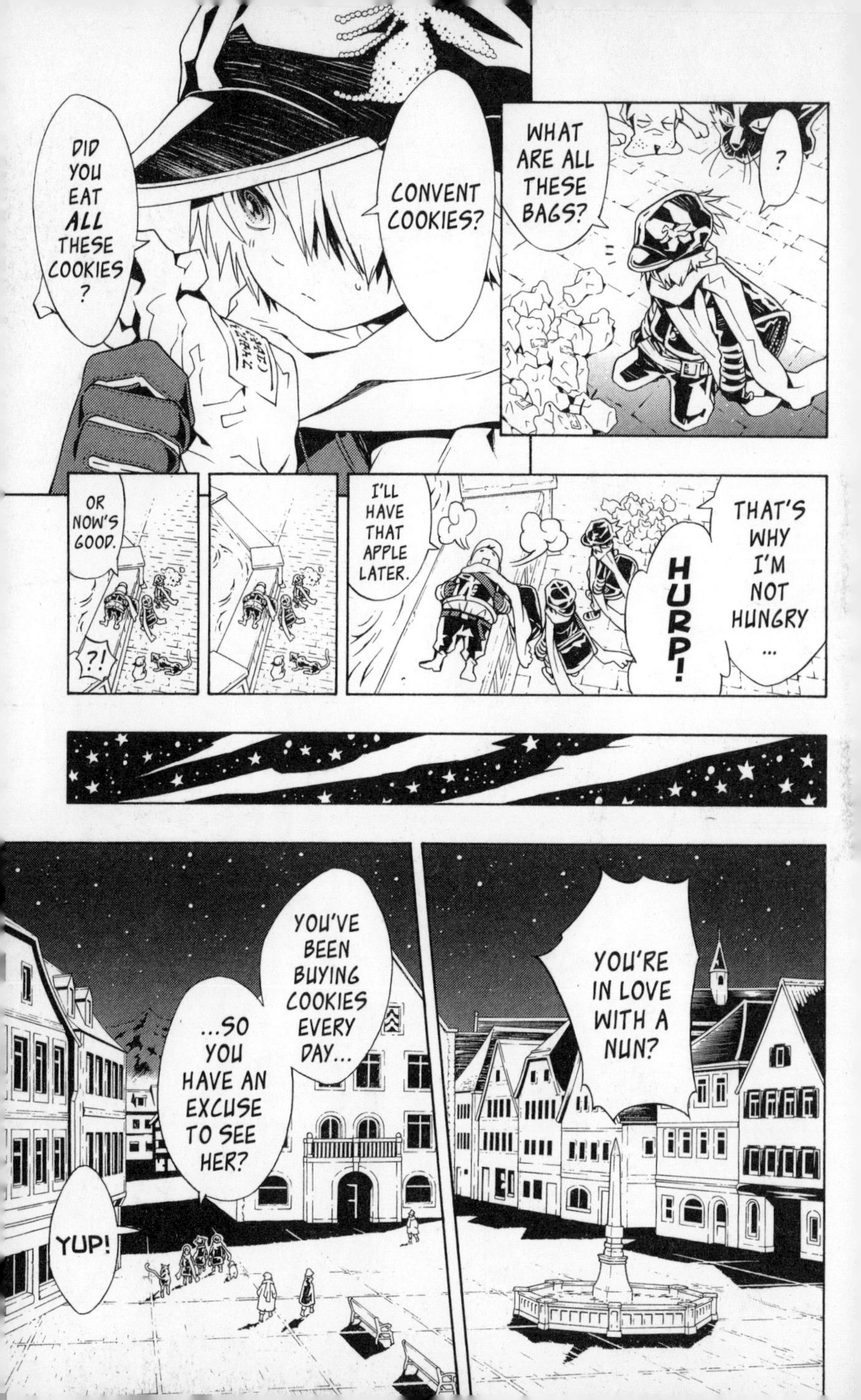
WHAT ARE ALL THESE BAGS?
?
CONVENT COOKIES?
DID YOU EAT ALL THESE COOKIES?
THAT'S WHY I'M NOT HUNGRY...
HURP!
I'LL HAVE THAT APPLE LATER.
OR NOW'S GOOD.
?!
YOU'RE IN LOVE WITH A NUN?
YOU'VE BEEN BUYING COOKIES EVERY DAY...
...SO YOU HAVE AN EXCUSE TO SEE HER?
YUP!

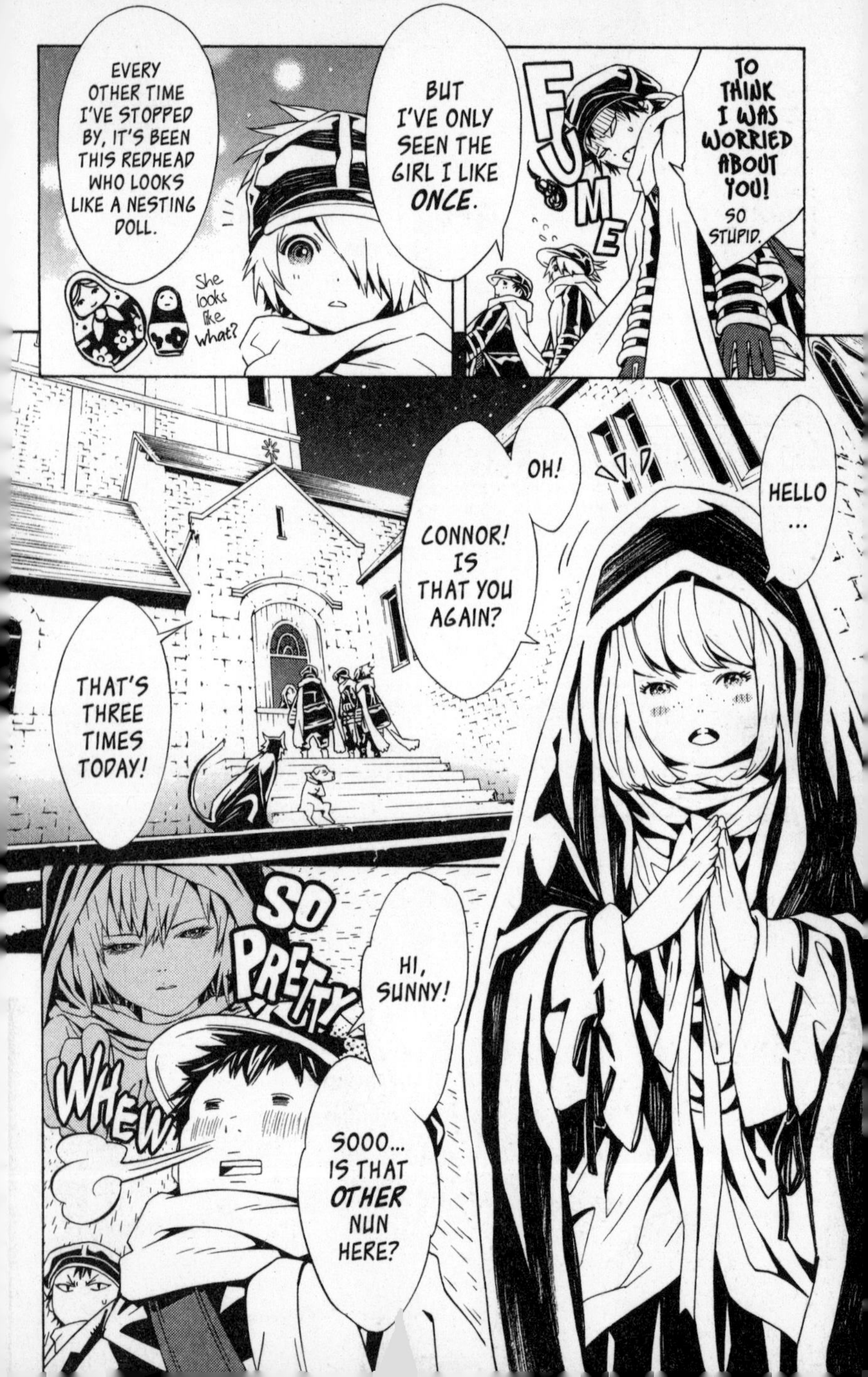
FUME
TO THINK I WAS WORRIED ABOUT YOU!
SO STUPID.
BUT I'VE ONLY SEEN THE GIRL I LIKE ONCE.
EVERY OTHER TIME I'VE STOPPED BY, IT'S BEEN THIS REDHEAD WHO LOOKS LIKE A NESTING DOLL.
She looks like what?
HELLO ...
OH!
CONNOR! IS THAT YOU AGAIN?
THAT'S THREE TIMES TODAY!
SO PRETTY
HI, SUNNY!
WHEW
SOOO... IS THAT OTHER NUN HERE?

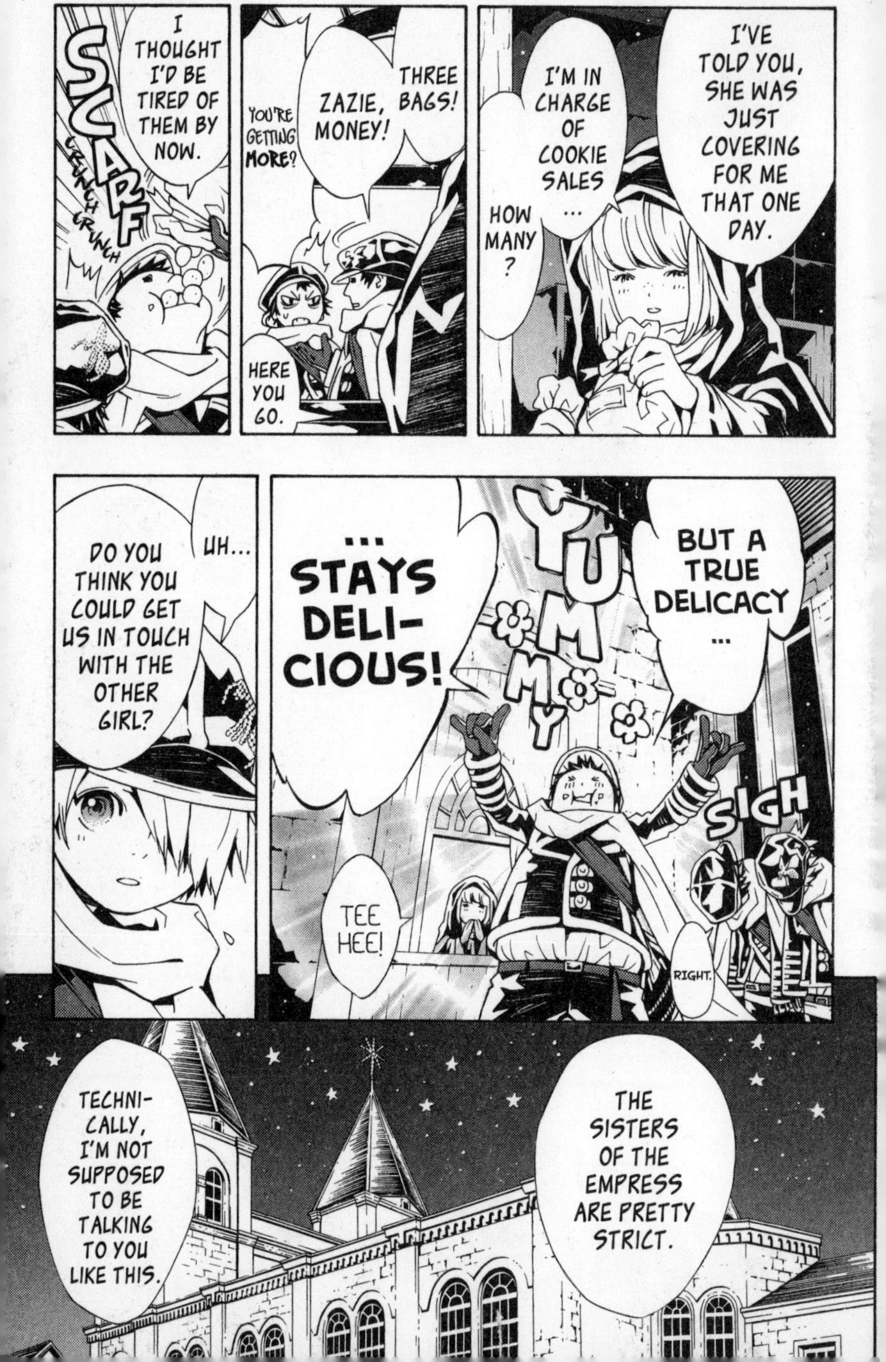
I'VE TOLD YOU, SHE WAS JUST COVERING FOR ME THAT ONE DAY.
I'M IN CHARGE OF COOKIE SALES...
HOW MANY?
THREE BAGS!
ZAZIE, MONEY!
YOU'RE GETTING MORE?
HERE YOU GO.
I THOUGHT I'D BE TIRED OF THEM BY NOW.
SCARF
CRUNCH CRUNCH
BUT A TRUE DELICACY...
YUMMY
...STAYS DELI-CIOUS!
SIGH
RIGHT.
TEE HEE!
UH...
DO YOU THINK YOU COULD GET US IN TOUCH WITH THE OTHER GIRL?
THE SISTERS OF THE EMPRESS ARE PRETTY STRICT.
TECHNI-CALLY, I'M NOT SUPPOSED TO BE TALKING TO YOU LIKE THIS.

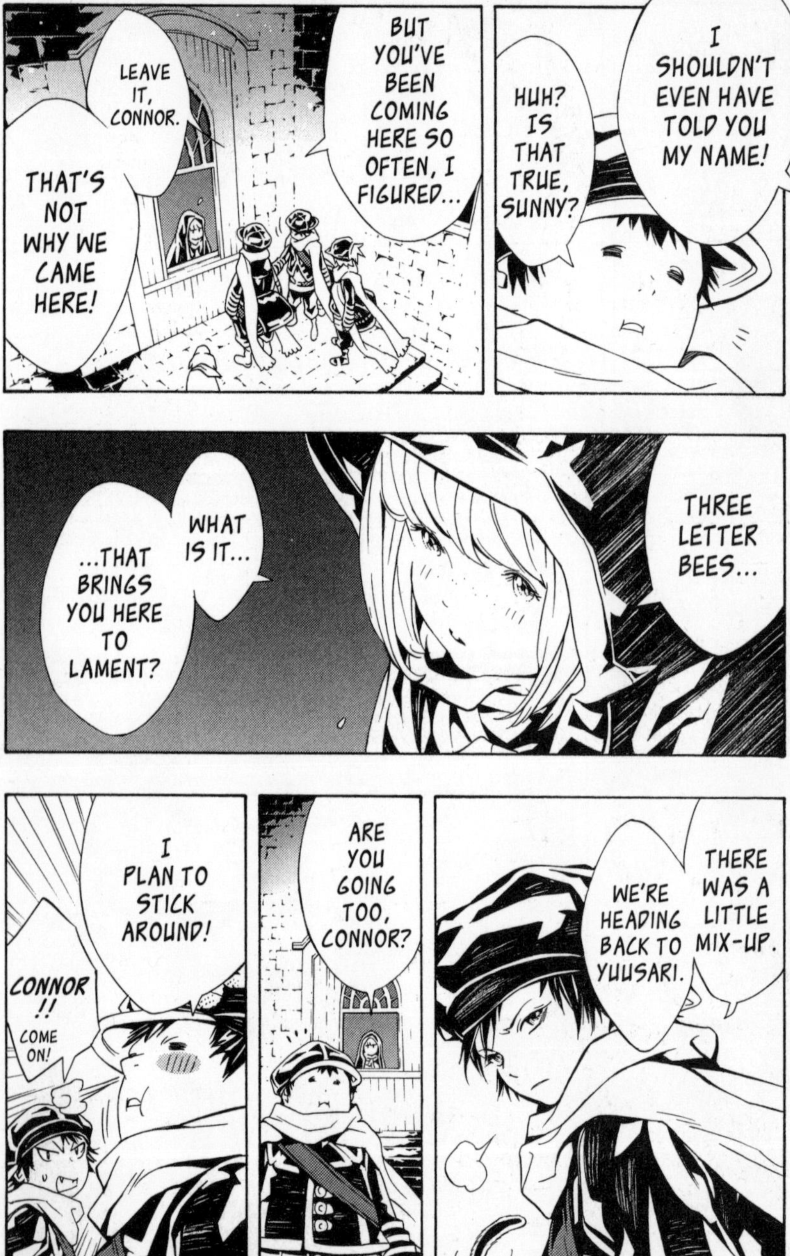
I SHOULDN'T EVEN HAVE TOLD YOU MY NAME!
HUH? IS THAT TRUE, SUNNY?
BUT YOU'VE BEEN COMING HERE SO OFTEN, I FIGURED...
LEAVE IT, CONNOR.
THAT'S NOT WHY WE CAME HERE!
THREE LETTER BEES...
WHAT IS IT...
...THAT BRINGS YOU HERE TO LAMENT?
THERE WAS A LITTLE MIX-UP.
WE'RE HEADING BACK TO YUUSARI.
ARE YOU GOING TOO, CONNOR?
I PLAN TO STICK AROUND!
CONNOR!!
COME ON!

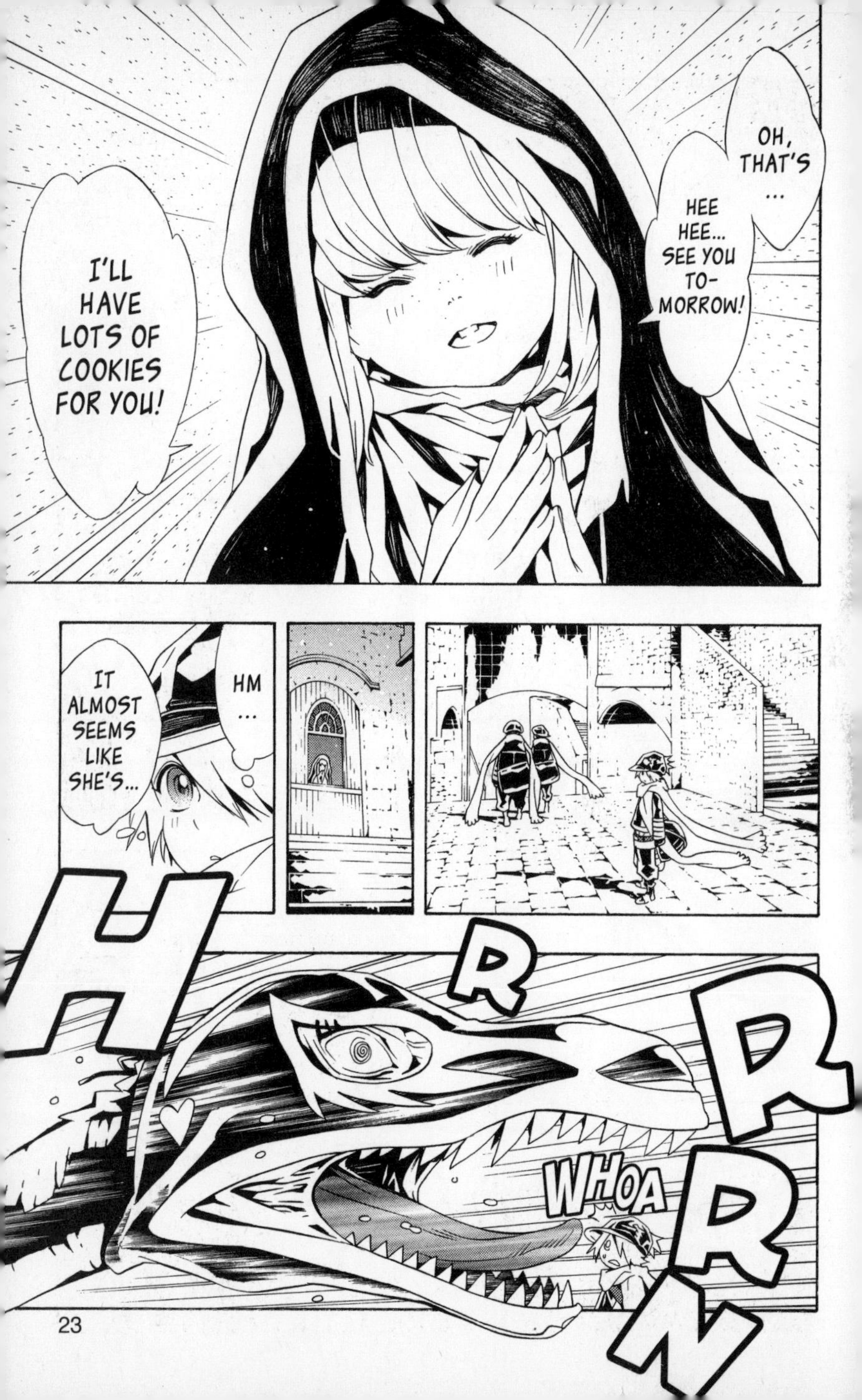
OH, THAT'S ...
HEE HEE... SEE YOU TO-MORROW!
I'LL HAVE LOTS OF COOKIES FOR YOU!
HM ...
IT ALMOST SEEMS LIKE SHE'S...
HRRRN
WHOA

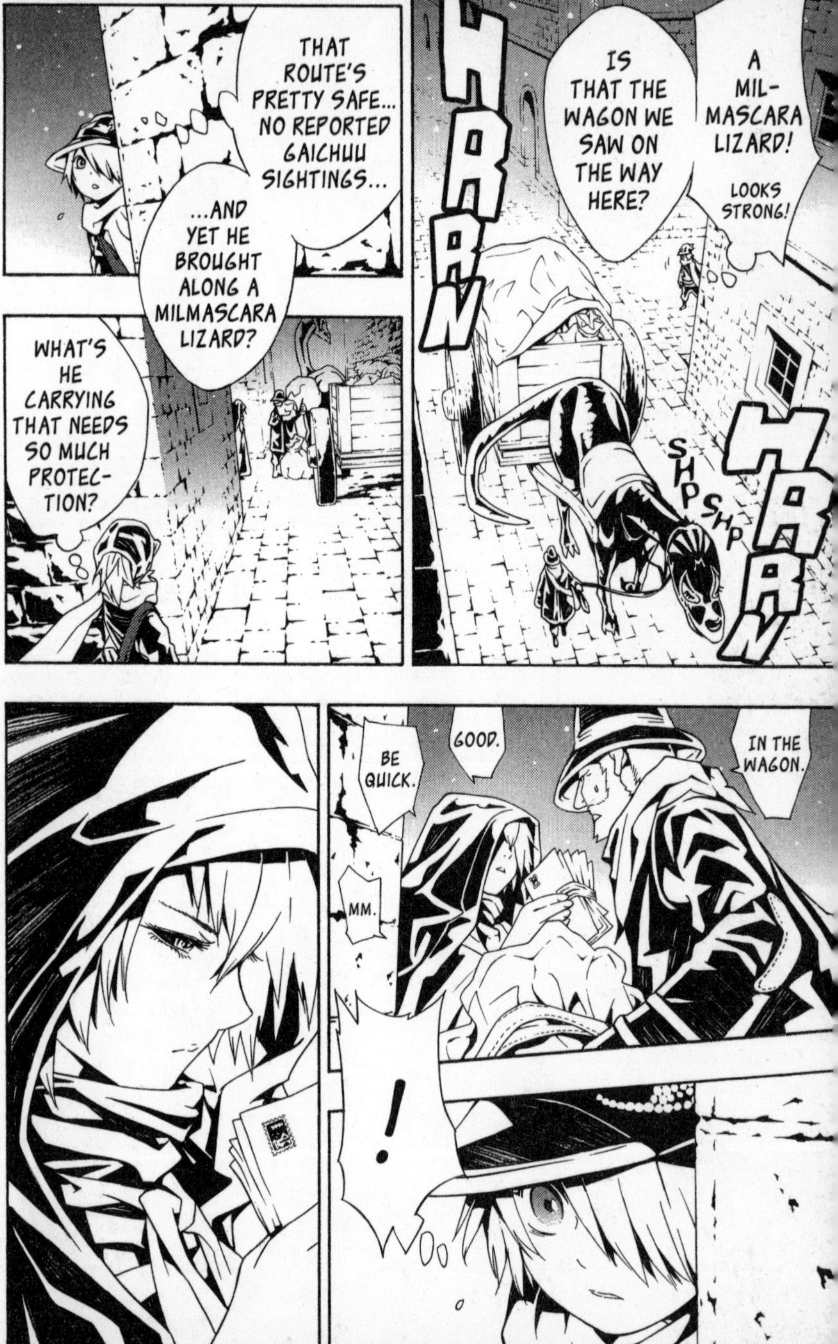
A MIL-MASCARA LIZARD!
LOOKS STRONG!
IS THAT THE WAGON WE SAW ON THE WAY HERE?
HRRN
SHP SHP
HRRN
THAT ROUTE'S PRETTY SAFE... NO REPORTED GAICHUU SIGHTINGS...
...AND YET HE BROUGHT ALONG A MILMASCARA LIZARD?
WHAT'S HE CARRYING THAT NEEDS SO MUCH PROTECTION?
IN THE WAGON.
GOOD.
BE QUICK.
MM.
!

ZAZIE!

SHUFFLE

HUH?

WHAT'RE YOU LOOKING AT?

....

RODA!

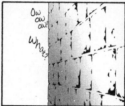

Ow ow ow!
What?

THAT CONVENT IS A *REVERSE BASE?*

I HEAR THEY HAVE HIDEOUTS ALL OVER, BUT...

I'M SURE OF IT!

CHEW CHEW

SIGH

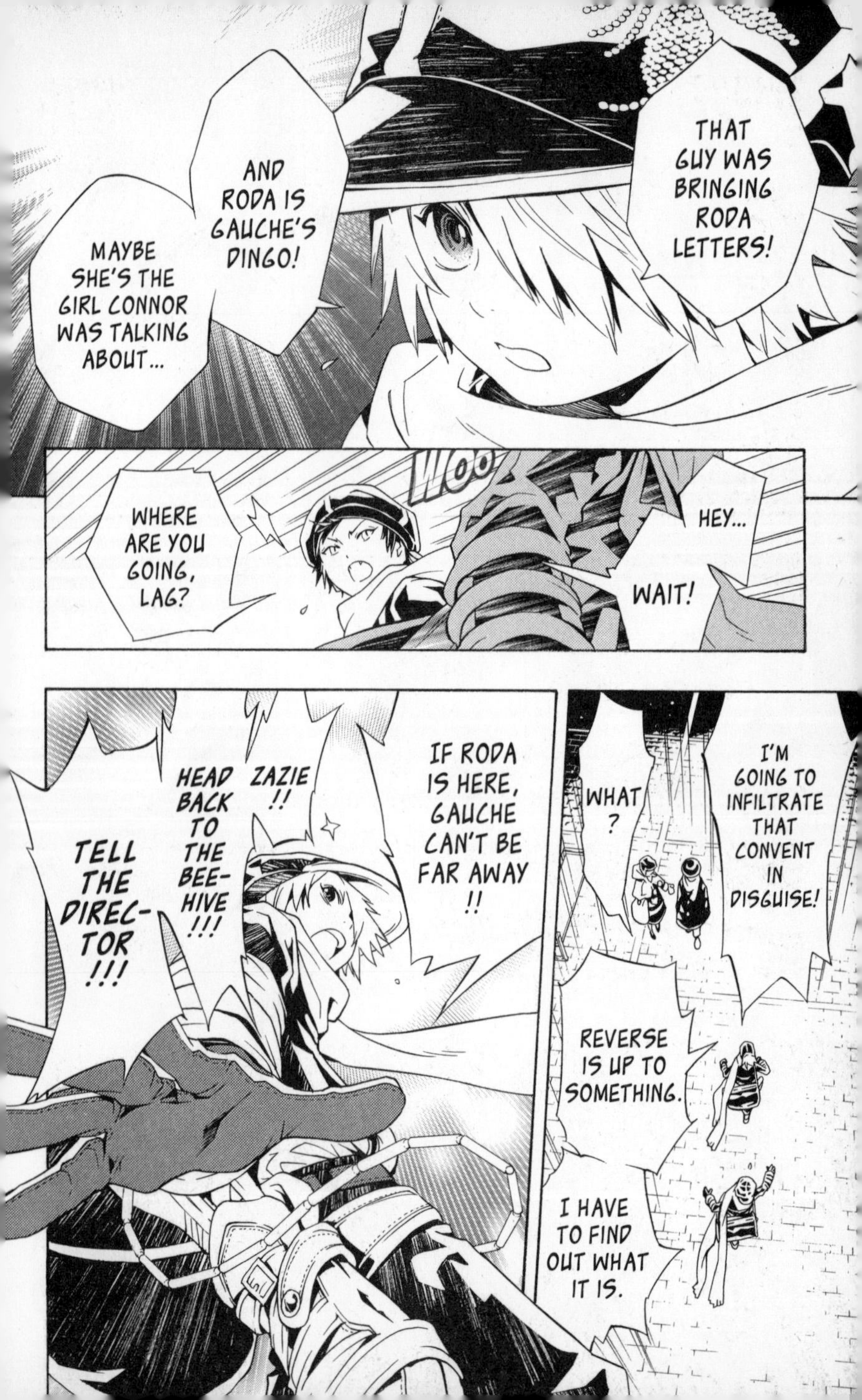
THAT GUY WAS BRINGING RODA LETTERS!
AND RODA IS GAUCHE'S DINGO!
MAYBE SHE'S THE GIRL CONNOR WAS TALKING ABOUT...
WOO
HEY... WAIT!
WHERE ARE YOU GOING, LAG?
I'M GOING TO INFILTRATE THAT CONVENT IN DISGUISE!
WHAT?
REVERSE IS UP TO SOMETHING.
I HAVE TO FIND OUT WHAT IT IS.
IF RODA IS HERE, GAUCHE CAN'T BE FAR AWAY!!
ZAZIE!!
HEAD BACK TO THE BEEHIVE!!!
TELL THE DIRECTOR!!!

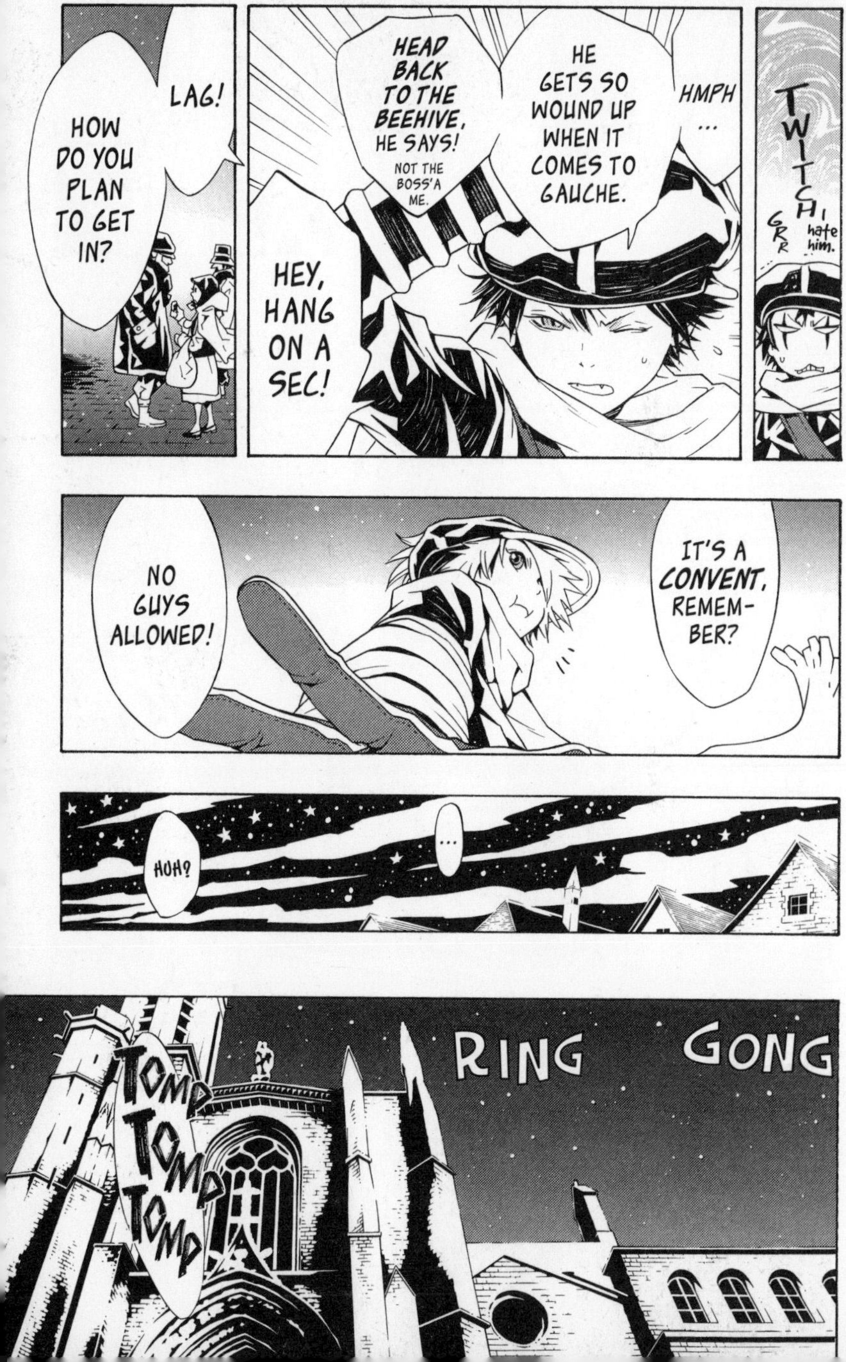
TWITCH
GRR
I hate him.
HMPH...
HE GETS SO WOUND UP WHEN IT COMES TO GAUCHE.
HEAD BACK TO THE BEEHIVE, HE SAYS!
NOT THE BOSS'A ME.
HEY, HANG ON A SEC!
LAG!
HOW DO YOU PLAN TO GET IN?
IT'S A CONVENT, REMEMBER?
NO GUYS ALLOWED!
...
HUH?
GONG
RING
TOMP TOMP TOMP TOMP

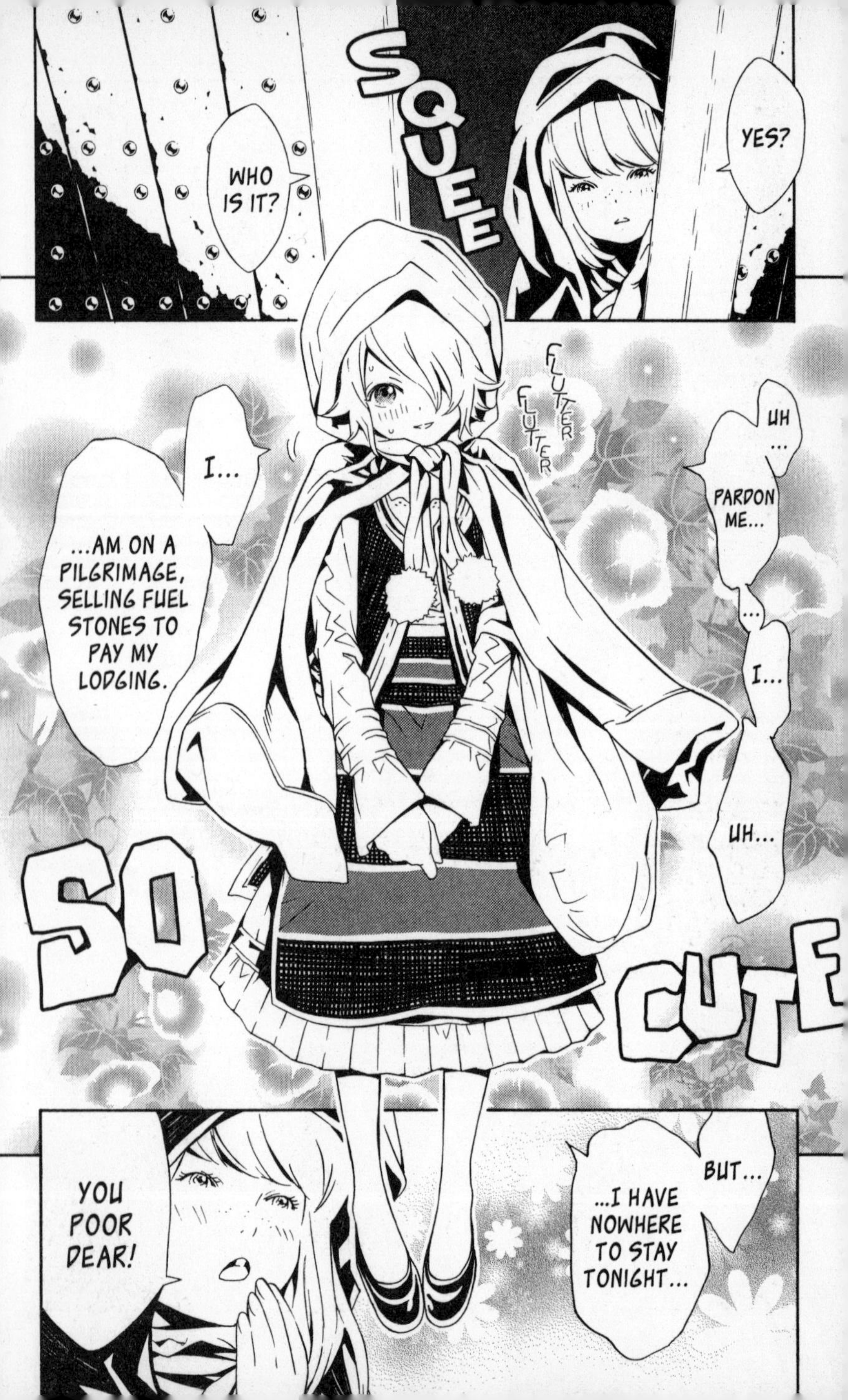
YES?
SQUEE
WHO IS IT?
UH ...
PARDON ME...
...
I...
UH...
FLUTTER FLUTTER
I...
...AM ON A PILGRIMAGE, SELLING FUEL STONES TO PAY MY LODGING.
SO CUTE
BUT...
...I HAVE NOWHERE TO STAY TONIGHT...
YOU POOR DEAR!

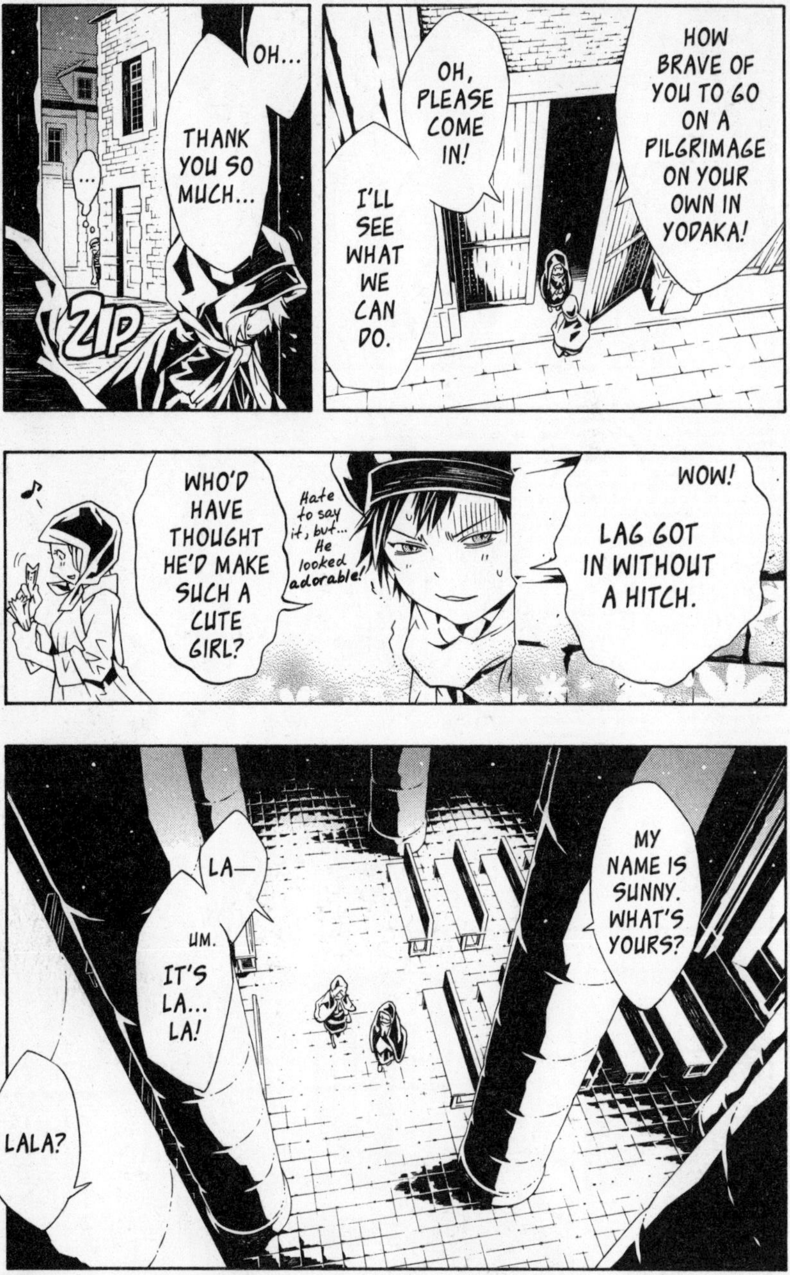
HOW BRAVE OF YOU TO GO ON A PILGRIMAGE ON YOUR OWN IN YODAKA!
OH, PLEASE COME IN!
I'LL SEE WHAT WE CAN DO.
OH...
THANK YOU SO MUCH...
...
ZIP
WOW!
LAG GOT IN WITHOUT A HITCH.
Hate to say it, but... He looked adorable!
WHO'D HAVE THOUGHT HE'D MAKE SUCH A CUTE GIRL?
MY NAME IS SUNNY. WHAT'S YOURS?
LA—
UM.
IT'S LA... LA!
LALA?

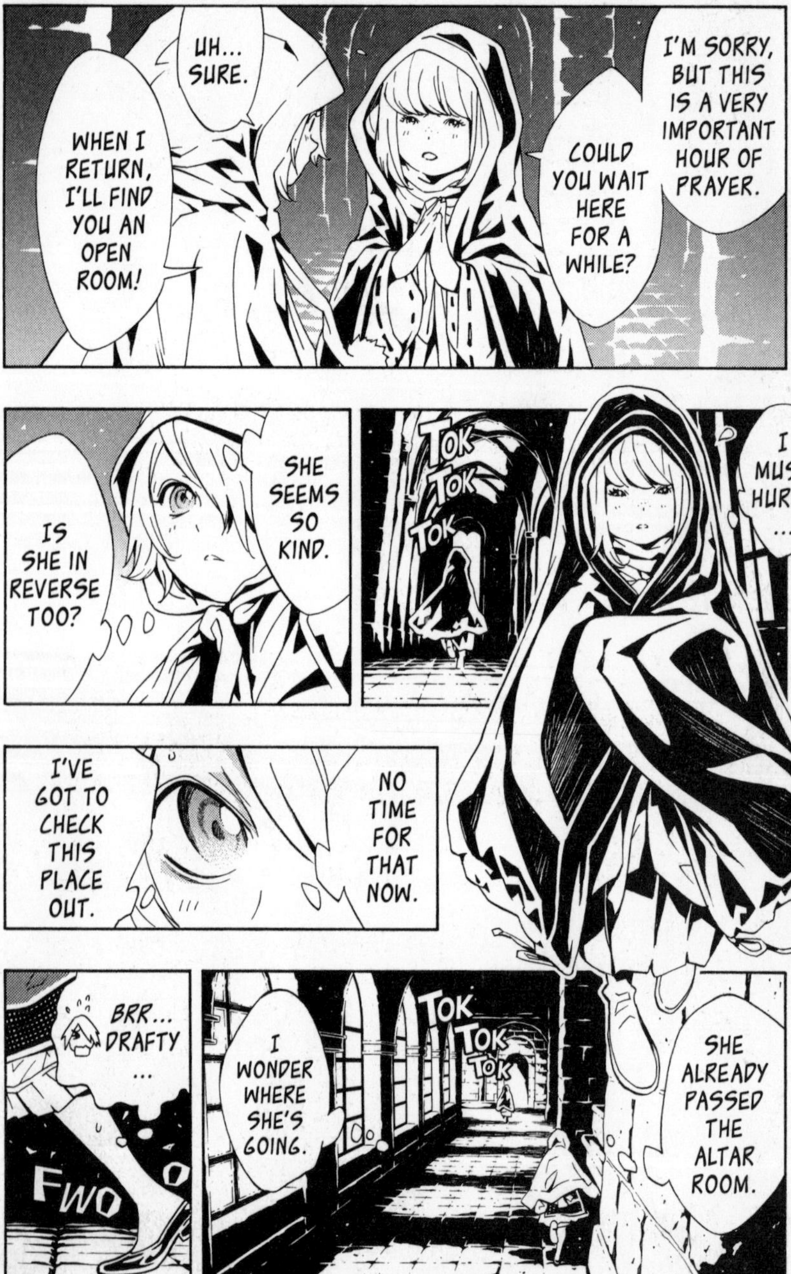
I'M SORRY, BUT THIS IS A VERY IMPORTANT HOUR OF PRAYER.
COULD YOU WAIT HERE FOR A WHILE?
UH... SURE.
WHEN I RETURN, I'LL FIND YOU AN OPEN ROOM!
I MUST HURRY...
TOK TOK TOK
SHE SEEMS SO KIND.
IS SHE IN REVERSE TOO?
NO TIME FOR THAT NOW.
I'VE GOT TO CHECK THIS PLACE OUT.
SHE ALREADY PASSED THE ALTAR ROOM.
TOK TOK TOK
I WONDER WHERE SHE'S GOING.
BRR... DRAFTY...
FWOO

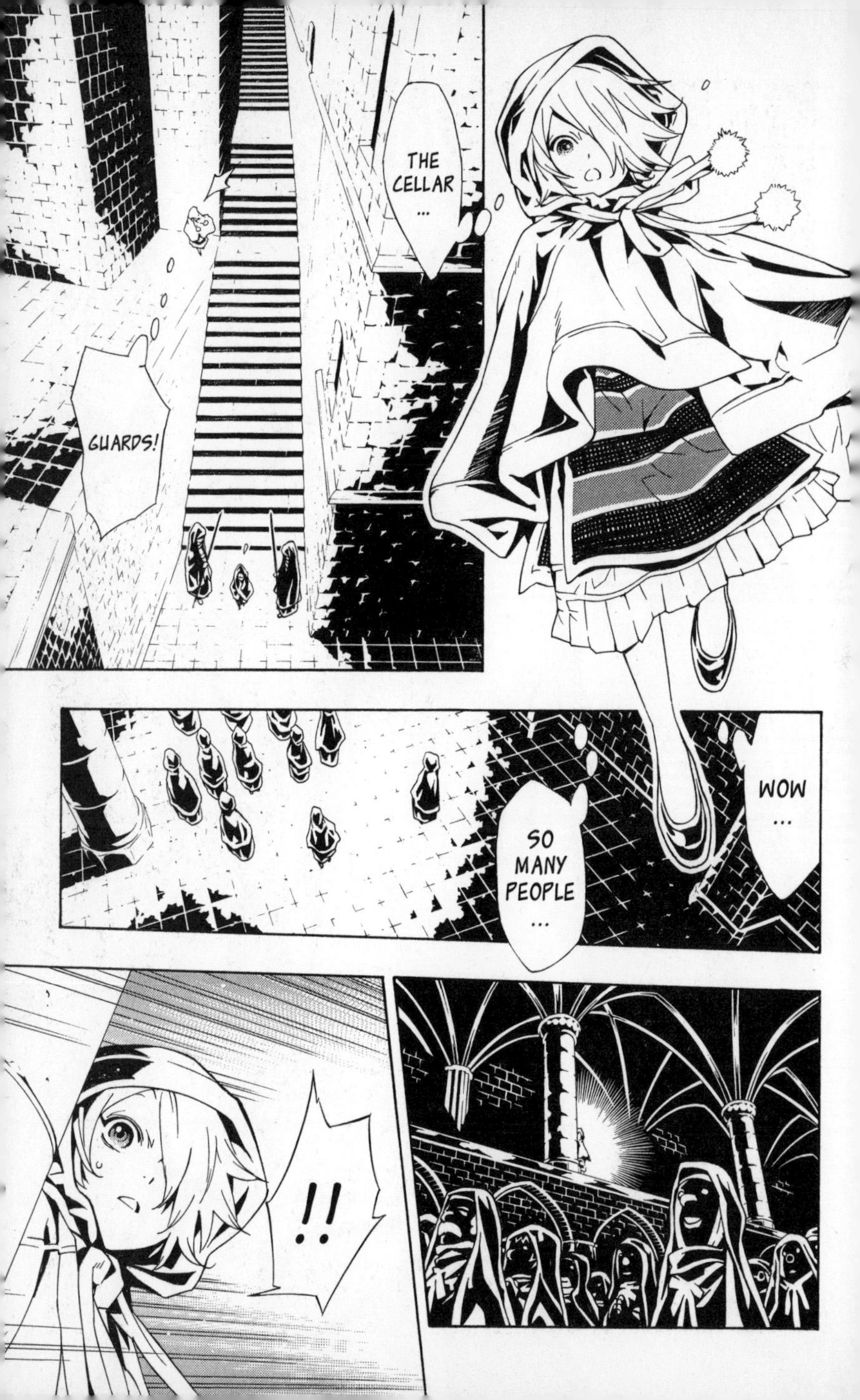
THE CELLAR ...
GUARDS!
WOW ...
SO MANY PEOPLE ...
!!

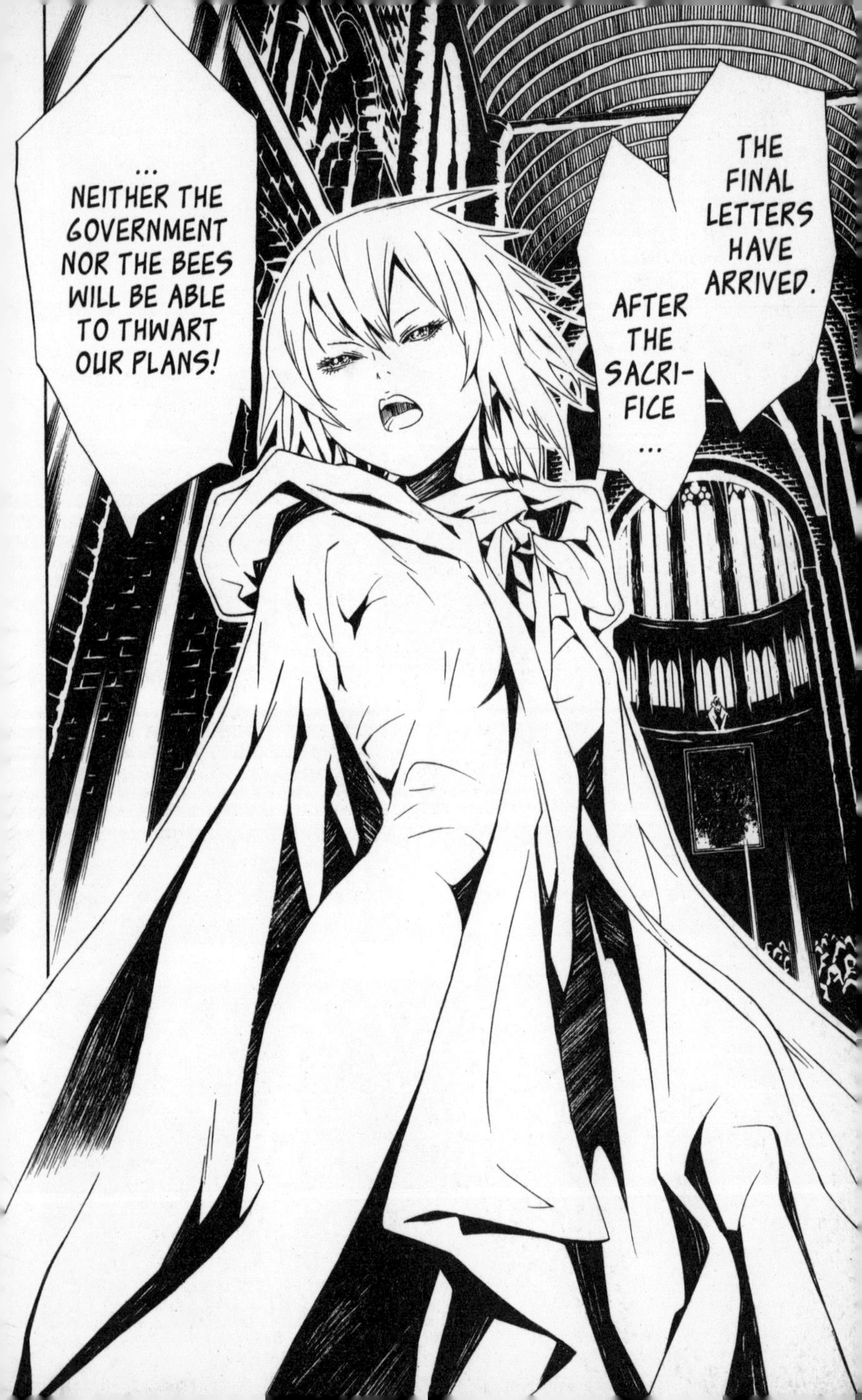
THE FINAL LETTERS HAVE ARRIVED.
AFTER THE SACRI-FICE ...
... NEITHER THE GOVERNMENT NOR THE BEES WILL BE ABLE TO THWART OUR PLANS!

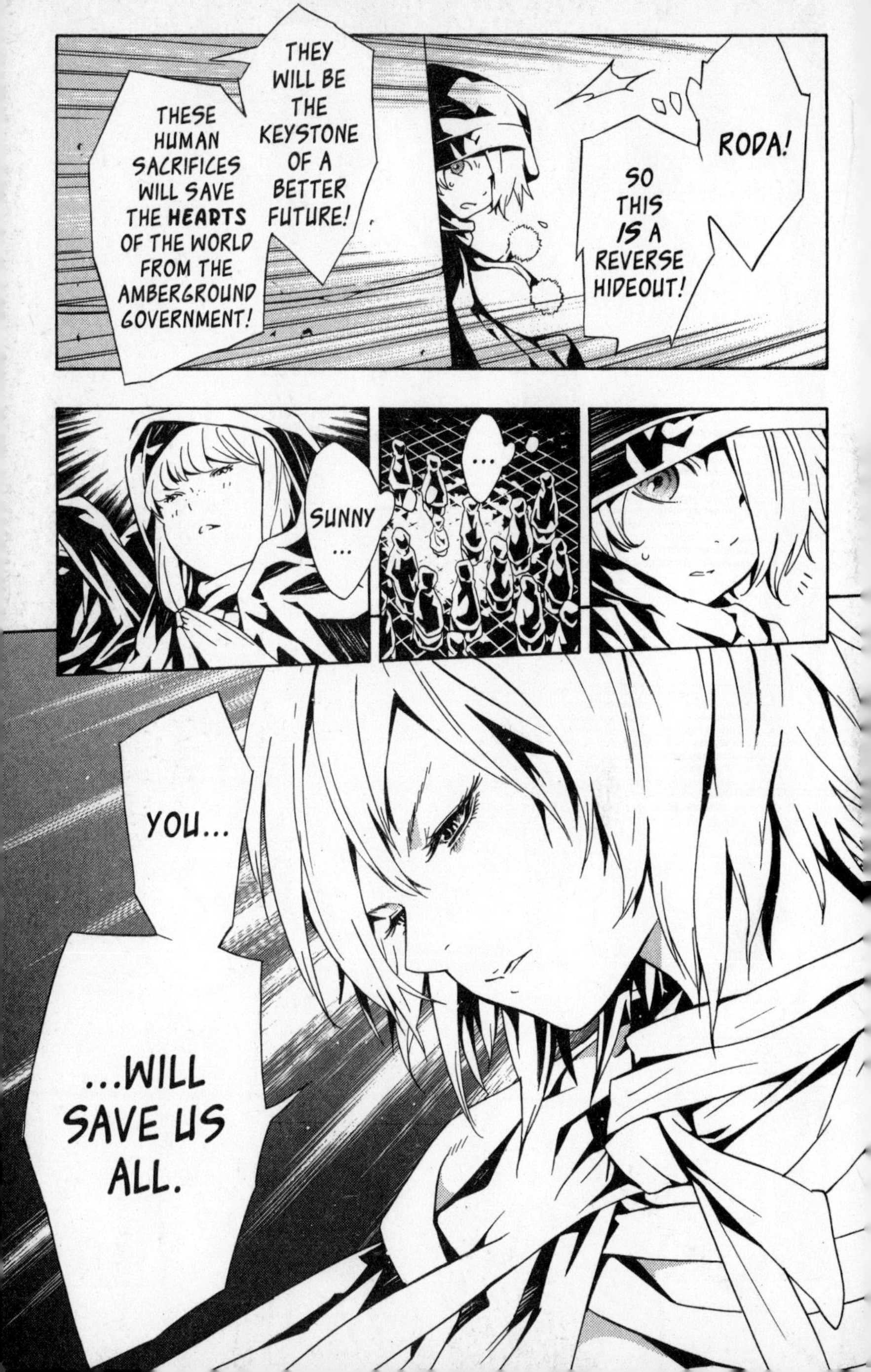
RODA!
SO THIS IS A REVERSE HIDEOUT!
THEY WILL BE THE KEYSTONE OF A BETTER FUTURE!
THESE HUMAN SACRIFICES WILL SAVE THE **HEARTS** OF THE WORLD FROM THE AMBERGROUND GOVERNMENT!
...
SUNNY ...
YOU...
...WILL SAVE US ALL.

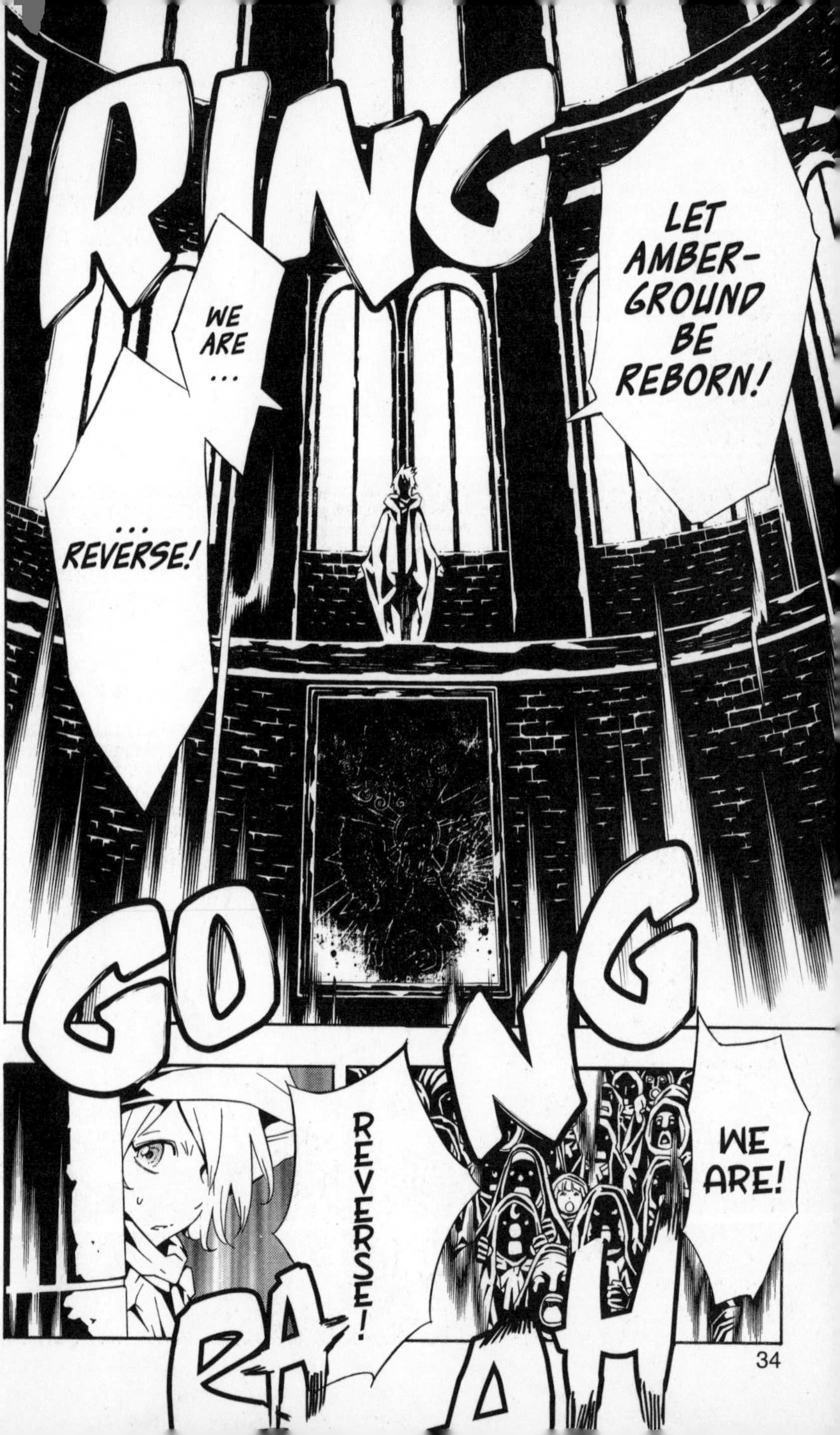
RING
LET AMBER-GROUND BE REBORN!
WE ARE...
...REVERSE!
GONG
WE ARE!
REVERSE!
RAAH

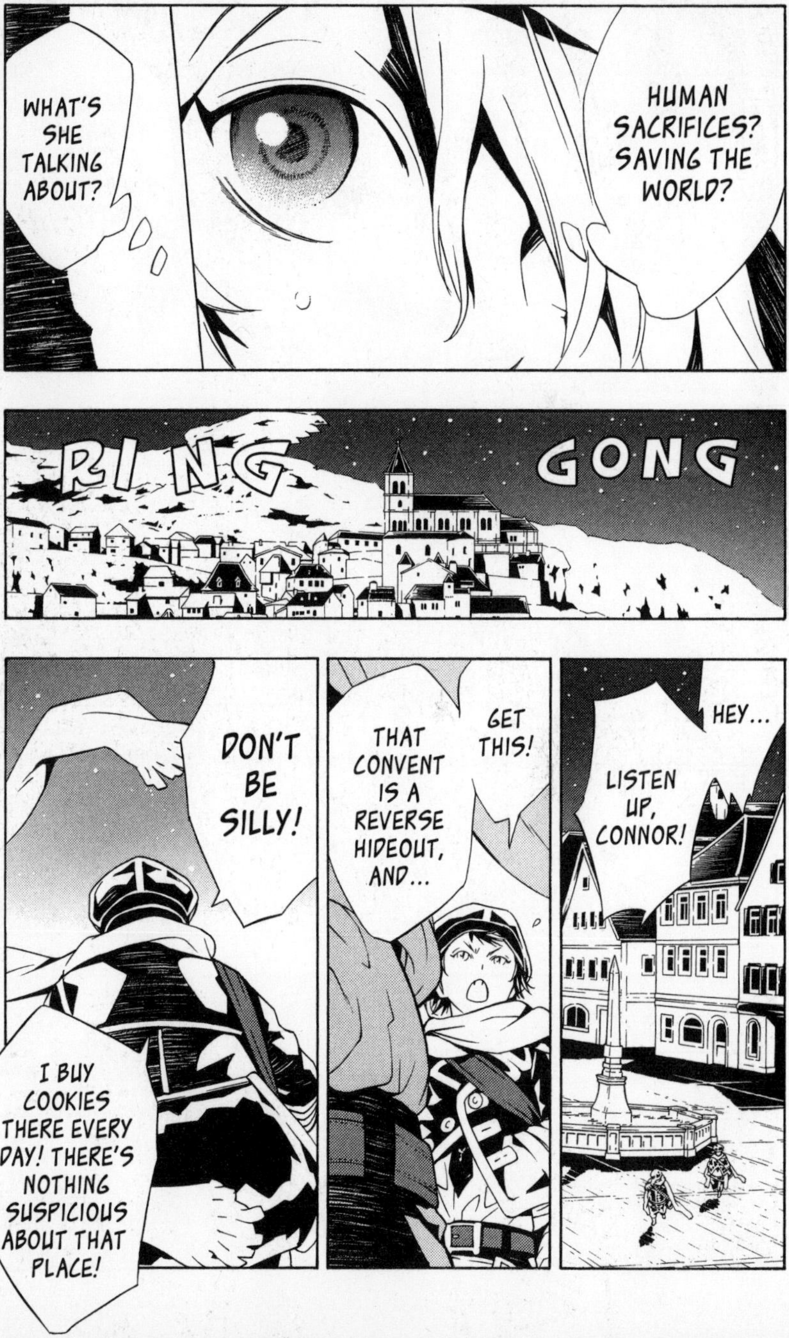
HUMAN SACRIFICES? SAVING THE WORLD?
WHAT'S SHE TALKING ABOUT?
GONG
RING
HEY...
LISTEN UP, CONNOR!
GET THIS!
THAT CONVENT IS A REVERSE HIDEOUT, AND...
DON'T BE SILLY!
I BUY COOKIES THERE EVERY DAY! THERE'S NOTHING SUSPICIOUS ABOUT THAT PLACE!

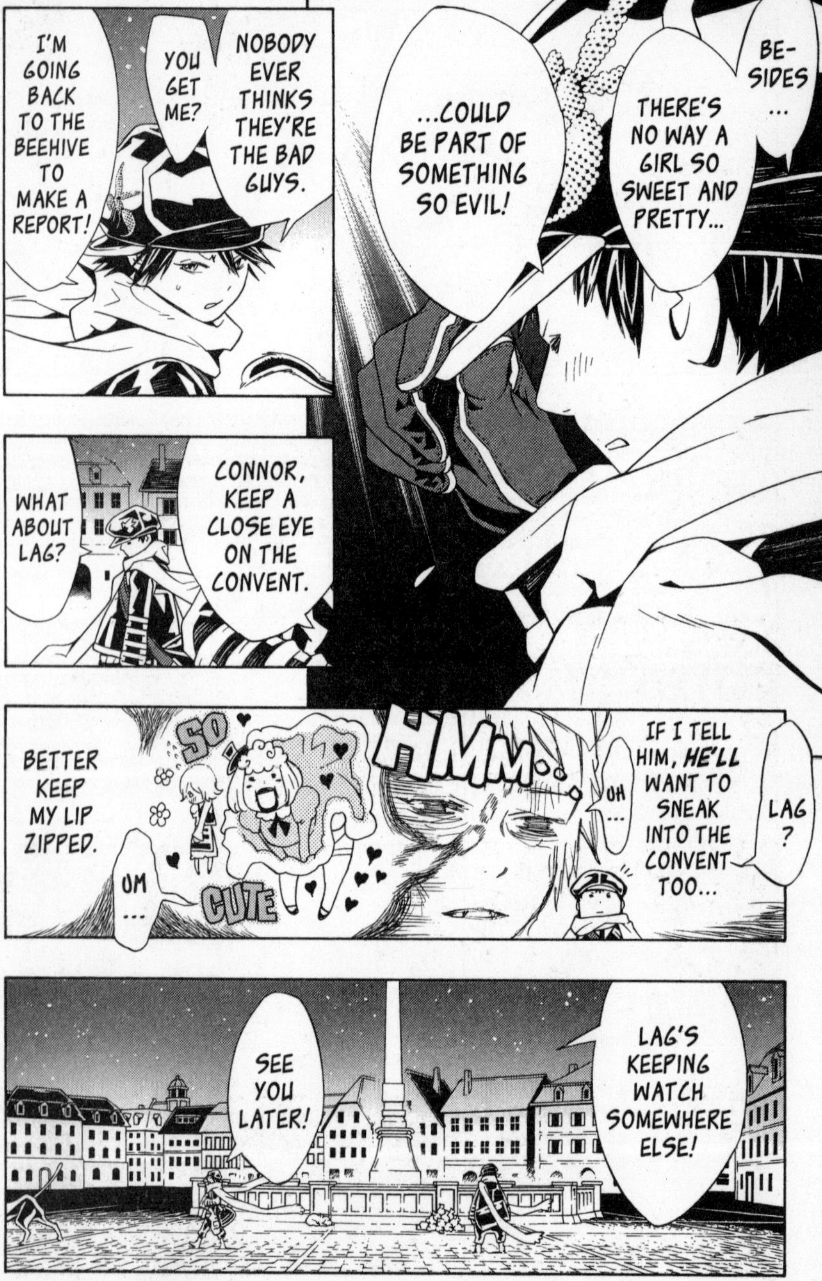
BE-SIDES...
THERE'S NO WAY A GIRL SO SWEET AND PRETTY...
...COULD BE PART OF SOMETHING SO EVIL!
NOBODY EVER THINKS THEY'RE THE BAD GUYS.
YOU GET ME?
I'M GOING BACK TO THE BEEHIVE TO MAKE A REPORT!
CONNOR, KEEP A CLOSE EYE ON THE CONVENT.
WHAT ABOUT LAG?
LAG?
IF I TELL HIM, ***HE'LL*** WANT TO SNEAK INTO THE CONVENT TOO...
OH...
HMM..
SO
CUTE
UM...
BETTER KEEP MY LIP ZIPPED.
LAG'S KEEPING WATCH SOMEWHERE ELSE!
SEE YOU LATER!

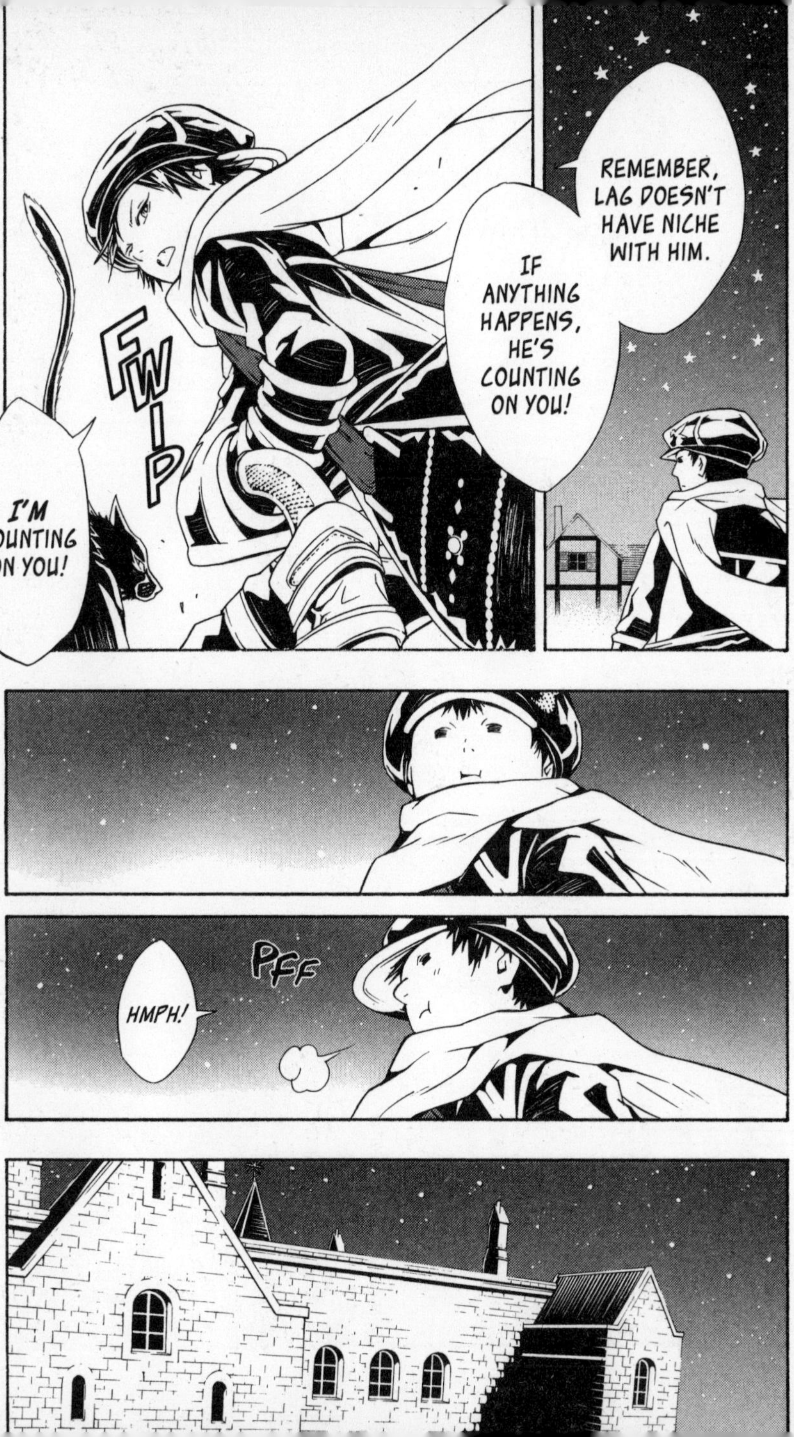
REMEMBER, LAG DOESN'T HAVE NICHE WITH HIM.
IF ANYTHING HAPPENS, HE'S COUNTING ON YOU!
FWIP
I'M COUNTING ON YOU!
PFF
HMPH!

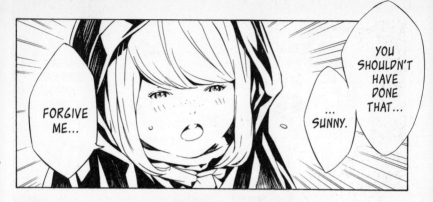

YOU SHOULDN'T HAVE DONE THAT...
... SUNNY.
FORGIVE ME...
HOW COULD YOU INVITE A STRANGER HERE AT SUCH A CRUCIAL TIME?
YOU KNOW WHAT AN IMPORTANT ROLE WE HAVE.
I THOUGHT IT WOULD BE ALL RIGHT...
...SINCE WE DON'T ACT FOR TWO MORE DAYS.
THE DATE HAS CHANGED.
WE MOVE *TODAY*.
...
TODAY? RIGHT NOW?
THE DELIVERY CAME EARLY.
EVERY-ONE'S HEADED FOR ANGEL'S WINGS.
AND NOW, SUNNY ...

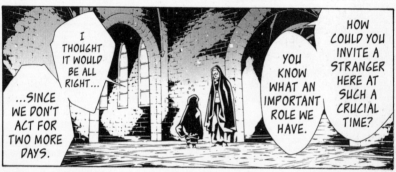

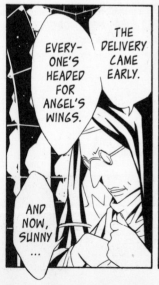

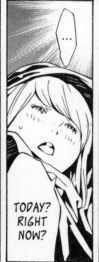

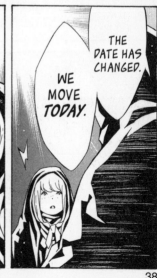

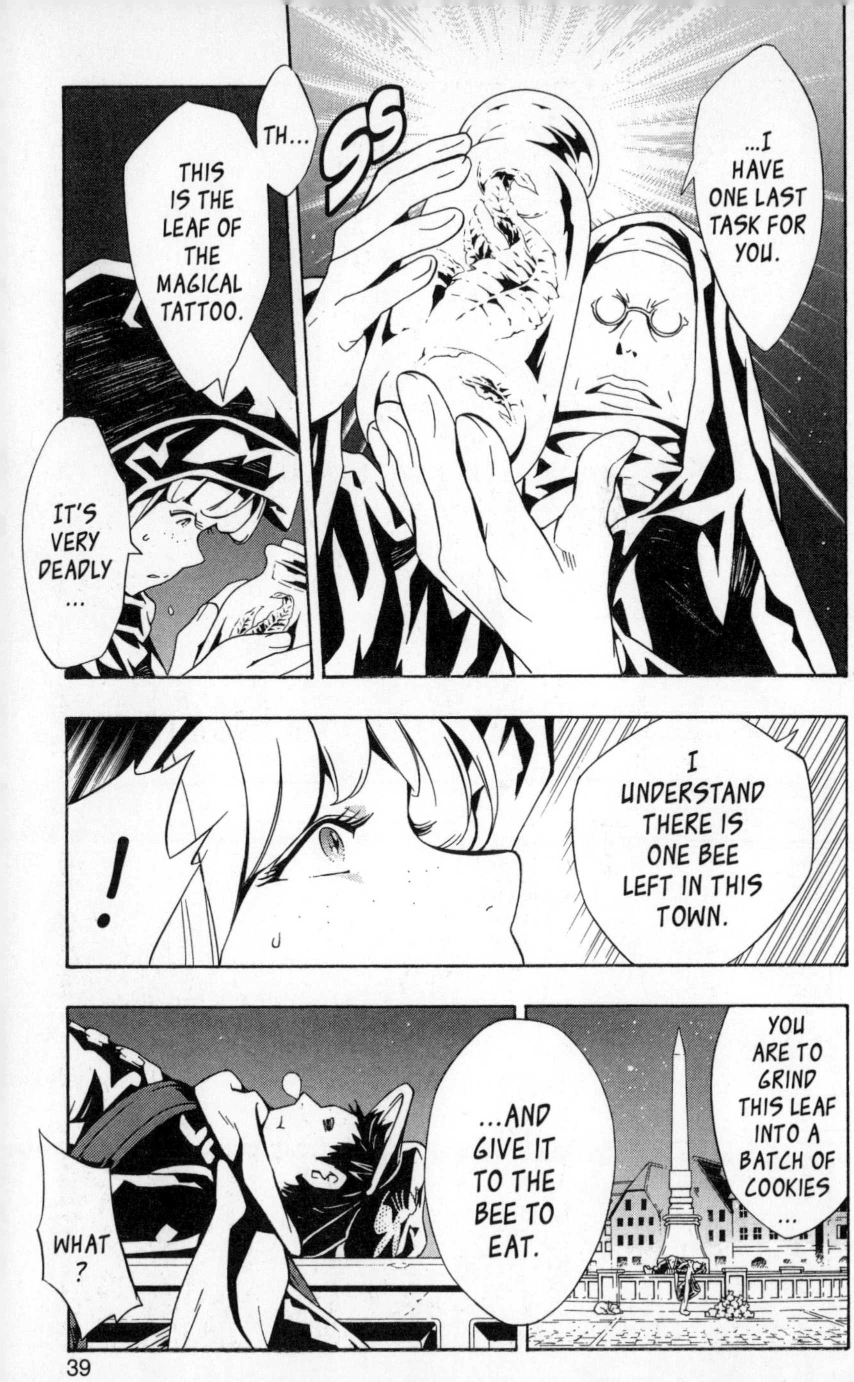
...I HAVE ONE LAST TASK FOR YOU.
SS
TH...
THIS IS THE LEAF OF THE MAGICAL TATTOO.
IT'S VERY DEADLY ...
I UNDERSTAND THERE IS ONE BEE LEFT IN THIS TOWN.
!
YOU ARE TO GRIND THIS LEAF INTO A BATCH OF COOKIES ...
...AND GIVE IT TO THE BEE TO EAT.
WHAT ?

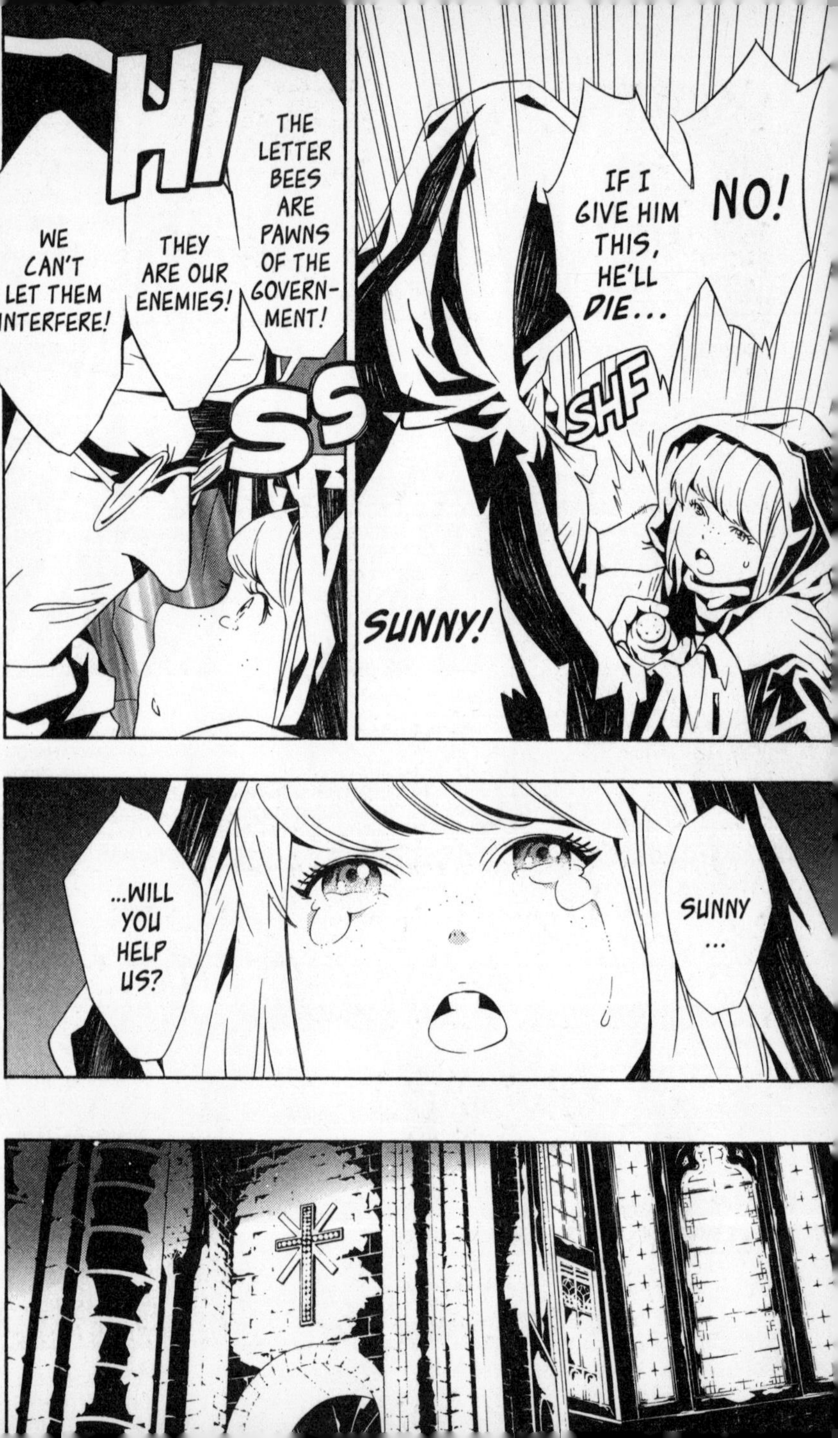
NO!
IF I GIVE HIM THIS, HE'LL DIE...
SHF
SUNNY!
HI
THE LETTER BEES ARE PAWNS OF THE GOVERN-MENT!
THEY ARE OUR ENEMIES!
WE CAN'T LET THEM INTERFERE!
SS
SUNNY ...
...WILL YOU HELP US?

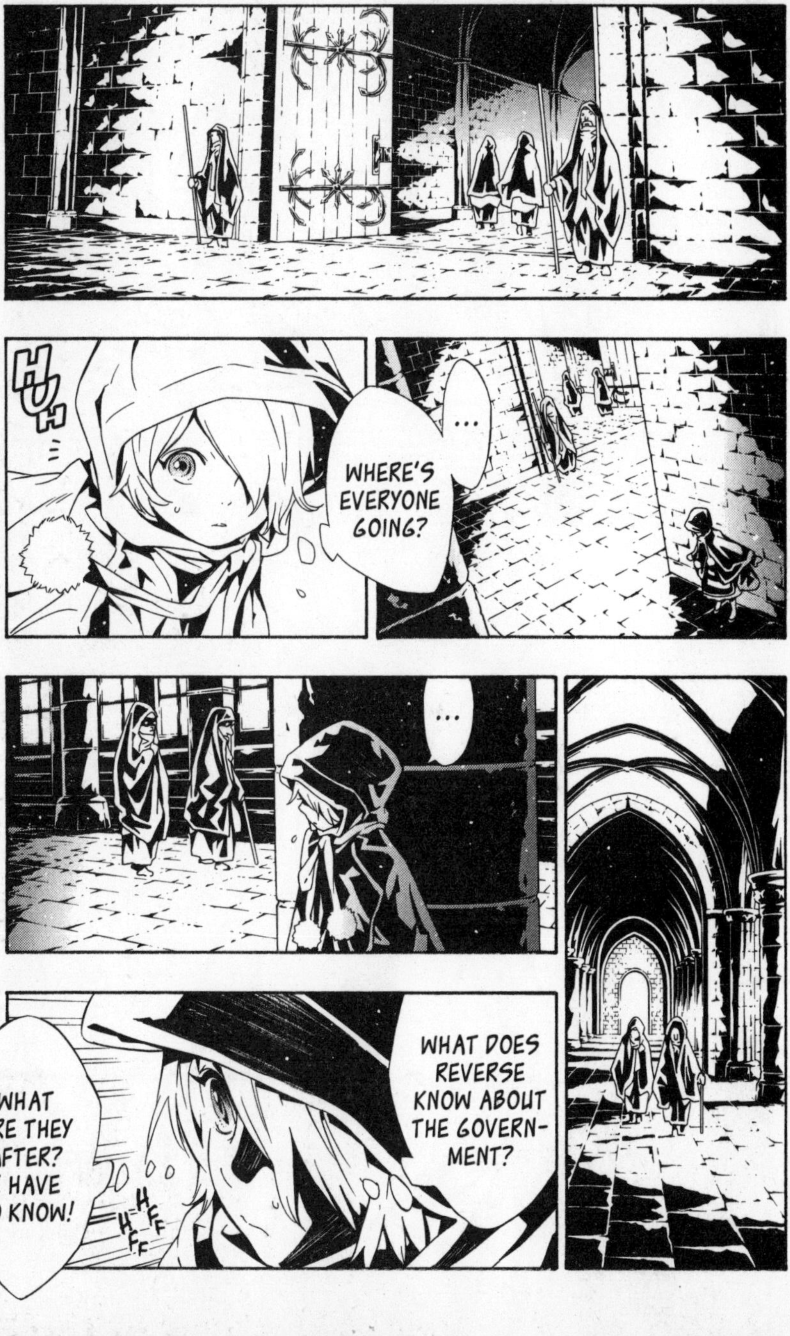
...
WHERE'S EVERYONE GOING?
HUH
...
WHAT DOES REVERSE KNOW ABOUT THE GOVERN-MENT?
WHAT ARE THEY AFTER? I HAVE TO KNOW!
HFF HFF

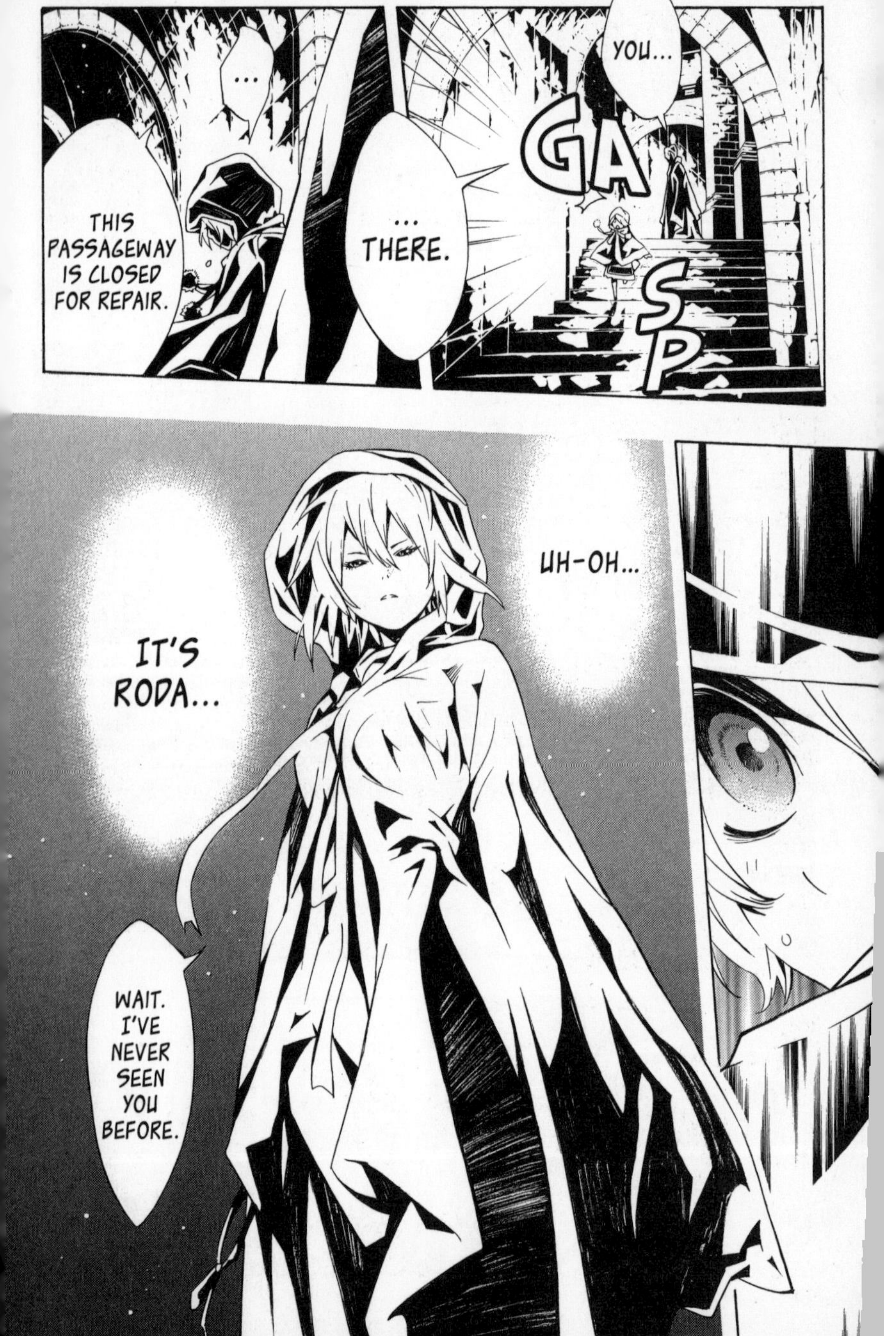
YOU...
GASP
...
... THERE.
THIS PASSAGEWAY IS CLOSED FOR REPAIR.
UH-OH...
IT'S RODA...
WAIT. I'VE NEVER SEEN YOU BEFORE.

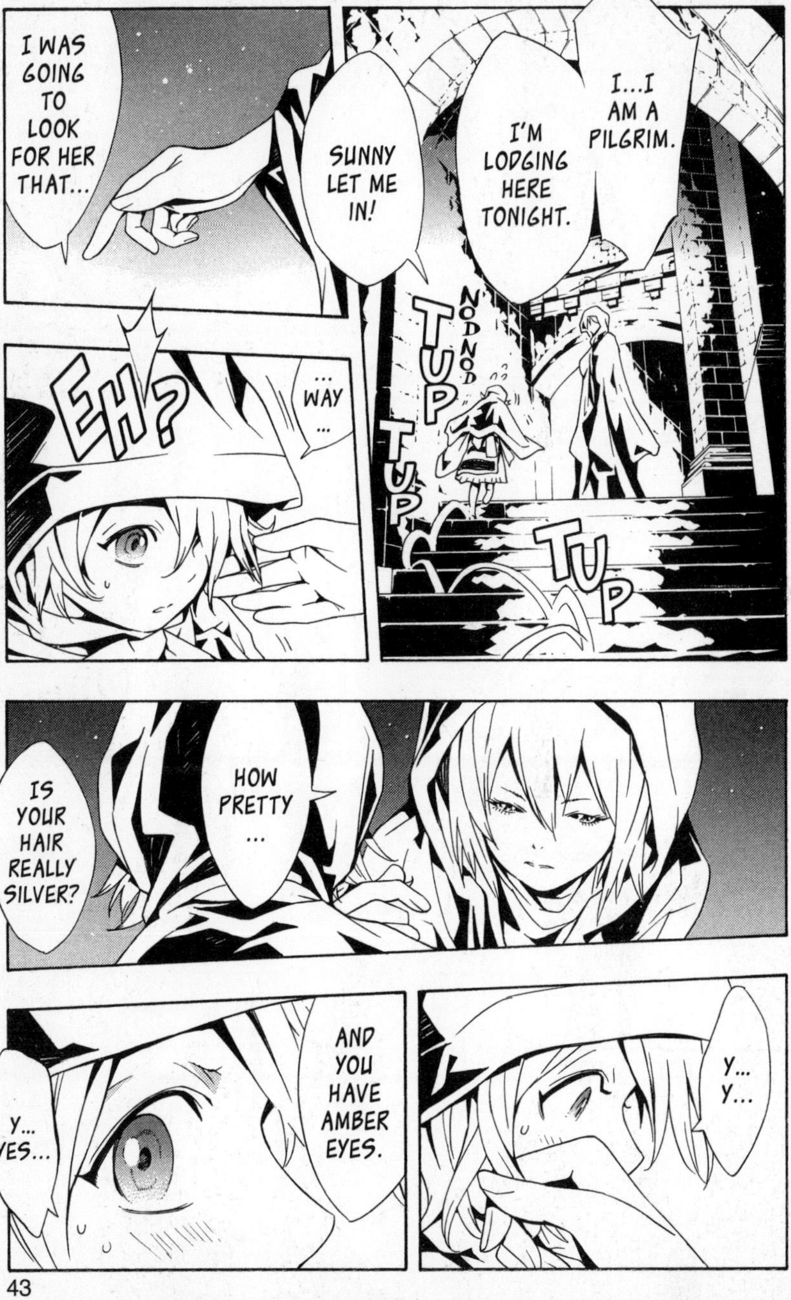
I...I AM A PILGRIM.
I'M LODGING HERE TONIGHT.
SUNNY LET ME IN!
NODNOD
TUP TUP
TUP TUP
TUP TUP
I WAS GOING TO LOOK FOR HER THAT...
...WAY...
EH?
HOW PRETTY...
IS YOUR HAIR REALLY SILVER?
Y... Y...
AND YOU HAVE AMBER EYES.
Y... YES...

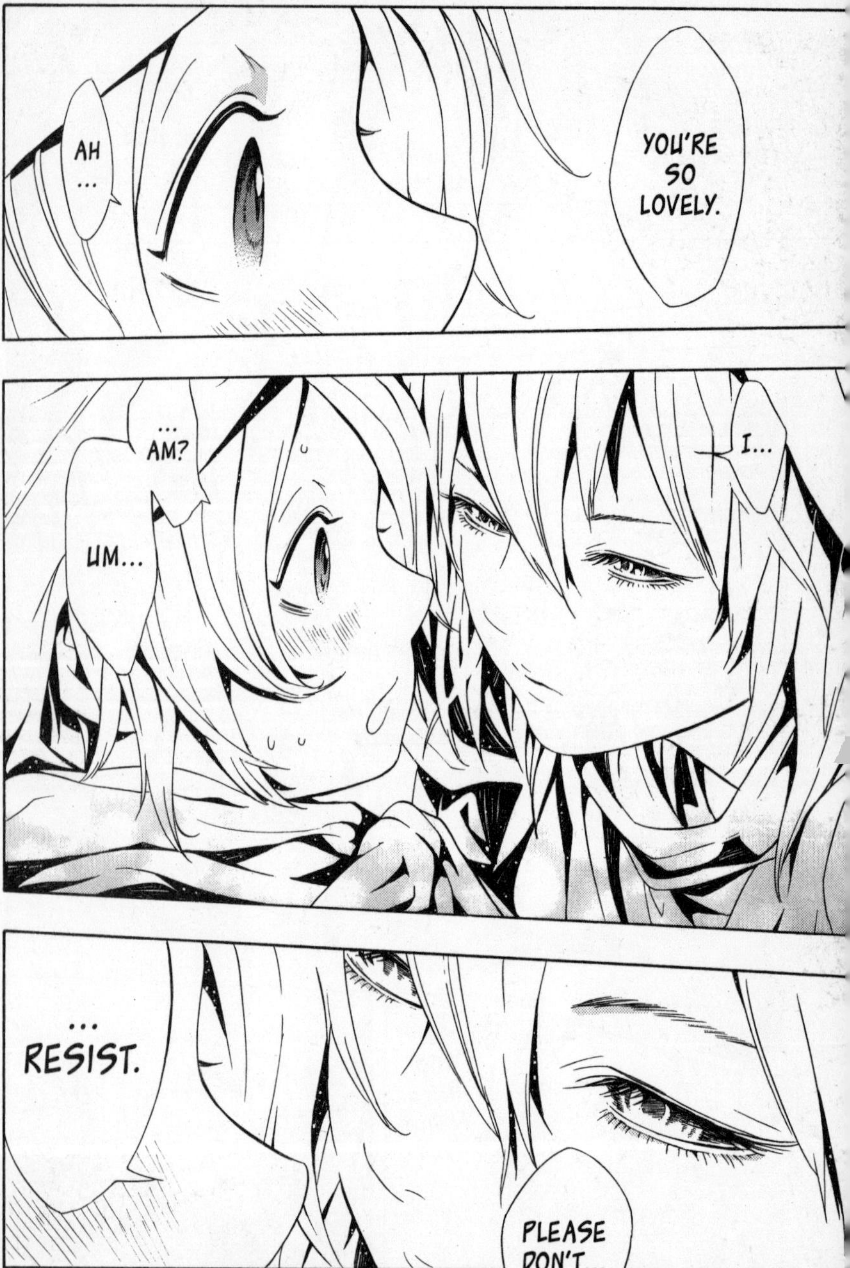
YOU'RE SO LOVELY.
AH ...
I...
... AM?
UM...
PLEASE DON'T...
... RESIST.

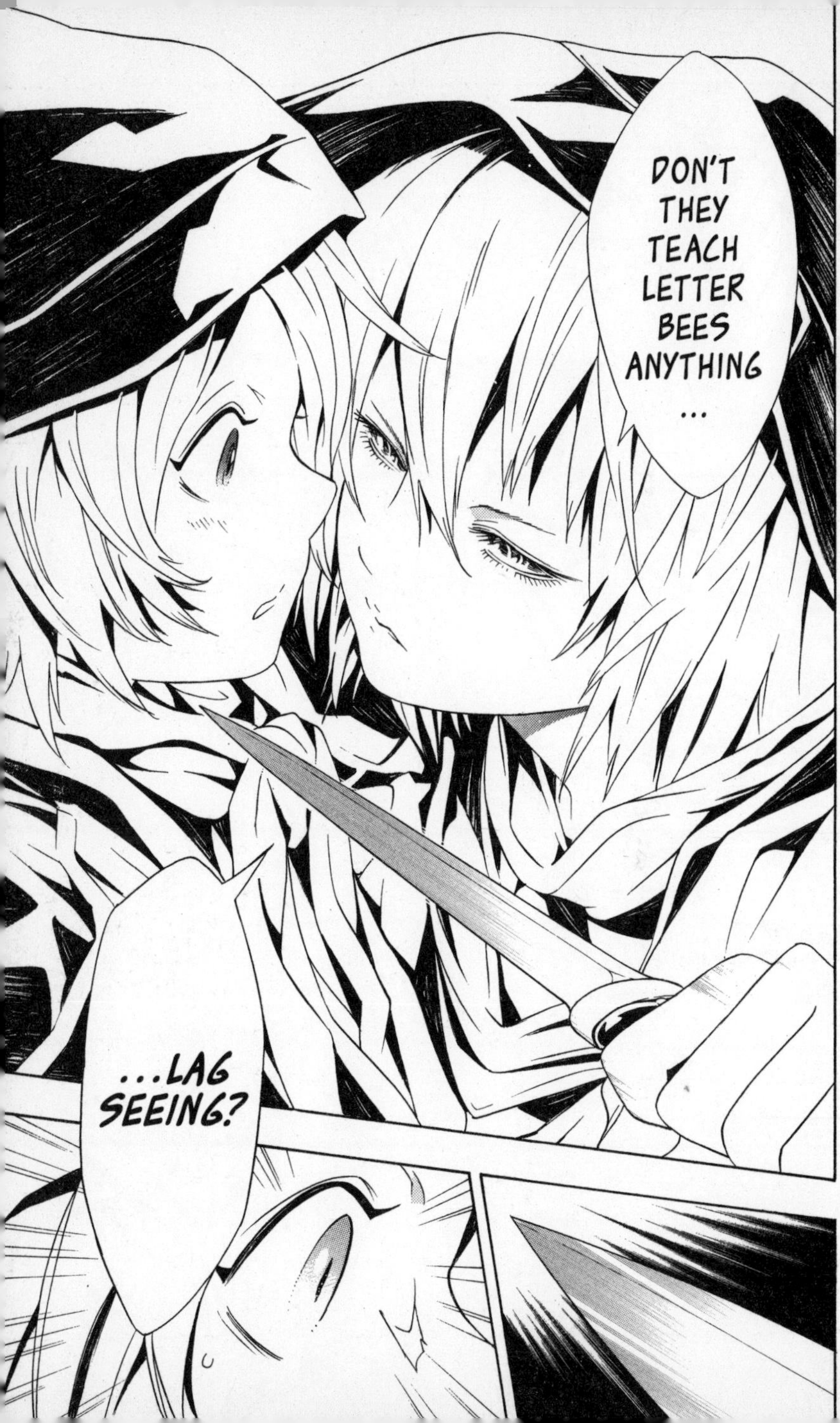
DON'T THEY TEACH LETTER BEES ANYTHING ...
...LAG SEEING?

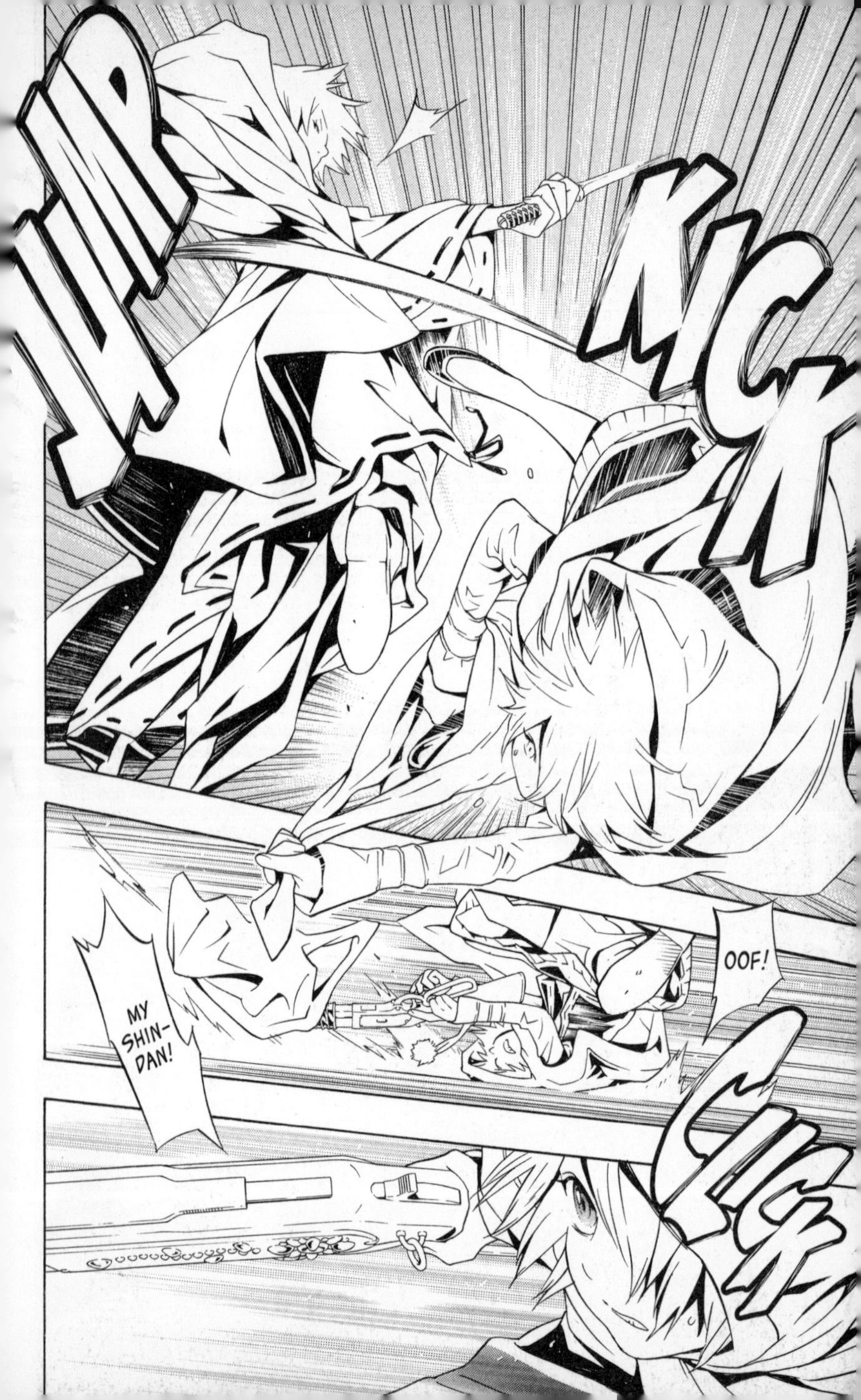
KICK
WHIP
OOF!
MY SHIN-DAN!
CLICK

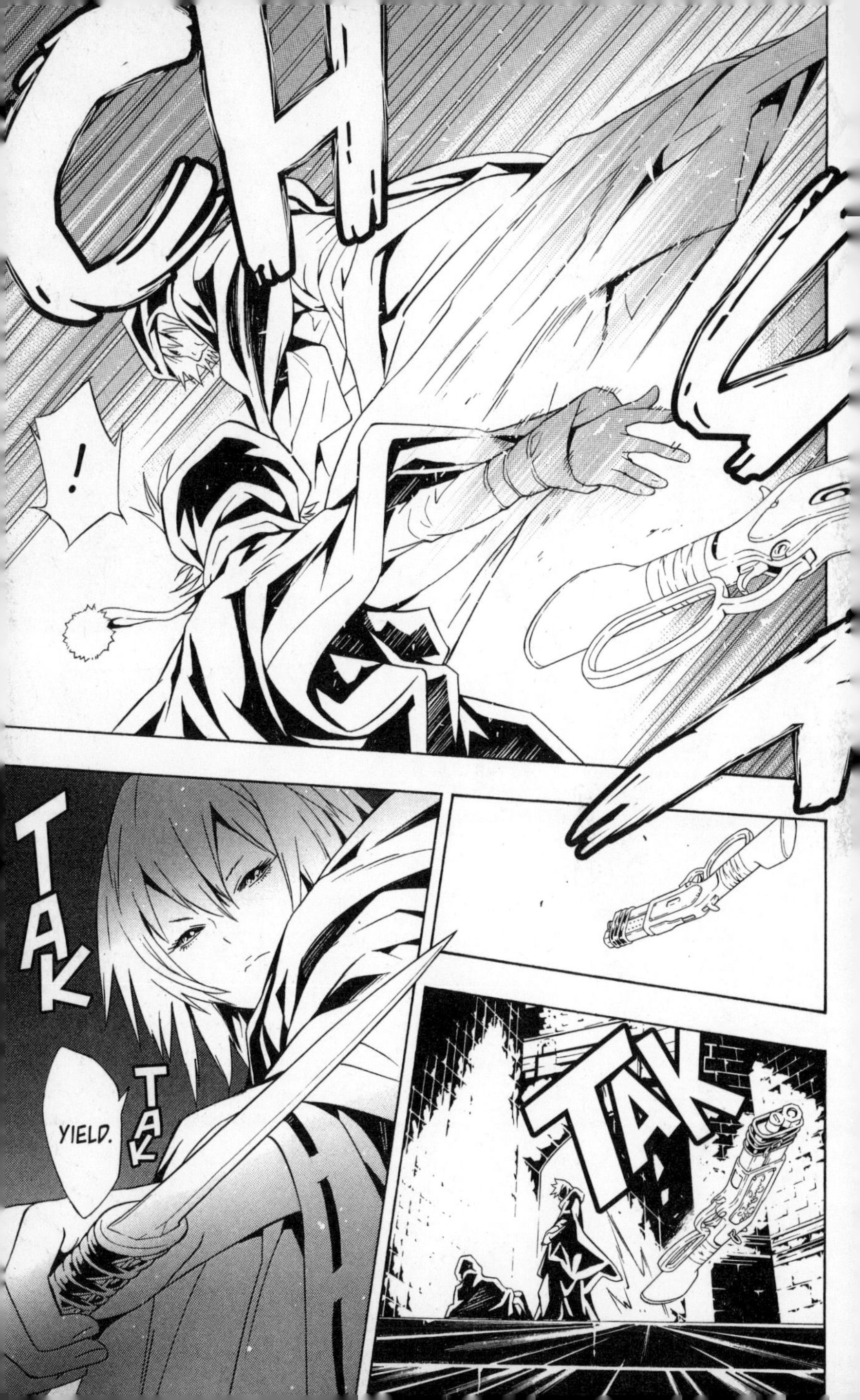
CHAK
!
TAK
TAK
YIELD.
TAK TAK

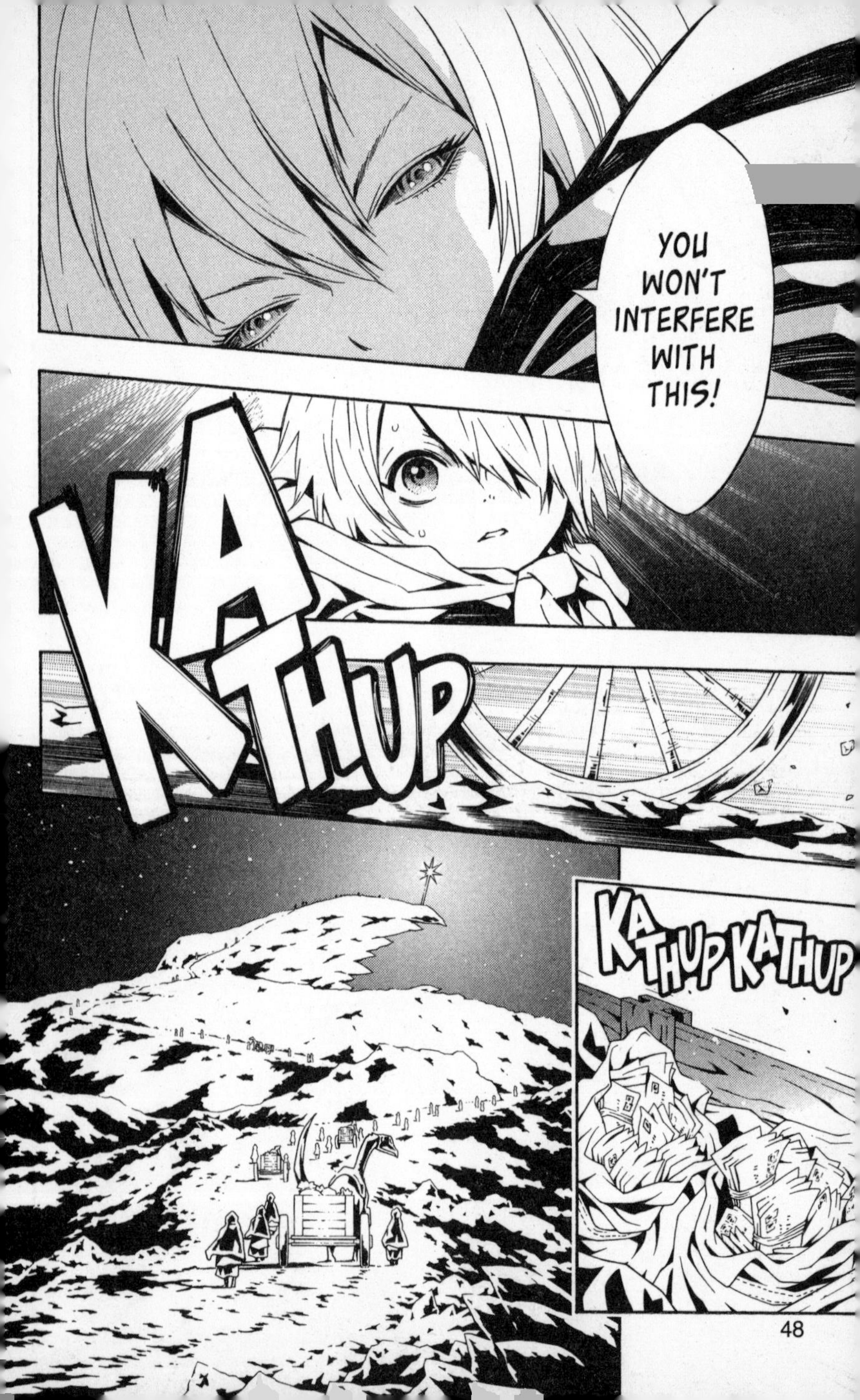
YOU WON'T INTERFERE WITH THIS!
KA THUP
KATHUP KATHUP

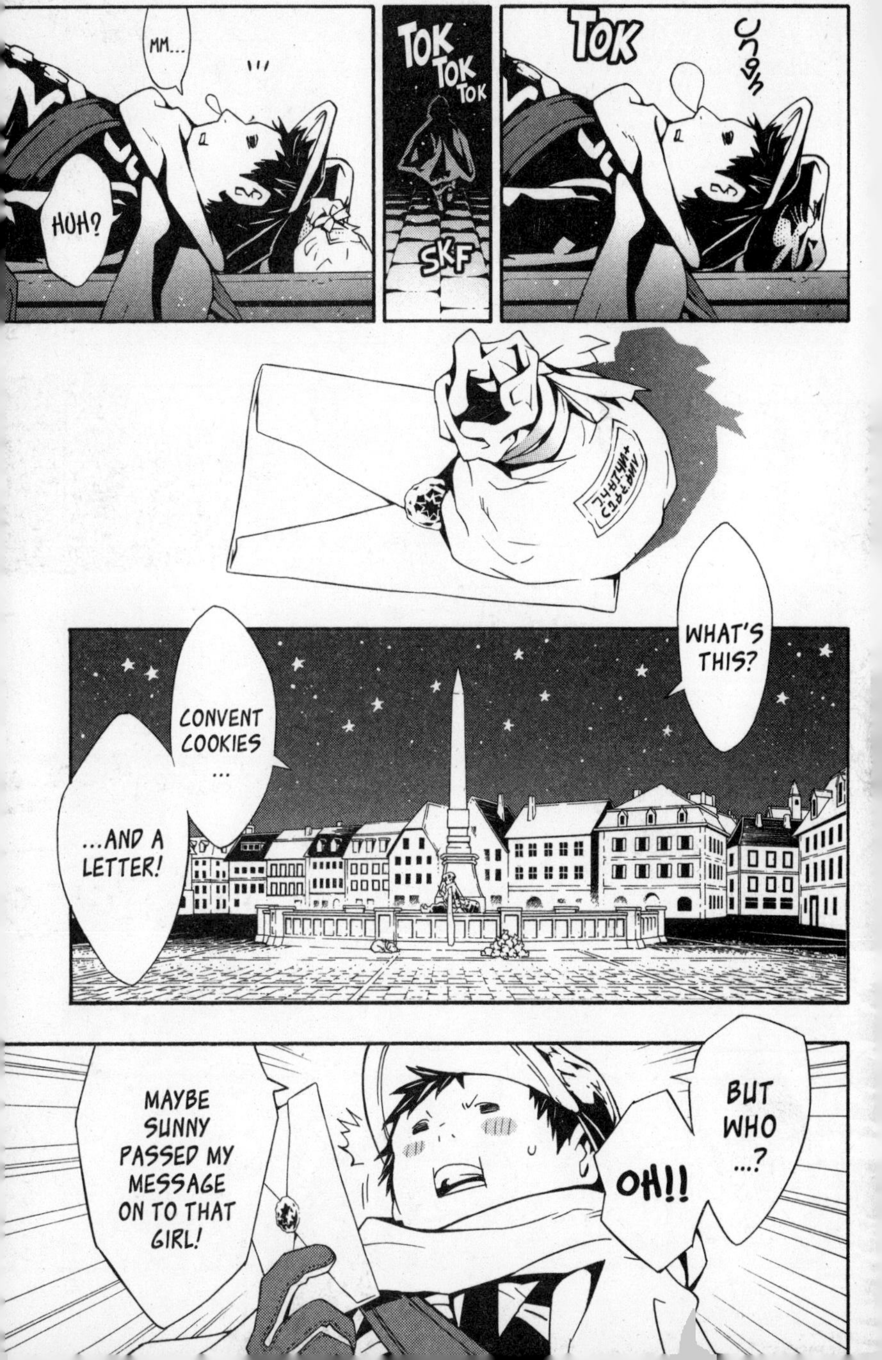
TOK
Ungh
TOK
TOK
TOK
SKF
MM...
HUH?
WHAT'S THIS?
CONVENT COOKIES ...
...AND A LETTER!
BUT WHO ...?
OH!!
MAYBE SUNNY PASSED MY MESSAGE ON TO THAT GIRL!

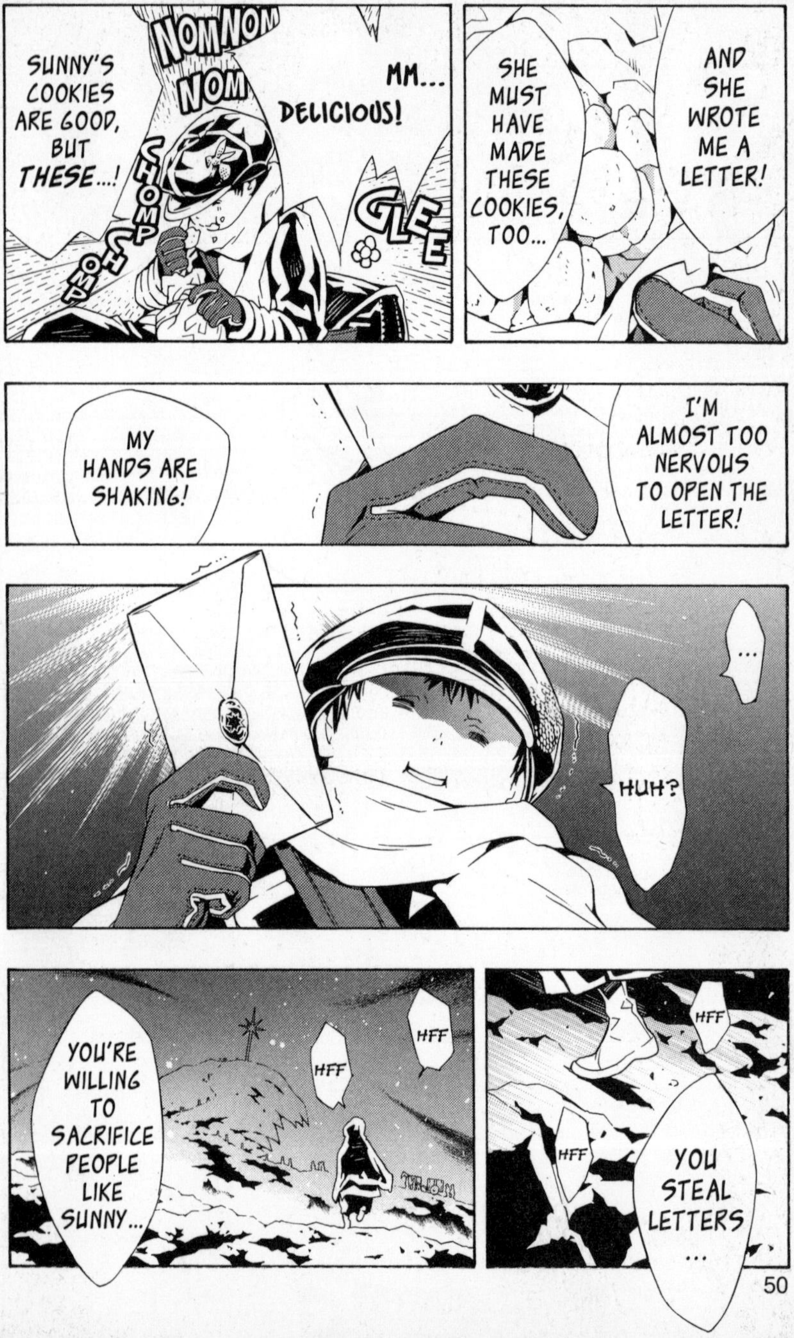
NOMNOM NOM
SUNNY'S COOKIES ARE GOOD, BUT THESE...!
CHOMP CHOMP
MM... DELICIOUS!
GLEE
SHE MUST HAVE MADE THESE COOKIES, TOO...
AND SHE WROTE ME A LETTER!
MY HANDS ARE SHAKING!
I'M ALMOST TOO NERVOUS TO OPEN THE LETTER!
...
HUH?
YOU'RE WILLING TO SACRIFICE PEOPLE LIKE SUNNY...
HFF
HFF
HFF
HFF
YOU STEAL LETTERS...

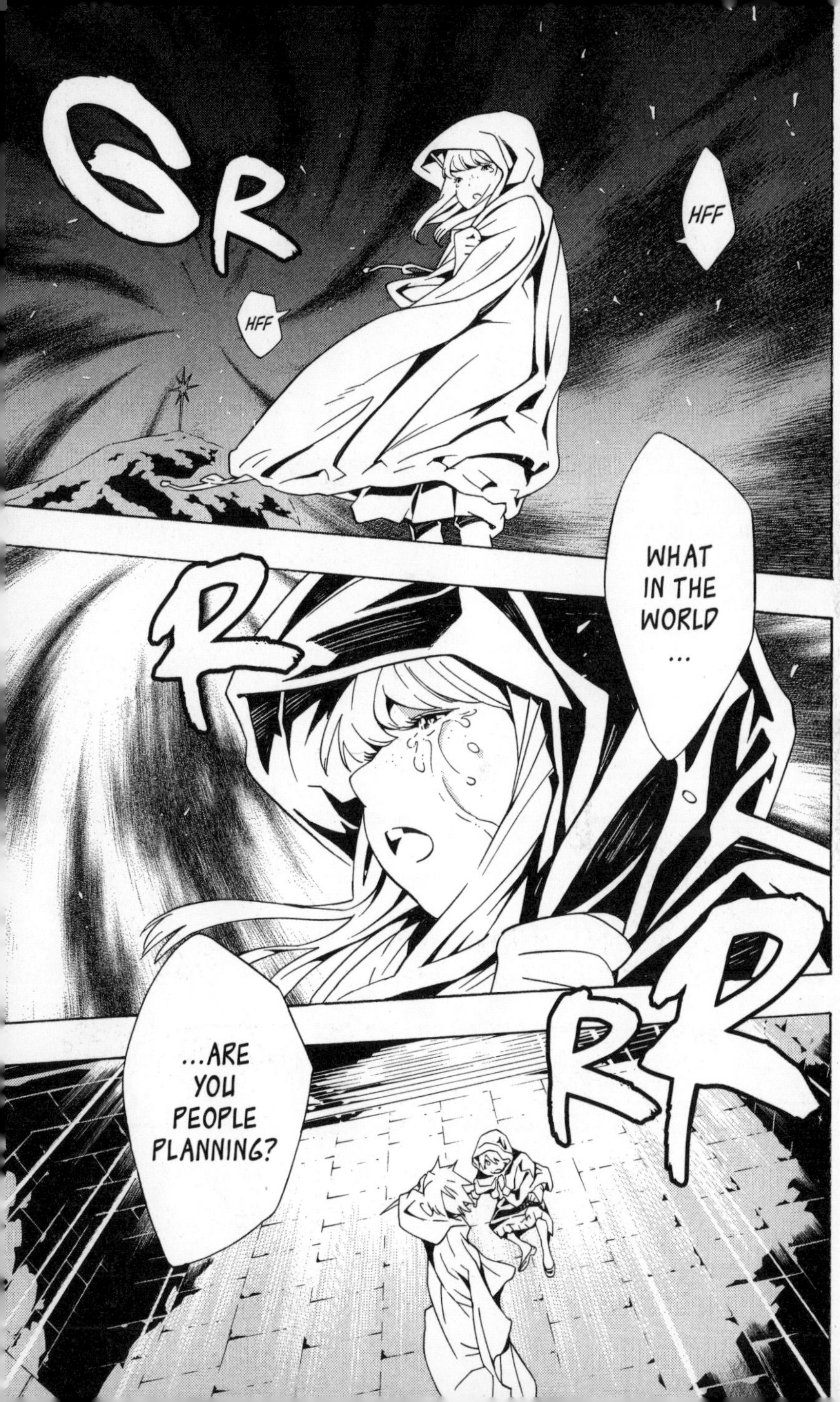
HFF
GR
HFF
WHAT IN THE WORLD ...
R
RR
...ARE YOU PEOPLE PLANNING?

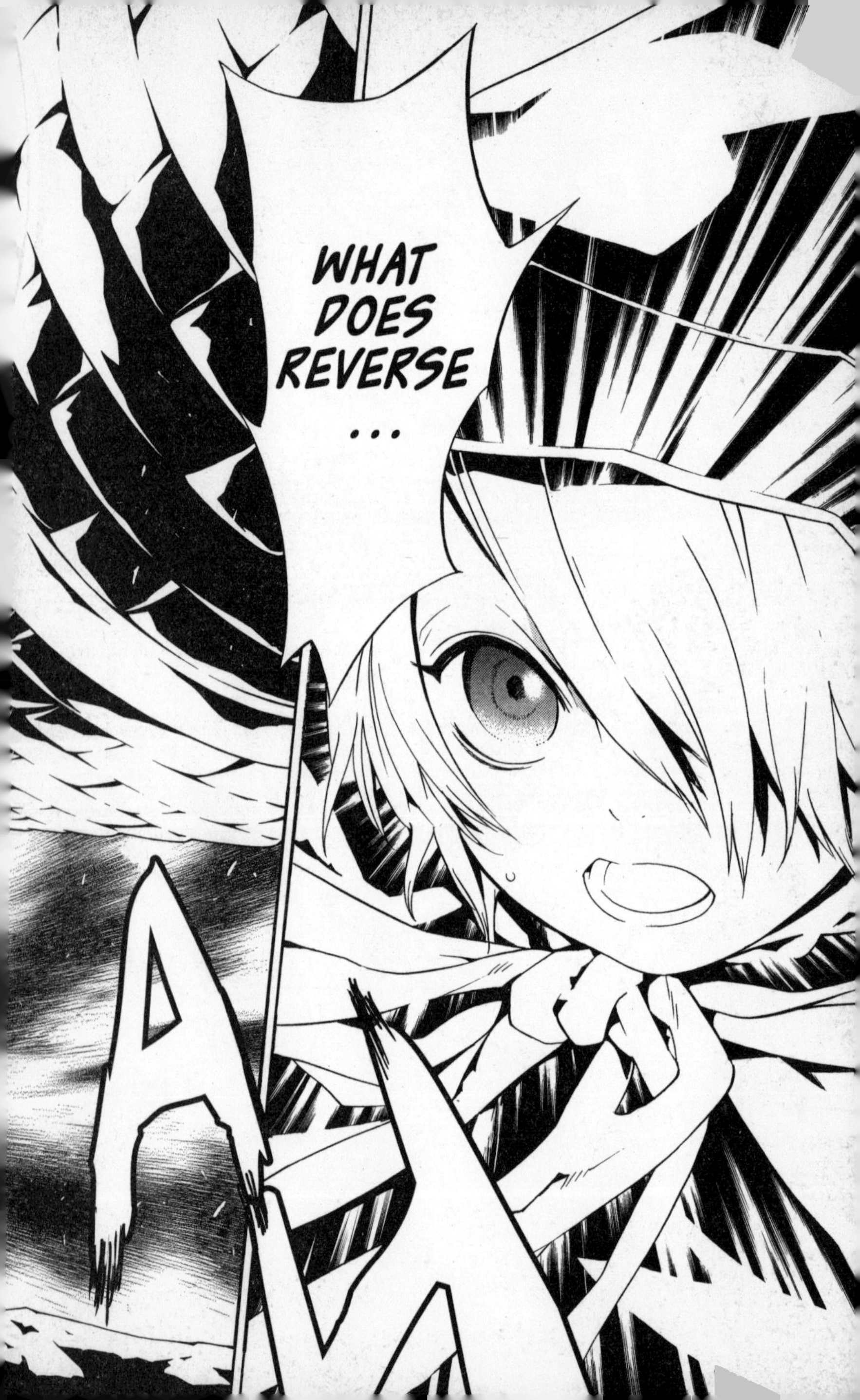
WHAT DOES REVERSE ...

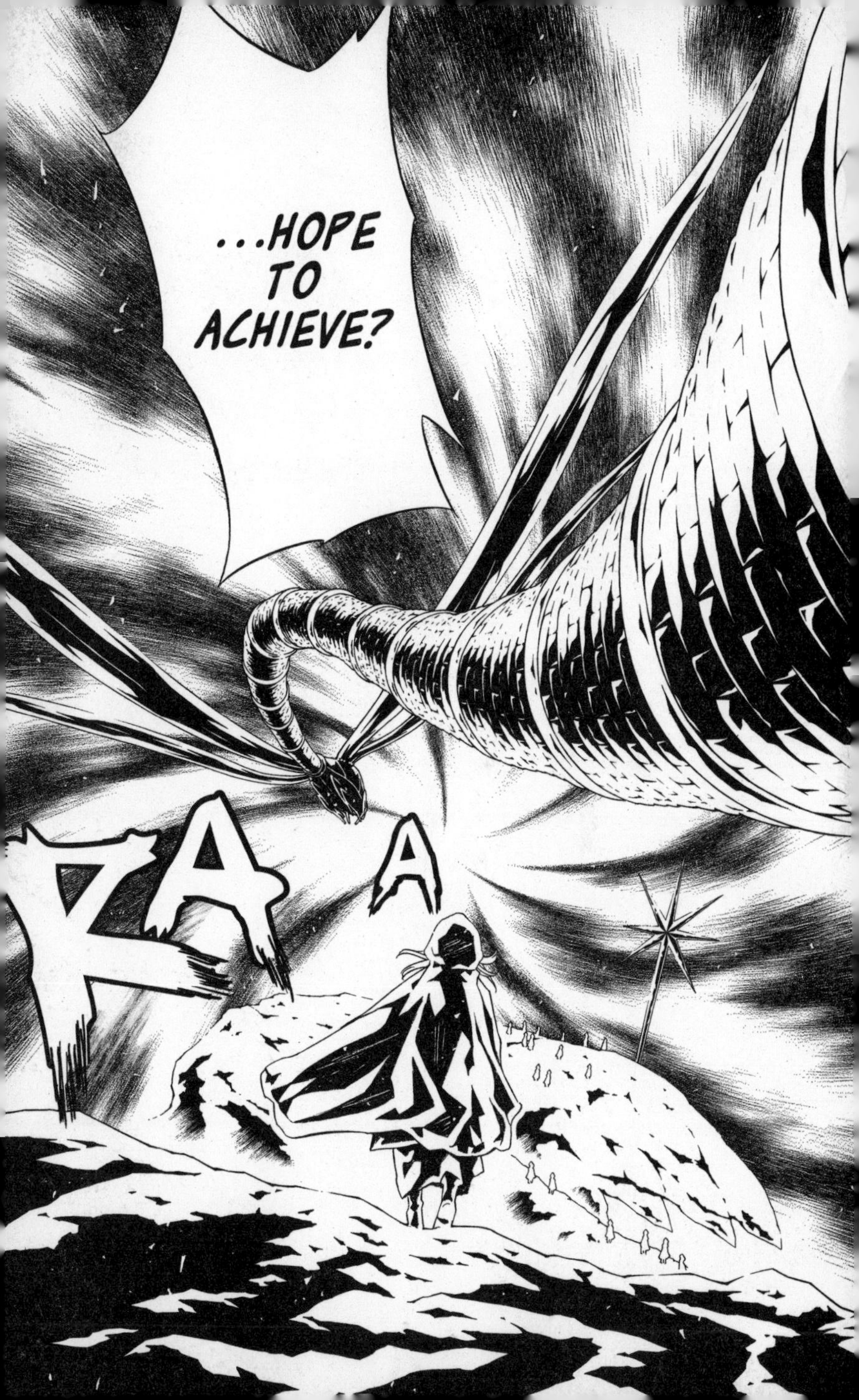
...HOPE TO ACHIEVE?
ZAA

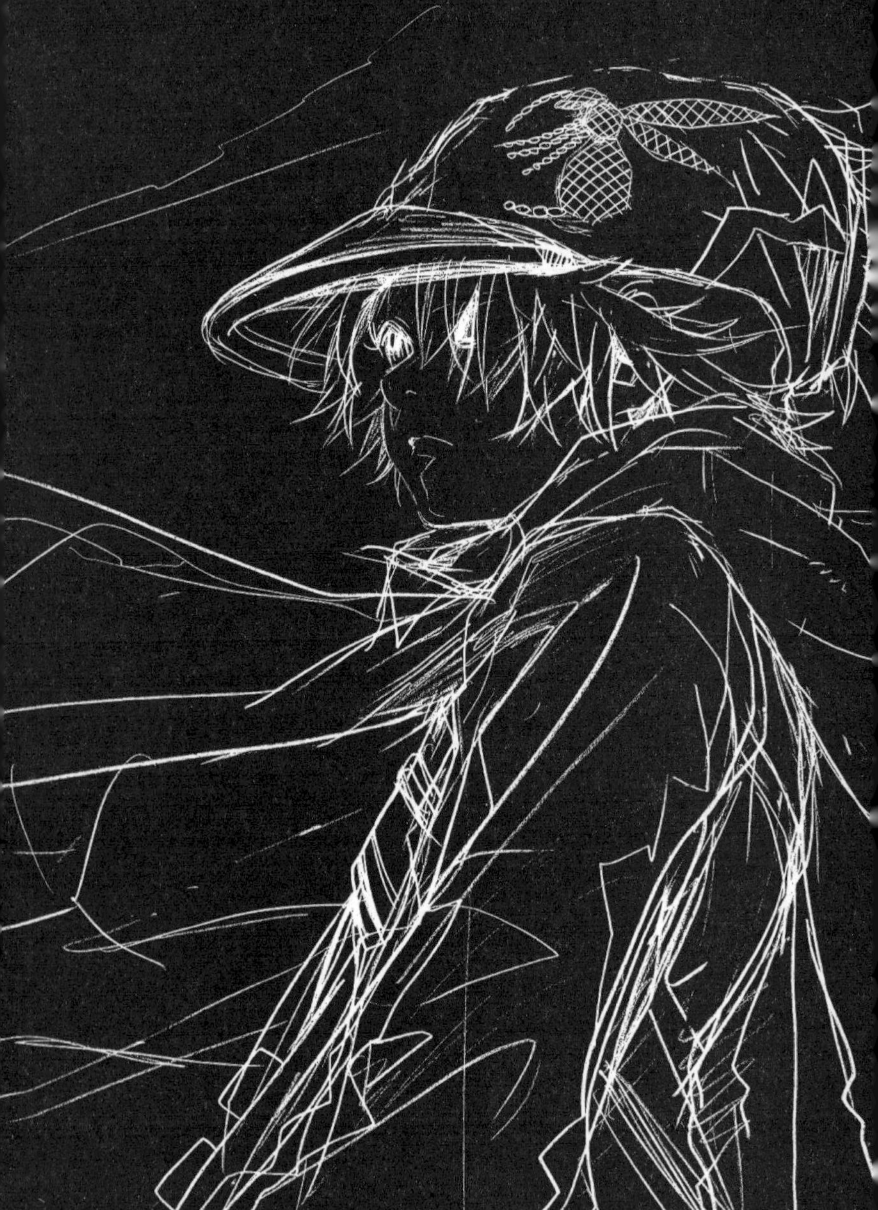

Rough Sketch
November 2009

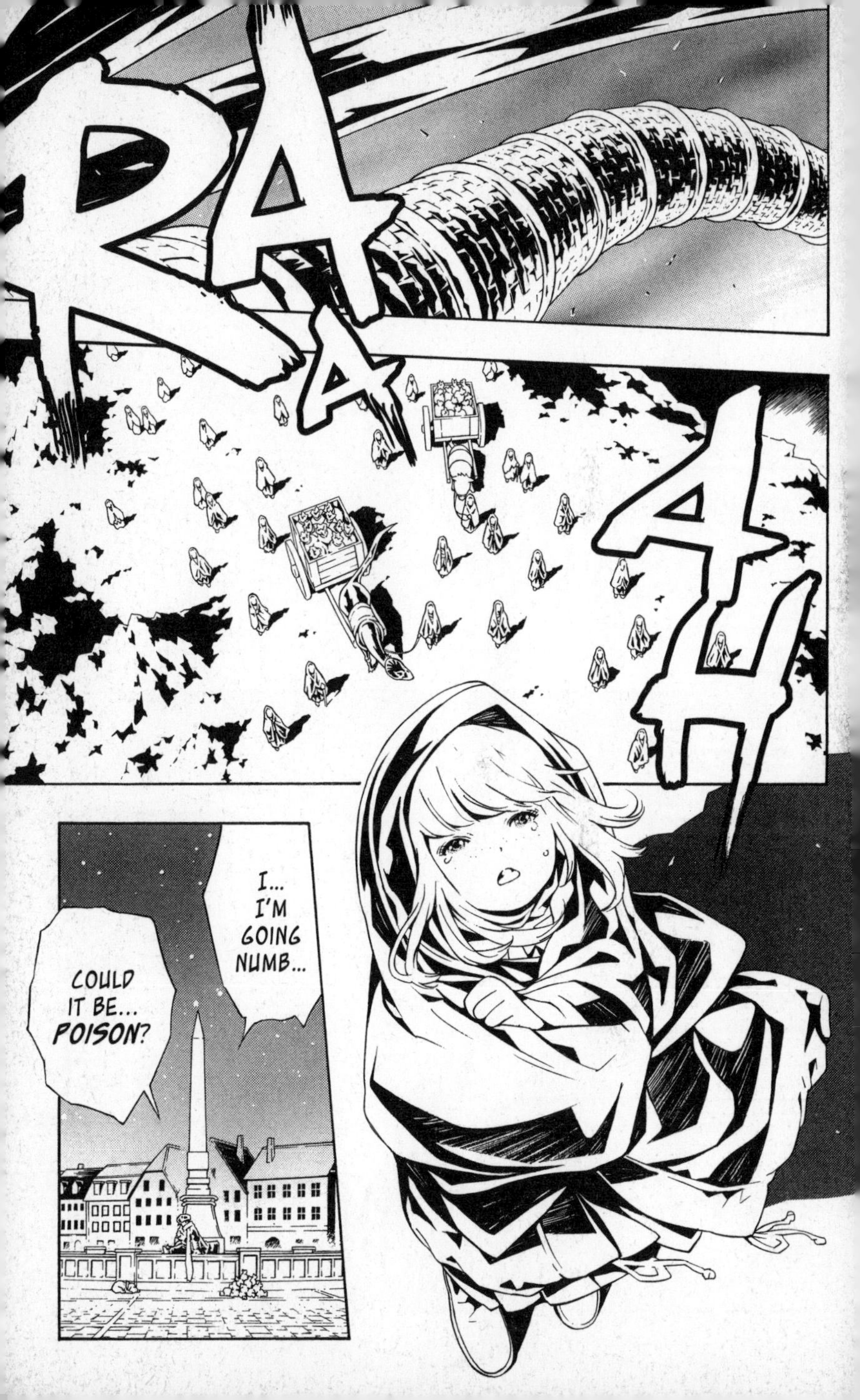
RAAAH
I... I'M GOING NUMB...
COULD IT BE... POISON?

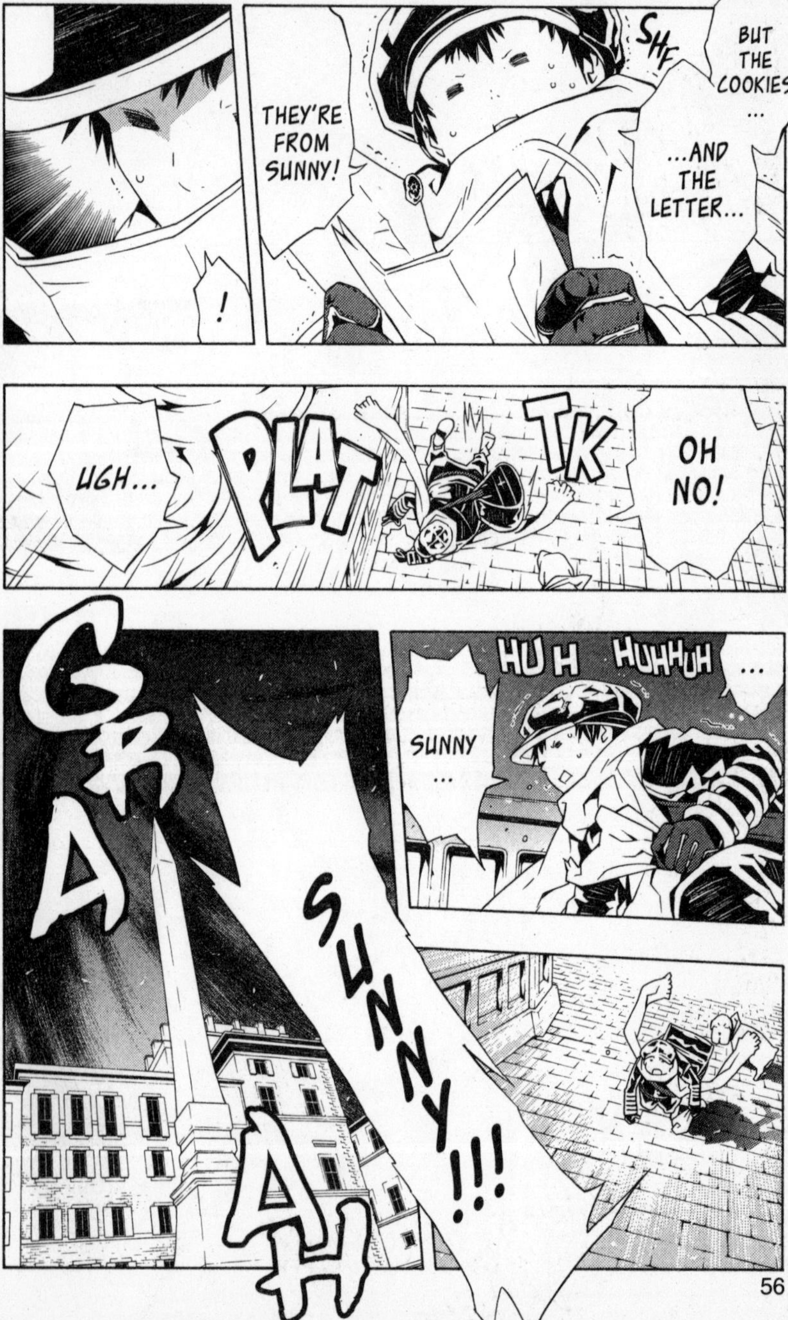
SHF
BUT THE COOKIES ...
...AND THE LETTER...
THEY'RE FROM SUNNY!
!
OH NO!
TK
PLAT
UGH...
HUH HUHHUH
...
SUNNY ...
SUNNY!!!
GRAAAH

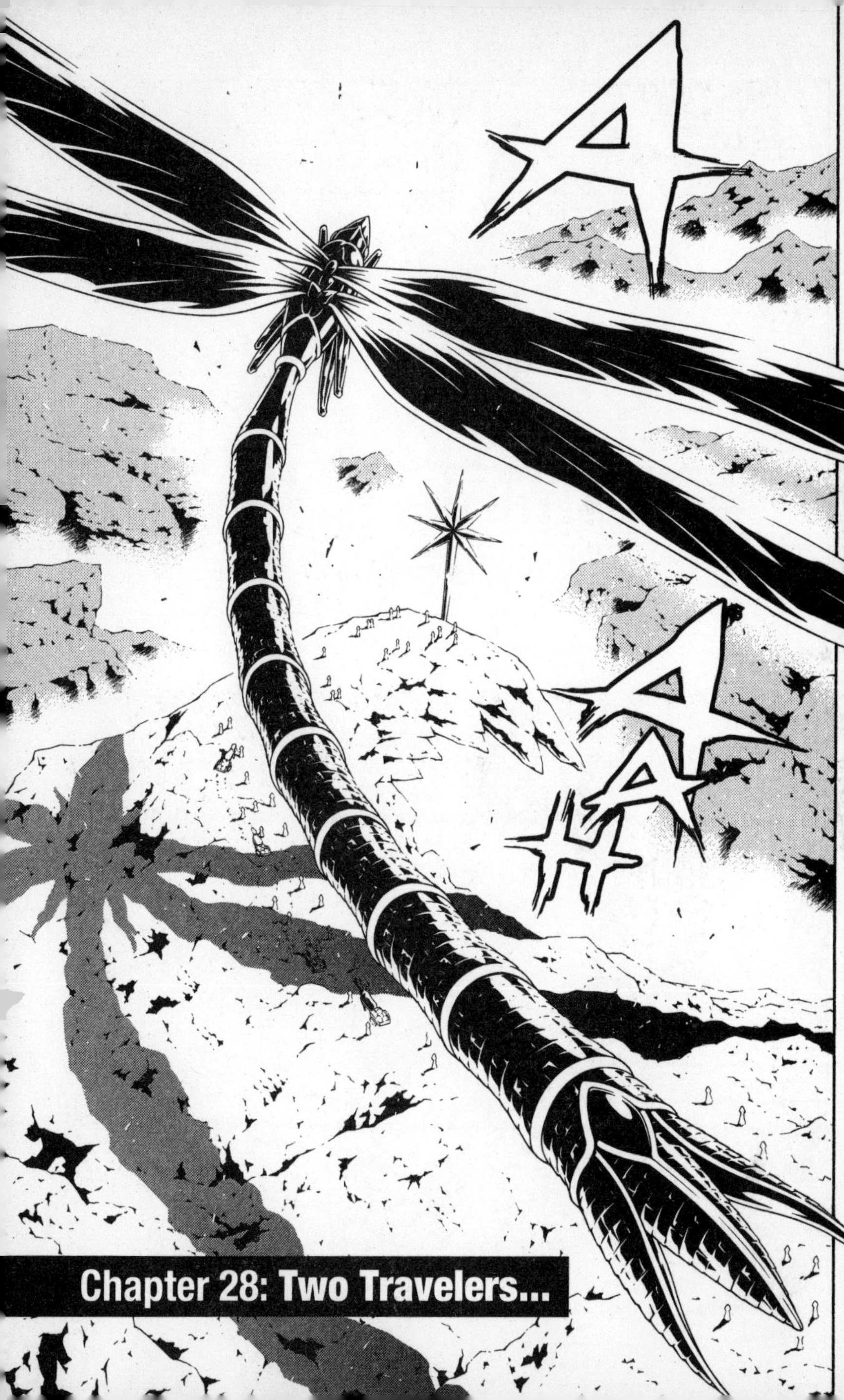
AAAH

Chapter 28: Two Travelers...

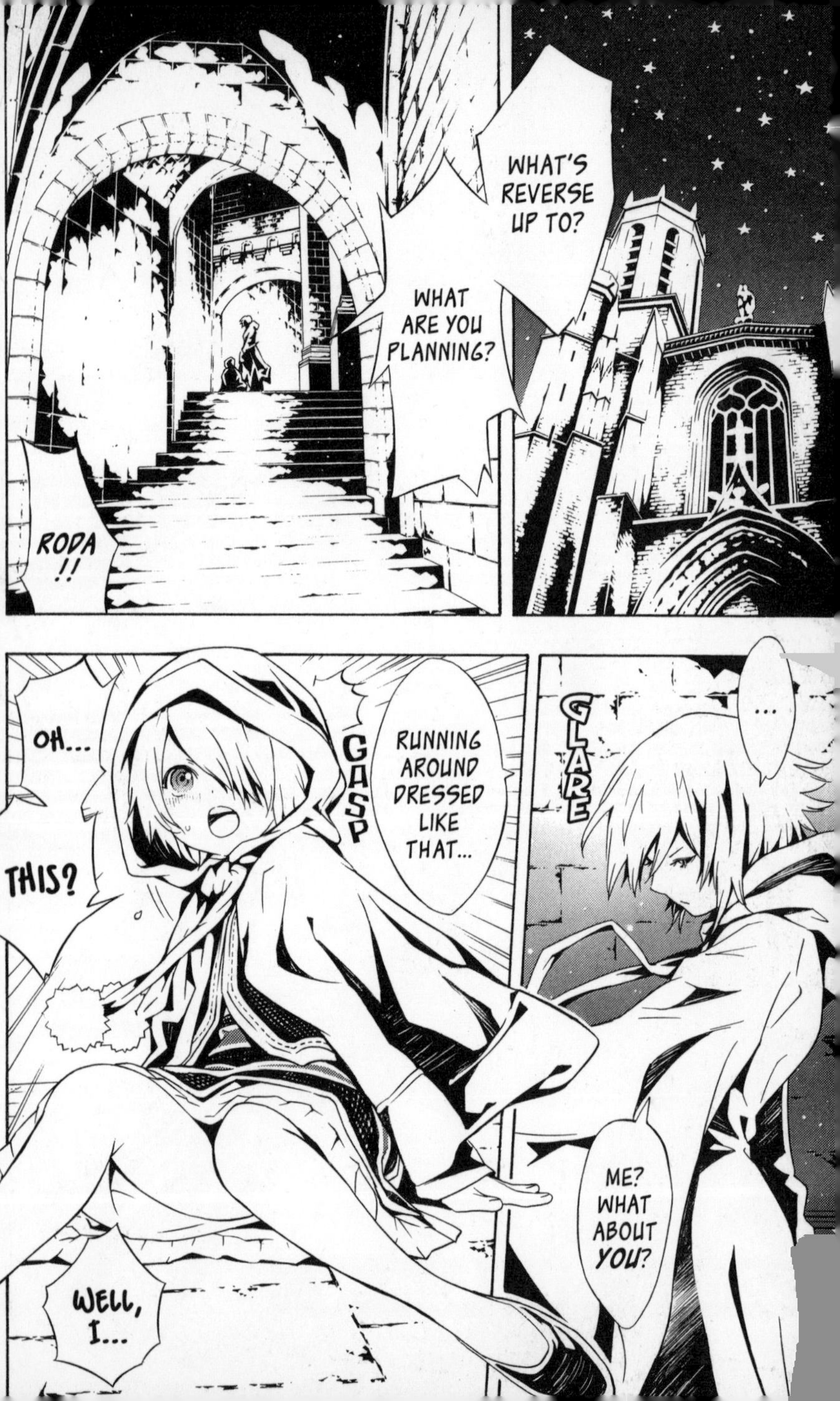
WHAT'S REVERSE UP TO?
WHAT ARE YOU PLANNING?
RODA!!
...
GLARE
ME? WHAT ABOUT YOU?
RUNNING AROUND DRESSED LIKE THAT...
GASP
OH... THIS?
WELL, I...

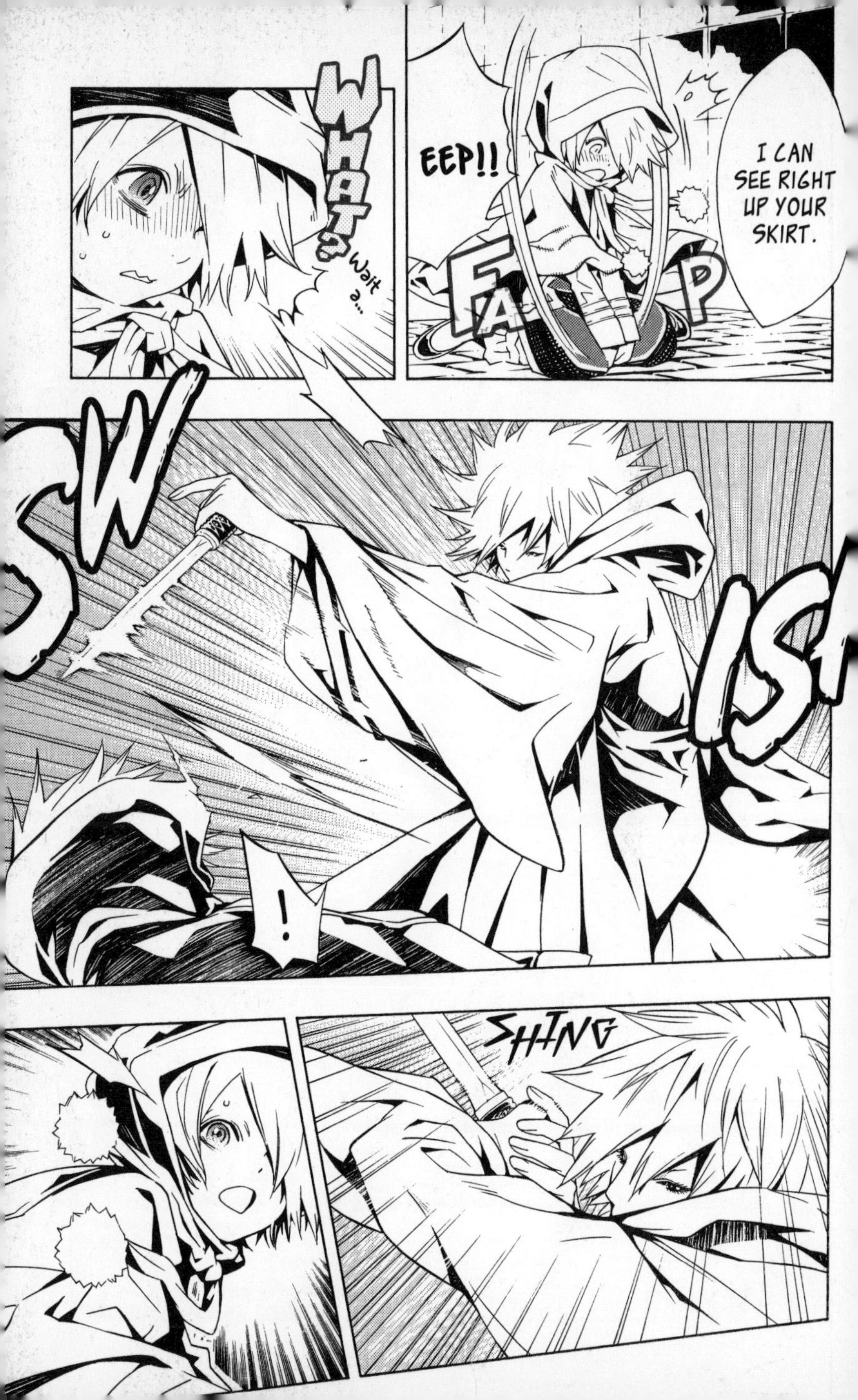
I CAN SEE RIGHT UP YOUR SKIRT.
EEP!!
FA P
WHAT?
Wait a...
SW
IS
!
SHING

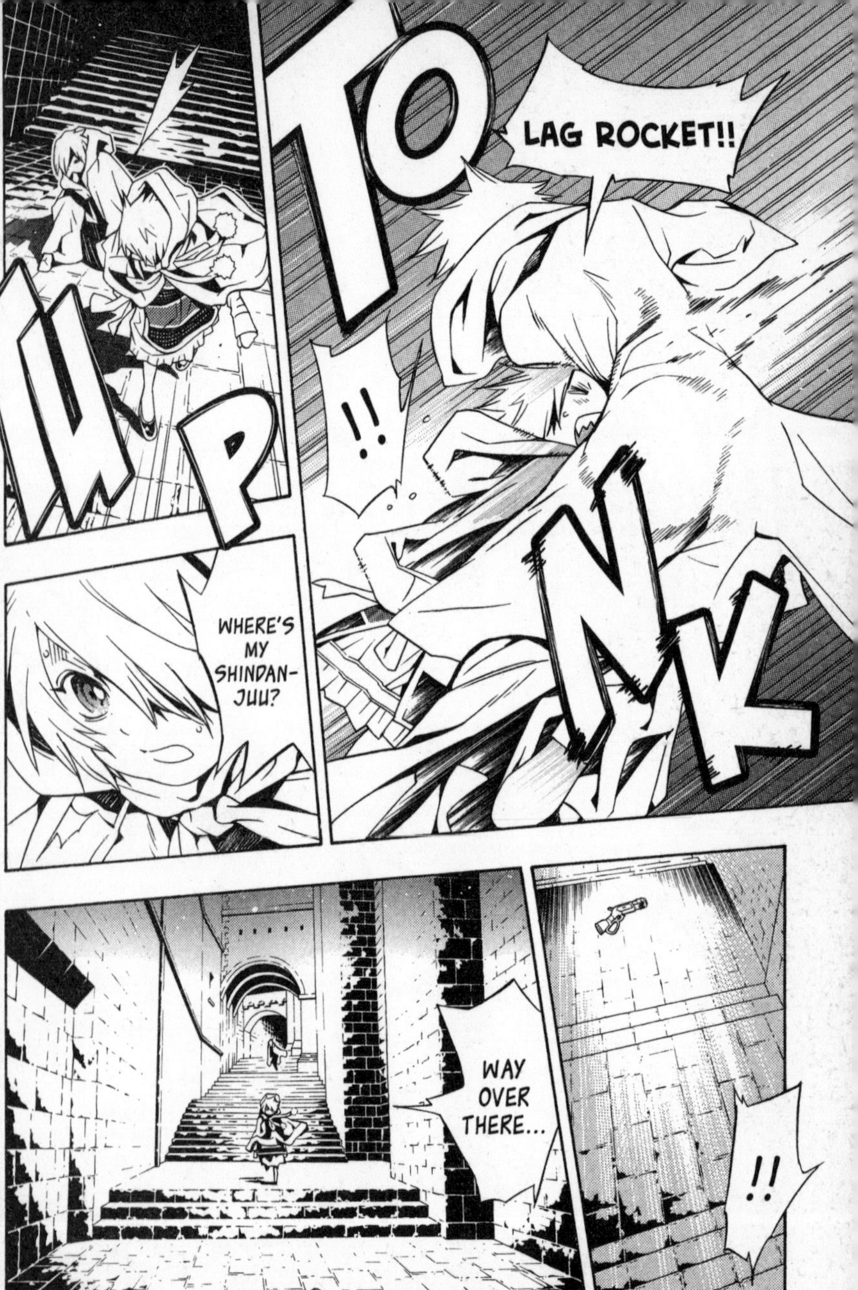
LAG ROCKET!!
!!
WHERE'S MY SHINDAN-JUU?
!!
WAY OVER THERE...

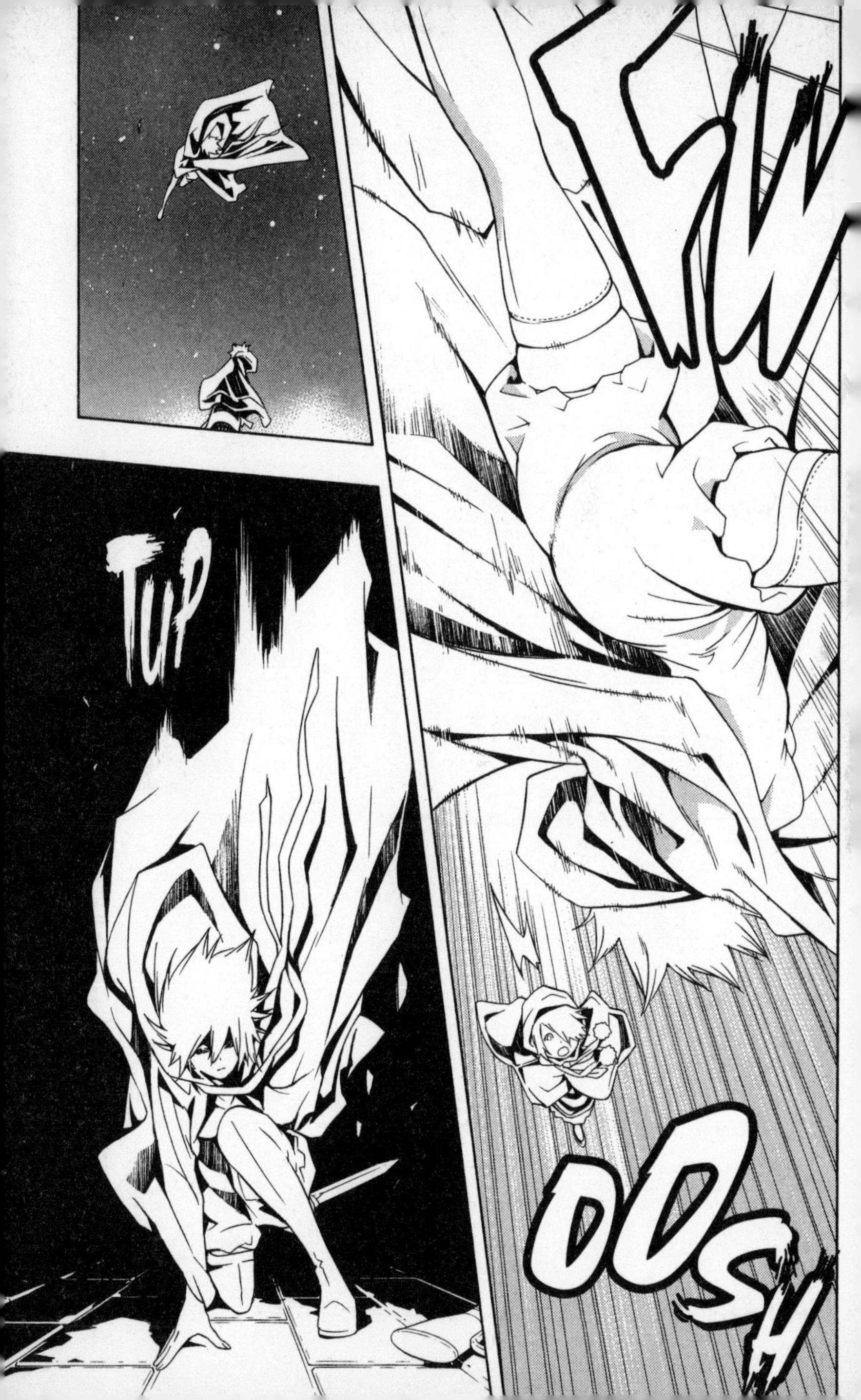
SW
OOSH
TUP

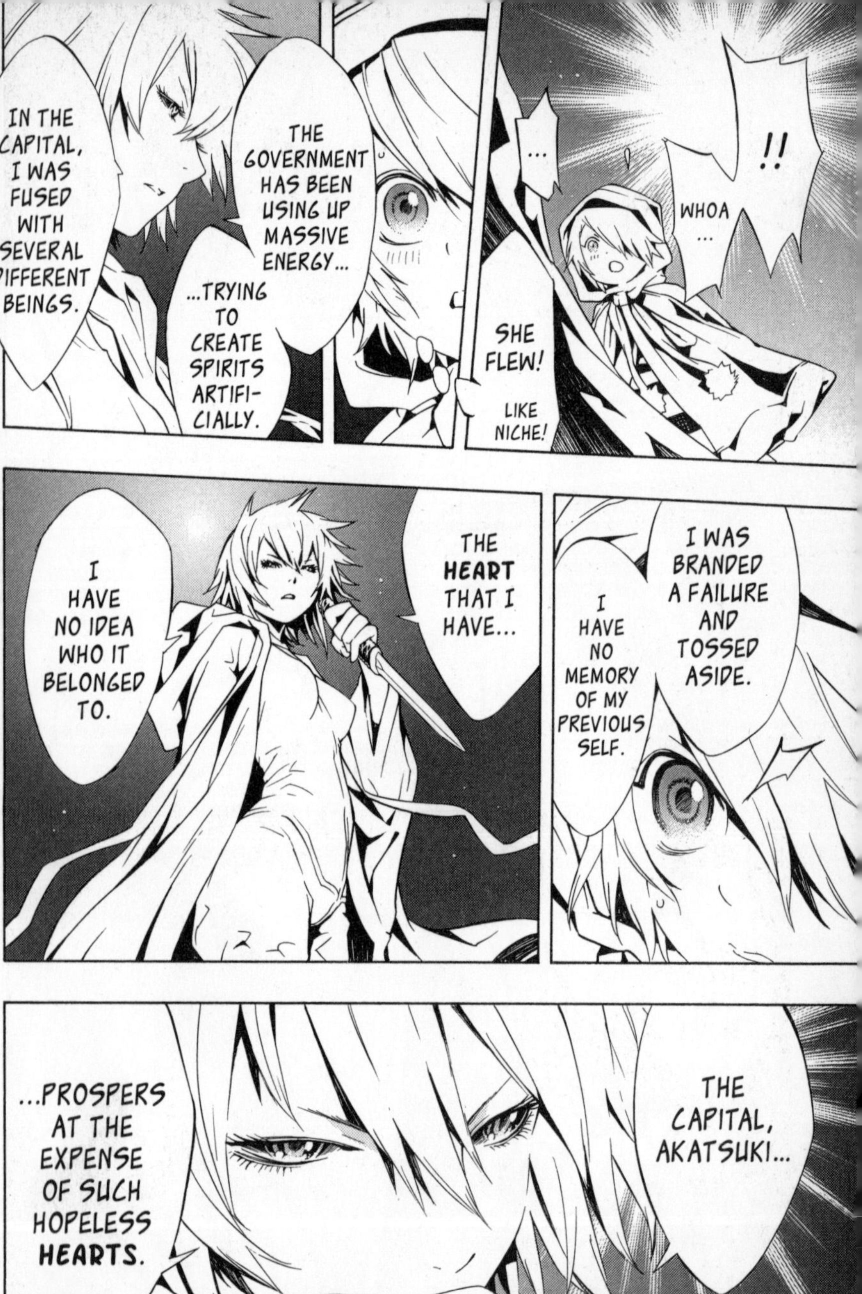
!!
WHOA...
...
SHE FLEW!
LIKE NICHE!
THE GOVERNMENT HAS BEEN USING UP MASSIVE ENERGY...
...TRYING TO CREATE SPIRITS ARTIFI-CIALLY.
IN THE CAPITAL, I WAS FUSED WITH SEVERAL DIFFERENT BEINGS.
I WAS BRANDED A FAILURE AND TOSSED ASIDE.
I HAVE NO MEMORY OF MY PREVIOUS SELF.
THE **HEART** THAT I HAVE...
I HAVE NO IDEA WHO IT BELONGED TO.
THE CAPITAL, AKATSUKI...
...PROSPERS AT THE EXPENSE OF SUCH HOPELESS **HEARTS**.

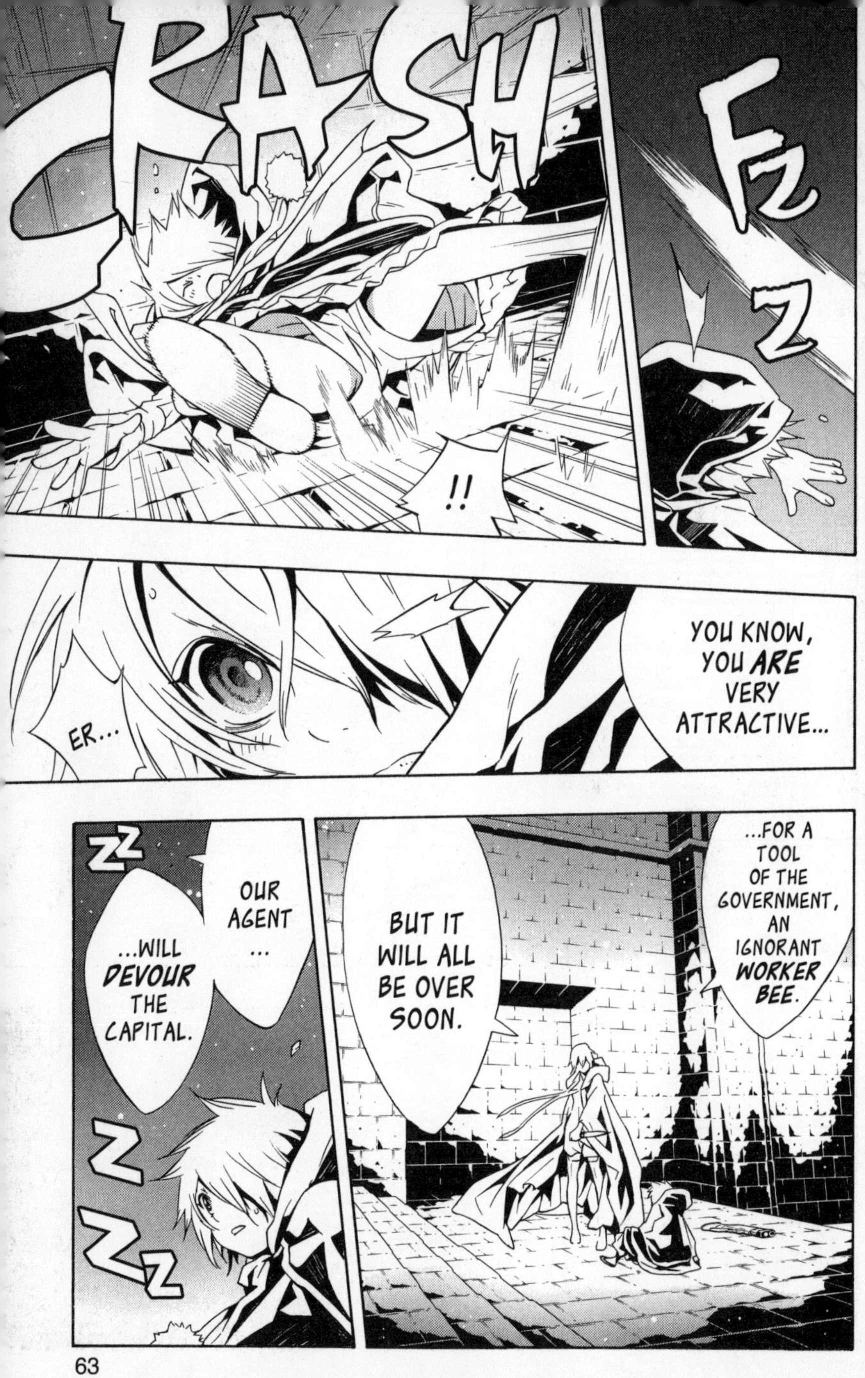
FZ
Z
CRASH
!!
YOU KNOW, YOU ARE VERY ATTRACTIVE...
ER...
...FOR A TOOL OF THE GOVERNMENT, AN IGNORANT WORKER BEE.
BUT IT WILL ALL BE OVER SOON.
OUR AGENT ...
...WILL DEVOUR THE CAPITAL.
ZZ
Z
ZZ

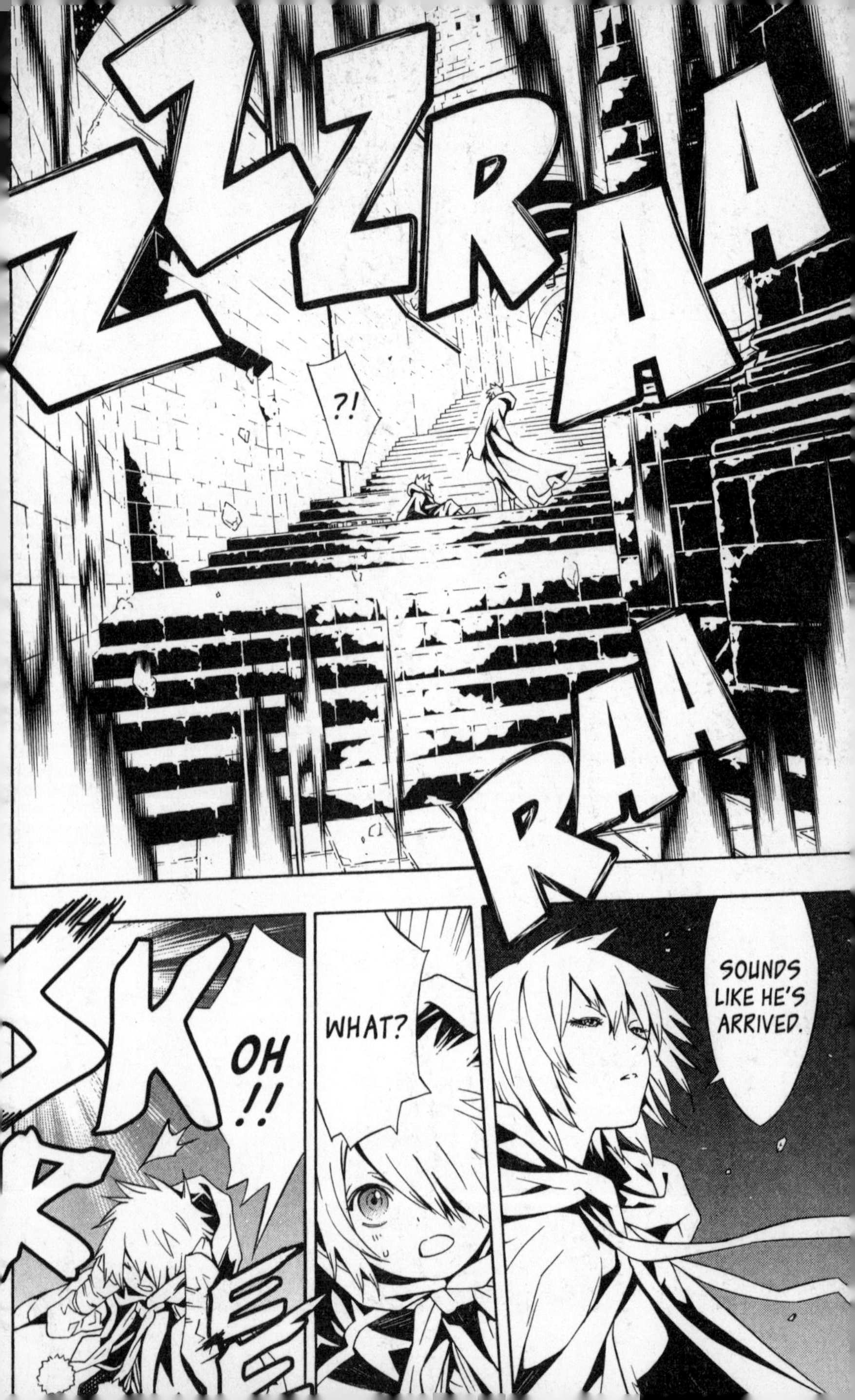
ZZRAA
?!
RAA
SOUNDS LIKE HE'S ARRIVED.
WHAT?
OH!!

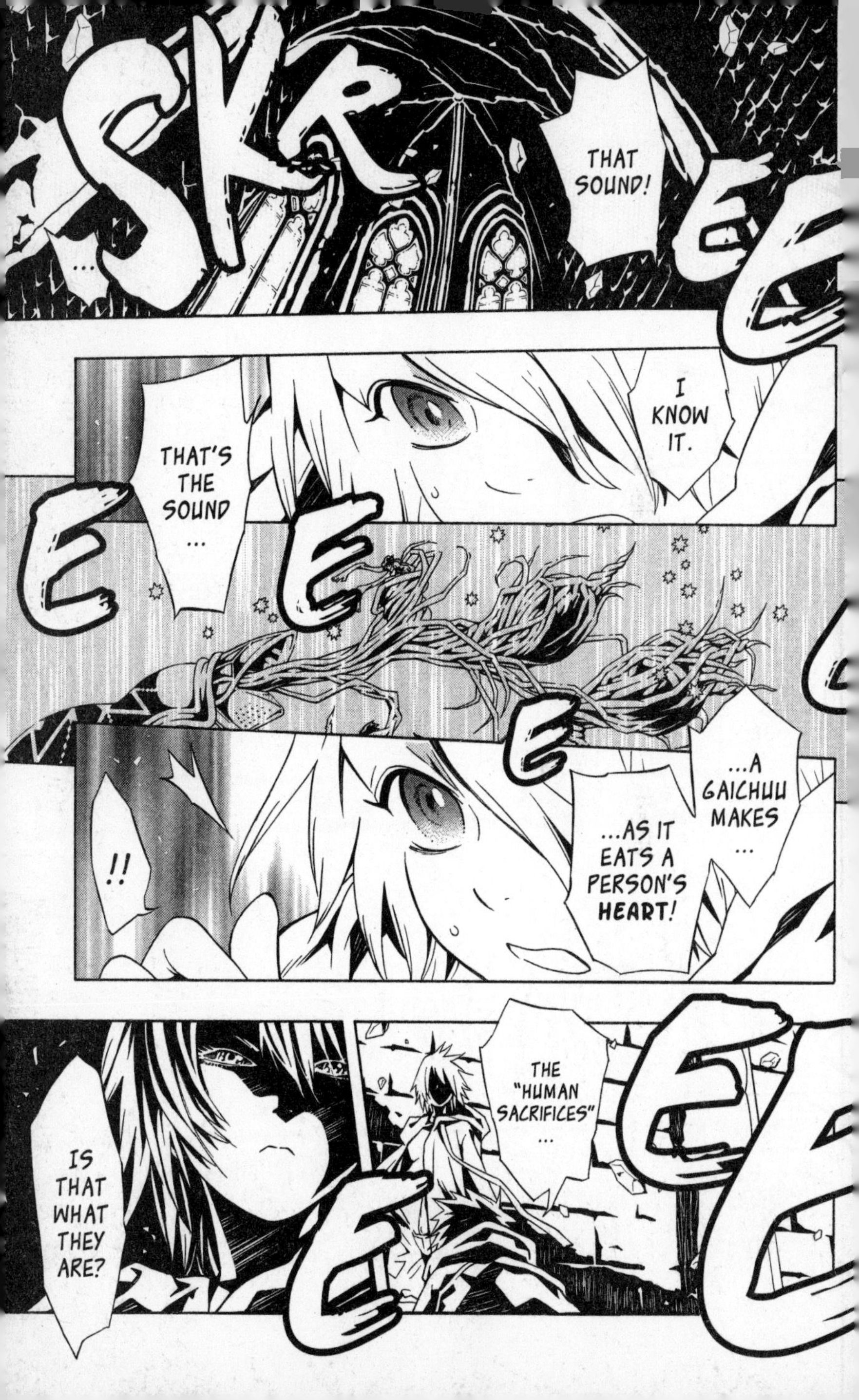
THAT SOUND!
...
SKREEEEEEEEEE
I KNOW IT.
THAT'S THE SOUND ...
...A GAICHUU MAKES ...
...AS IT EATS A PERSON'S HEART!
!!
THE "HUMAN SACRIFICES" ...
IS THAT WHAT THEY ARE?

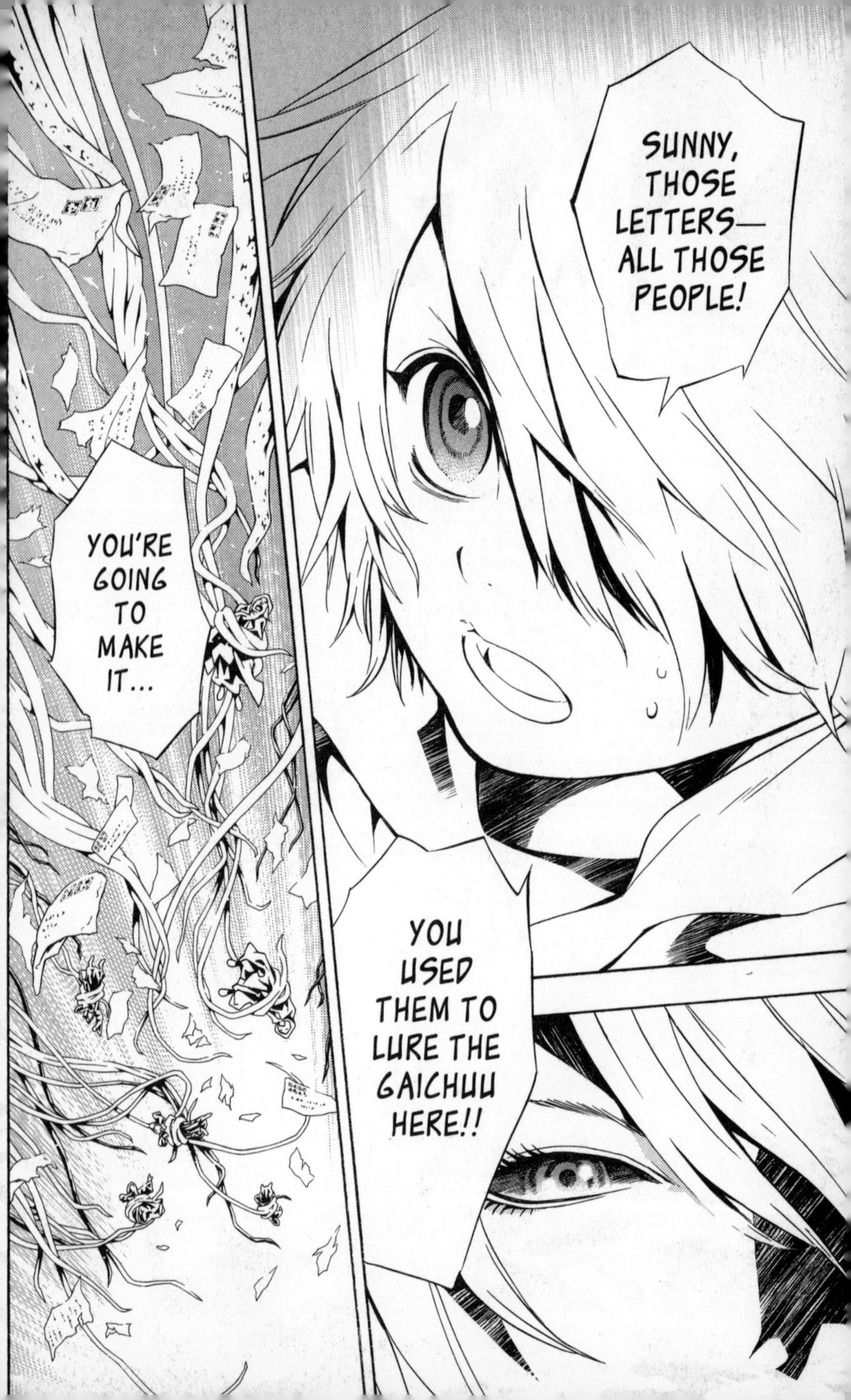
SUNNY, THOSE LETTERS— ALL THOSE PEOPLE!
YOU USED THEM TO LURE THE GAICHUU HERE!!
YOU'RE GOING TO MAKE IT...

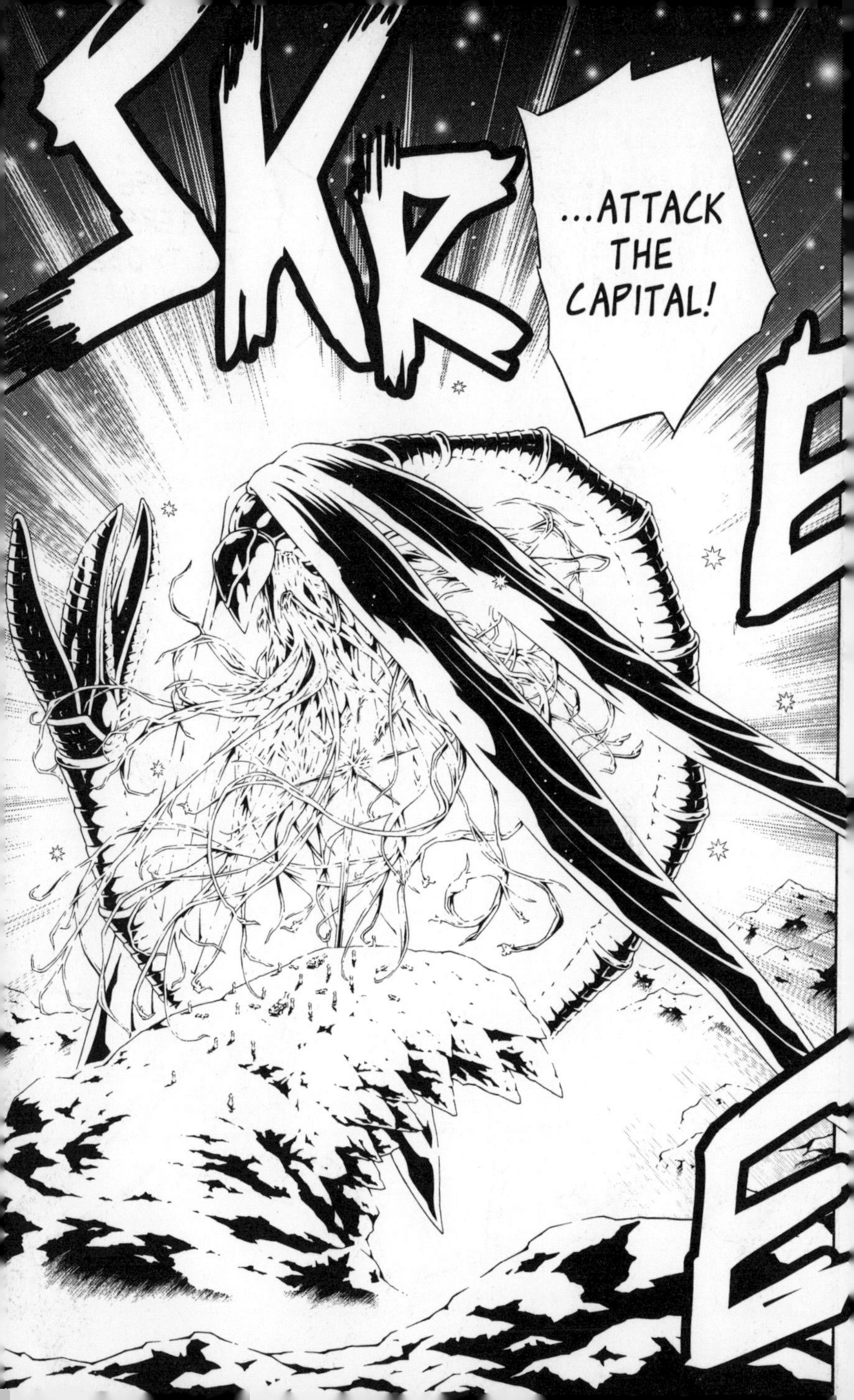
...ATTACK THE CAPITAL!

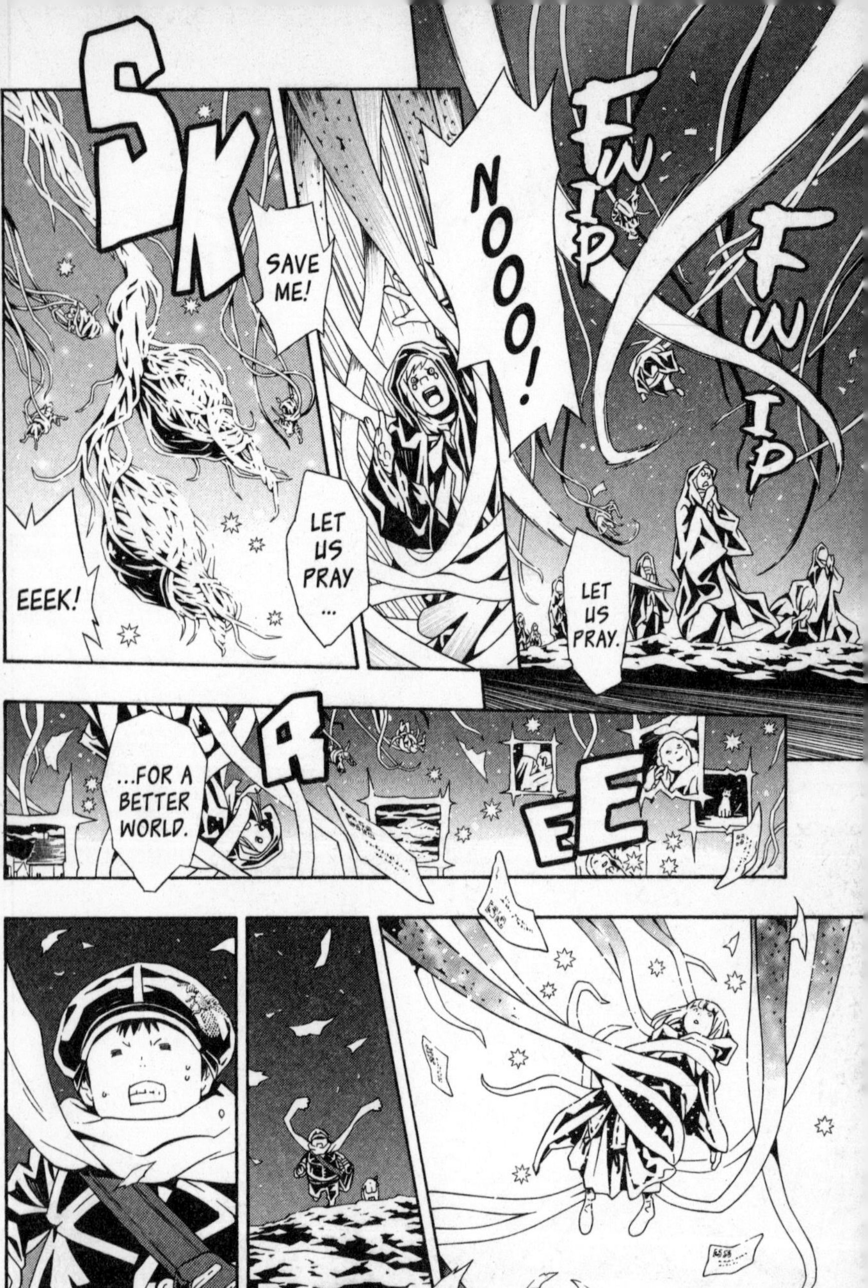
FWIP
FWIP
LET US PRAY.
NOOOO!!
SAVE ME!
LET US PRAY ...
SK
EEEK!
EE
R
...FOR A BETTER WORLD.

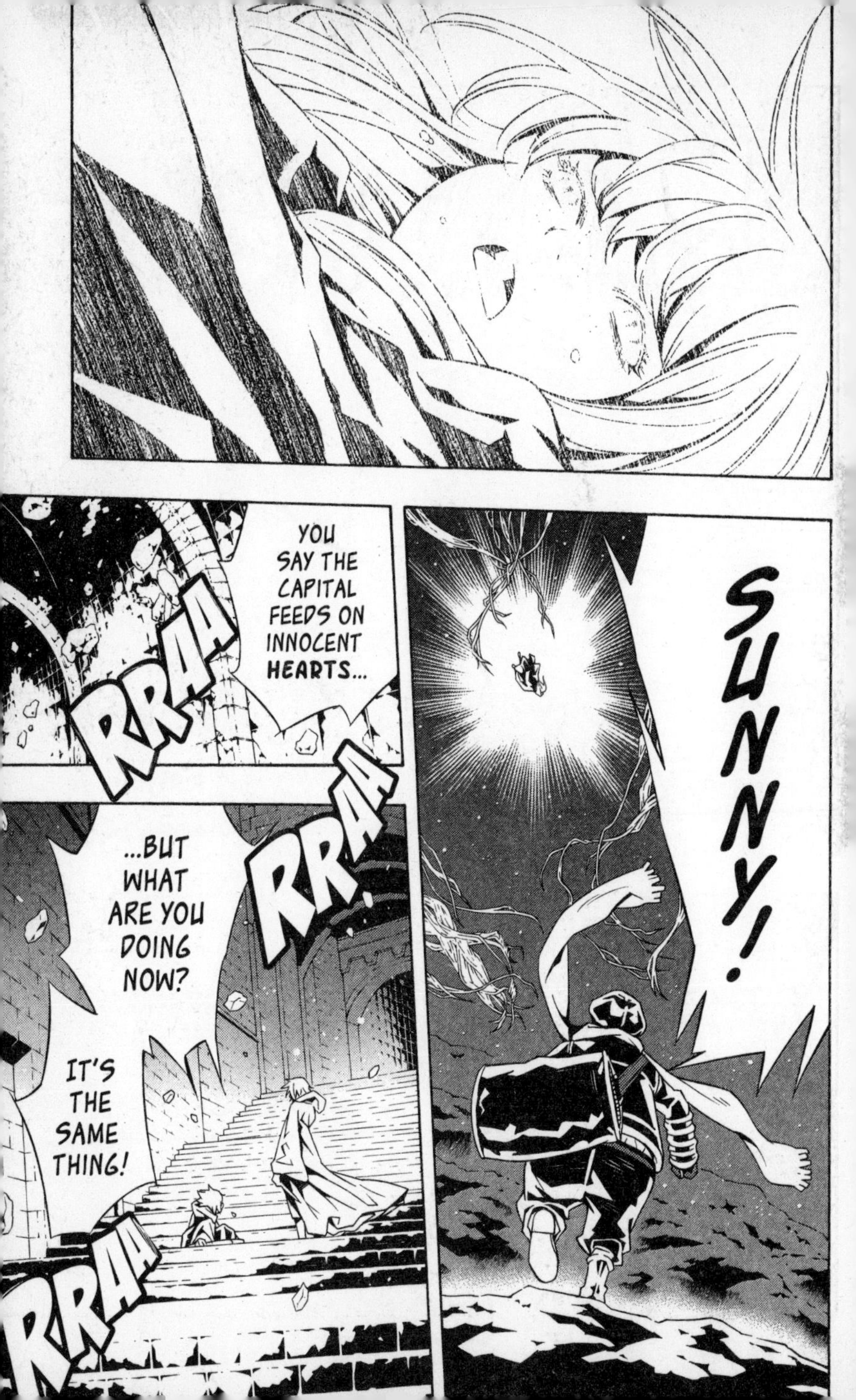
SUNNY!!
YOU SAY THE CAPITAL FEEDS ON INNOCENT HEARTS...
RRAA
RRAA
...BUT WHAT ARE YOU DOING NOW?
IT'S THE SAME THING!
RRAA

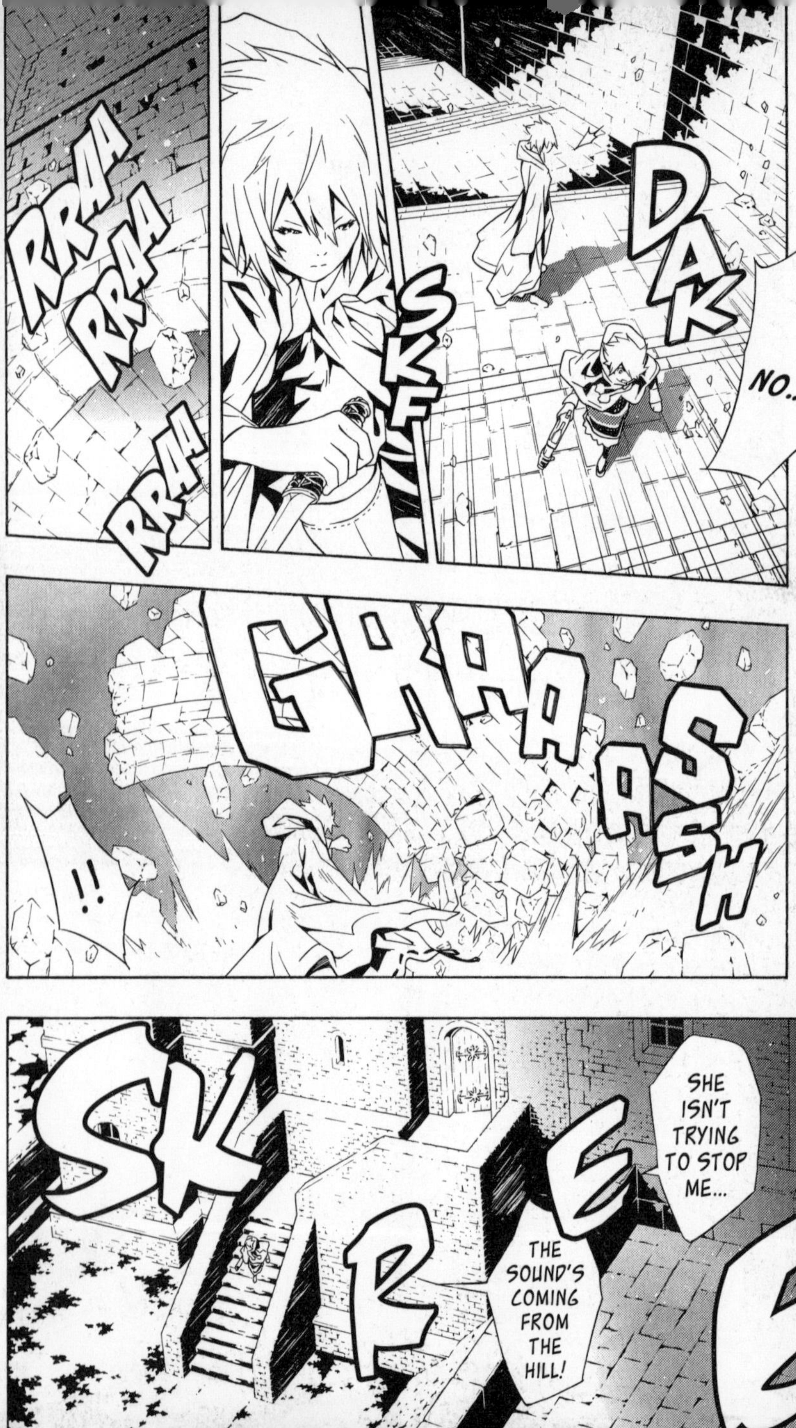
DAK
NO...
SKF
RRAA
RRAA
RRAA
GRAAASH
!!
SKRE
SHE ISN'T TRYING TO STOP ME...
THE SOUND'S COMING FROM THE HILL!

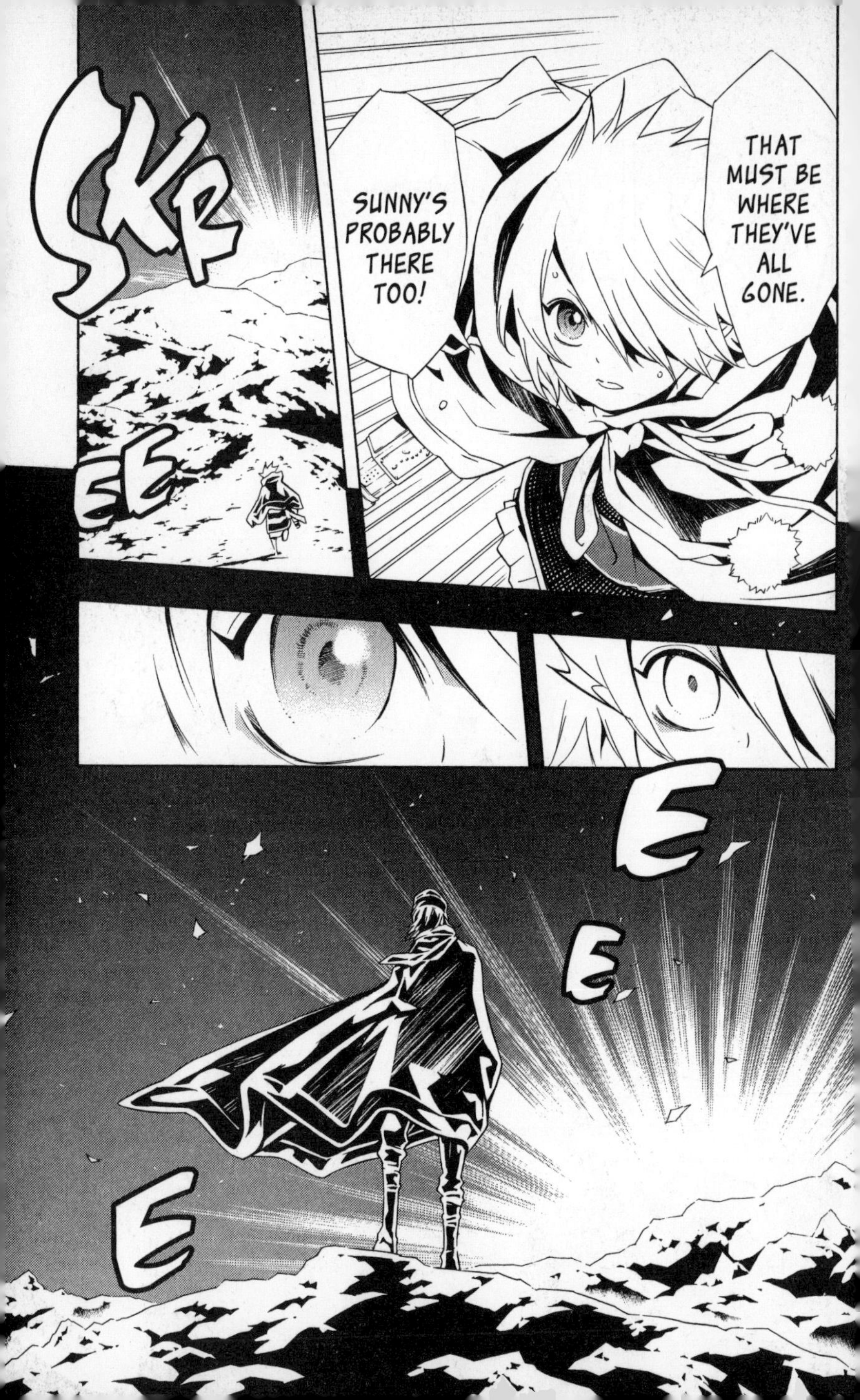
THAT MUST BE WHERE THEY'VE ALL GONE.
SUNNY'S PROBABLY THERE TOO!
SKR
EE
E
E
E

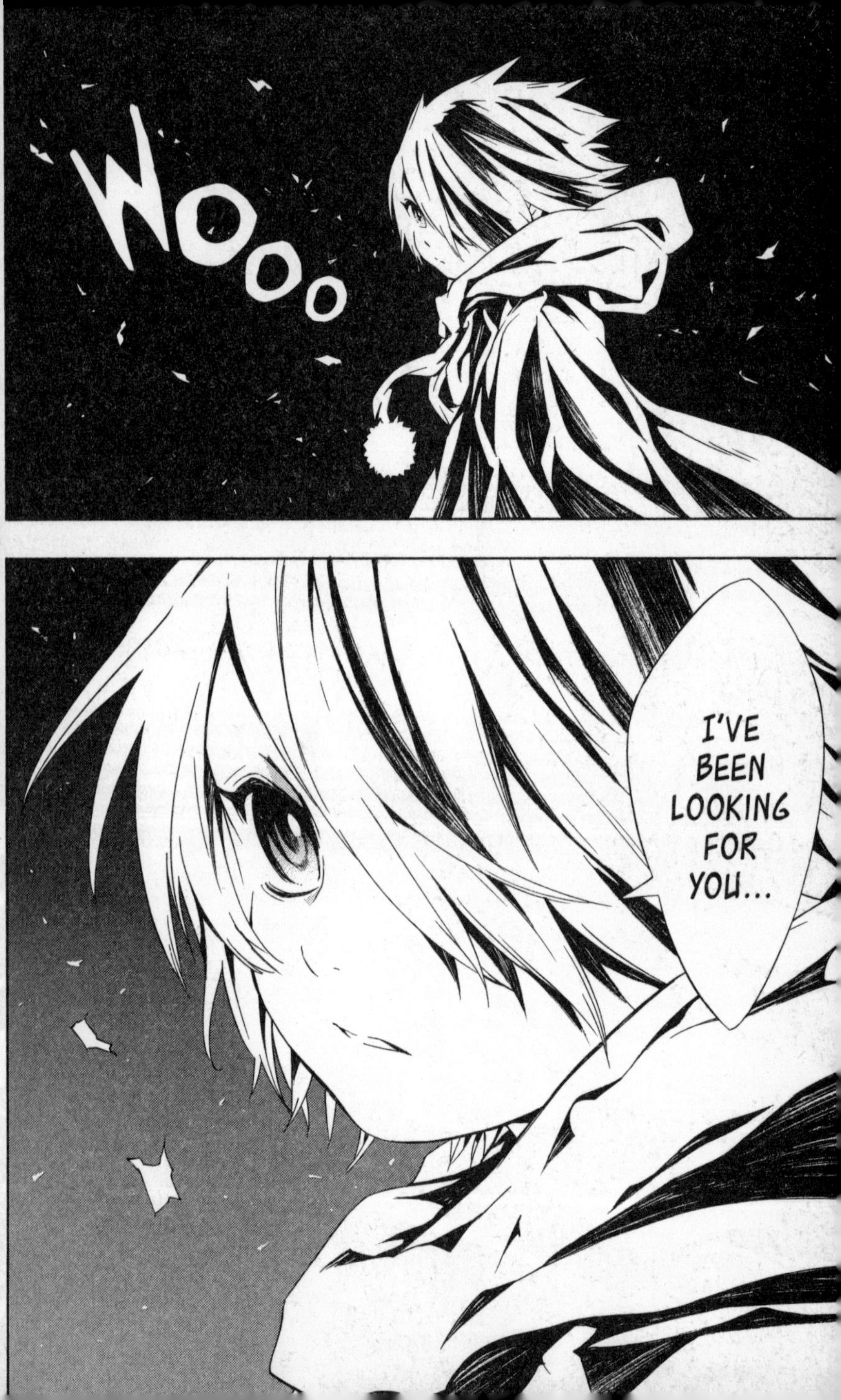
WOOO
I'VE BEEN LOOKING FOR YOU...

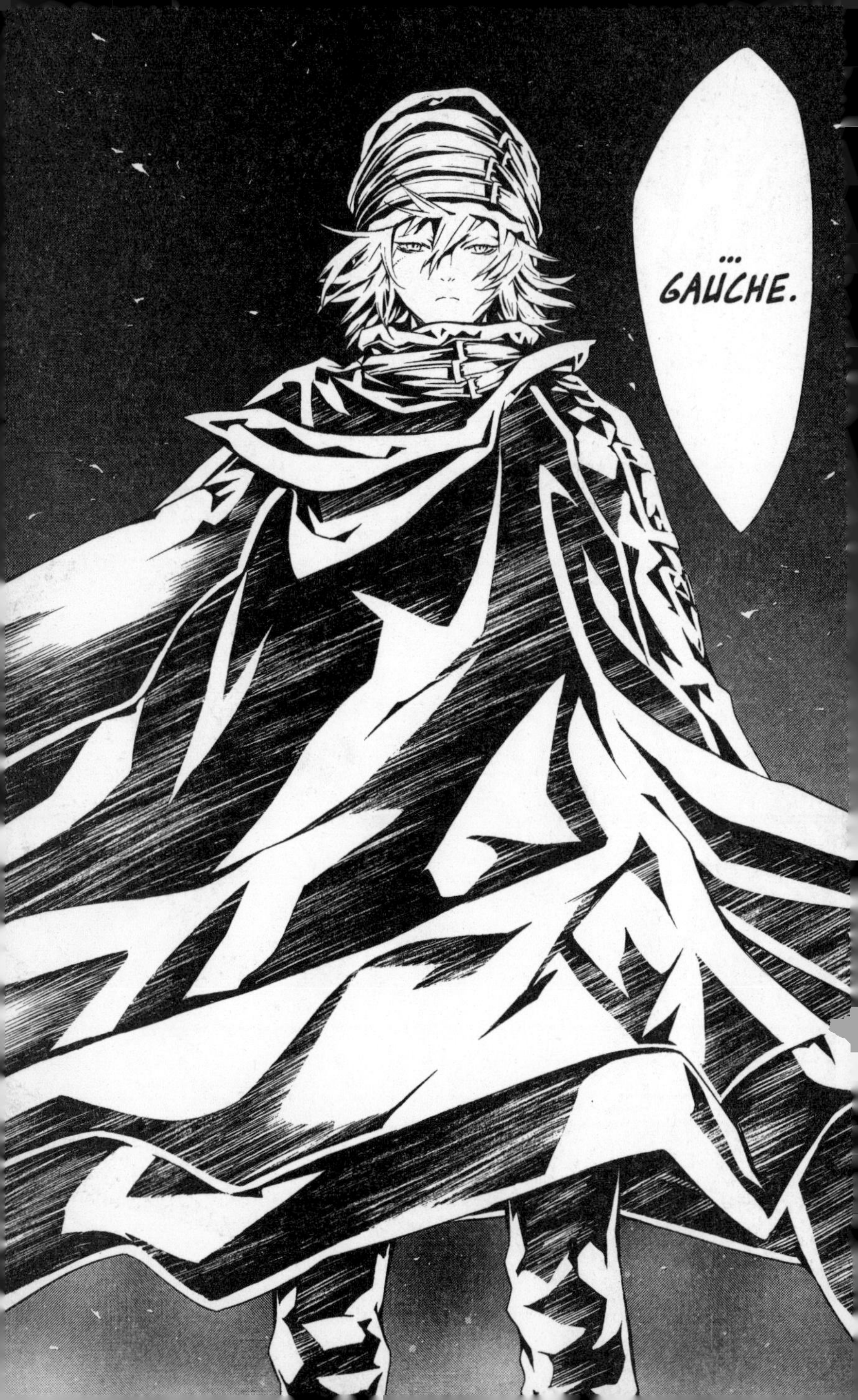

... GAÜCHE.

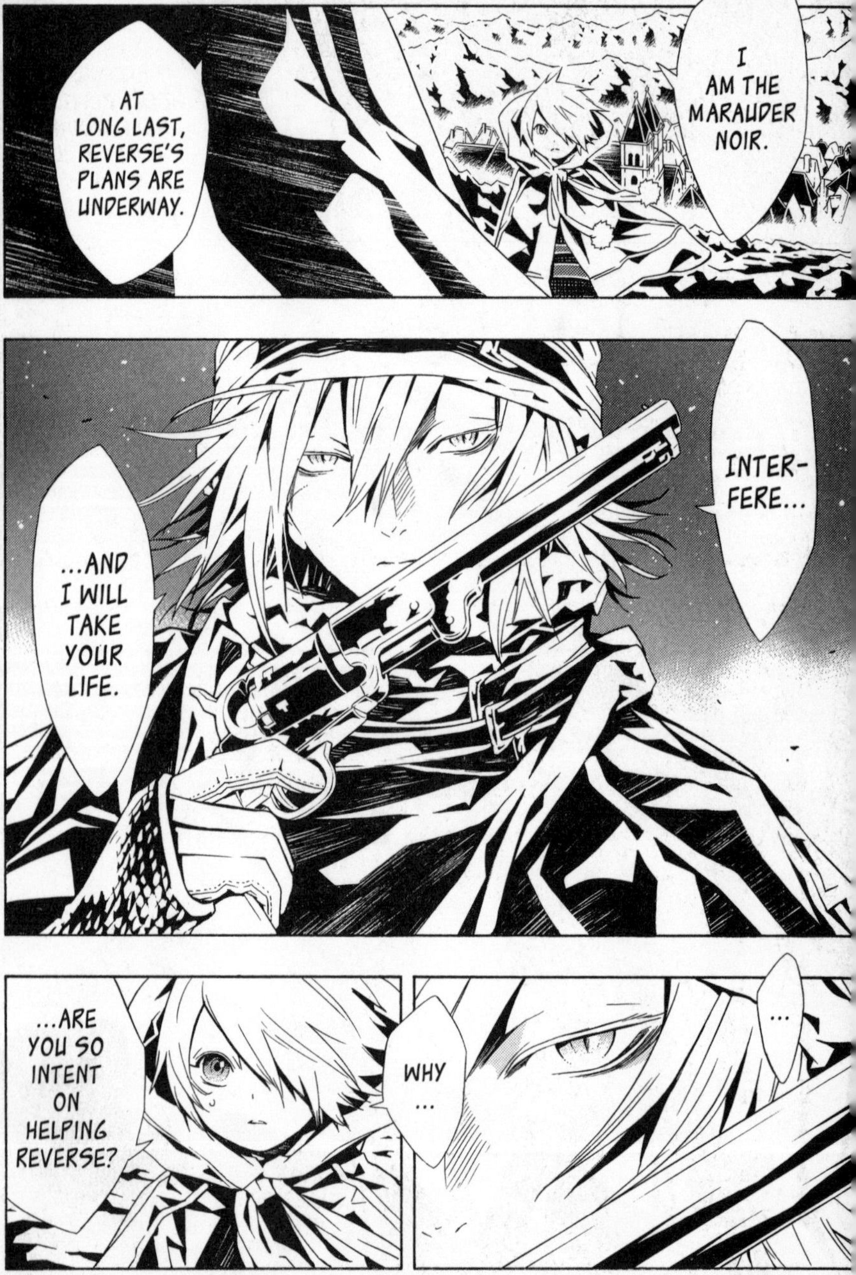
I AM THE MARAUDER NOIR.
AT LONG LAST, REVERSE'S PLANS ARE UNDERWAY.
INTER-FERE...
...AND I WILL TAKE YOUR LIFE.
...
WHY...
...ARE YOU SO INTENT ON HELPING REVERSE?

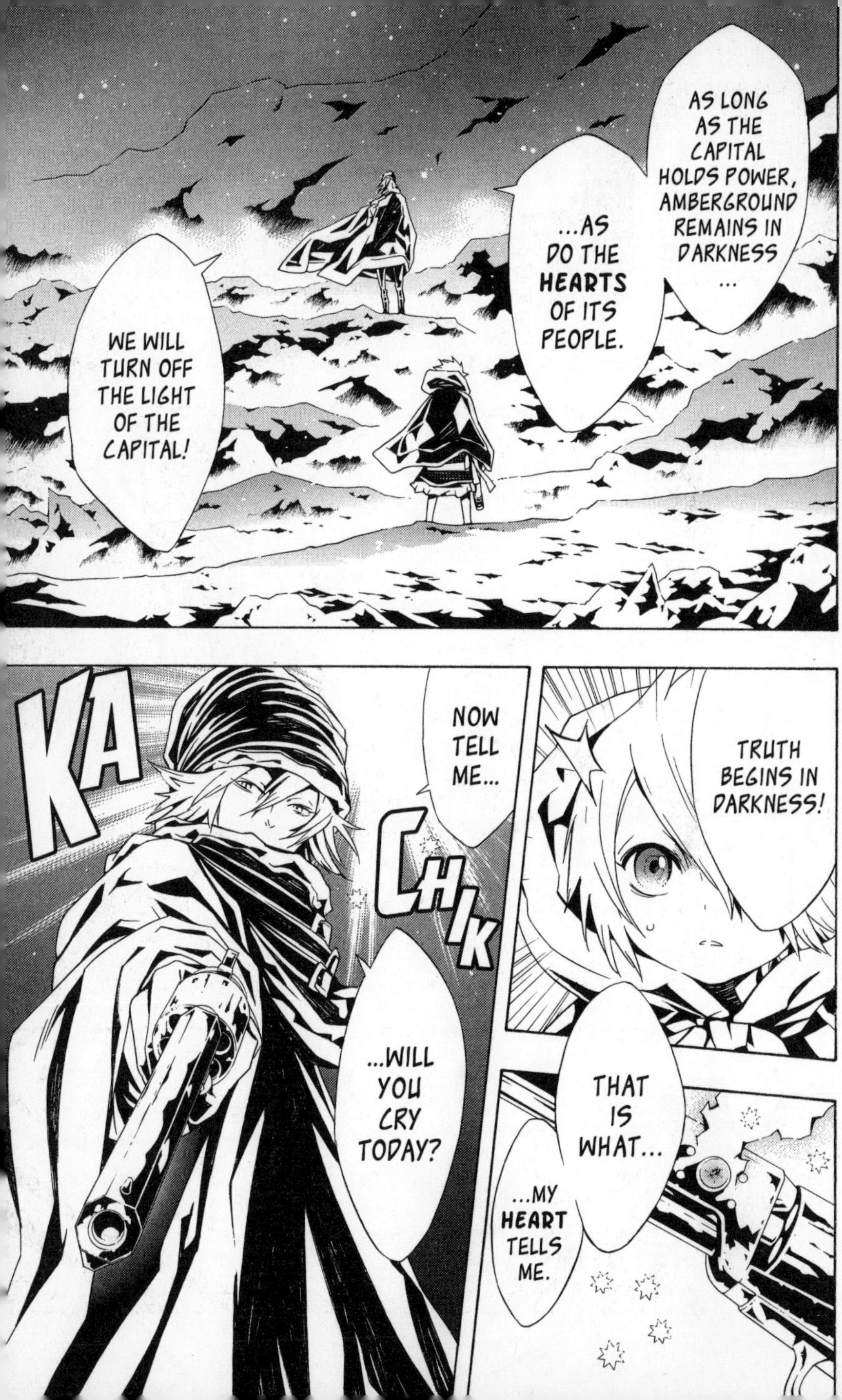
AS LONG AS THE CAPITAL HOLDS POWER, AMBERGROUND REMAINS IN DARKNESS ...
...AS DO THE HEARTS OF ITS PEOPLE.
WE WILL TURN OFF THE LIGHT OF THE CAPITAL!
TRUTH BEGINS IN DARKNESS!
THAT IS WHAT...
...MY HEART TELLS ME.
KA
NOW TELL ME...
CHIK
...WILL YOU CRY TODAY?

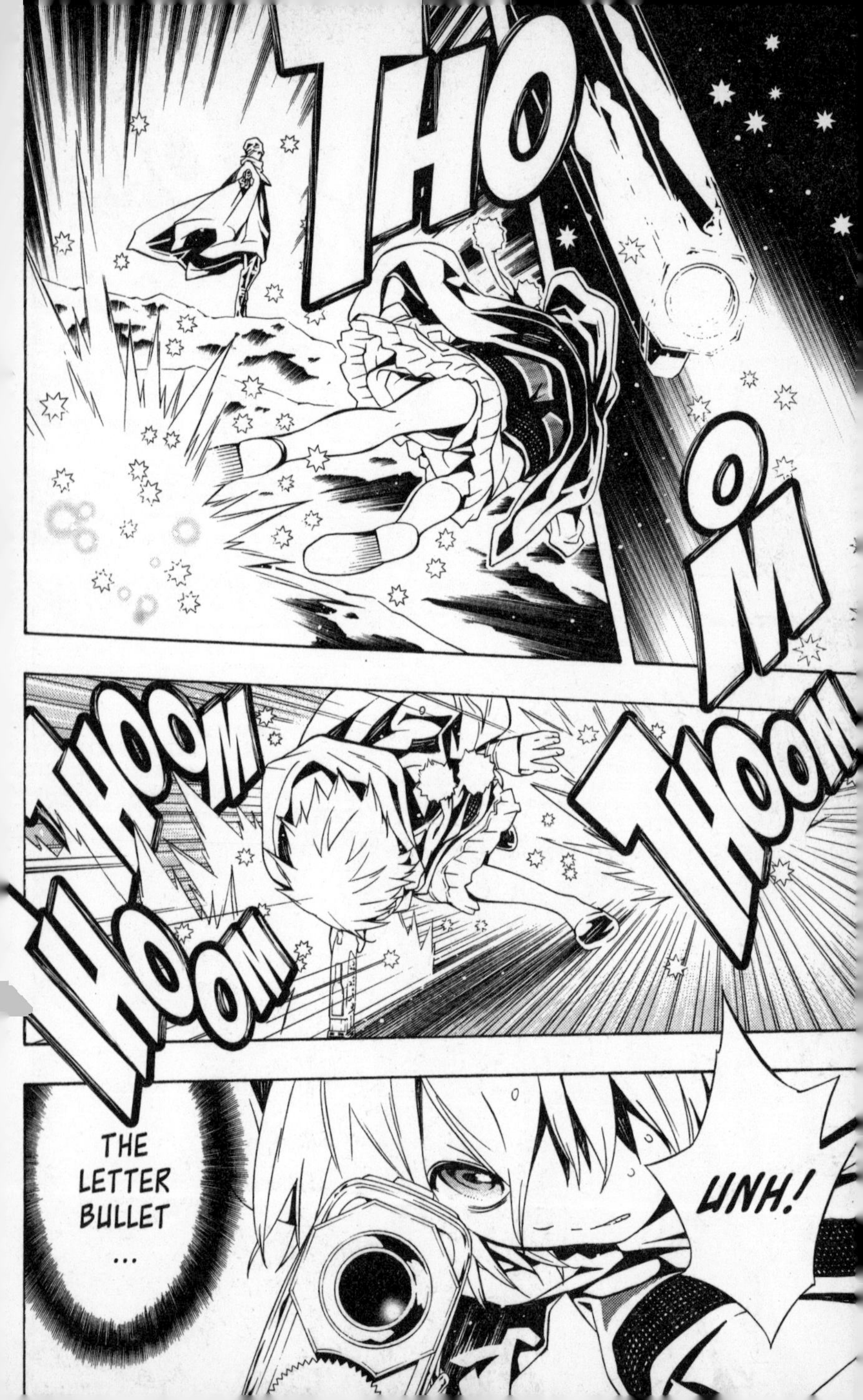

THOOM
THOOM
THOOM
THOOM
UNH!
THE LETTER BULLET ...

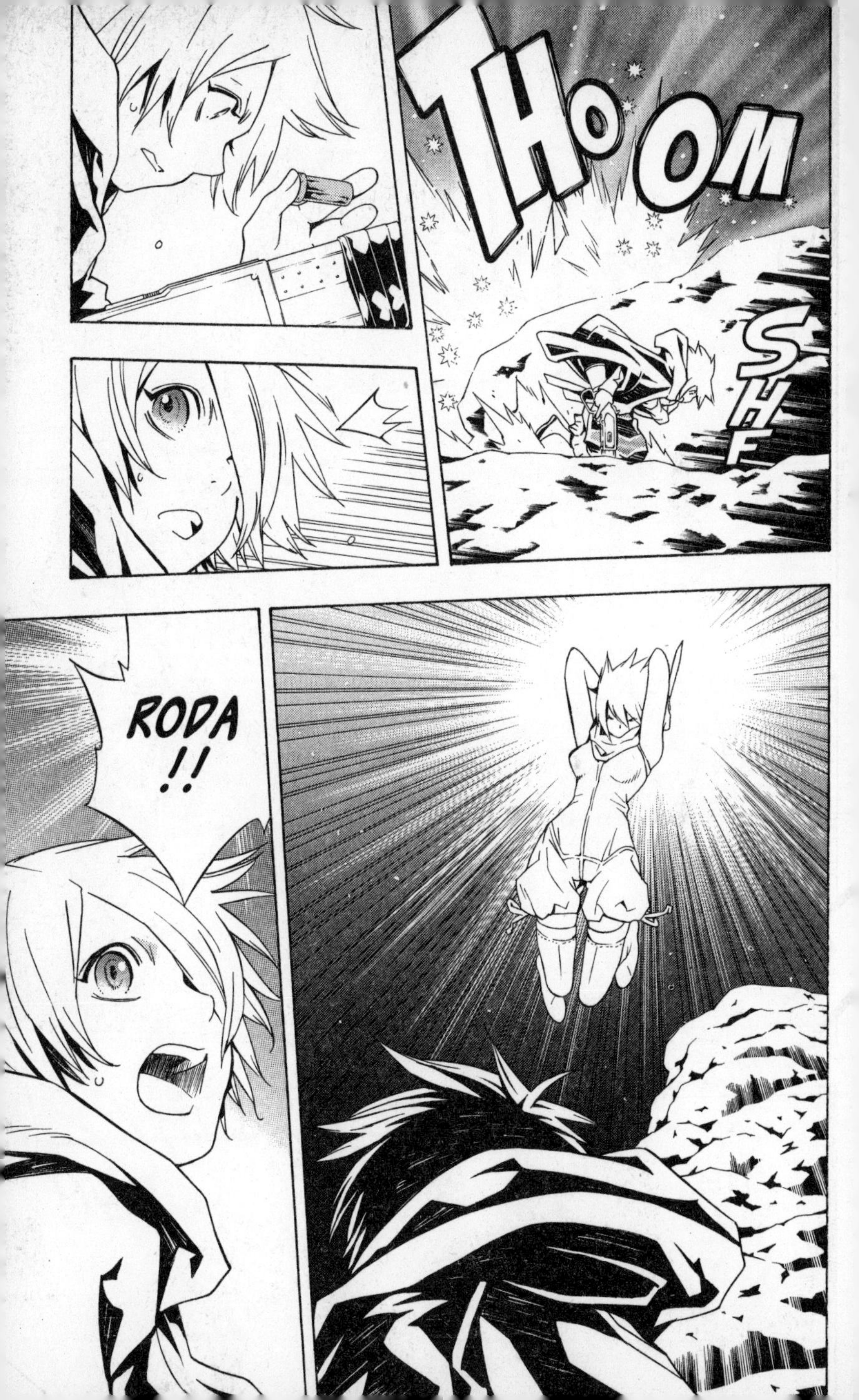
THOOM
SHF
RODA !!

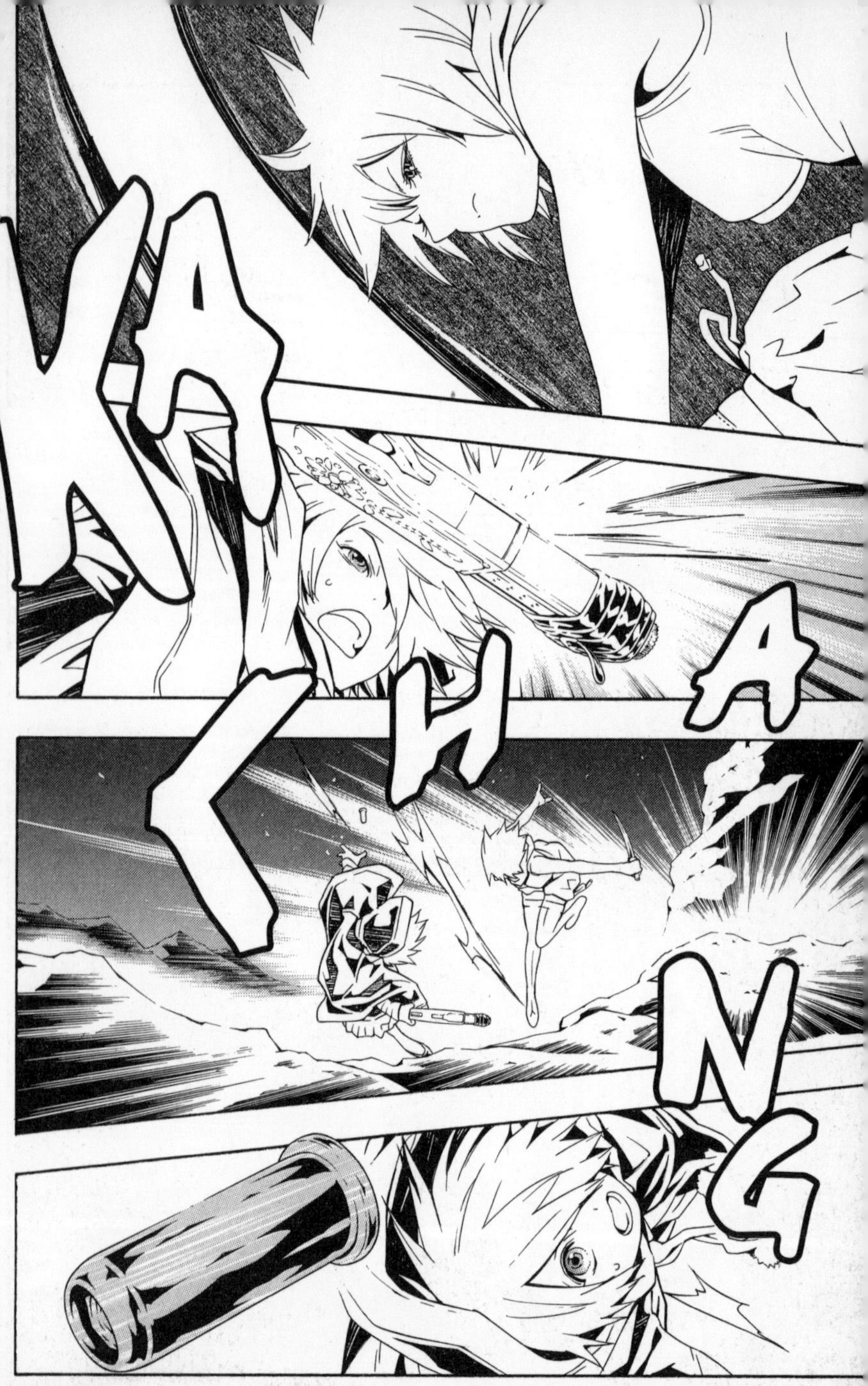
KACHANG

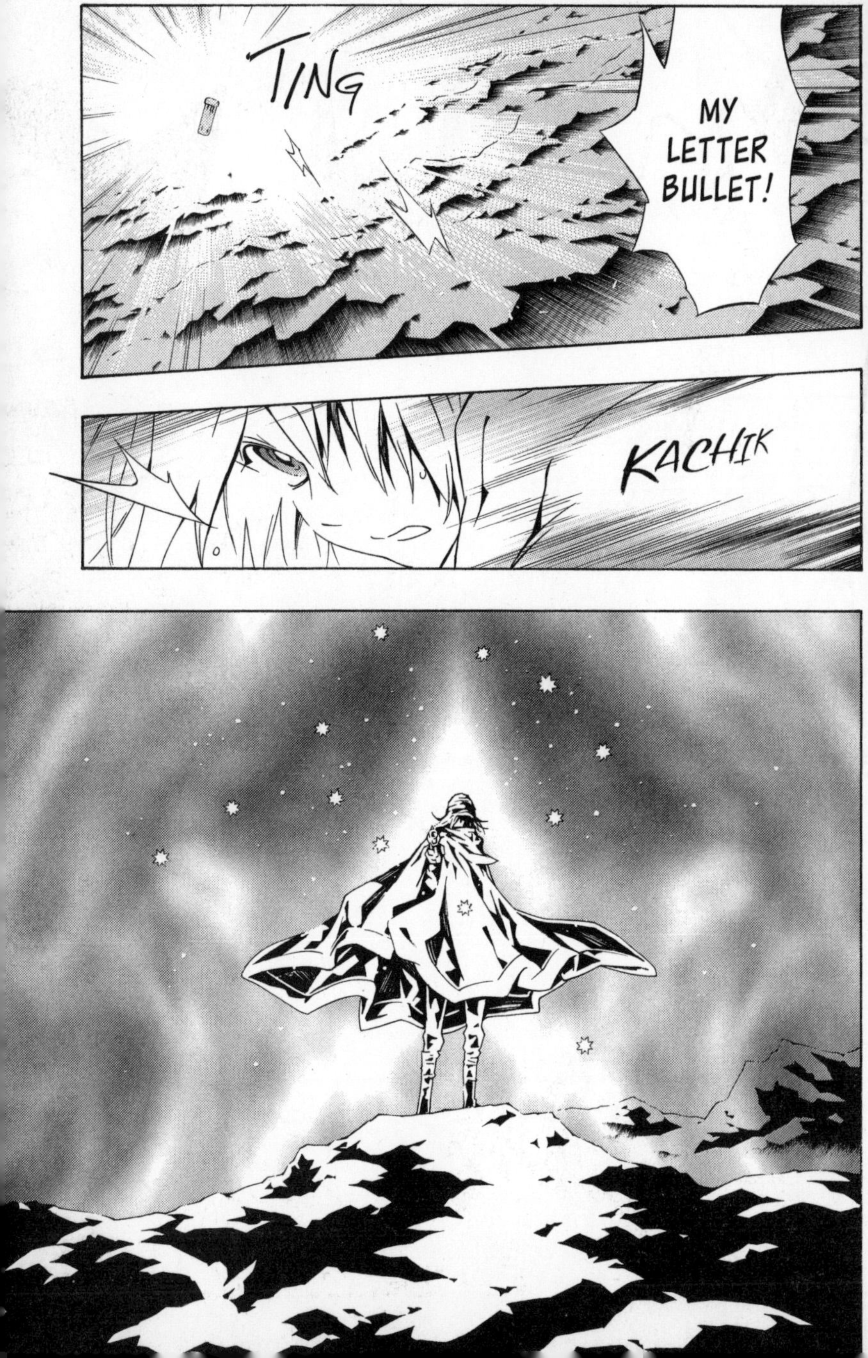
MY LETTER BULLET!
TING
KACHIK

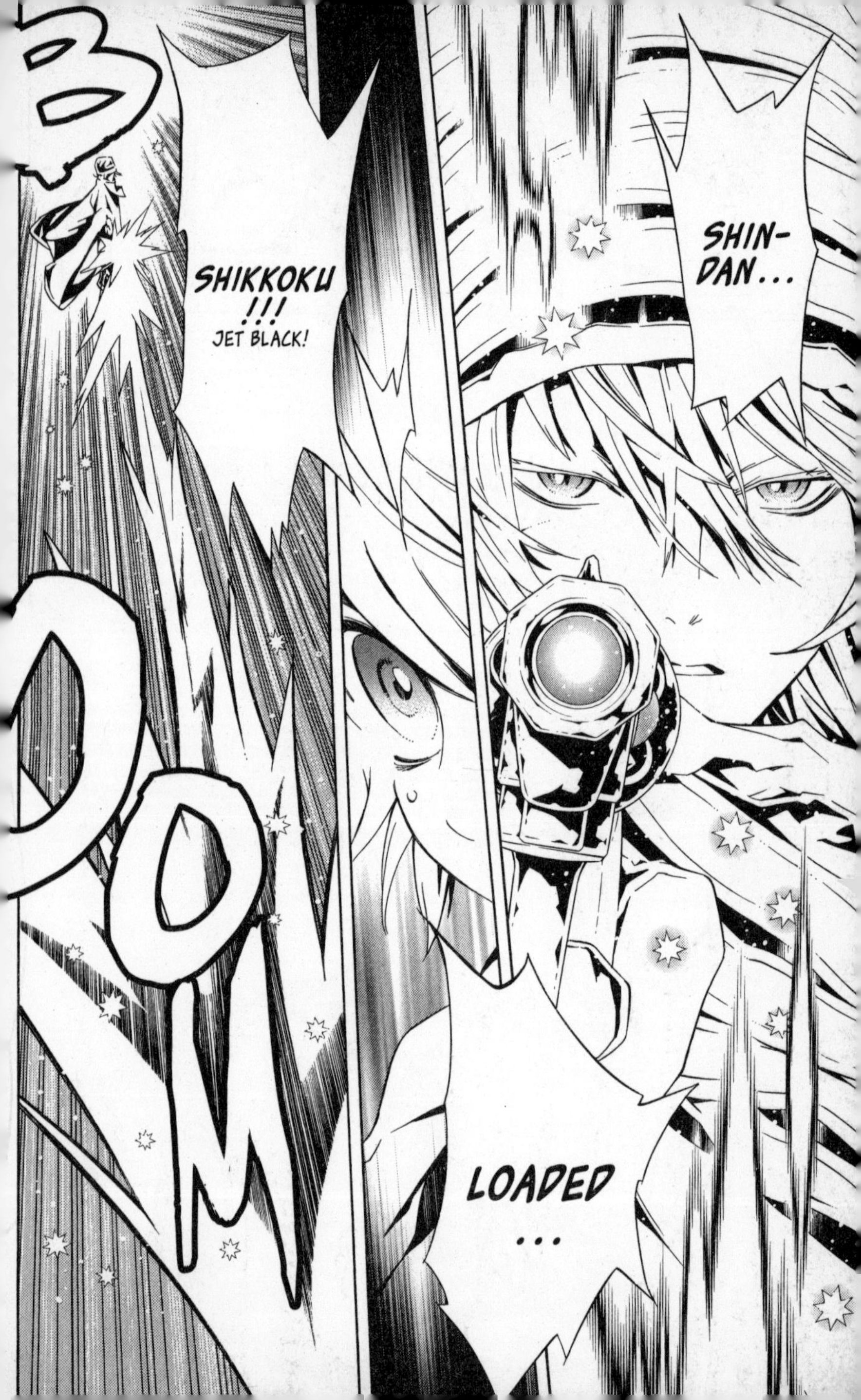
SHIN-DAN...
LOADED...
SHIKKOKU!!!
JET BLACK!

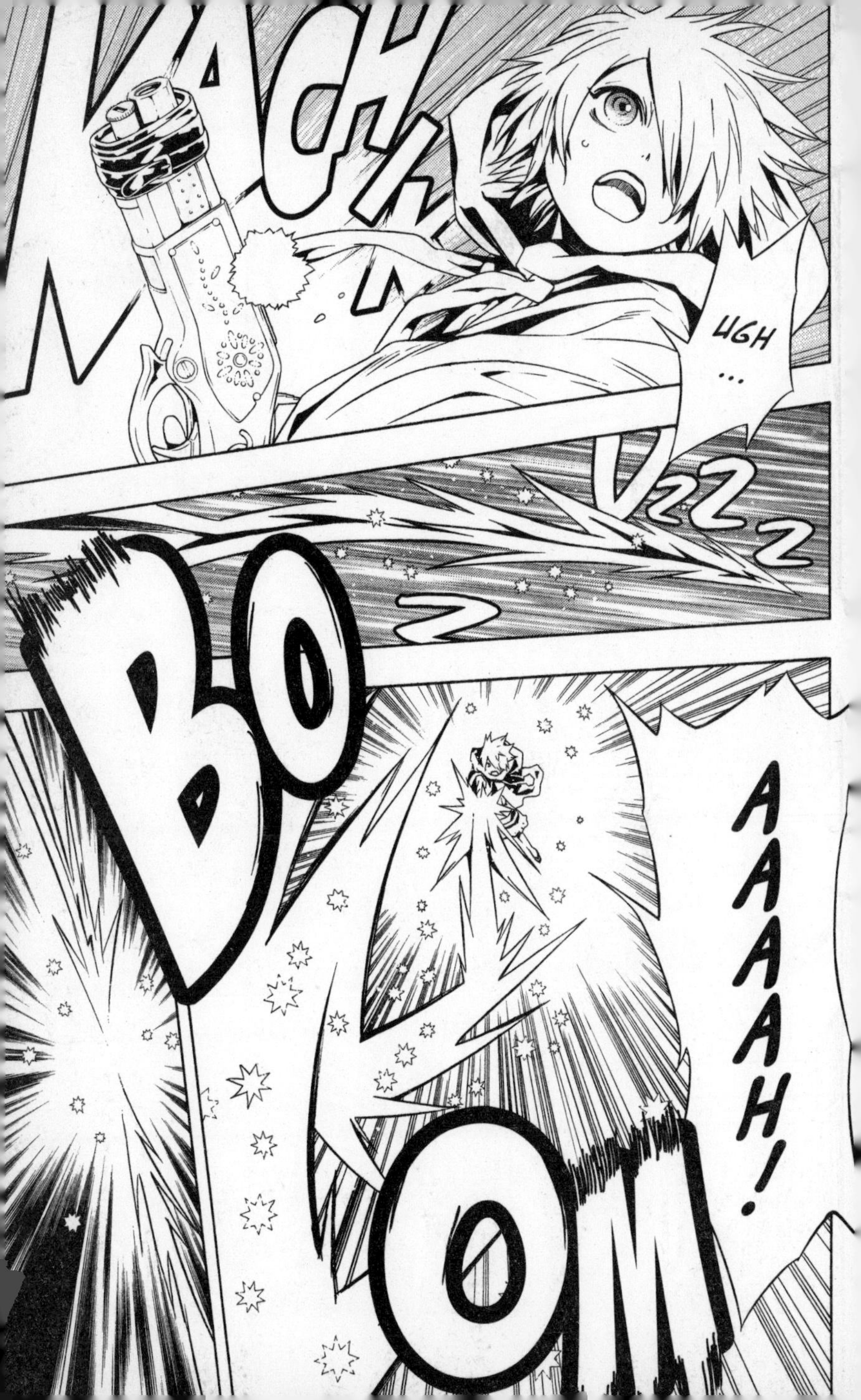
UGH ...
KACH
VZZZZZ
AAAAAH!
BOOM

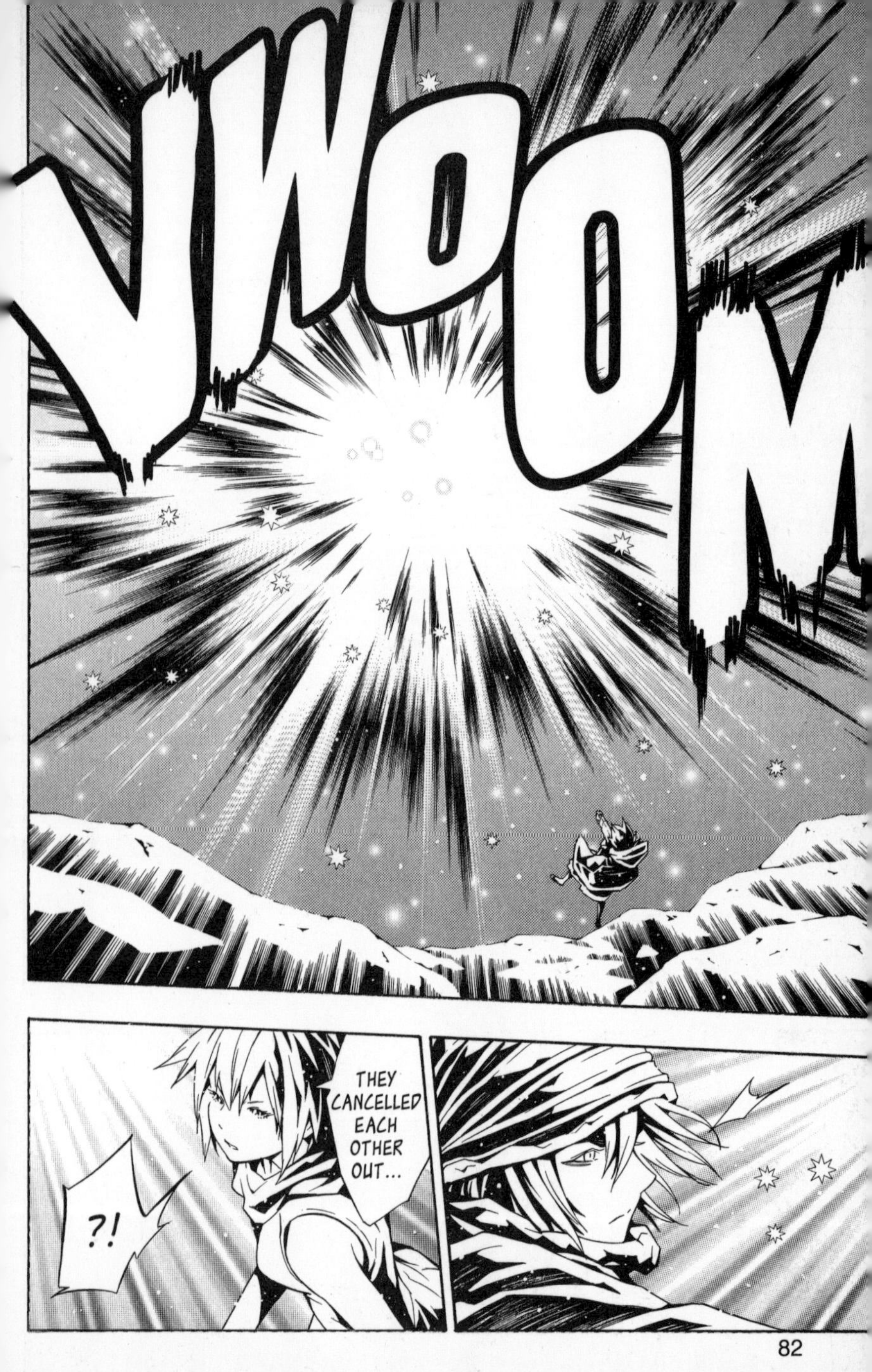
VWOOM
THEY CANCELLED EACH OTHER OUT...
?!

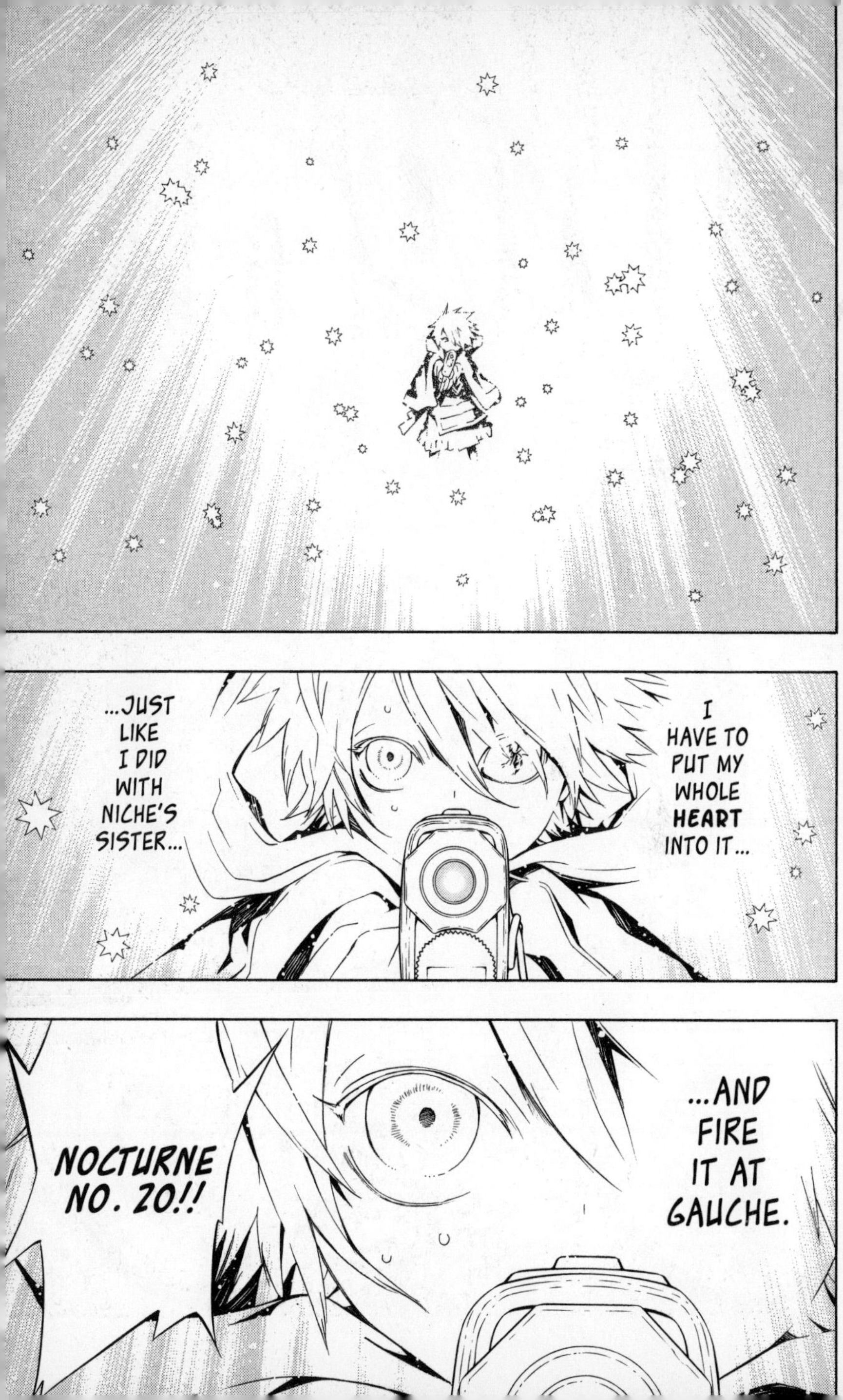
I HAVE TO PUT MY WHOLE HEART INTO IT...
...JUST LIKE I DID WITH NICHE'S SISTER...
...AND FIRE IT AT GAUCHE.
NOCTURNE NO. 20!!

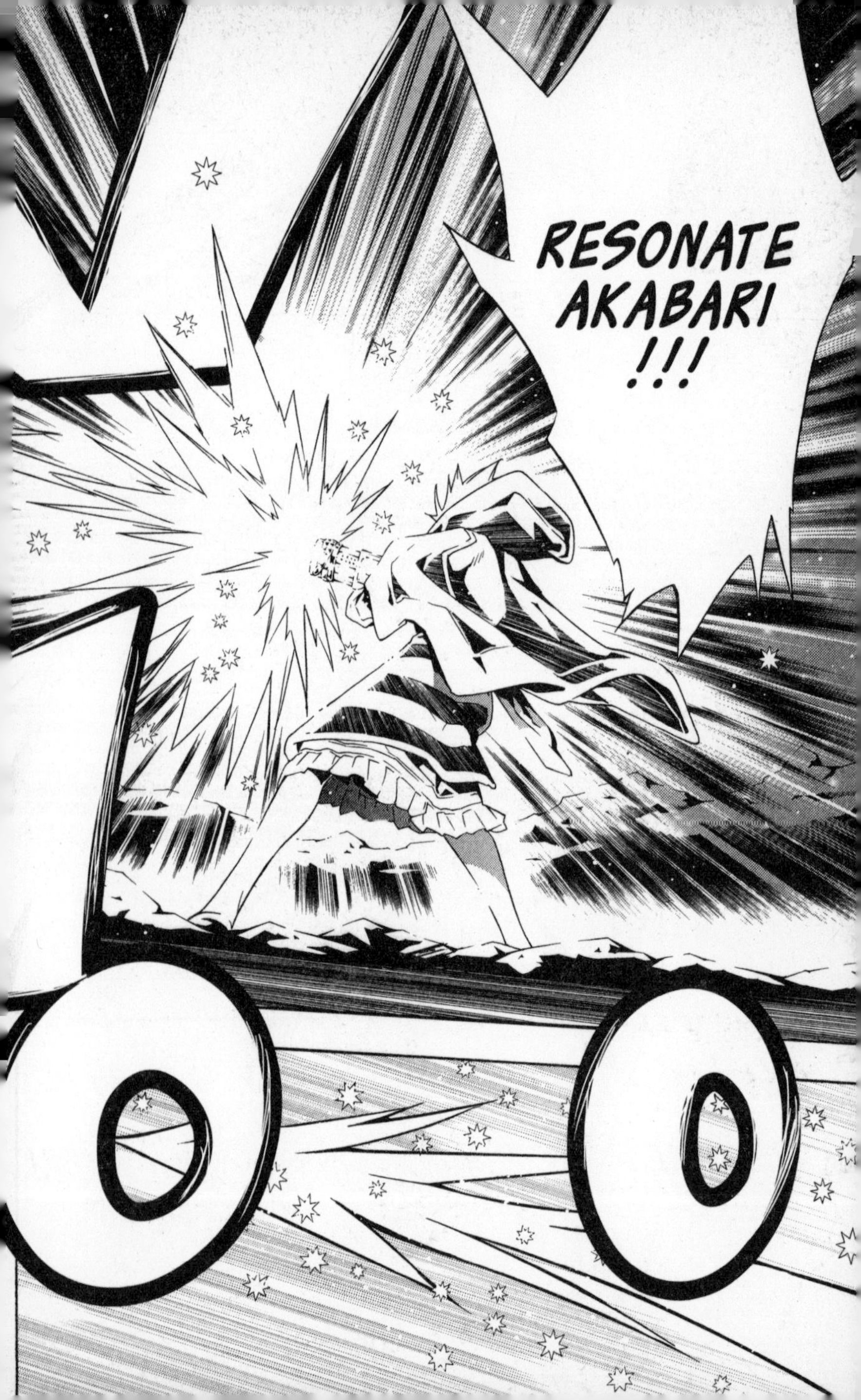
RESONATE AKABARI !!!

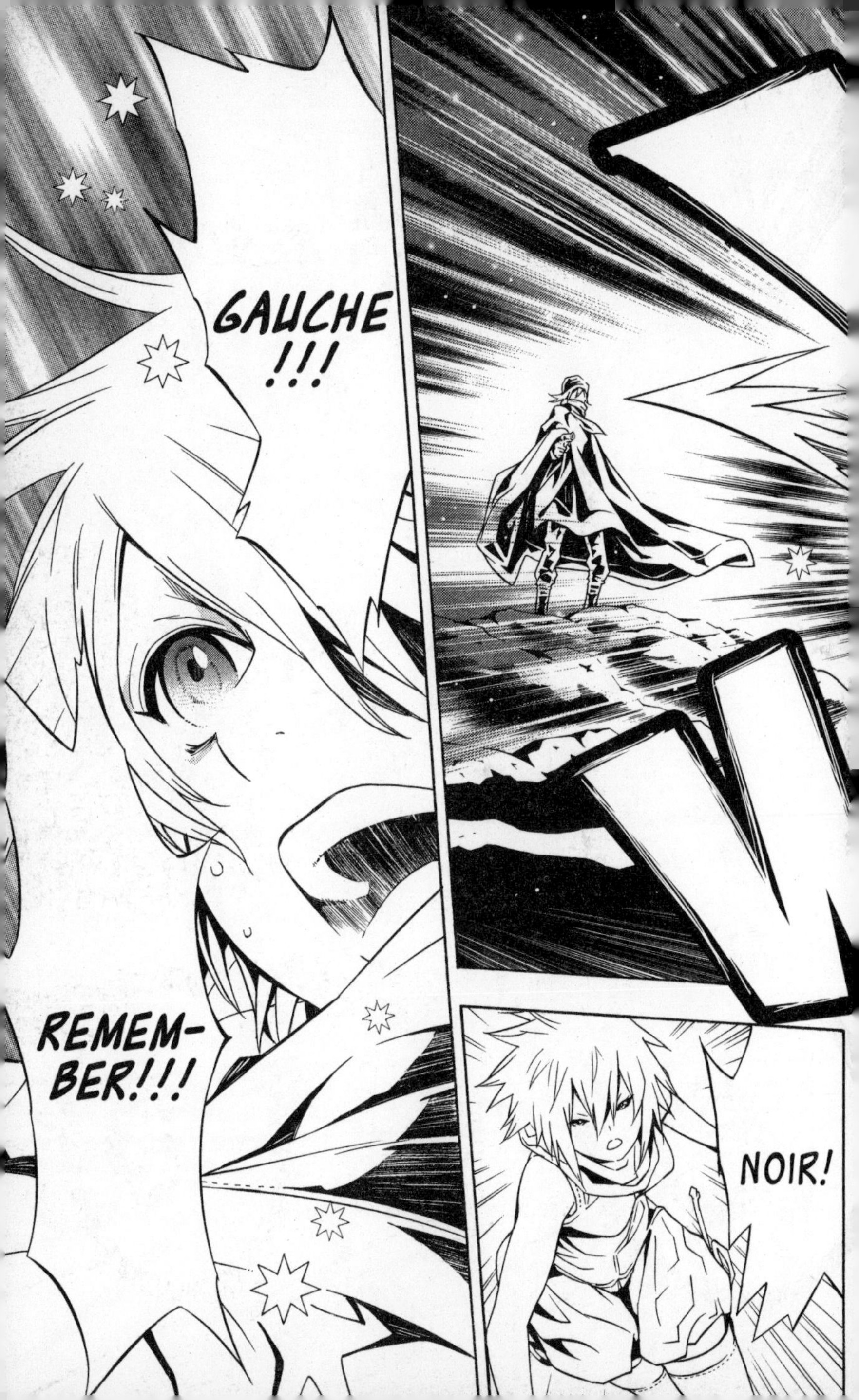
NOIR!
GAUCHE !!!
REMEM-
BER!!!

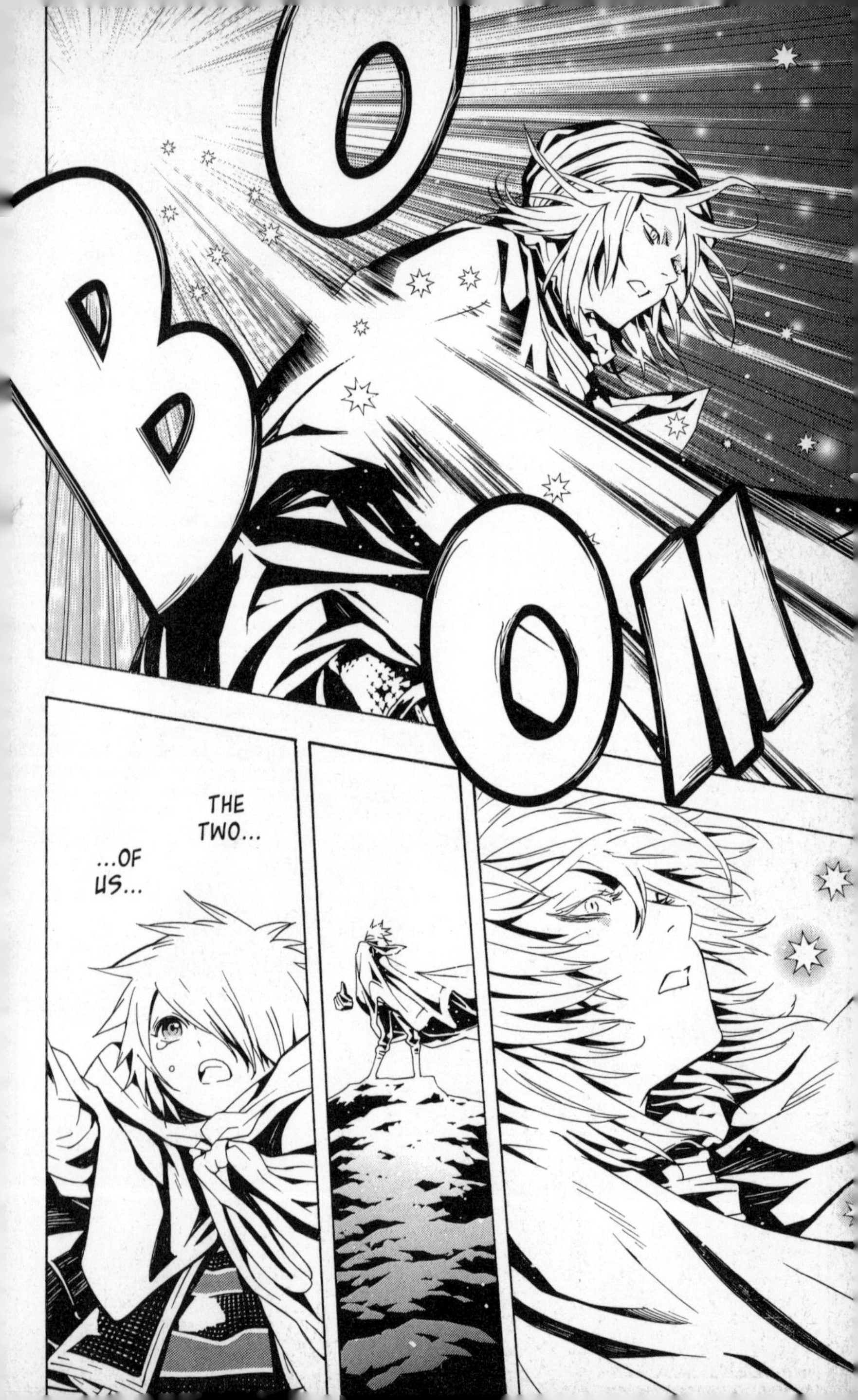
BOOM
THE TWO...
...OF US...

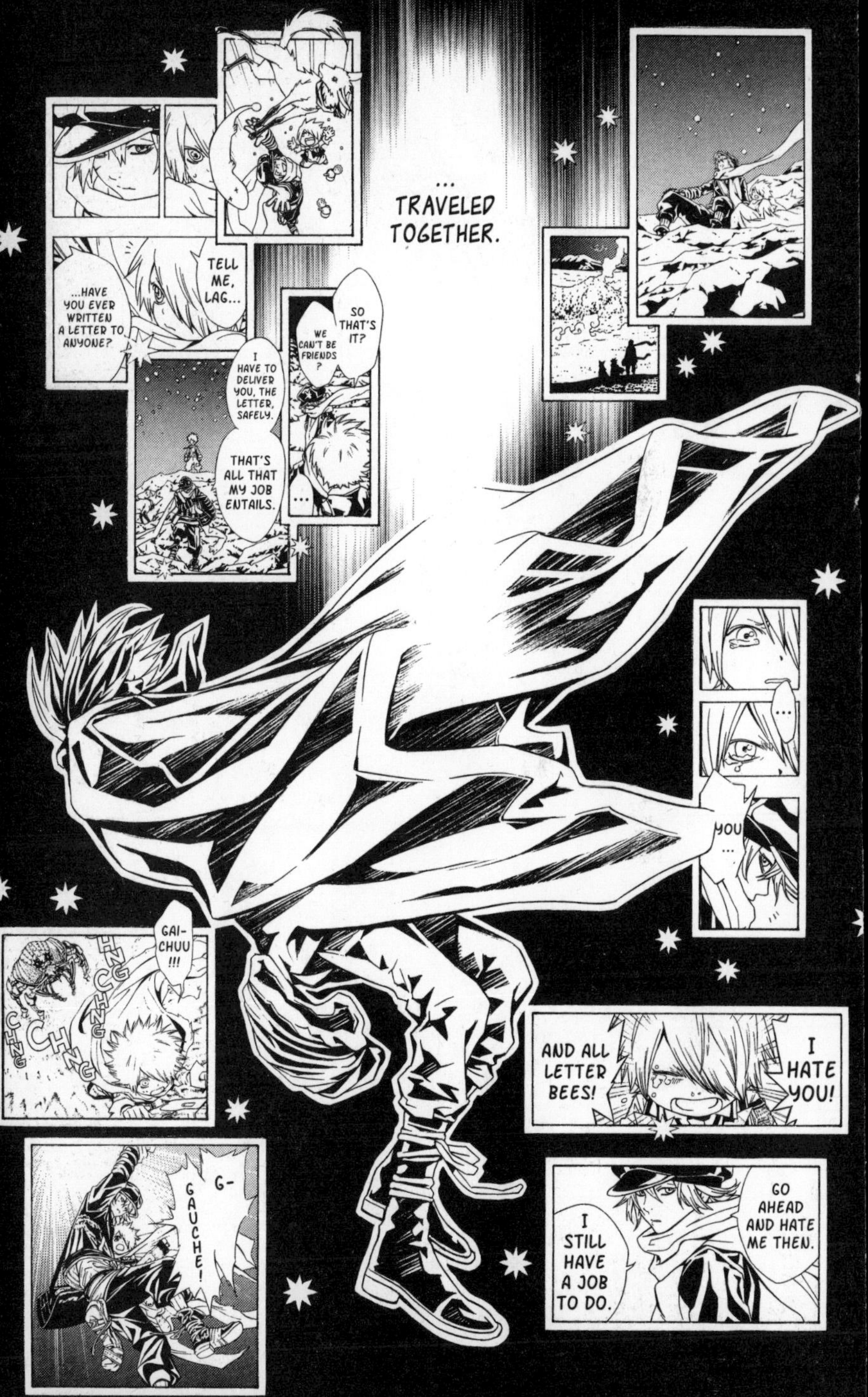
... TRAVELED TOGETHER.
TELL ME, LAG...
...HAVE YOU EVER WRITTEN A LETTER TO ANYONE?
SO THAT'S IT?
WE CAN'T BE FRIENDS ?
...
I HAVE TO DELIVER YOU, THE LETTER, SAFELY.
THAT'S ALL THAT MY JOB ENTAILS.
...
YOU ...
I HATE YOU!
AND ALL LETTER BEES!
GO AHEAD AND HATE ME THEN.
I STILL HAVE A JOB TO DO.
GAI-CHUU !!!
CHNG CHNG CHNG CHNG
G-GAUCHE!

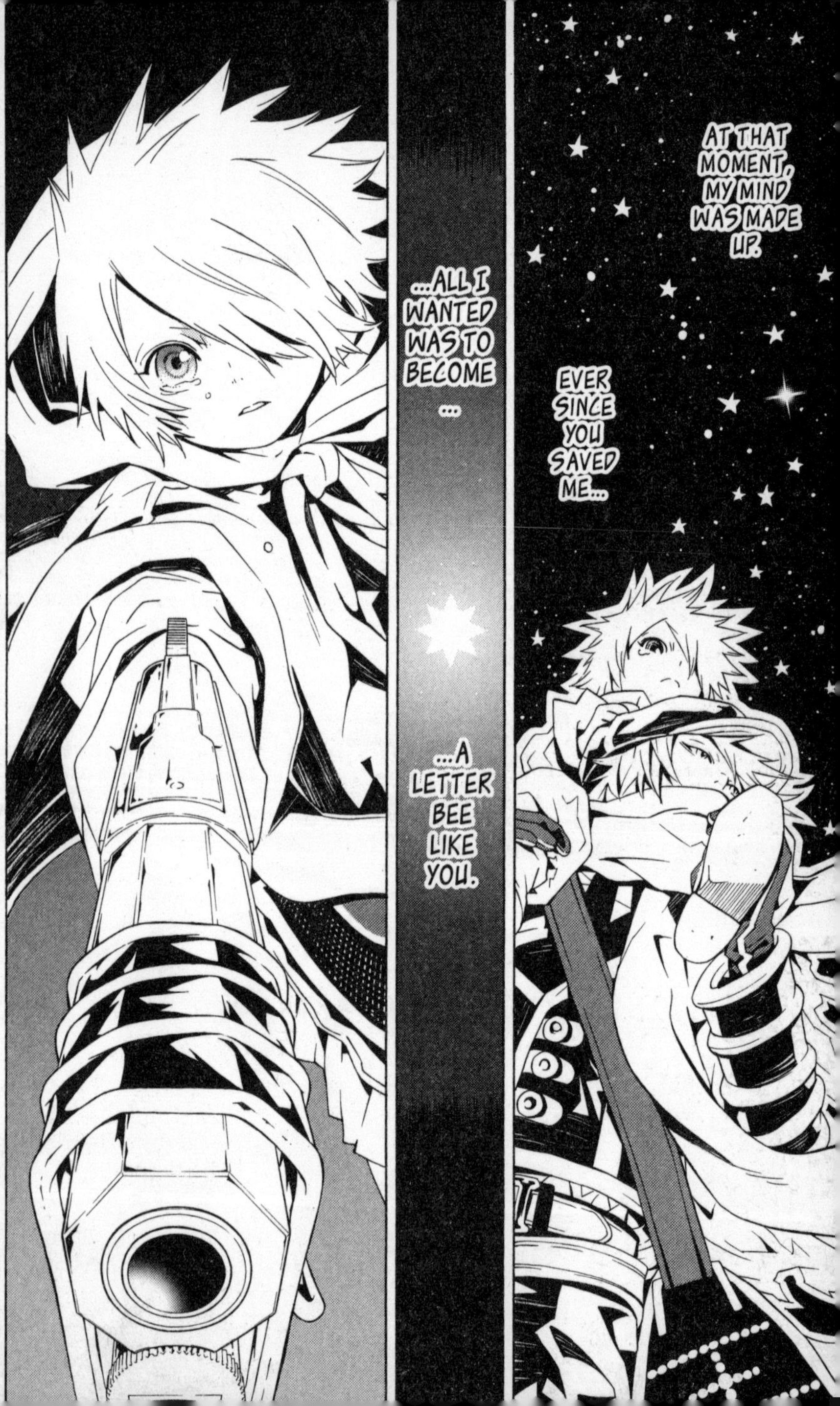
AT THAT MOMENT, MY MIND WAS MADE UP.
EVER SINCE YOU SAVED ME...
...ALL I WANTED WAS TO BECOME...
...A LETTER BEE LIKE YOU.

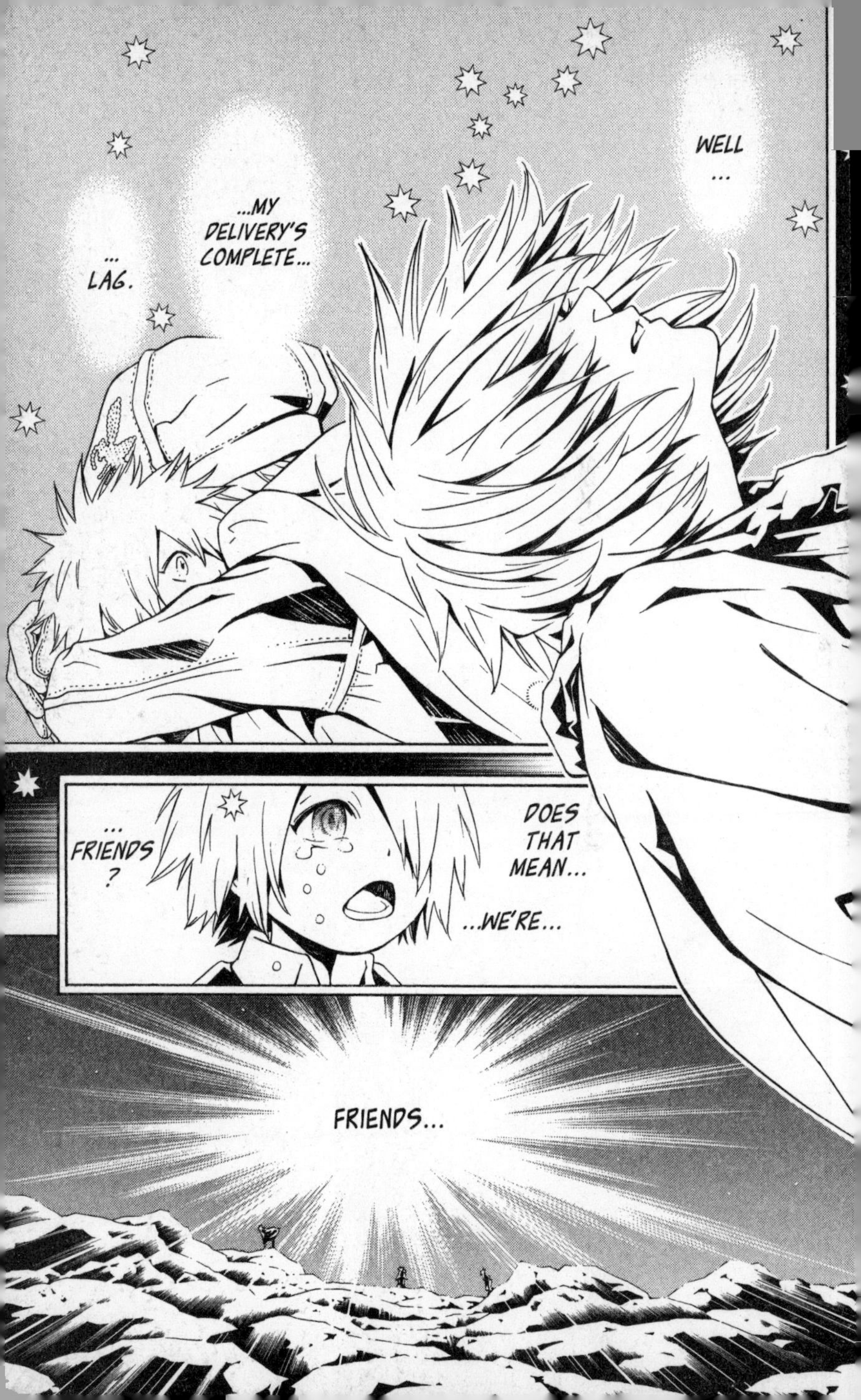
WELL ...
...MY DELIVERY'S COMPLETE...
... LAG.
DOES THAT MEAN...
...WE'RE...
... FRIENDS ?
FRIENDS...

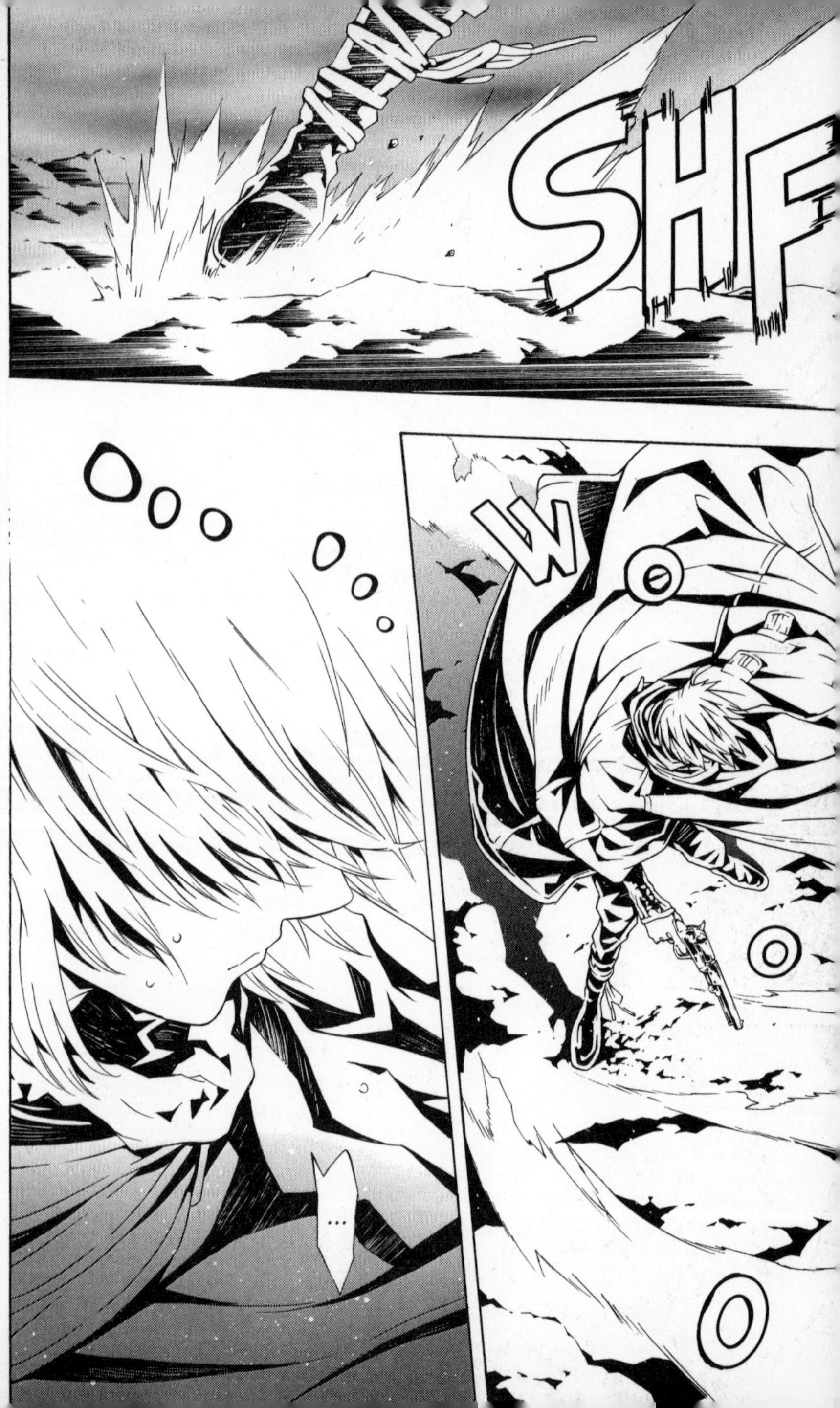
SHF
WOOO
OOOOOO
...

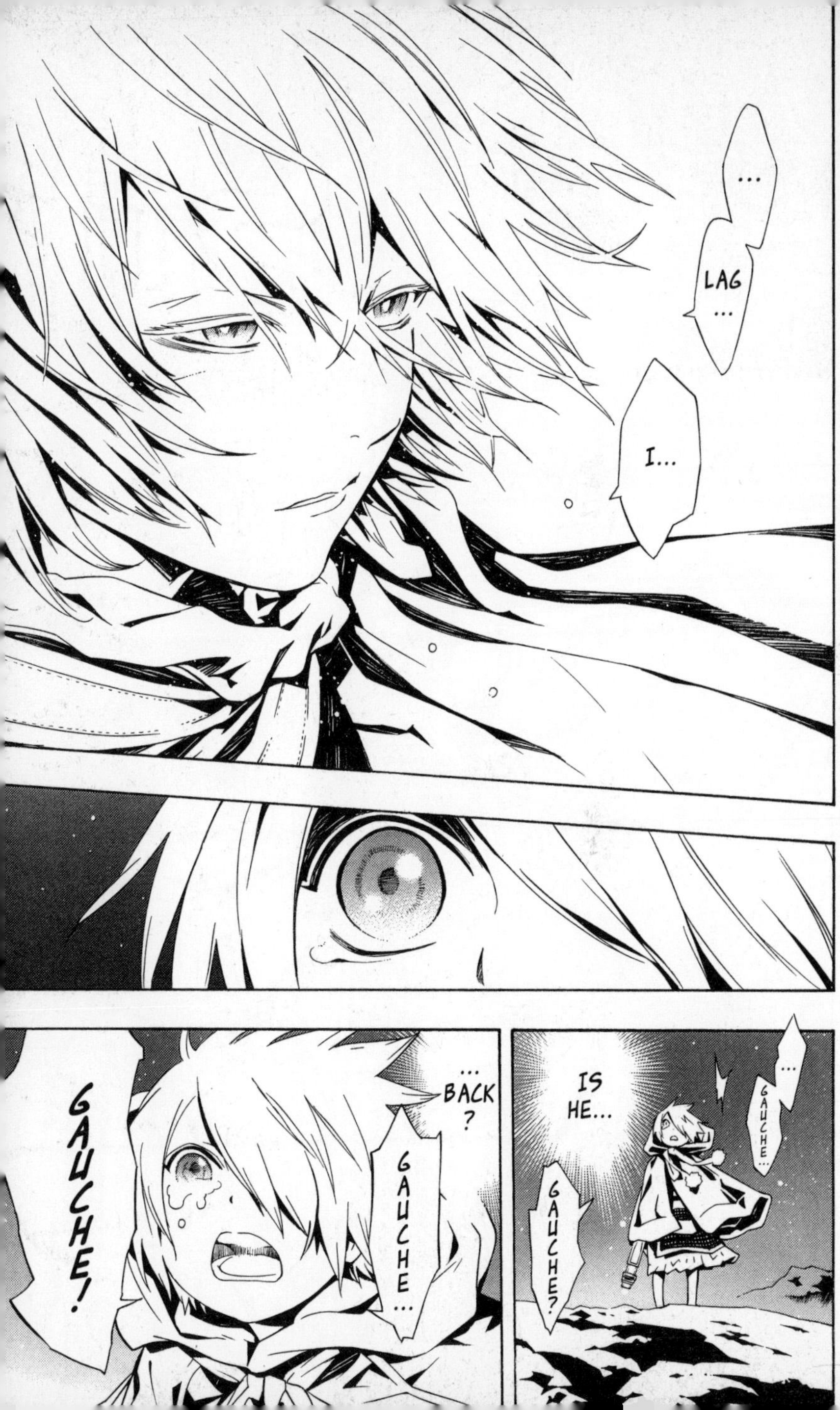
...
LAG...
I...
...GAUCHE...
IS HE...
GAUCHE?
...BACK?
GAUCHE...
GAUCHE!

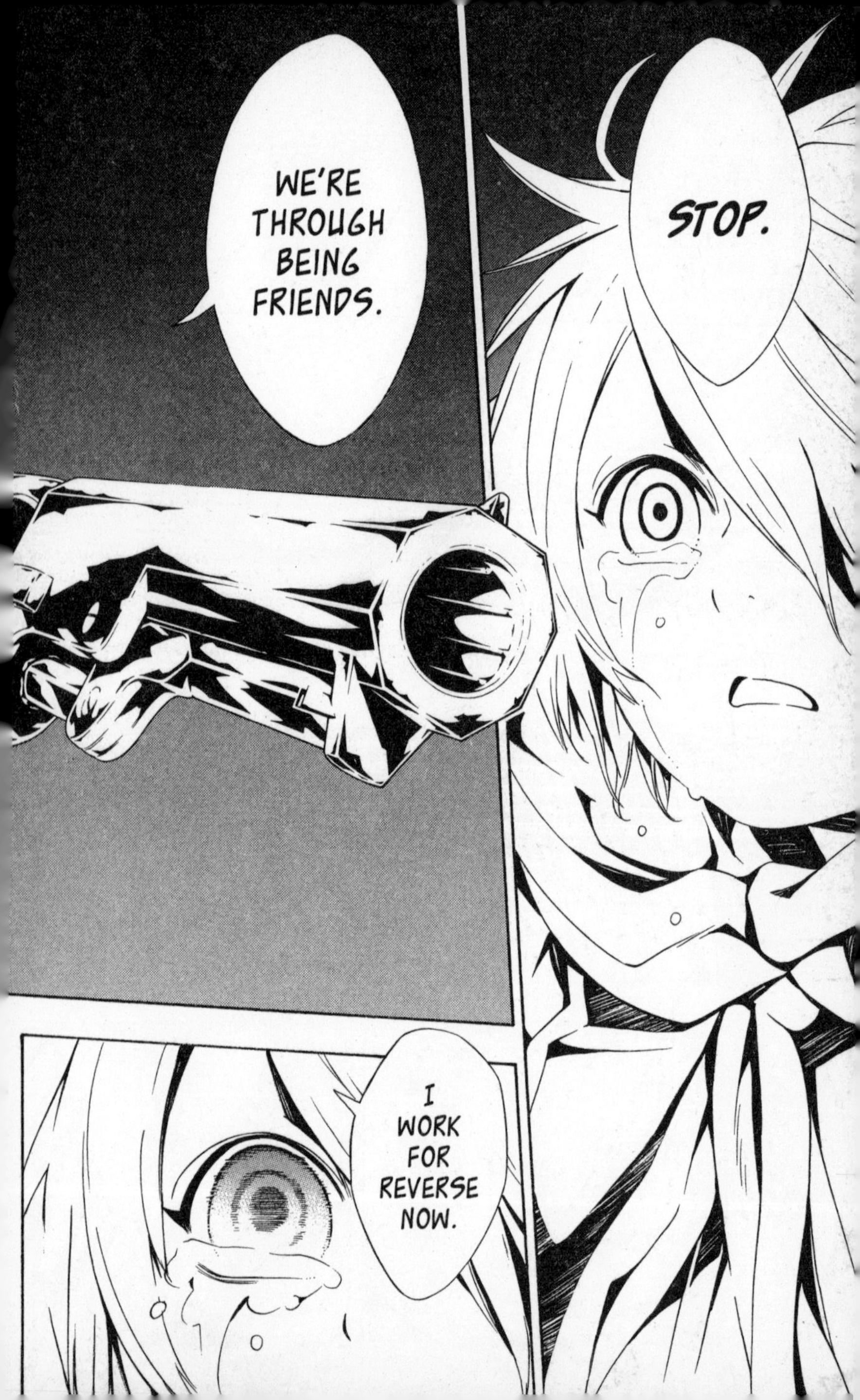
STOP.
WE'RE THROUGH BEING FRIENDS.
I WORK FOR REVERSE NOW.

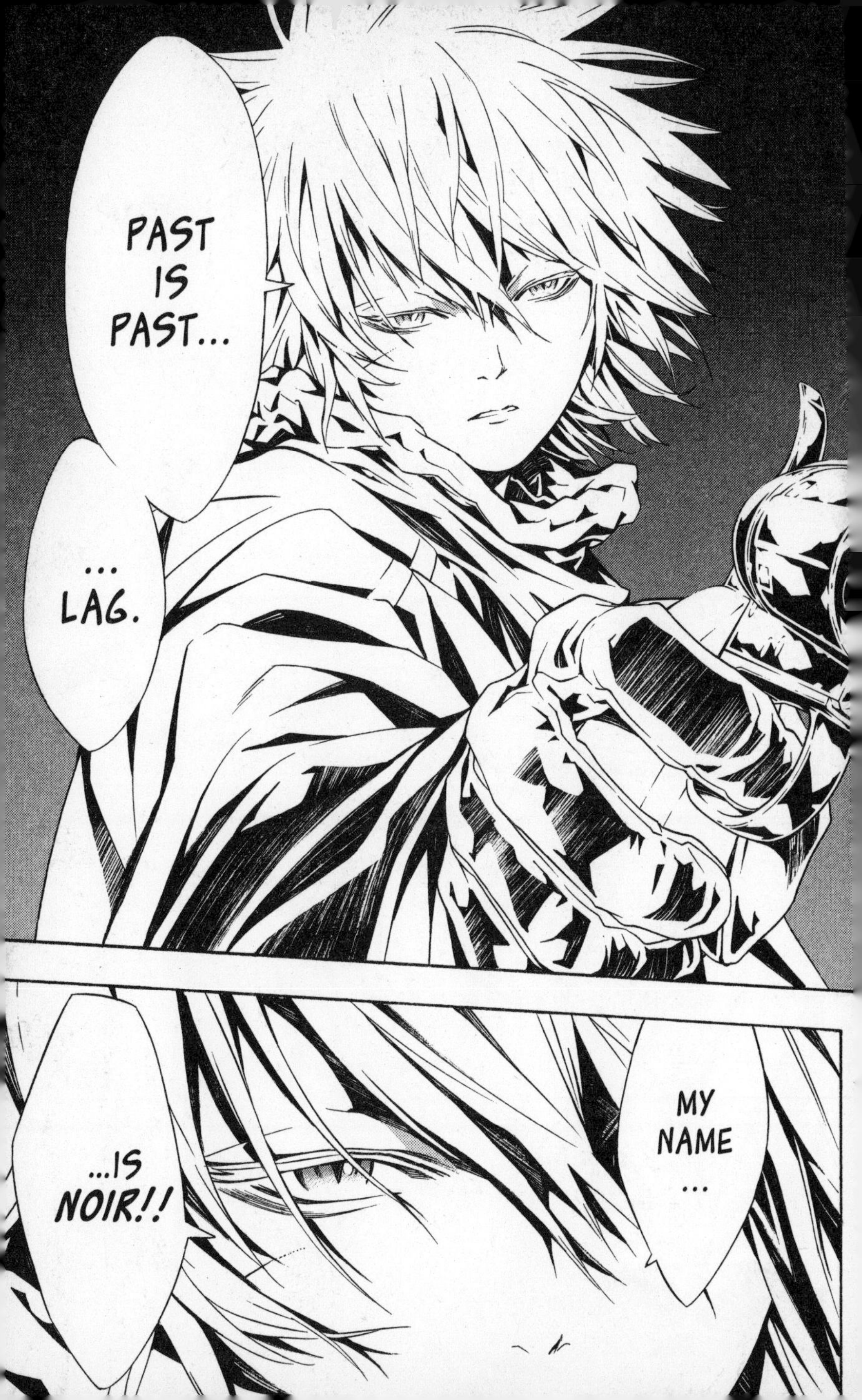
PAST IS PAST...
... LAG.
MY NAME ...
...IS NOIR!!

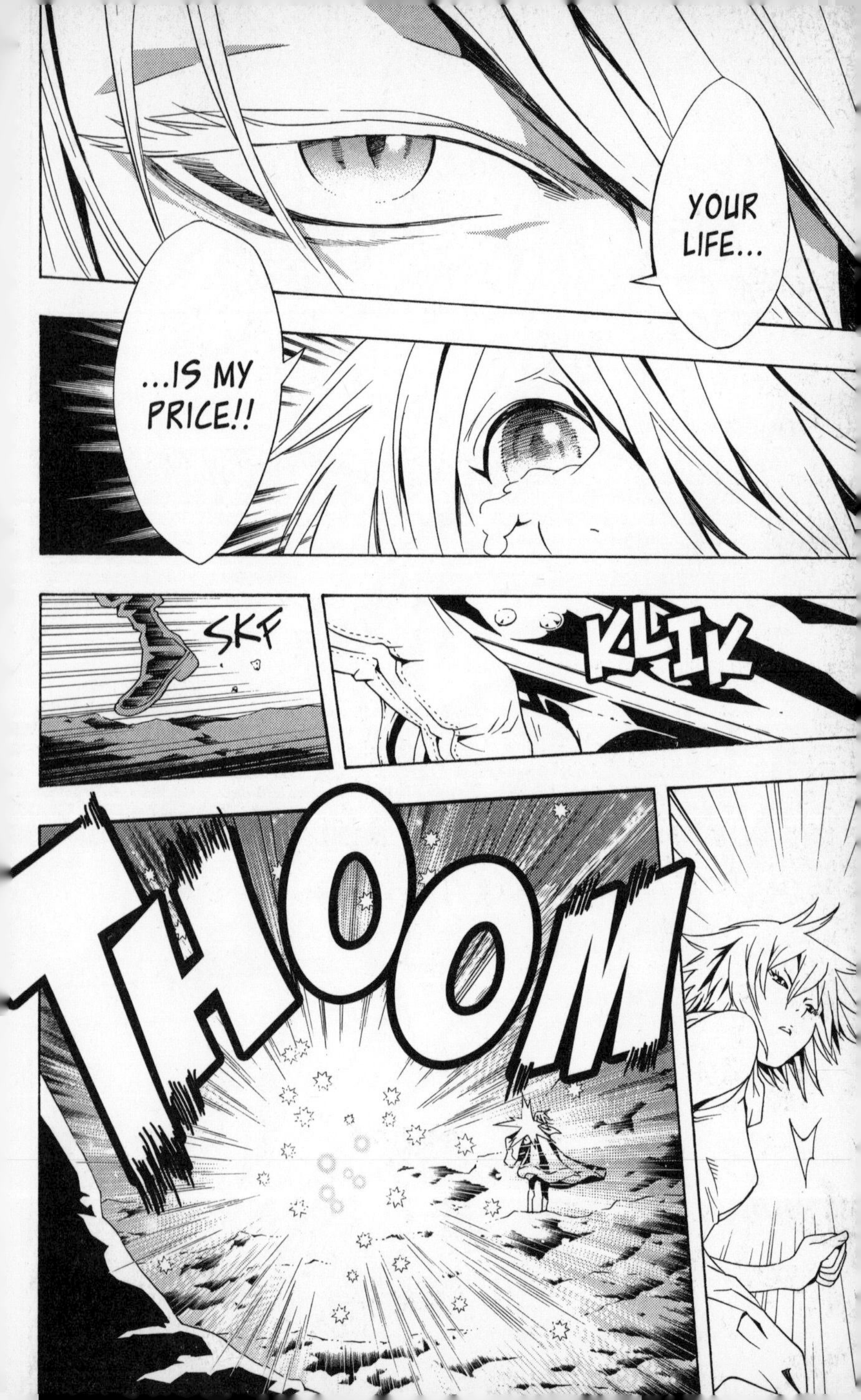
YOUR LIFE...
...IS MY PRICE!!
KLIK
SKF
THOOM

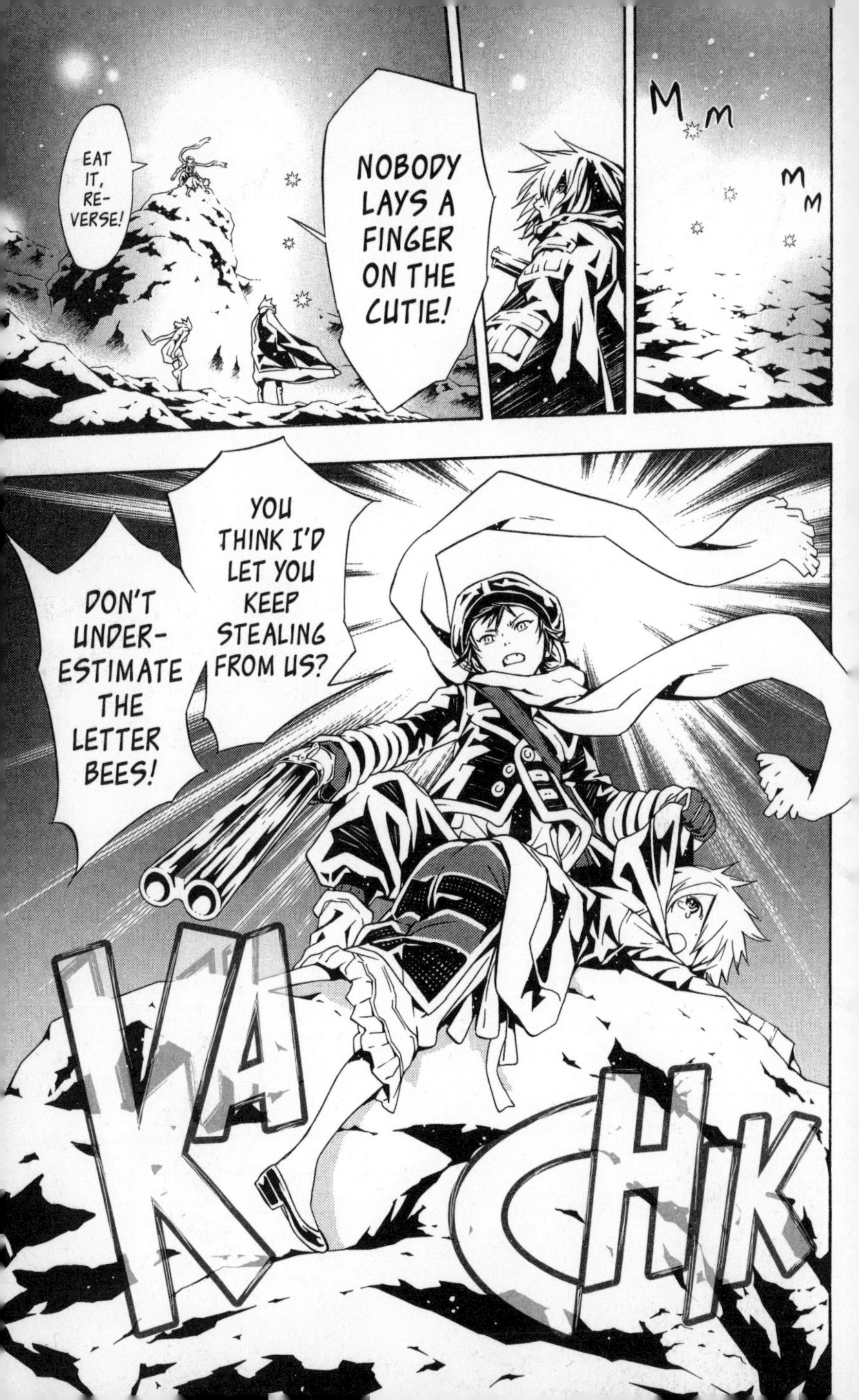
MM
MM
NOBODY LAYS A FINGER ON THE CUTIE!
EAT IT, RE-VERSE!
YOU THINK I'D LET YOU KEEP STEALING FROM US?
DON'T UNDER-ESTIMATE THE LETTER BEES!
KA CHIK

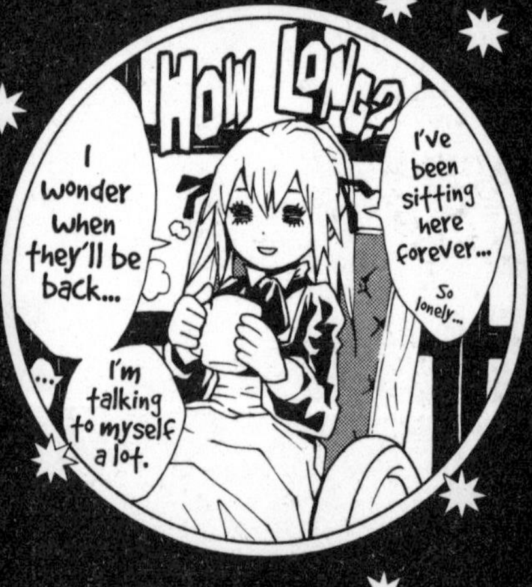
HOW LONG?
I've been sitting here forever...
So lonely...
I wonder when they'll be back...
I'm talking to myself a lot.
...

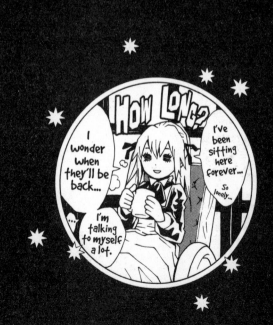

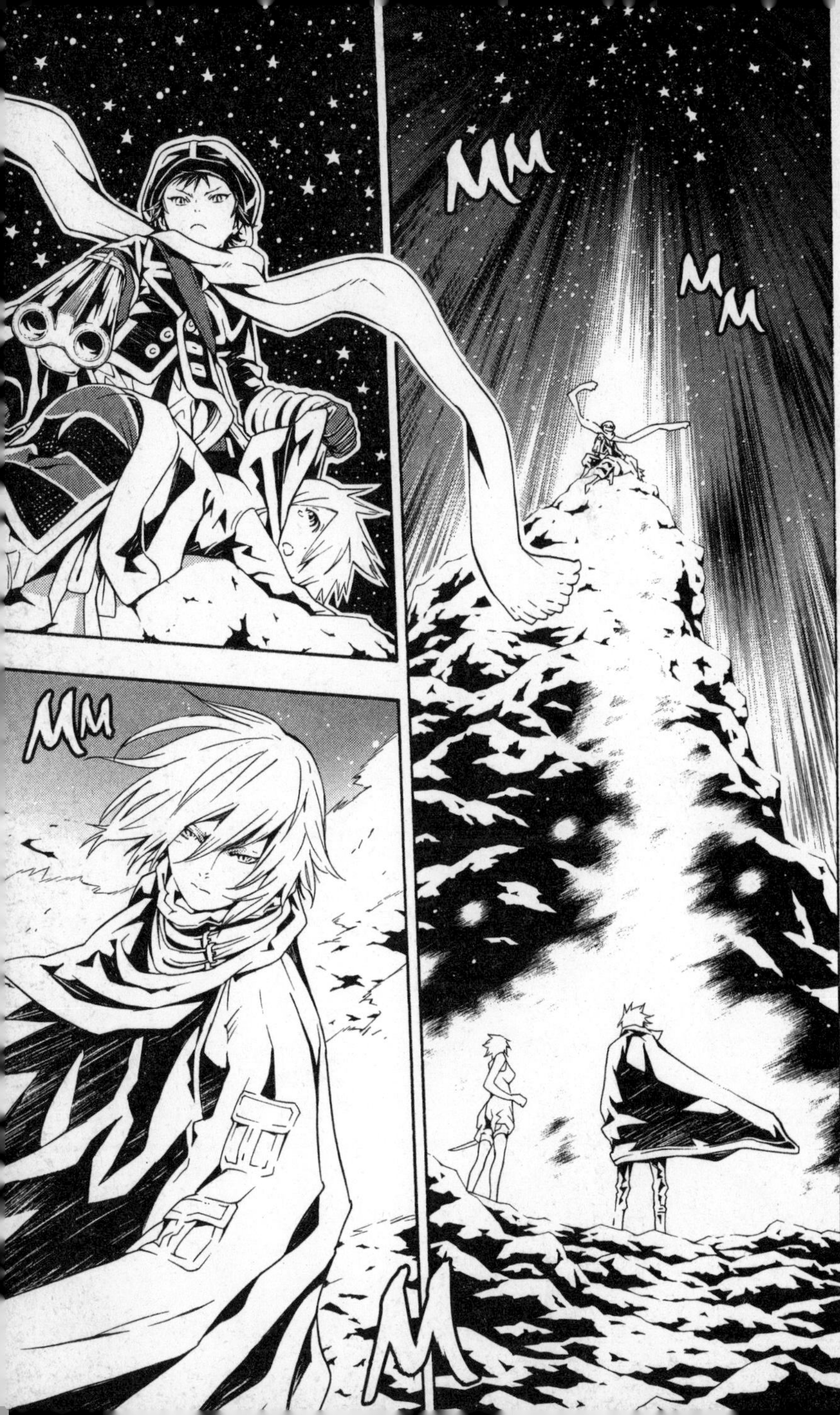
MM
MM
M
MM

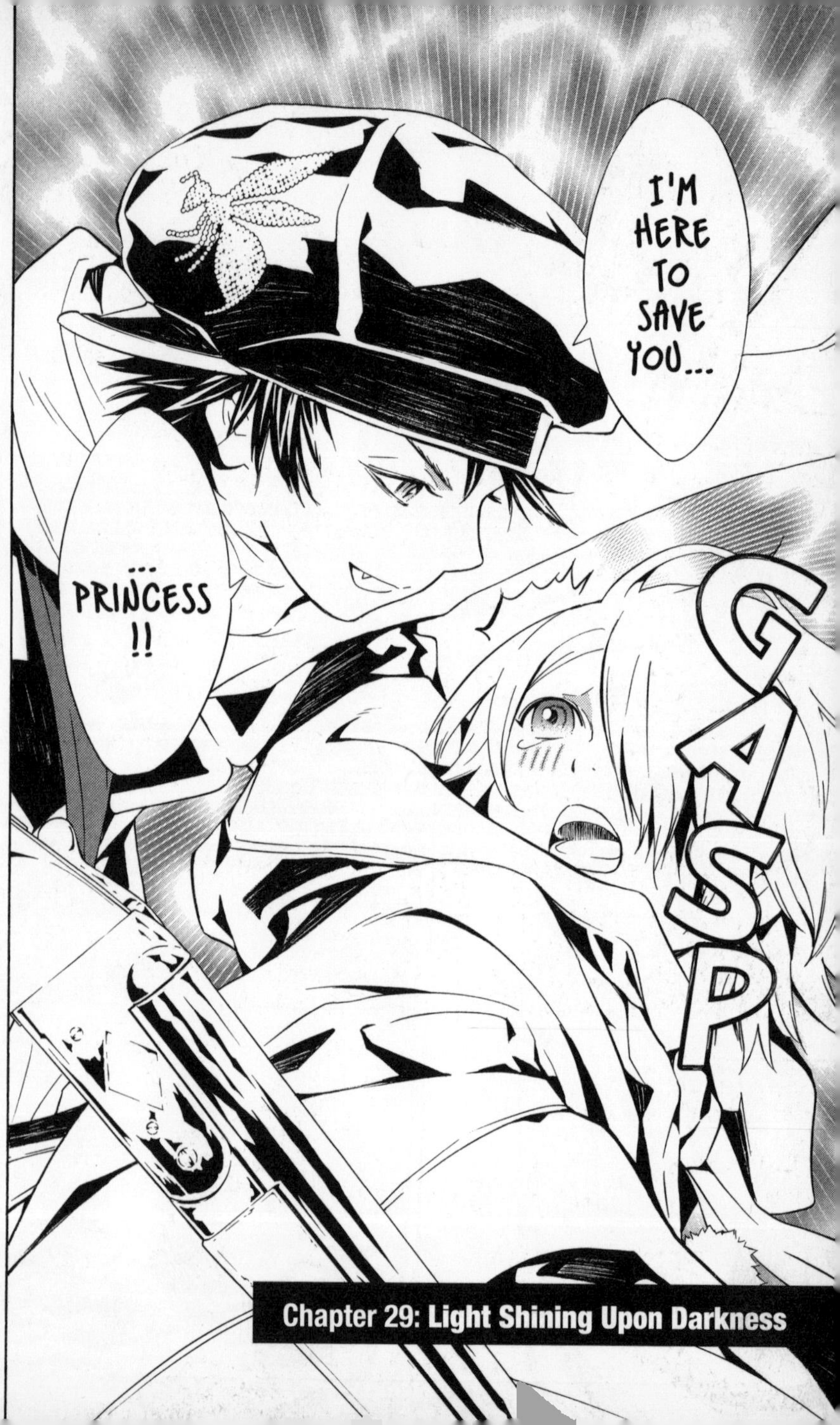
I'M HERE TO SAVE YOU...
...PRINCESS!!
GASP

Chapter 29: Light Shining Upon Darkness

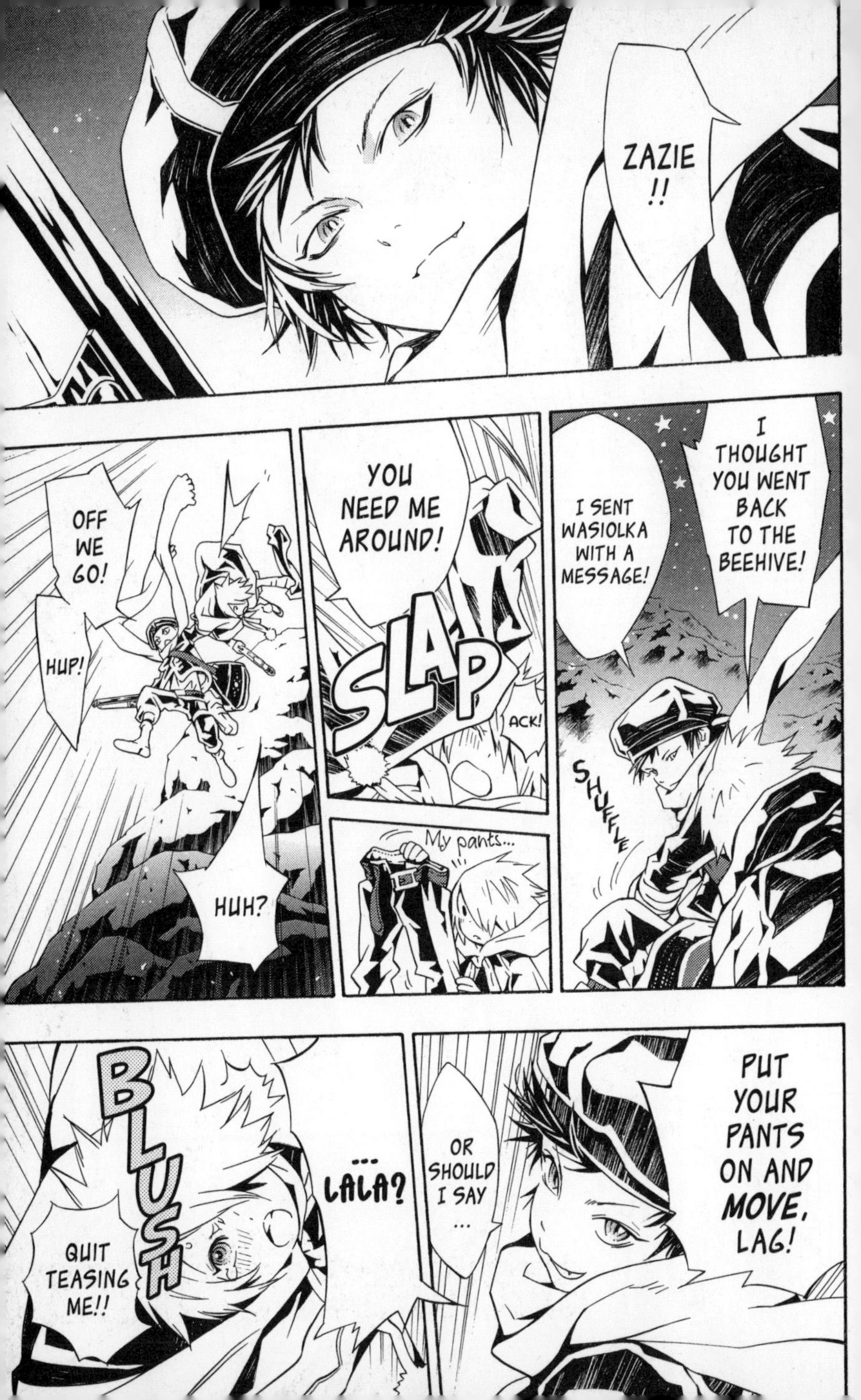
ZAZIE !!
I THOUGHT YOU WENT BACK TO THE BEEHIVE!
I SENT WASIOLKA WITH A MESSAGE!
SHUFFLE
YOU NEED ME AROUND!
SLAP
ACK!
My pants...
OFF WE GO!
HUP!
HUH?
PUT YOUR PANTS ON AND MOVE, LAG!
OR SHOULD I SAY ...
... LALA?
BLUSH
QUIT TEASING ME!!

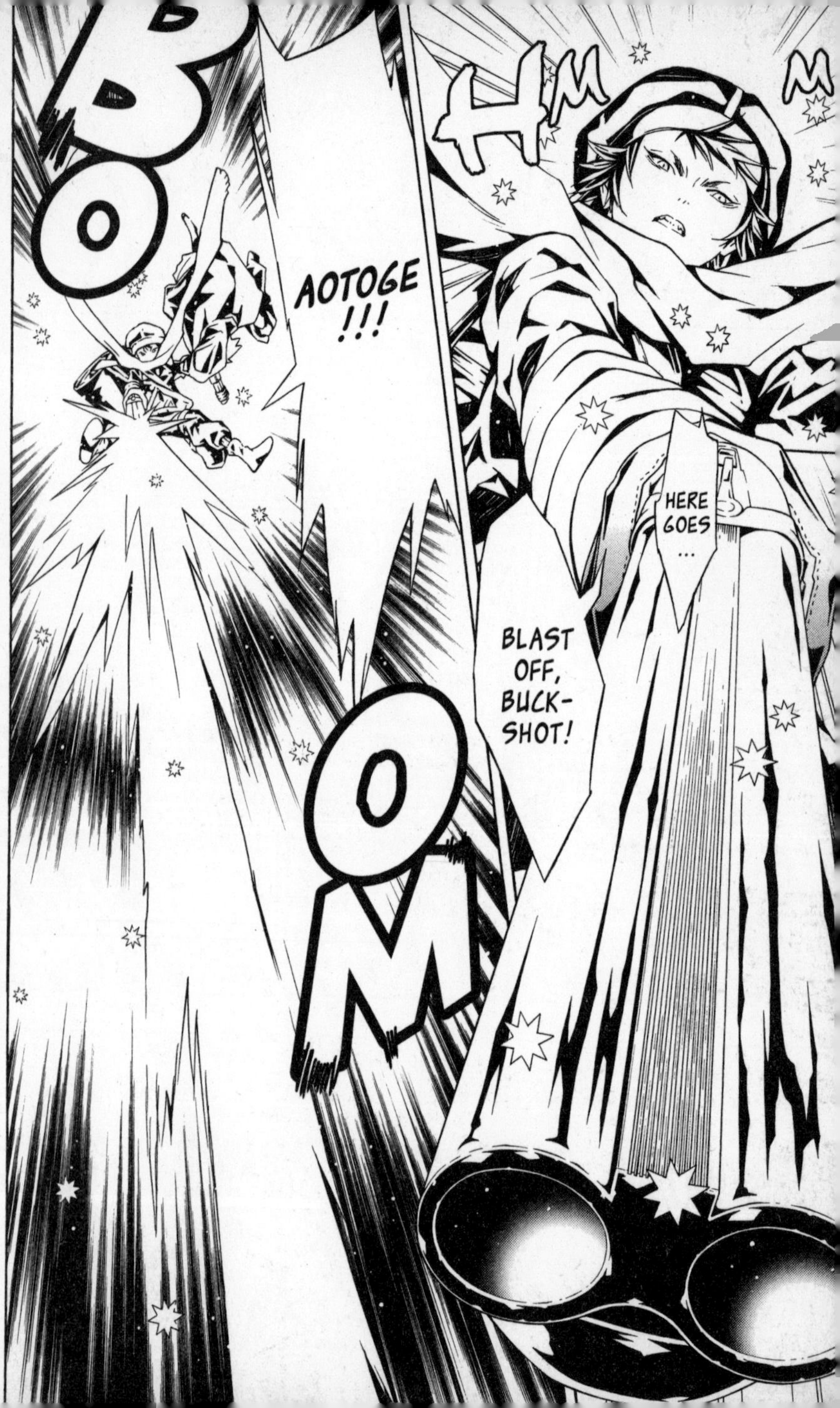
HMM
HERE GOES...
BLAST OFF, BUCK-SHOT!
BOOM
AOTOGE!!!

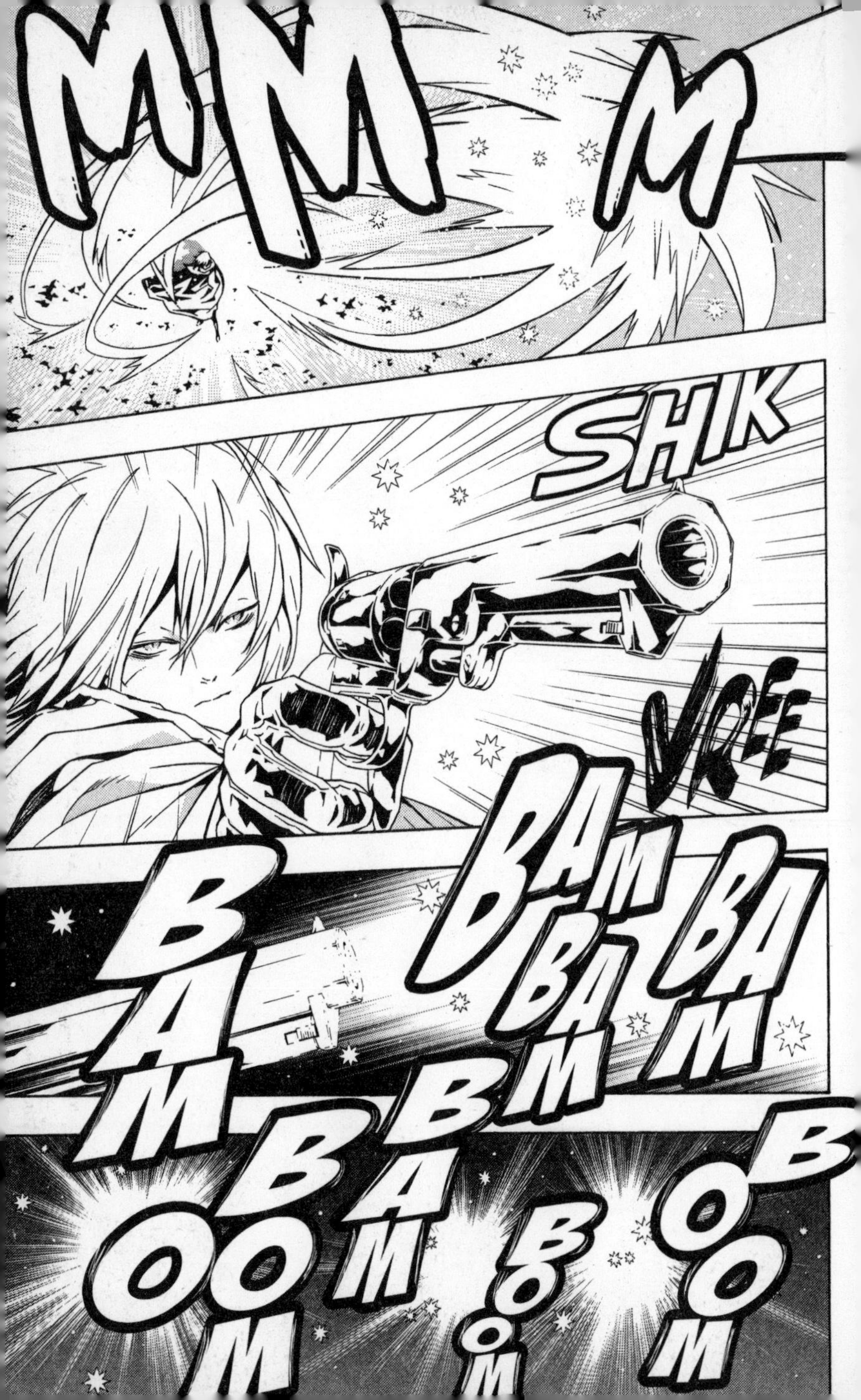
MMMM
SHIK
VREE
BABAM
BABAM
BAM
BAM
BAM
BOOM
BOOM
BOOM
BOOM

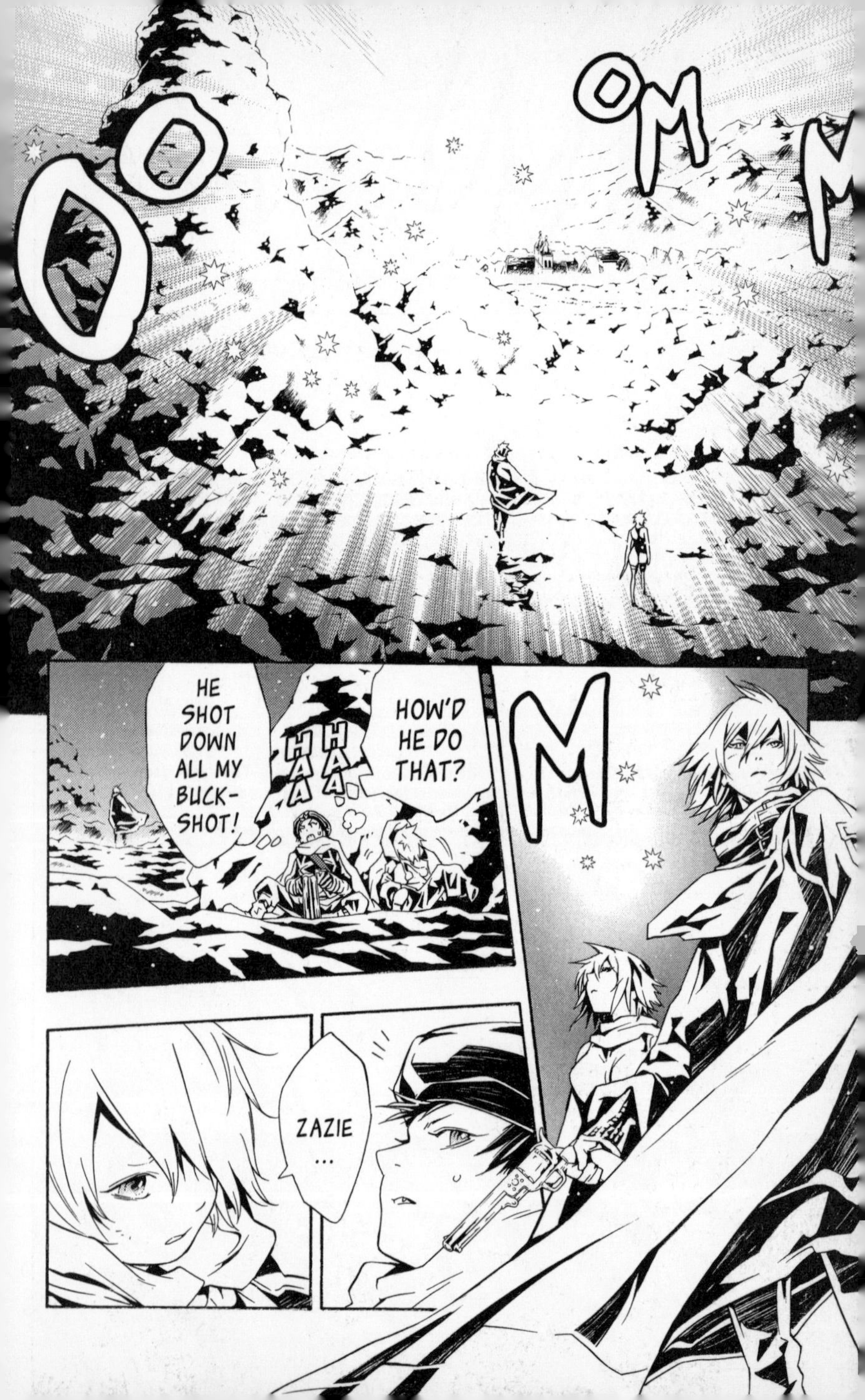
OOOMM
M
HOW'D HE DO THAT?
HAA HAA
HE SHOT DOWN ALL MY BUCK-SHOT!
ZAZIE ...

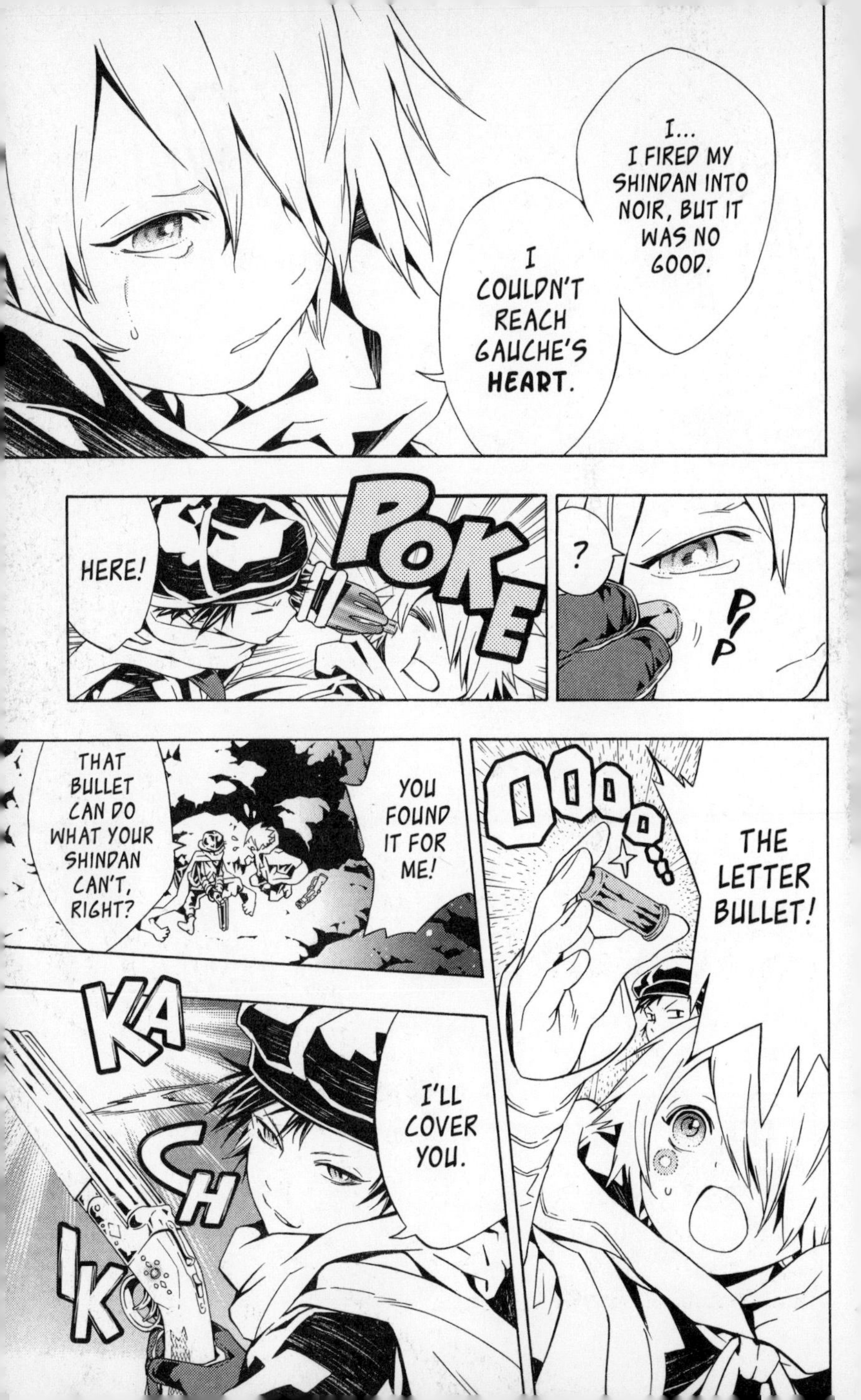

I... I FIRED MY SHINDAN INTO NOIR, BUT IT WAS NO GOOD.
I COULDN'T REACH GAUCHE'S **HEART**.
?
PIP
POKE
HERE!
OOOO
THE LETTER BULLET!
YOU FOUND IT FOR ME!
THAT BULLET CAN DO WHAT YOUR SHINDAN CAN'T, RIGHT?
I'LL COVER YOU.
KA CHIK

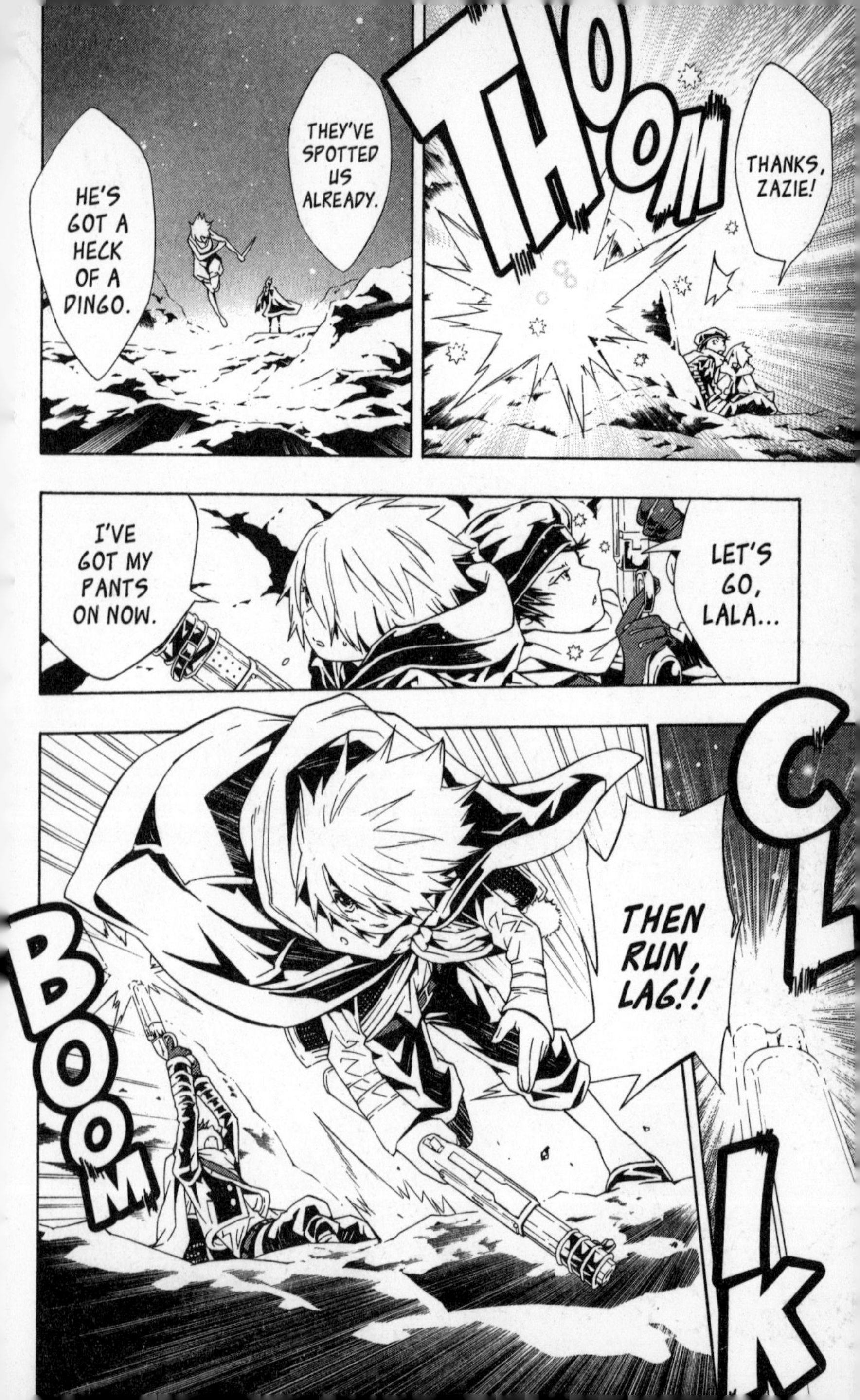
THANKS, ZAZIE!
THOOM
THEY'VE SPOTTED US ALREADY.
HE'S GOT A HECK OF A DINGO.
LET'S GO, LALA...
I'VE GOT MY PANTS ON NOW.
CLIK
THEN RUN, LAG!!
BOOM

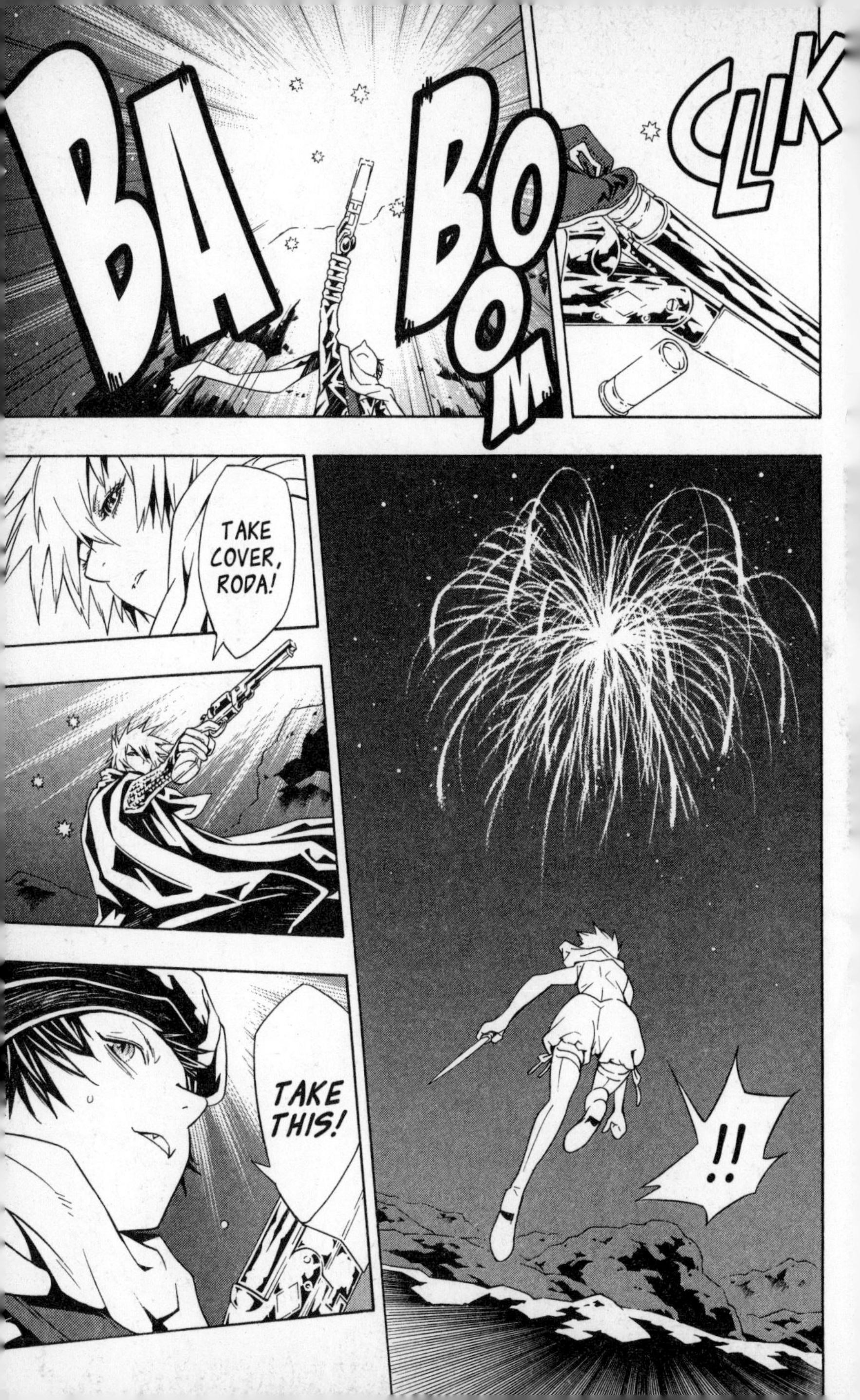
CLIK
BA
BOOM
!!
TAKE COVER, RODA!
TAKE THIS!

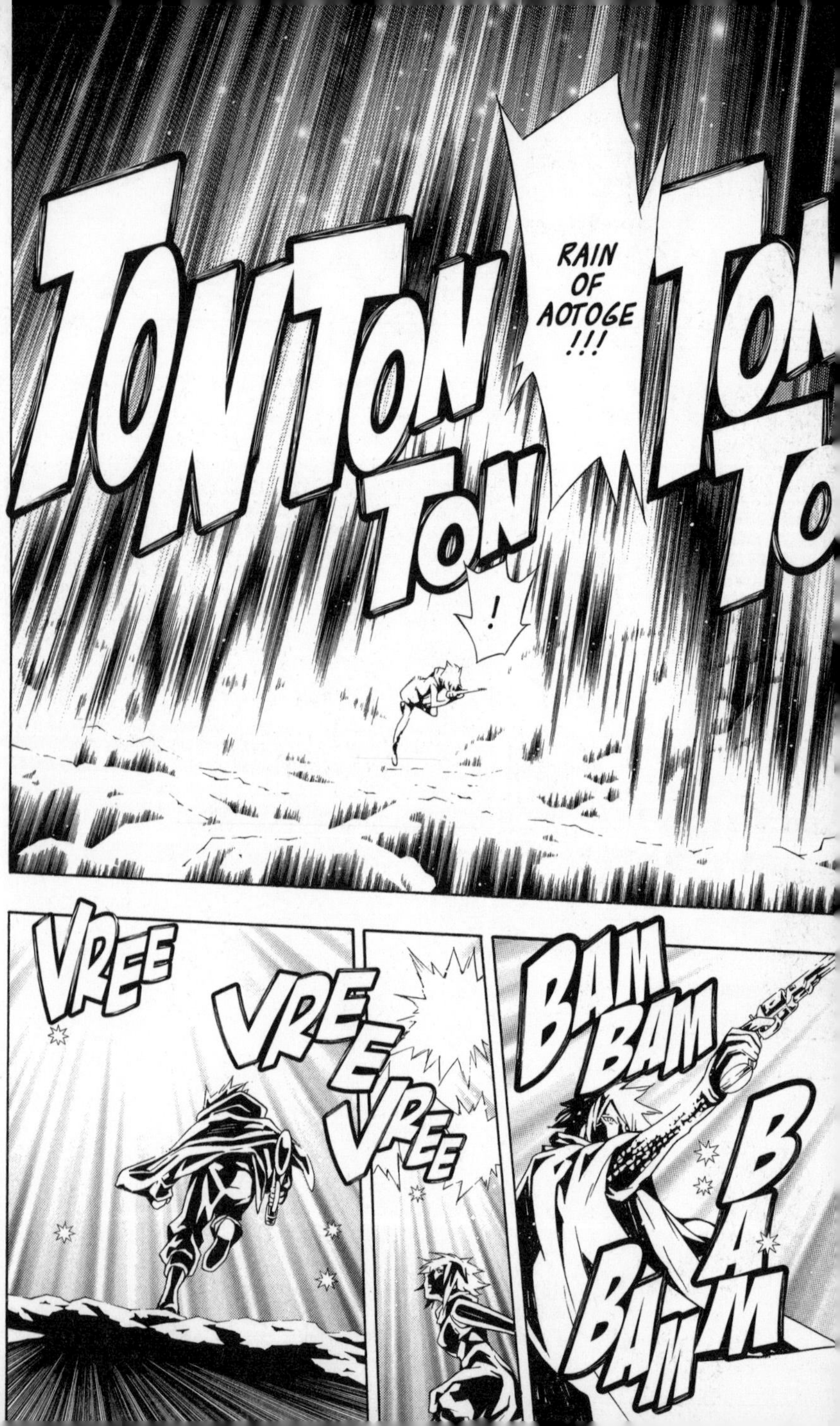
TON TON
RAIN OF AOTOGE!!!
TON TON TON
!
BAM BAM
BAM
BAM BAM
VREE VREE
VREE

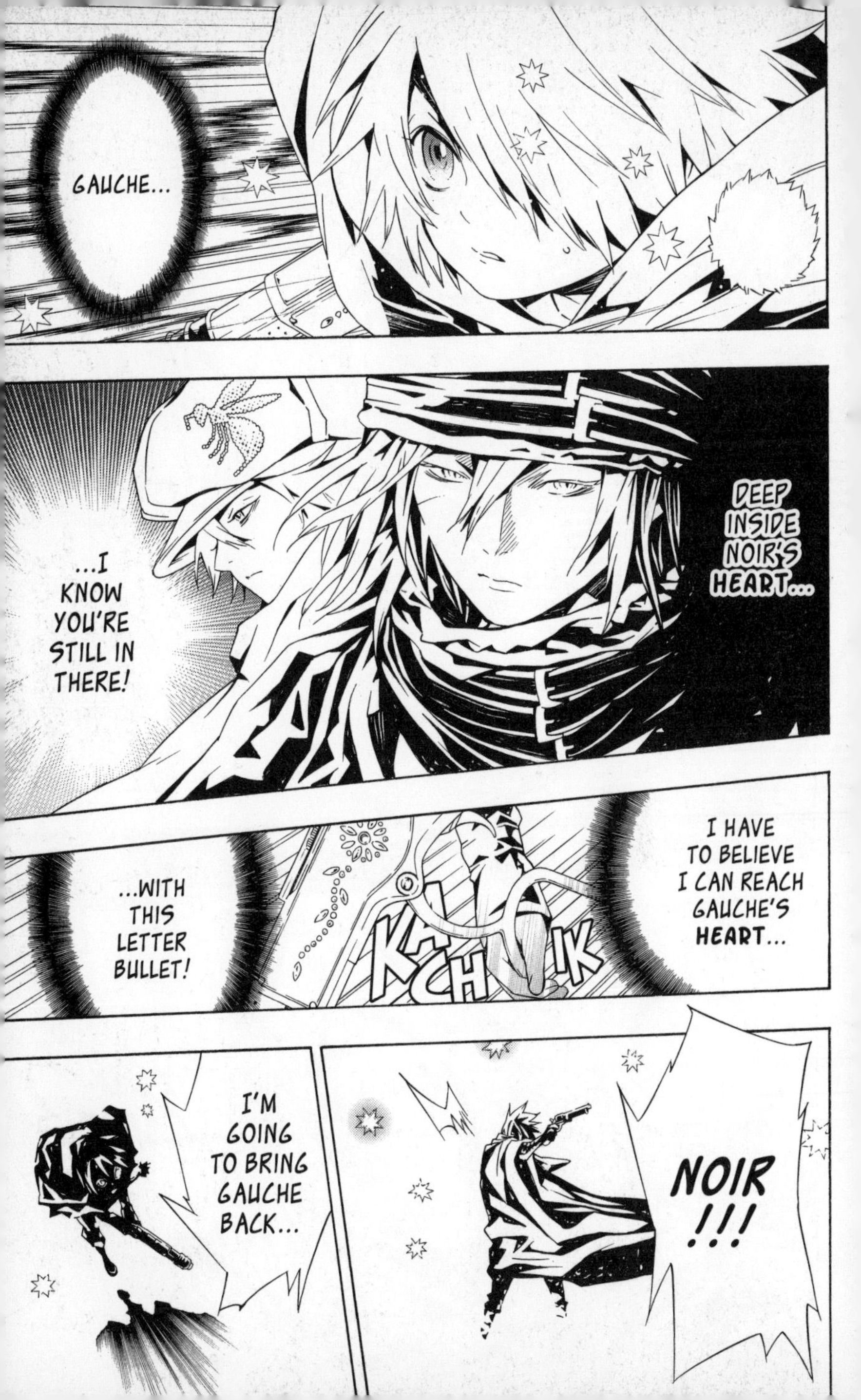
GAUCHE...
DEEP INSIDE NOIR'S HEART...
...I KNOW YOU'RE STILL IN THERE!
I HAVE TO BELIEVE I CAN REACH GAUCHE'S HEART...
...WITH THIS LETTER BULLET!
NOIR !!!
I'M GOING TO BRING GAUCHE BACK...

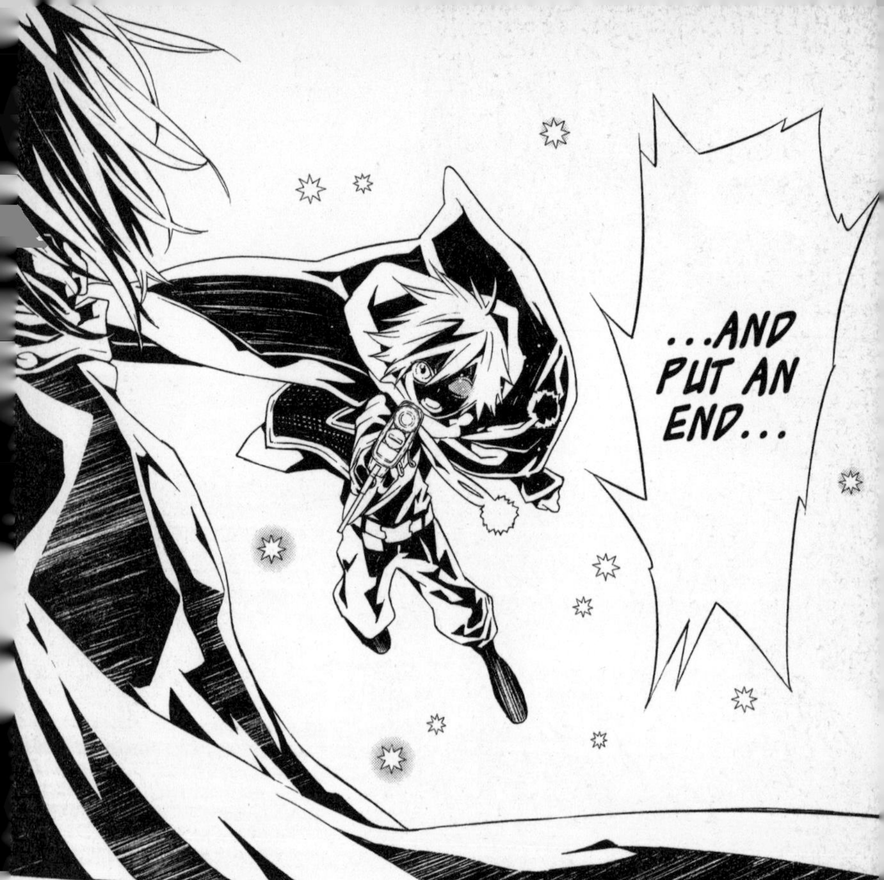
...AND PUT AN END...
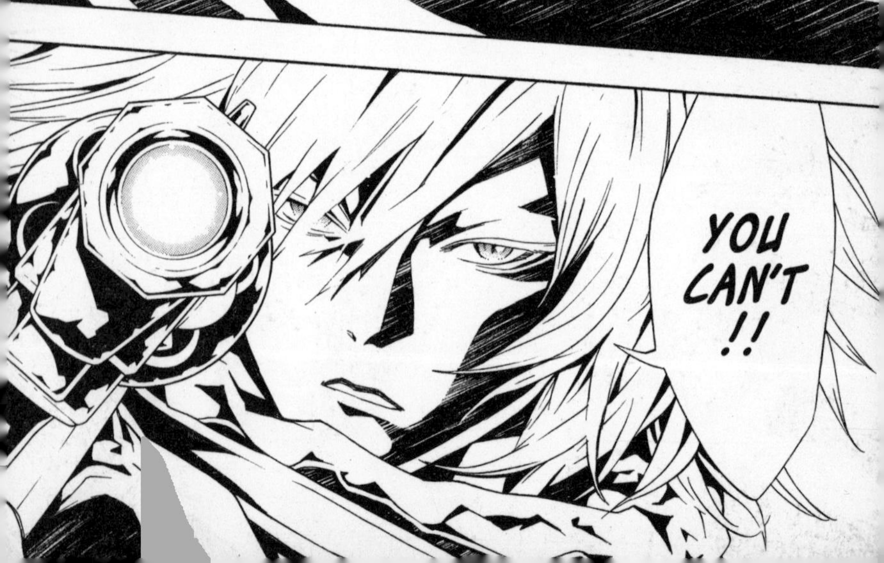
YOU CAN'T !!

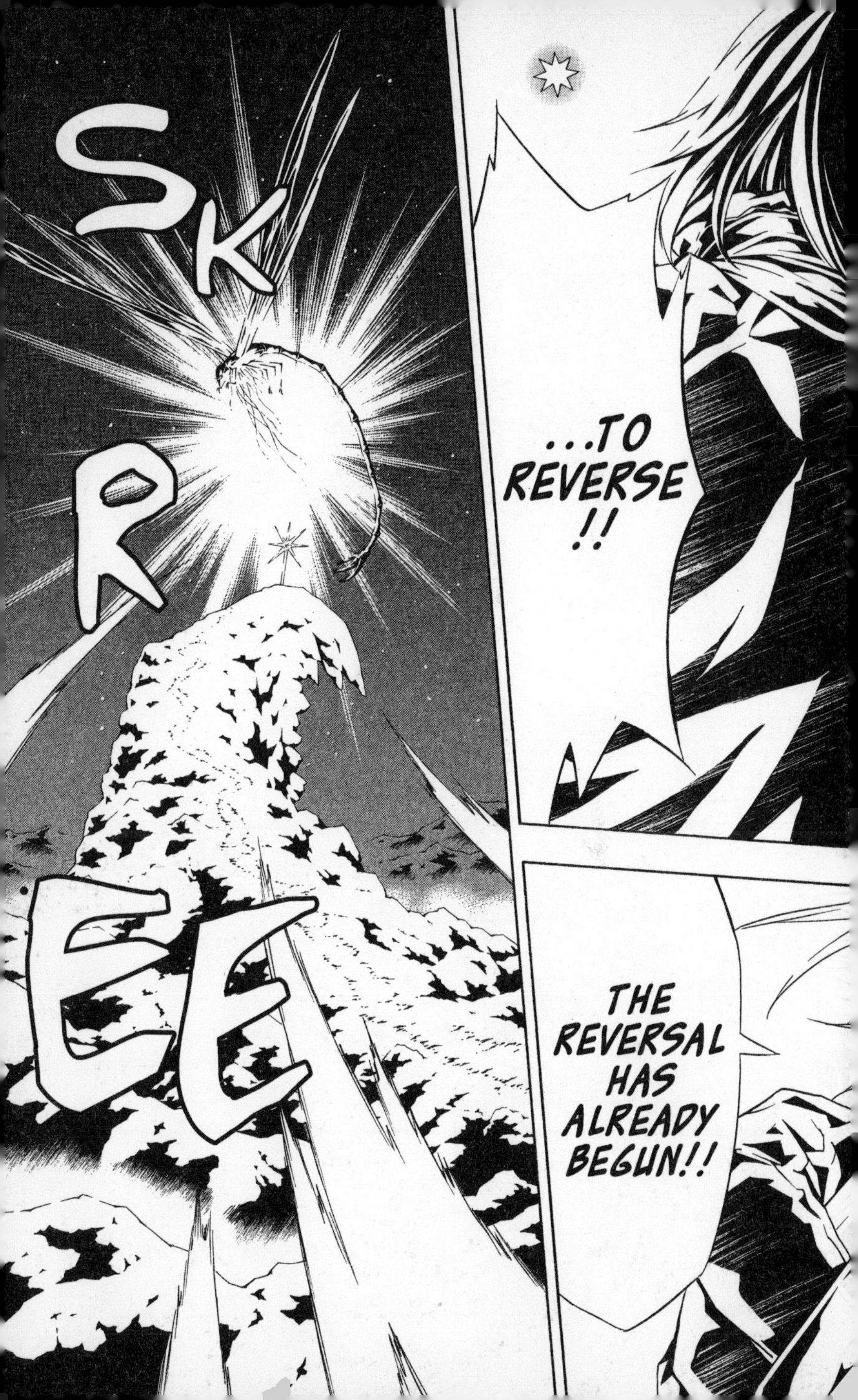
...TO REVERSE!!
THE REVERSAL HAS ALREADY BEGUN!!
SKREE

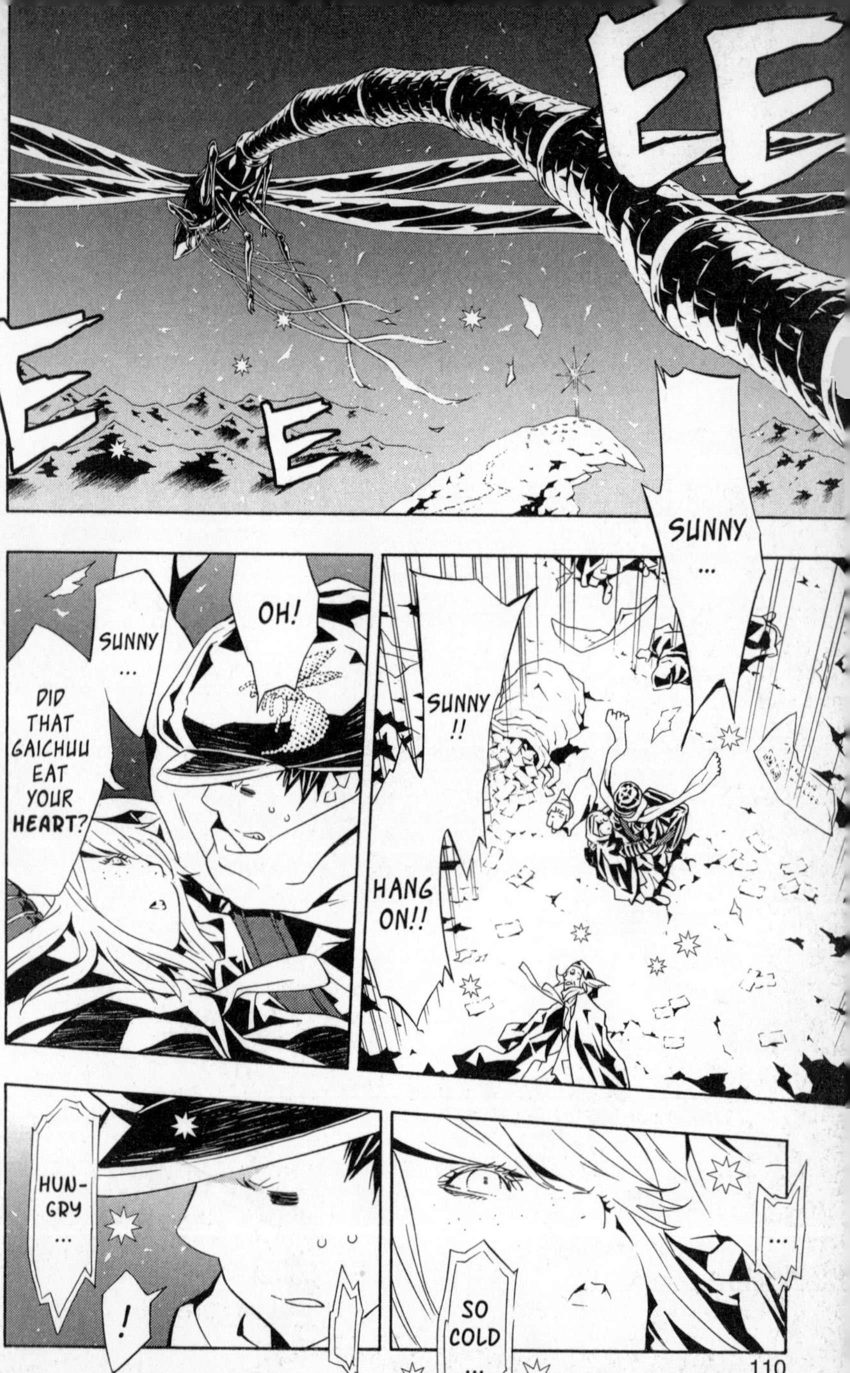
EE
E
E
SUNNY ...
SUNNY !!
HANG ON!!
OH!
SUNNY ...
DID THAT GAICHUU EAT YOUR HEART?
...
SO COLD ...
!
HUN-GRY ...

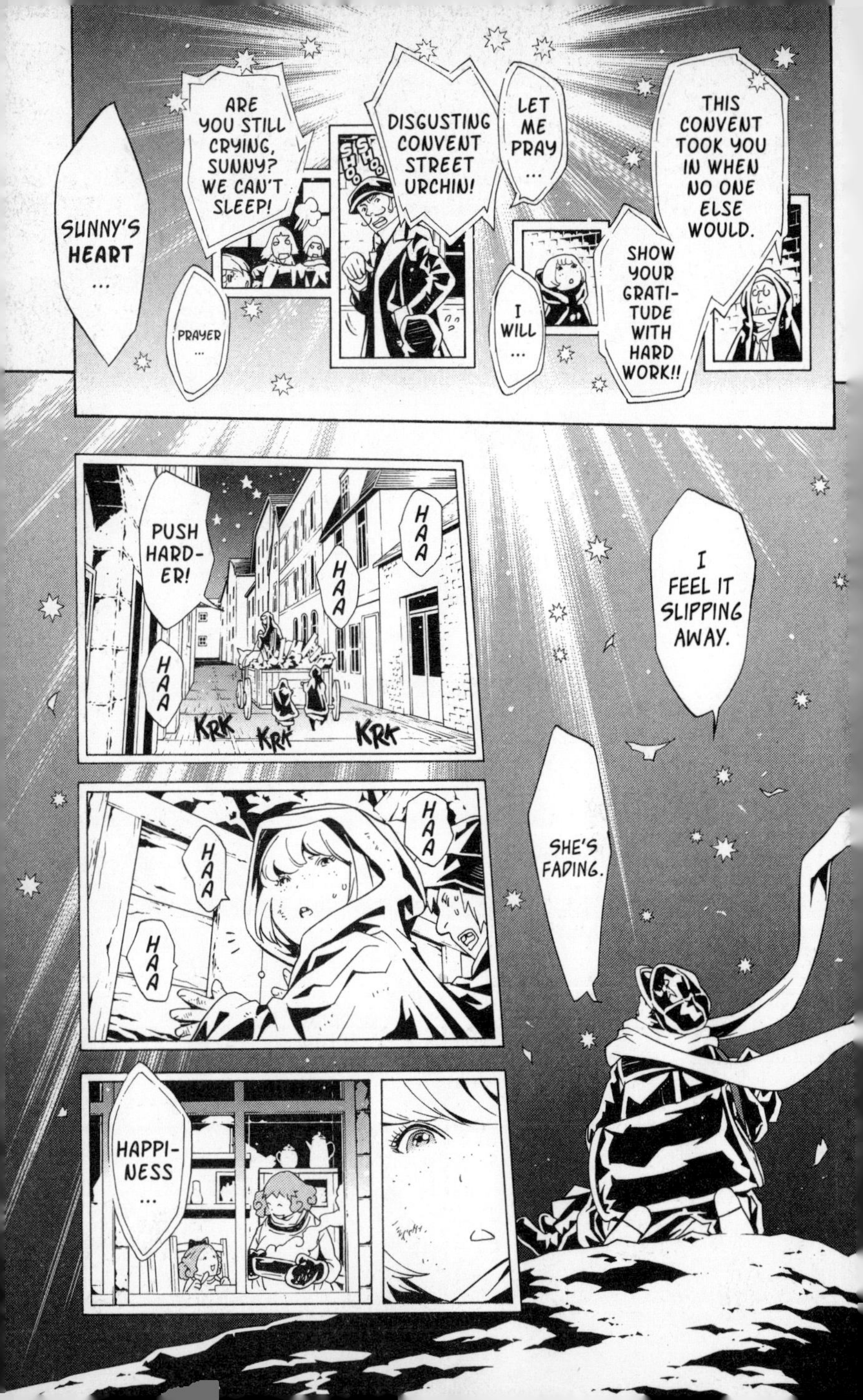
THIS CONVENT TOOK YOU IN WHEN NO ONE ELSE WOULD.
SHOW YOUR GRATITUDE WITH HARD WORK!!
LET ME PRAY ...
I WILL ...
DISGUSTING CONVENT STREET URCHIN!
SHOO SHOO
ARE YOU STILL CRYING, SUNNY? WE CAN'T SLEEP!
PRAYER ...
SUNNY'S HEART ...
I FEEL IT SLIPPING AWAY.
SHE'S FADING.
HAA
HAA
PUSH HARDER!
HAA
KRK KRK KRK
HAA
HAA
HAA
HAPPINESS ...

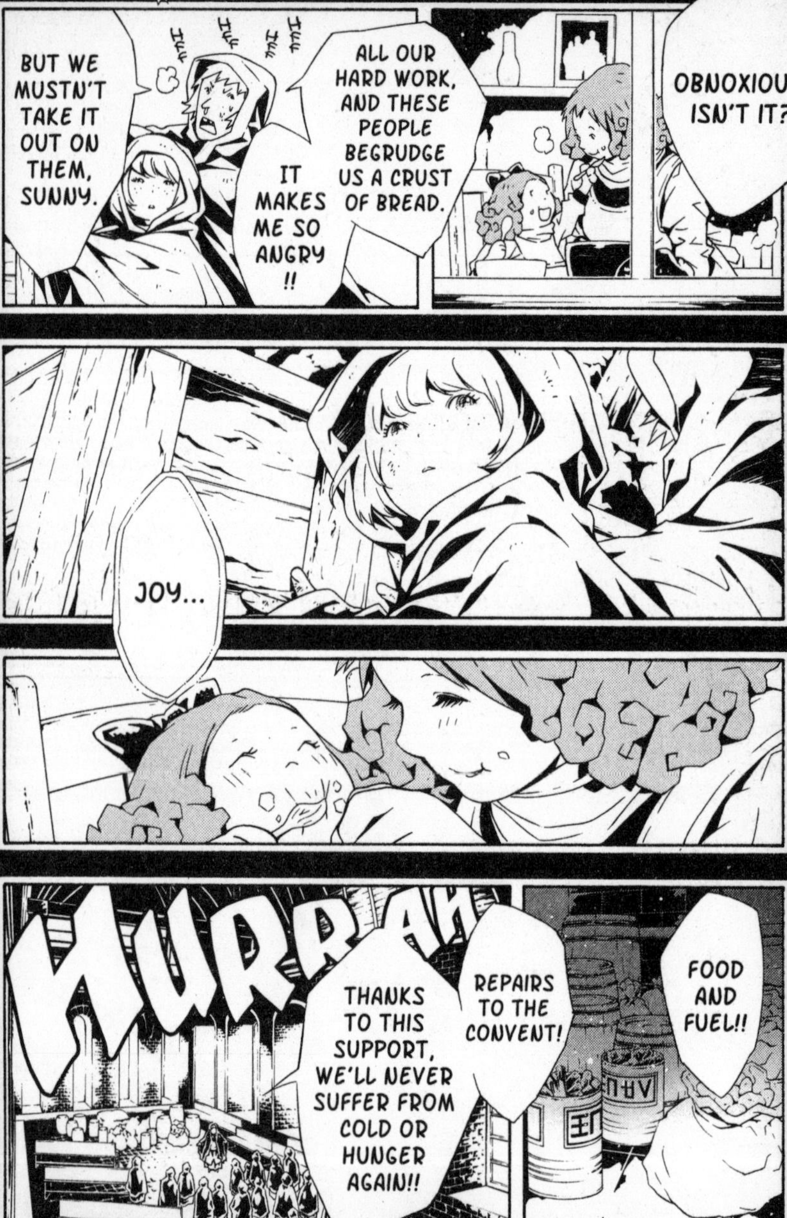
OBNOXIOUS, ISN'T IT?
HFF HFF
HFF HFF
ALL OUR HARD WORK, AND THESE PEOPLE BEGRUDGE US A CRUST OF BREAD.
IT MAKES ME SO ANGRY!!
BUT WE MUSTN'T TAKE IT OUT ON THEM, SUNNY.
JOY...
FOOD AND FUEL!!
REPAIRS TO THE CONVENT!
THANKS TO THIS SUPPORT, WE'LL NEVER SUFFER FROM COLD OR HUNGER AGAIN!!
HURRAH

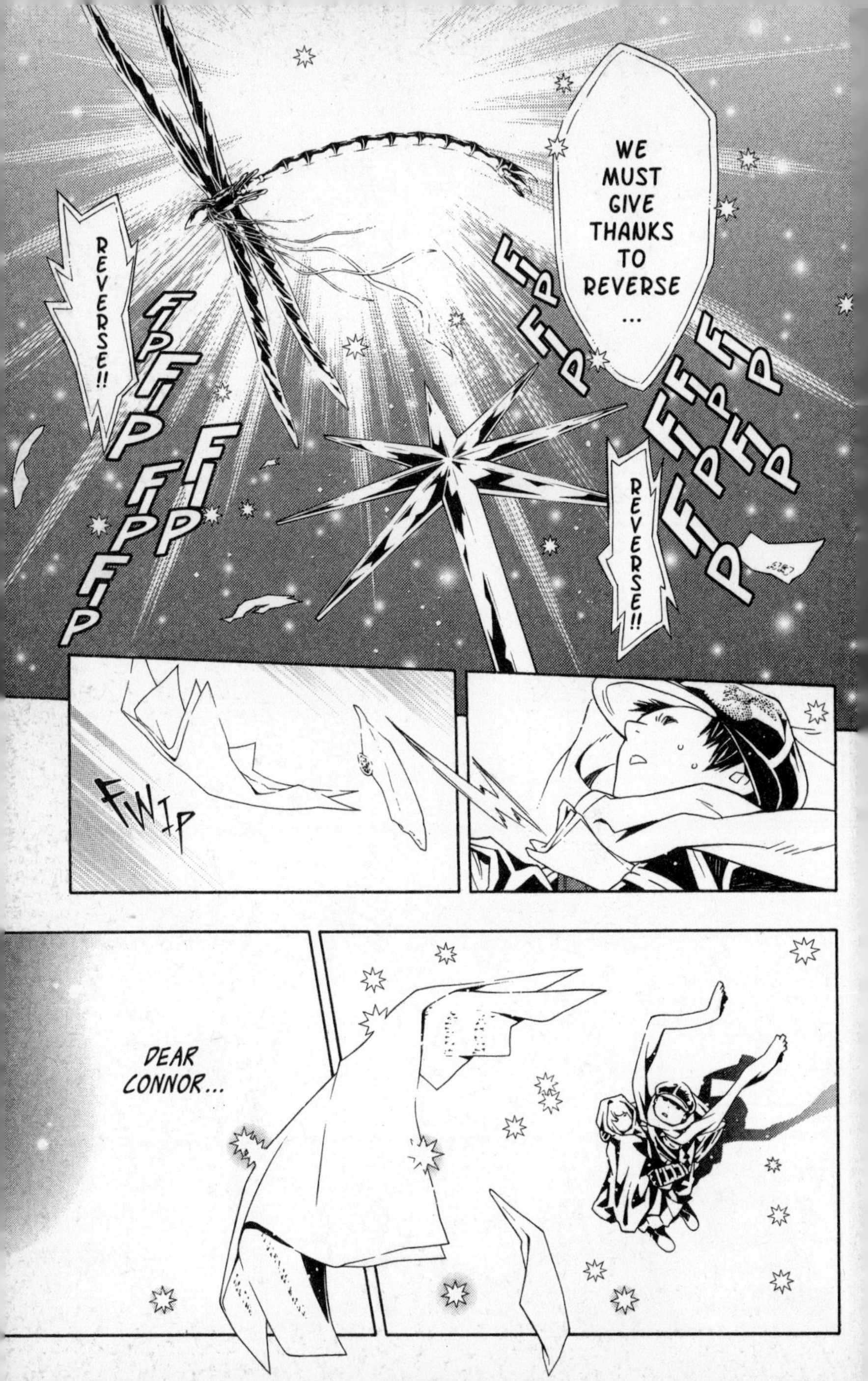
WE MUST GIVE THANKS TO REVERSE ...
FFFIP FFIP FFIP FFIP
REVERSE!!
FIP FIP
REVERSE!!
FIP FIP FIP FIP
FWIP
DEAR CONNOR...

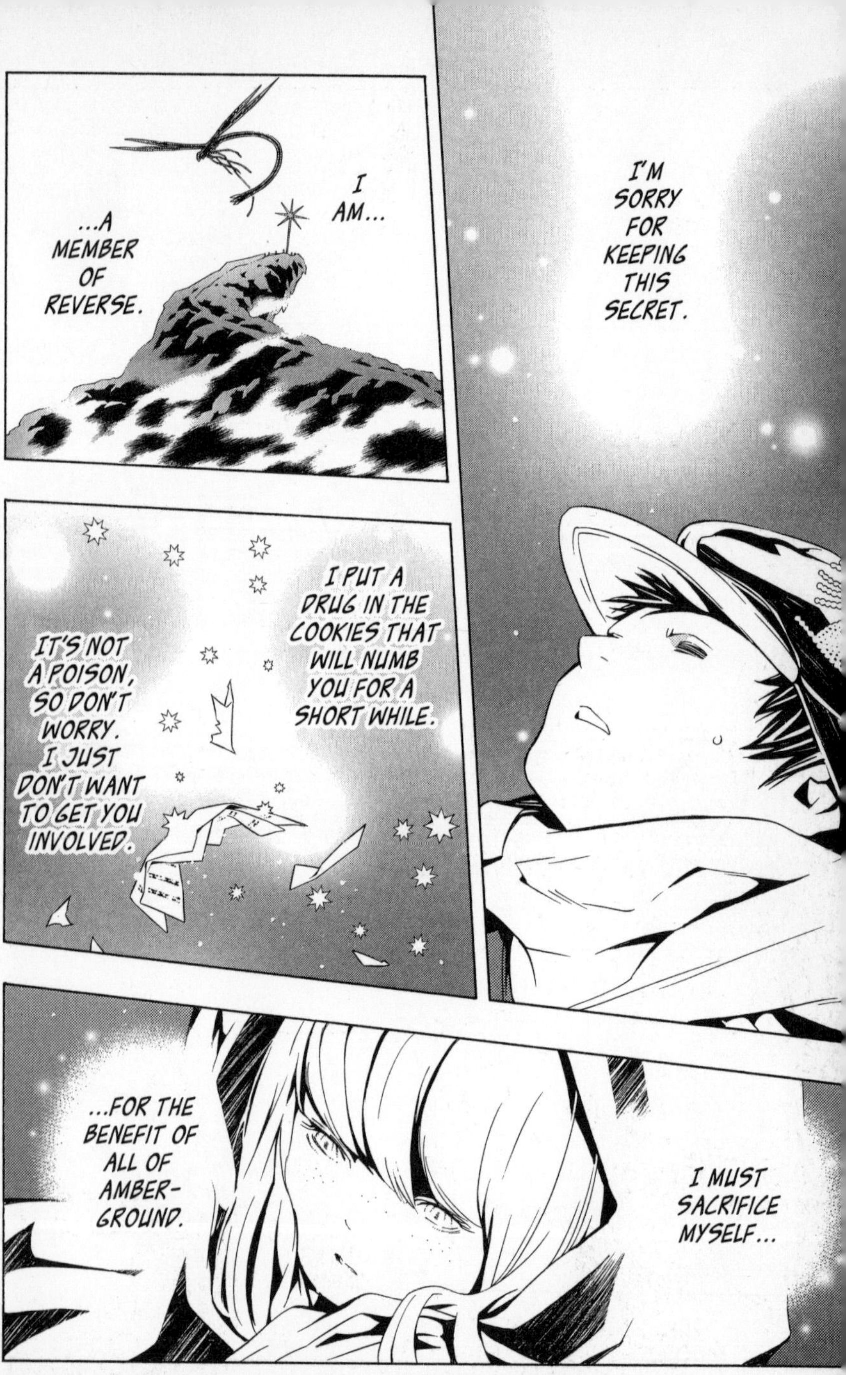
I'M SORRY FOR KEEPING THIS SECRET.
I AM...
...A MEMBER OF REVERSE.
I PUT A DRUG IN THE COOKIES THAT WILL NUMB YOU FOR A SHORT WHILE.
IT'S NOT A POISON, SO DON'T WORRY. I JUST DON'T WANT TO GET YOU INVOLVED.
I MUST SACRIFICE MYSELF...
...FOR THE BENEFIT OF ALL OF AMBER-GROUND.

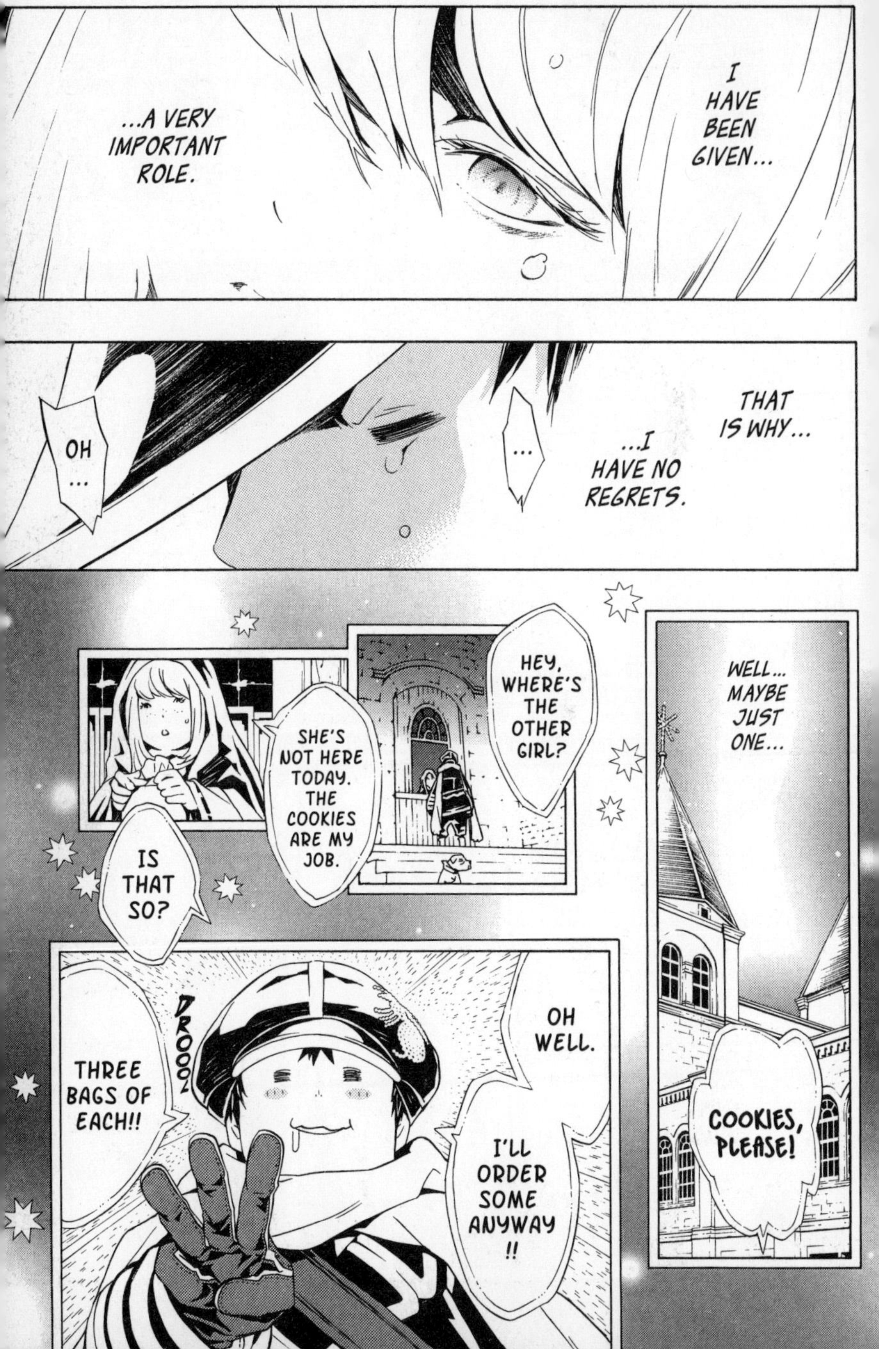
I HAVE BEEN GIVEN...
...A VERY IMPORTANT ROLE.
THAT IS WHY...
...I HAVE NO REGRETS.
...
OH ...
WELL... MAYBE JUST ONE...
COOKIES, PLEASE!
HEY, WHERE'S THE OTHER GIRL?
SHE'S NOT HERE TODAY. THE COOKIES ARE MY JOB.
IS THAT SO?
OH WELL.
I'LL ORDER SOME ANYWAY!!
DROOOL
THREE BAGS OF EACH!!

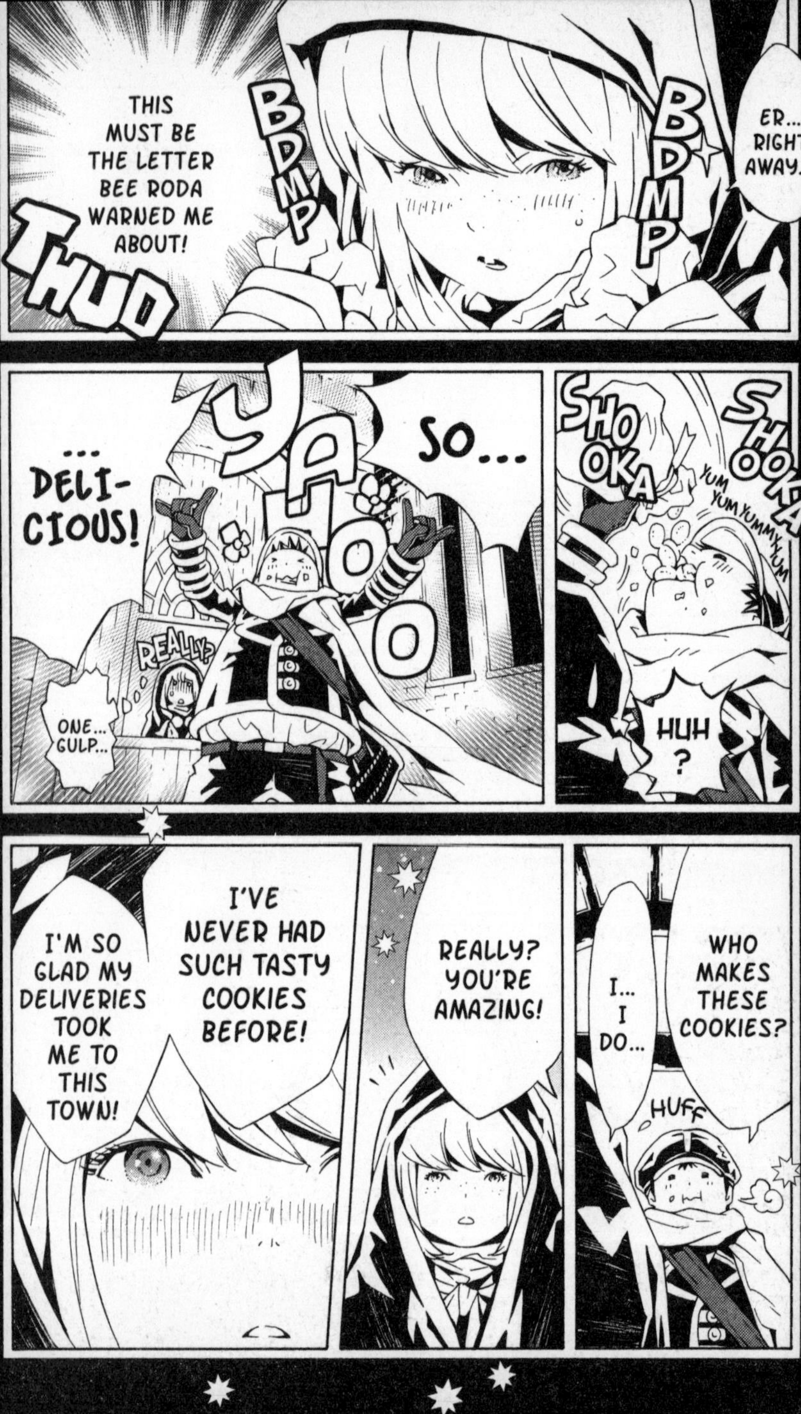
ER... RIGHT AWAY...
BDMP
BDMP
THIS MUST BE THE LETTER BEE RODA WARNED ME ABOUT!
THUD
SHOOKA
SHOOKA
YUM YUM YUMMY YUM
HUH ?
SO...
YAHOO
... DELI-CIOUS!
REALLY?
ONE... GULP...
WHO MAKES THESE COOKIES?
I... I DO...
HUFF
REALLY? YOU'RE AMAZING!
I'VE NEVER HAD SUCH TASTY COOKIES BEFORE!
I'M SO GLAD MY DELIVERIES TOOK ME TO THIS TOWN!

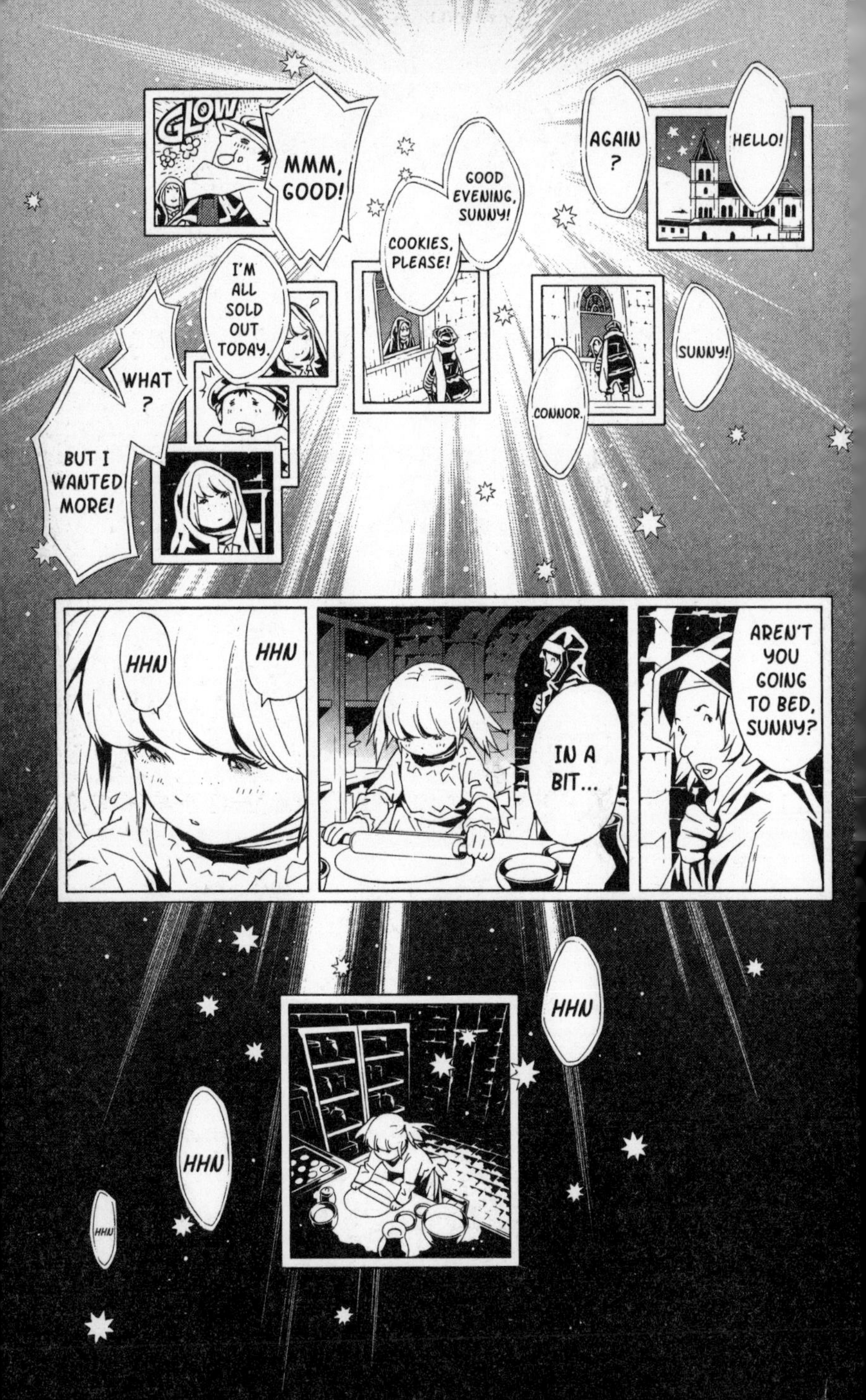
HELLO!
AGAIN ?
GOOD EVENING, SUNNY!
COOKIES, PLEASE!
MMM, GOOD!
GLOW
SUNNY!
CONNOR.
I'M ALL SOLD OUT TODAY.
WHAT ?
BUT I WANTED MORE!
AREN'T YOU GOING TO BED, SUNNY?
IN A BIT...
HHN
HHN
HHN
HHN
HHN

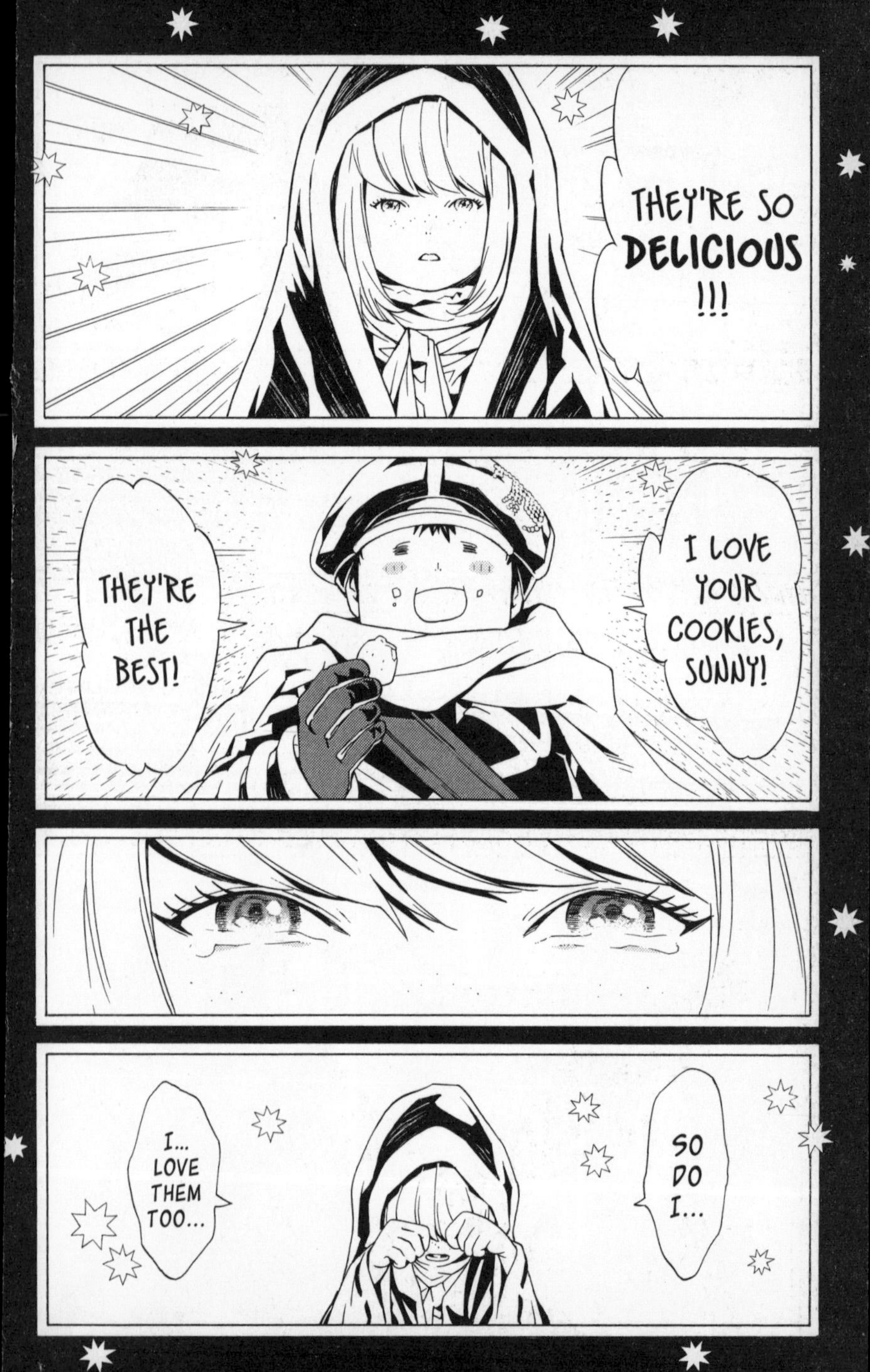
THEY'RE SO DELICIOUS !!!
I LOVE YOUR COOKIES, SUNNY!
THEY'RE THE BEST!
SO DO I...
I... LOVE THEM TOO...

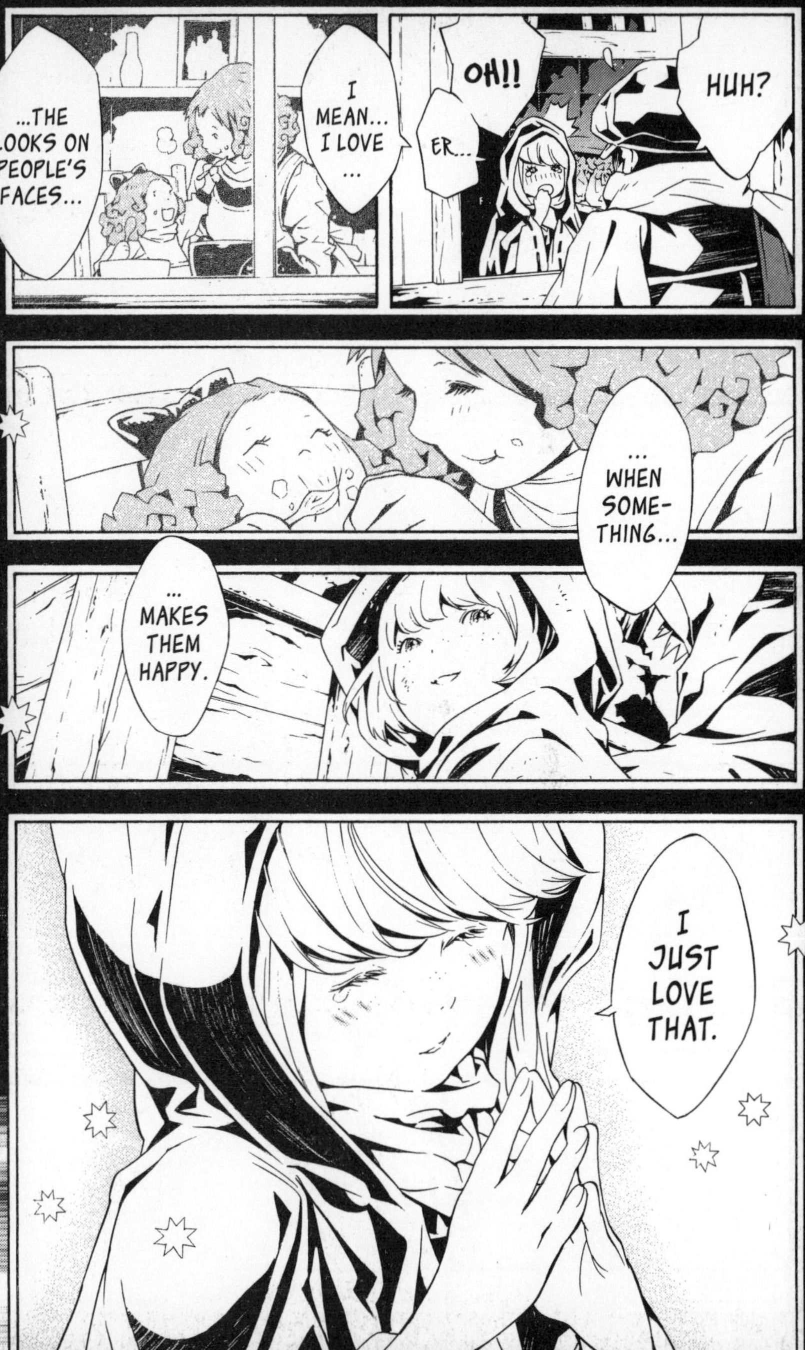
HUH?
OH!!
ER...
I MEAN... I LOVE ...
...THE LOOKS ON PEOPLE'S FACES...
... WHEN SOME-THING...
... MAKES THEM HAPPY.
I JUST LOVE THAT.

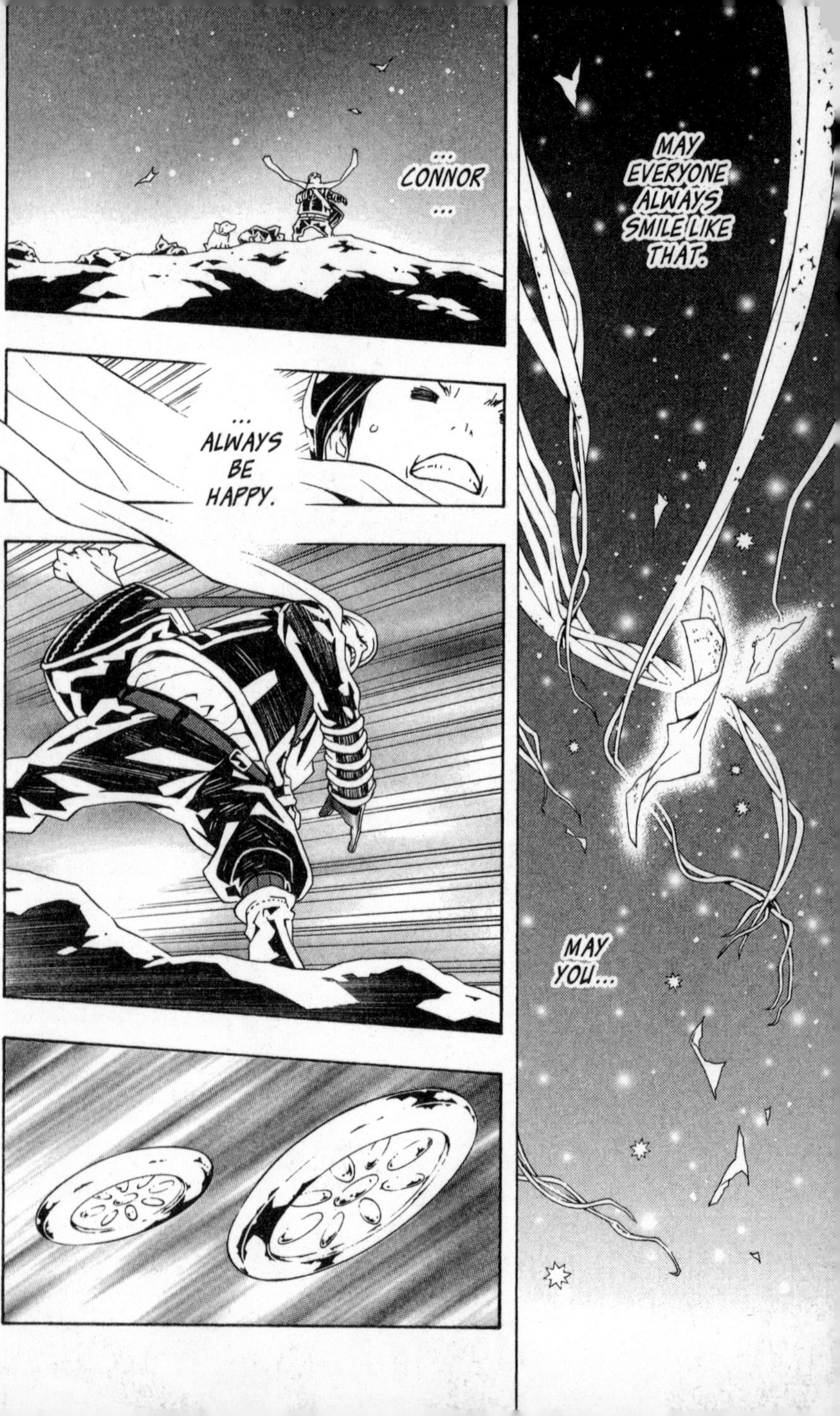
MAY EVERYONE ALWAYS SMILE LIKE THAT.
MAY YOU...
...CONNOR...
...ALWAYS BE HAPPY.

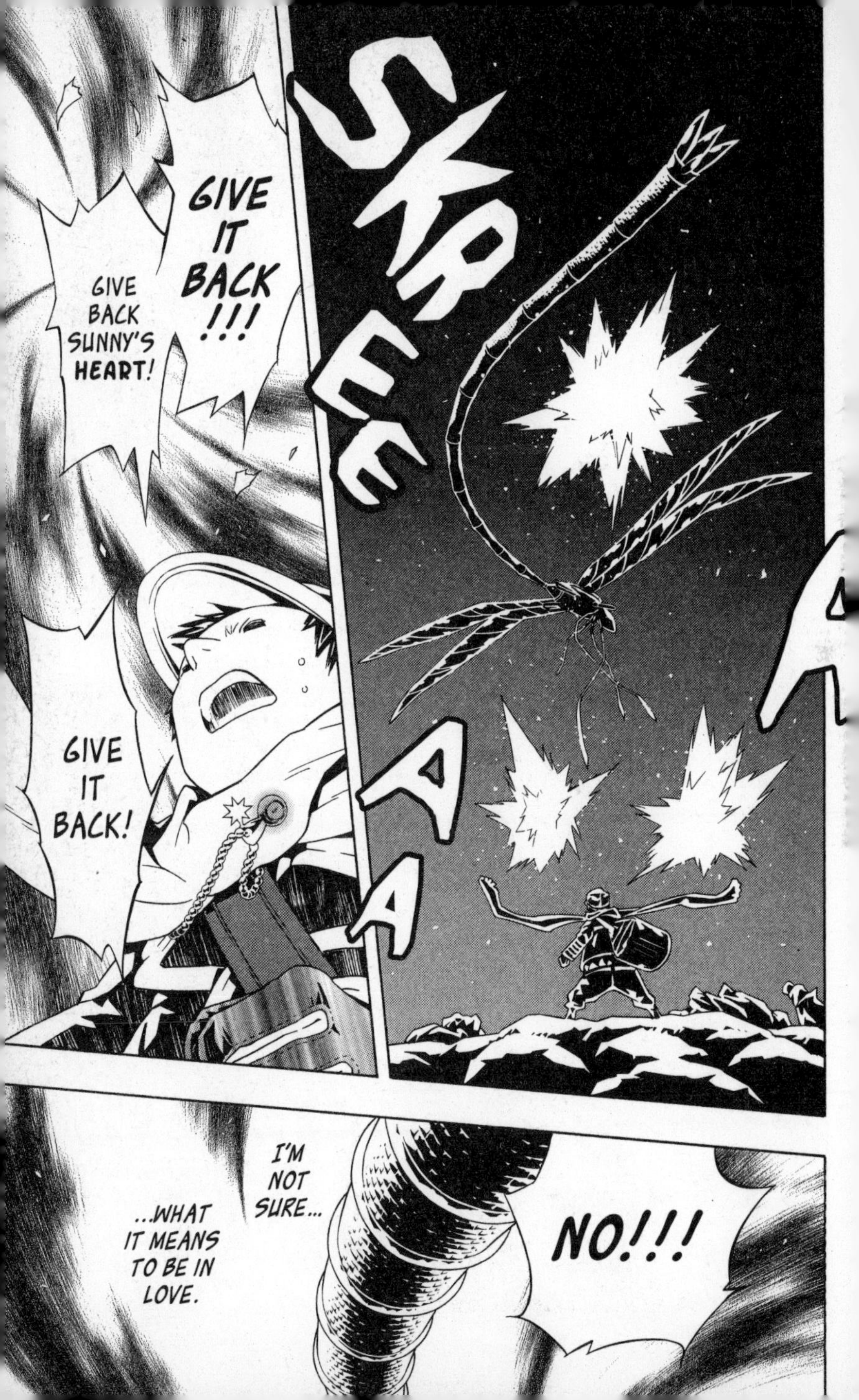
SKREEAAA
GIVE IT BACK!!!
GIVE BACK SUNNY'S HEART!
GIVE IT BACK!
NO!!!
I'M NOT SURE...
...WHAT IT MEANS TO BE IN LOVE.

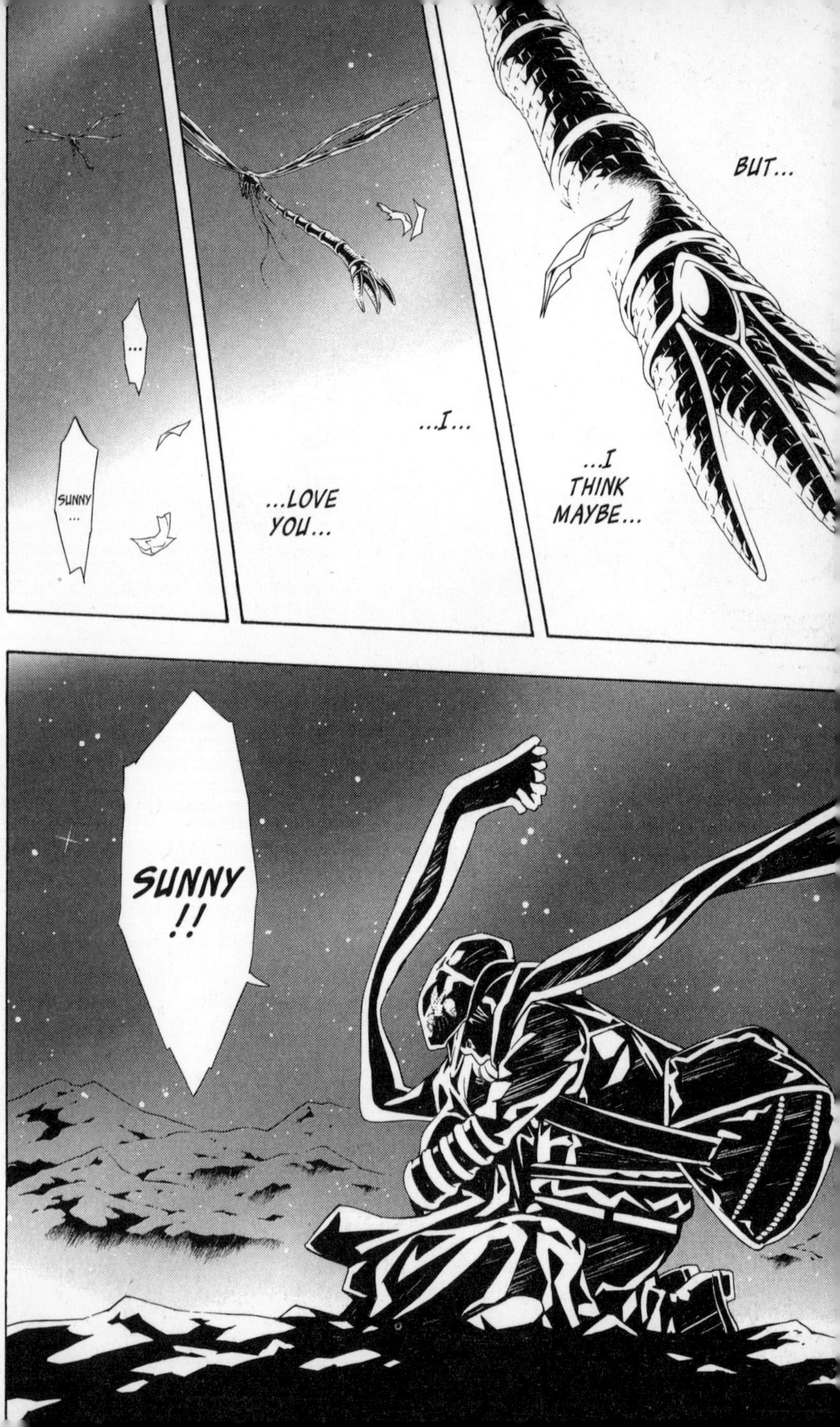
BUT...
...I THINK MAYBE...
...I...
...LOVE YOU...
...
SUNNY ...
SUNNY !!

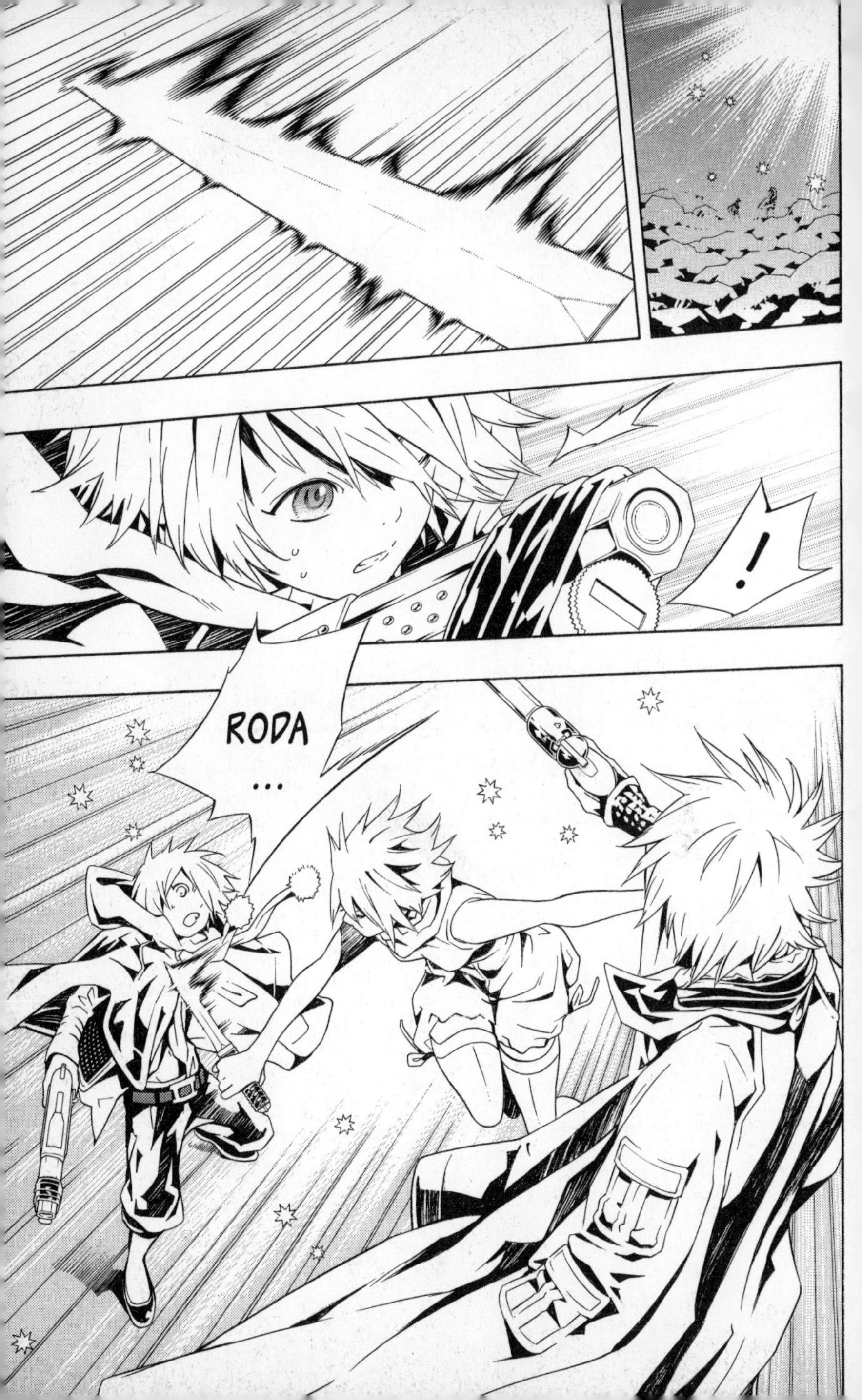
!
RODA
...

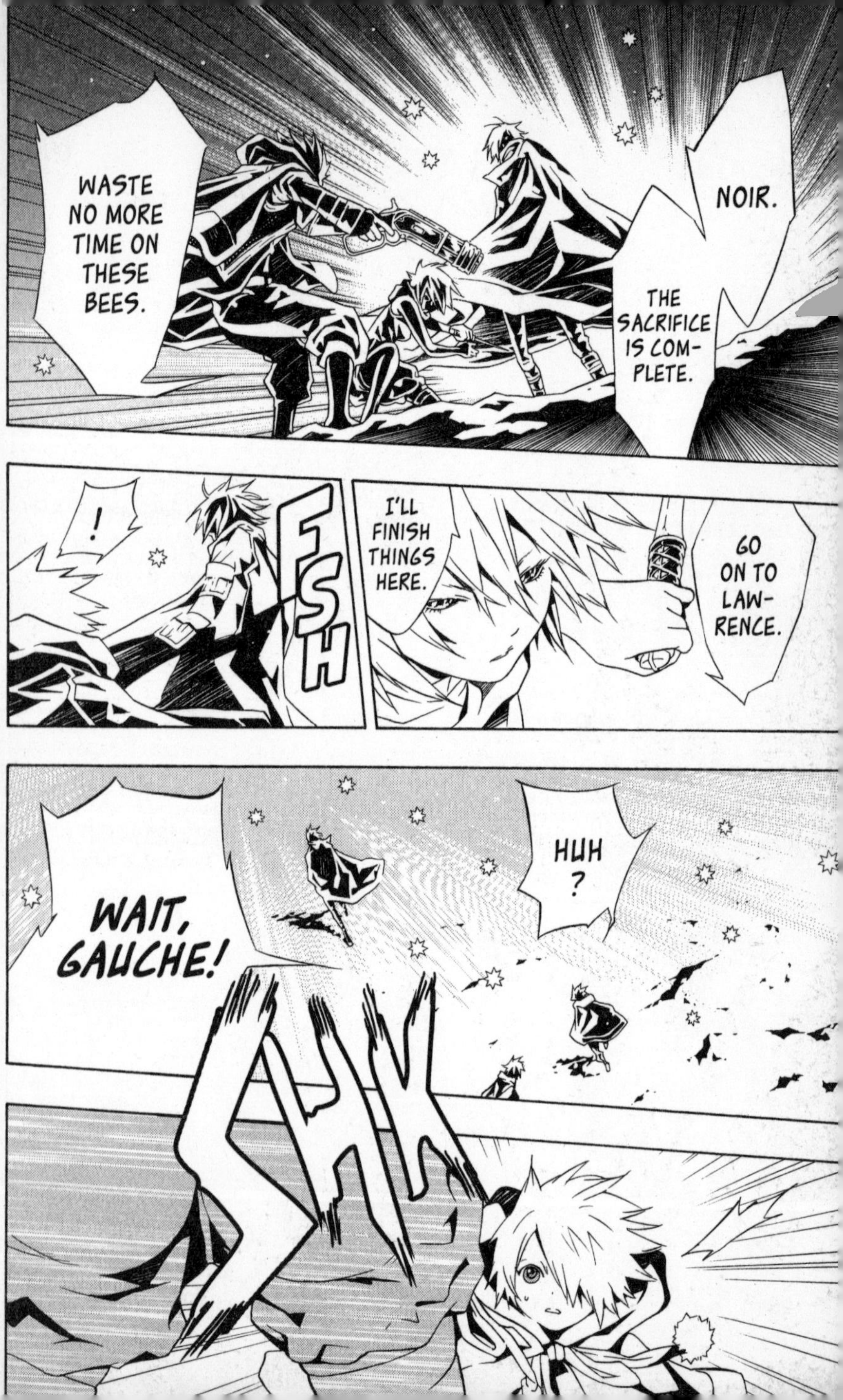
NOIR.
THE SACRIFICE IS COMPLETE.
WASTE NO MORE TIME ON THESE BEES.
GO ON TO LAWRENCE.
I'LL FINISH THINGS HERE.
FSH
!
HUH ?
WAIT, GAUCHE!
SHK

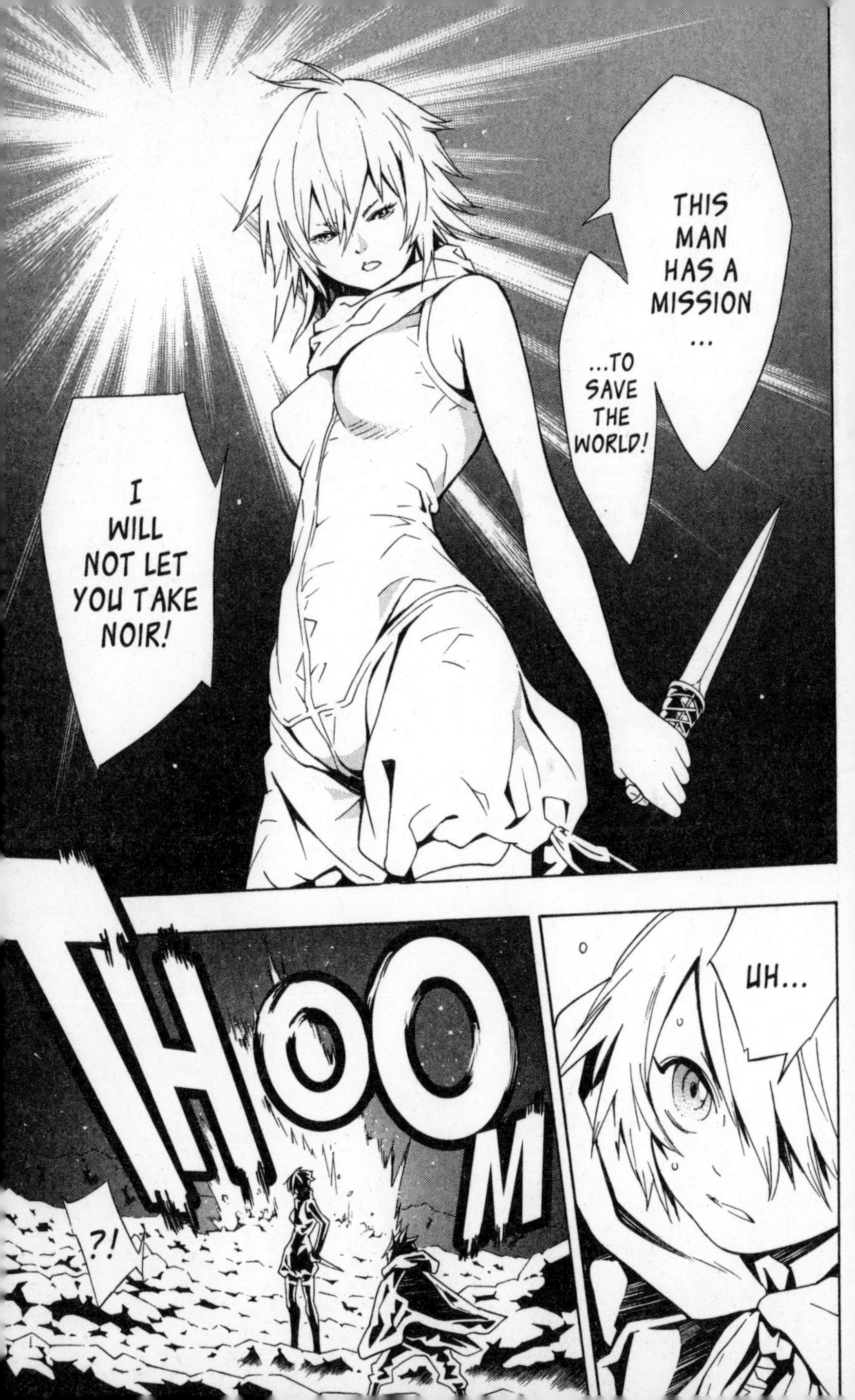
THIS MAN HAS A MISSION...
...TO SAVE THE WORLD!
I WILL NOT LET YOU TAKE NOIR!
UH...
WHOOM
?!

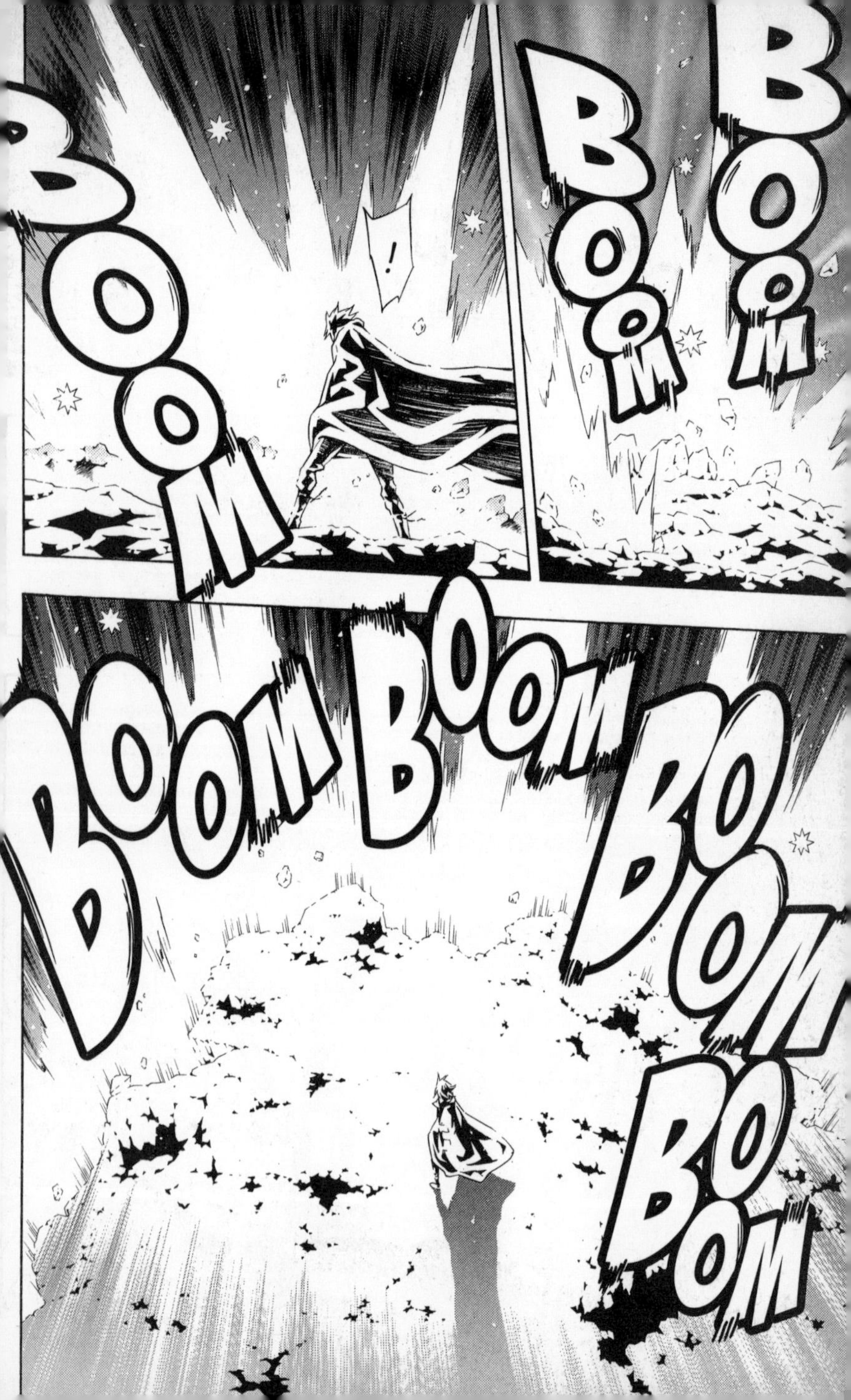
BOOM
BOOM
!
BOOM
BOOM
BOOM
BOOM
BOOM

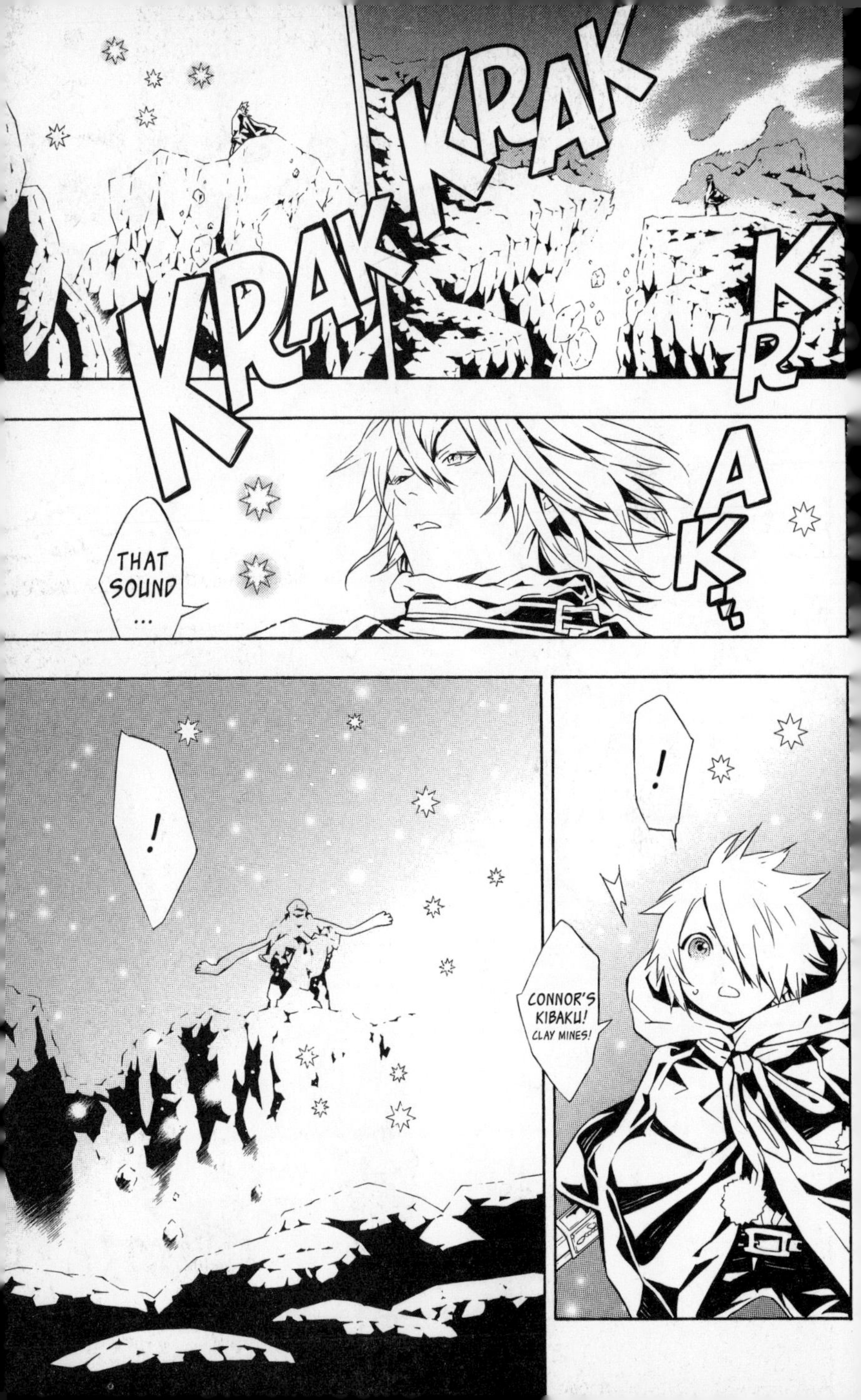
KRAK
KRAK
KRAK...
THAT SOUND ...
!
CONNOR'S KIBAKU!
CLAY MINES!
!

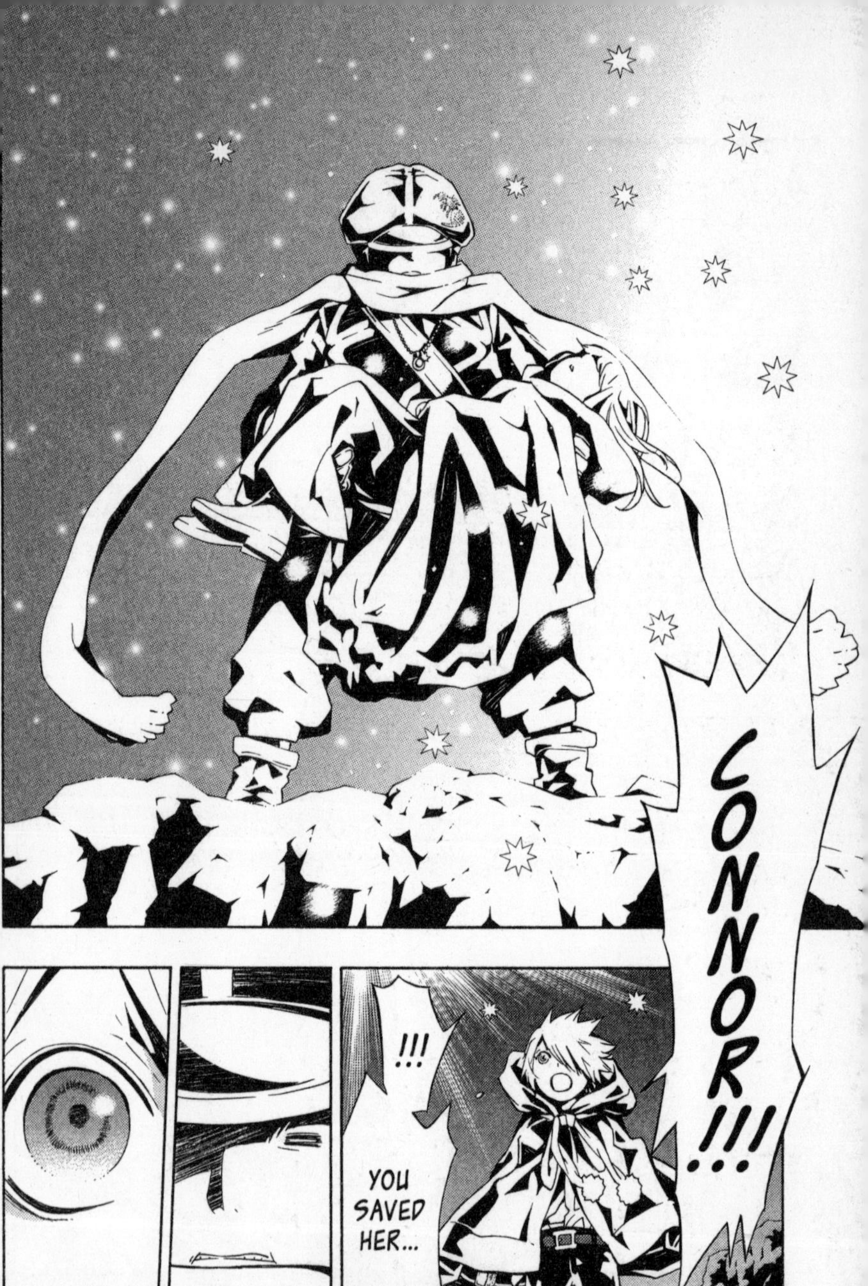
CONNOR!!!!
!!!
YOU SAVED HER...

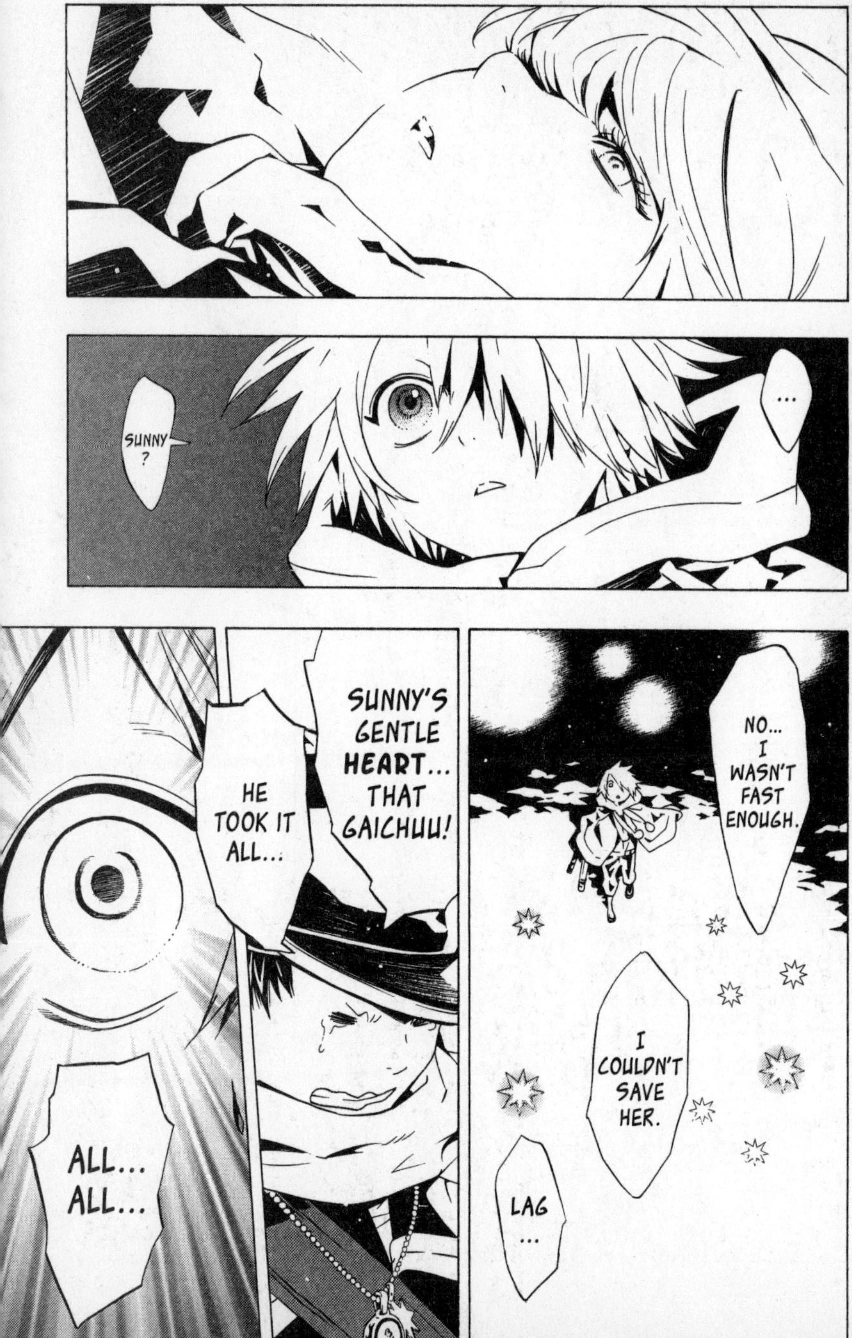
...
SUNNY ?
NO... I WASN'T FAST ENOUGH.
I COULDN'T SAVE HER.
LAG ...
SUNNY'S GENTLE HEART... THAT GAICHUU!
HE TOOK IT ALL...
ALL... ALL...

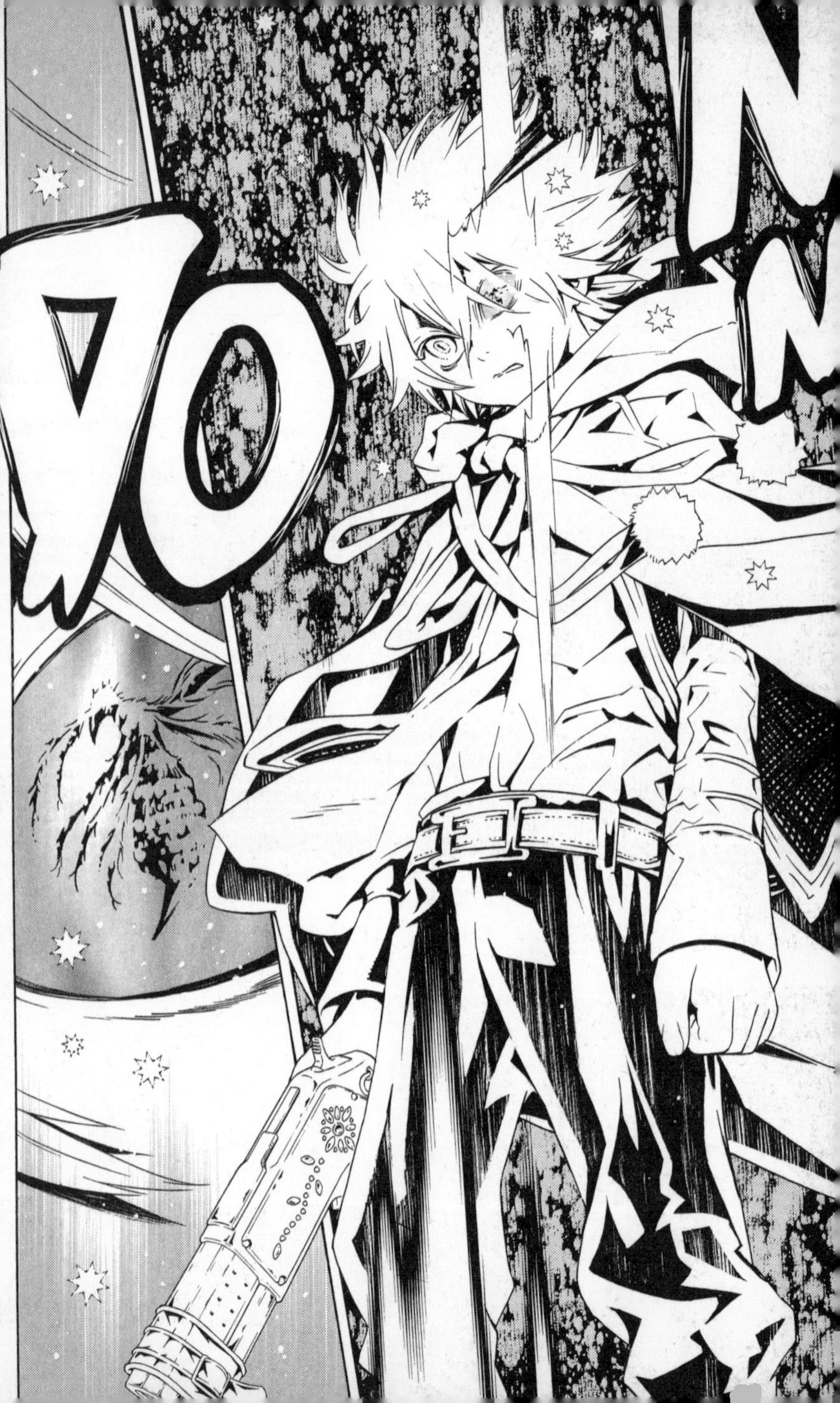

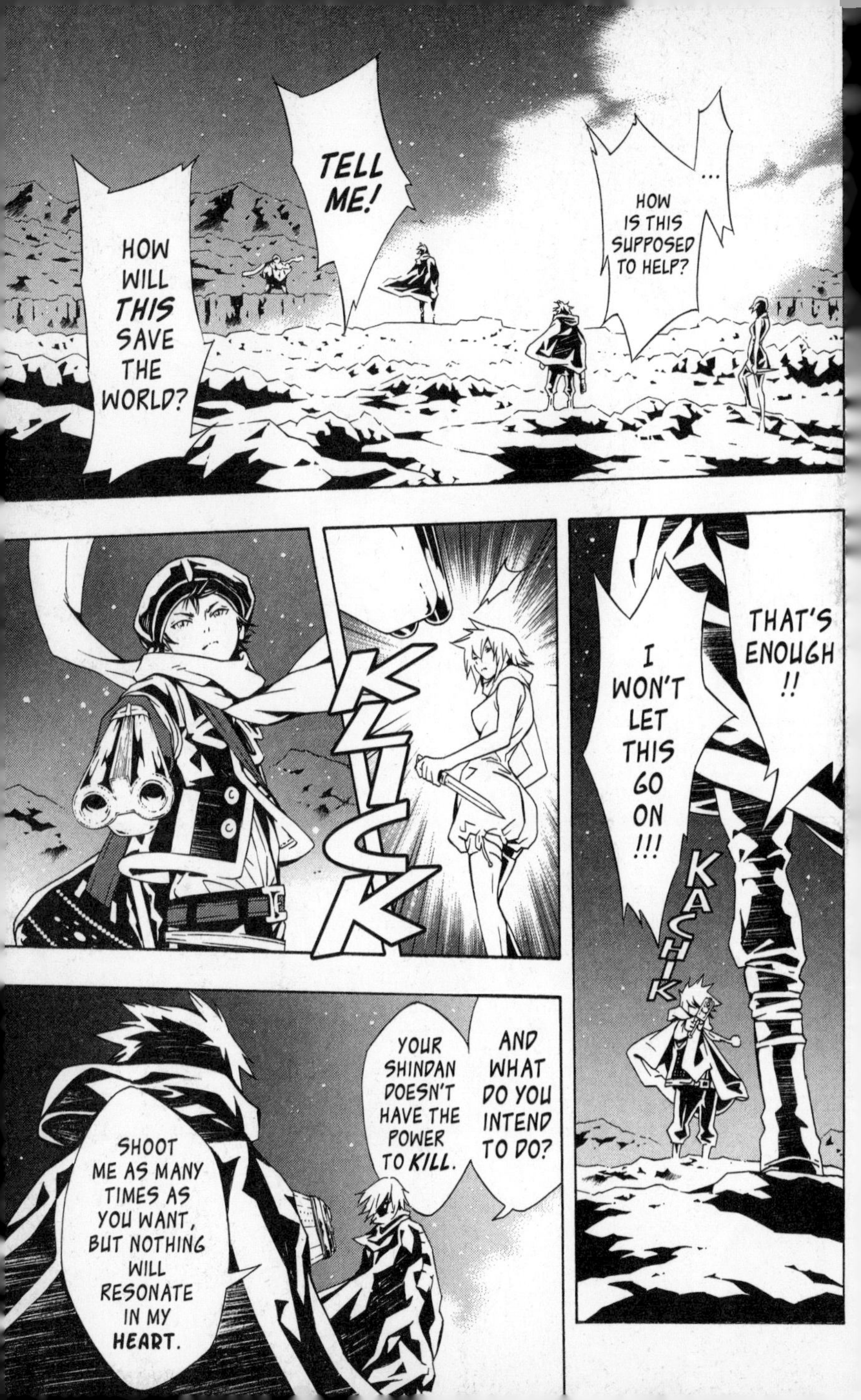

... HOW IS THIS SUPPOSED TO HELP?
TELL ME!
HOW WILL THIS SAVE THE WORLD?
THAT'S ENOUGH!!
I WON'T LET THIS GO ON!!!
KACHIK
KLICK
AND WHAT DO YOU INTEND TO DO?
YOUR SHINDAN DOESN'T HAVE THE POWER TO KILL.
SHOOT ME AS MANY TIMES AS YOU WANT, BUT NOTHING WILL RESONATE IN MY HEART.

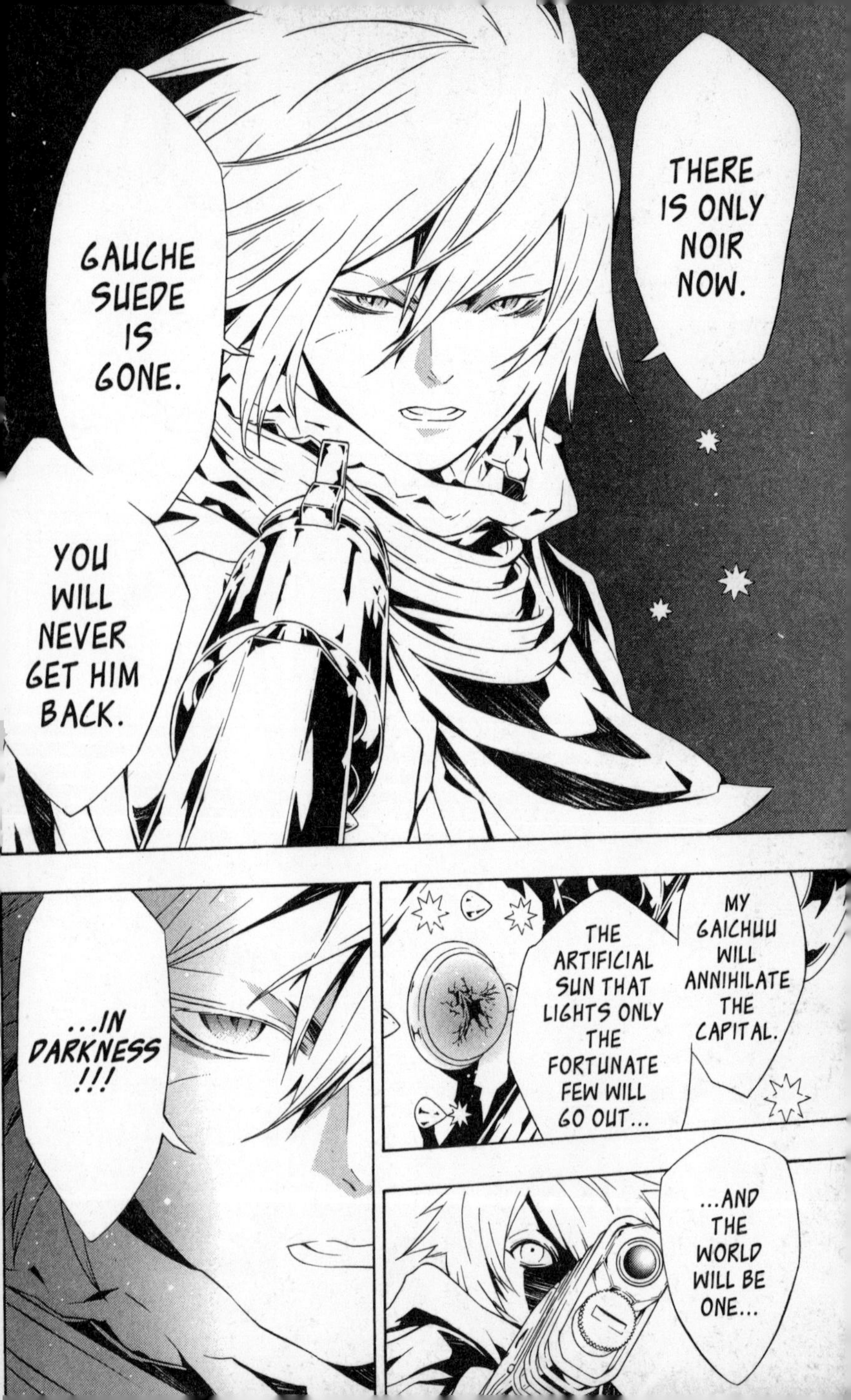
THERE IS ONLY NOIR NOW.
GAUCHE SUEDE IS GONE.
YOU WILL NEVER GET HIM BACK.
MY GAICHUU WILL ANNIHILATE THE CAPITAL.
THE ARTIFICIAL SUN THAT LIGHTS ONLY THE FORTUNATE FEW WILL GO OUT...
...AND THE WORLD WILL BE ONE...
...IN DARKNESS!!!

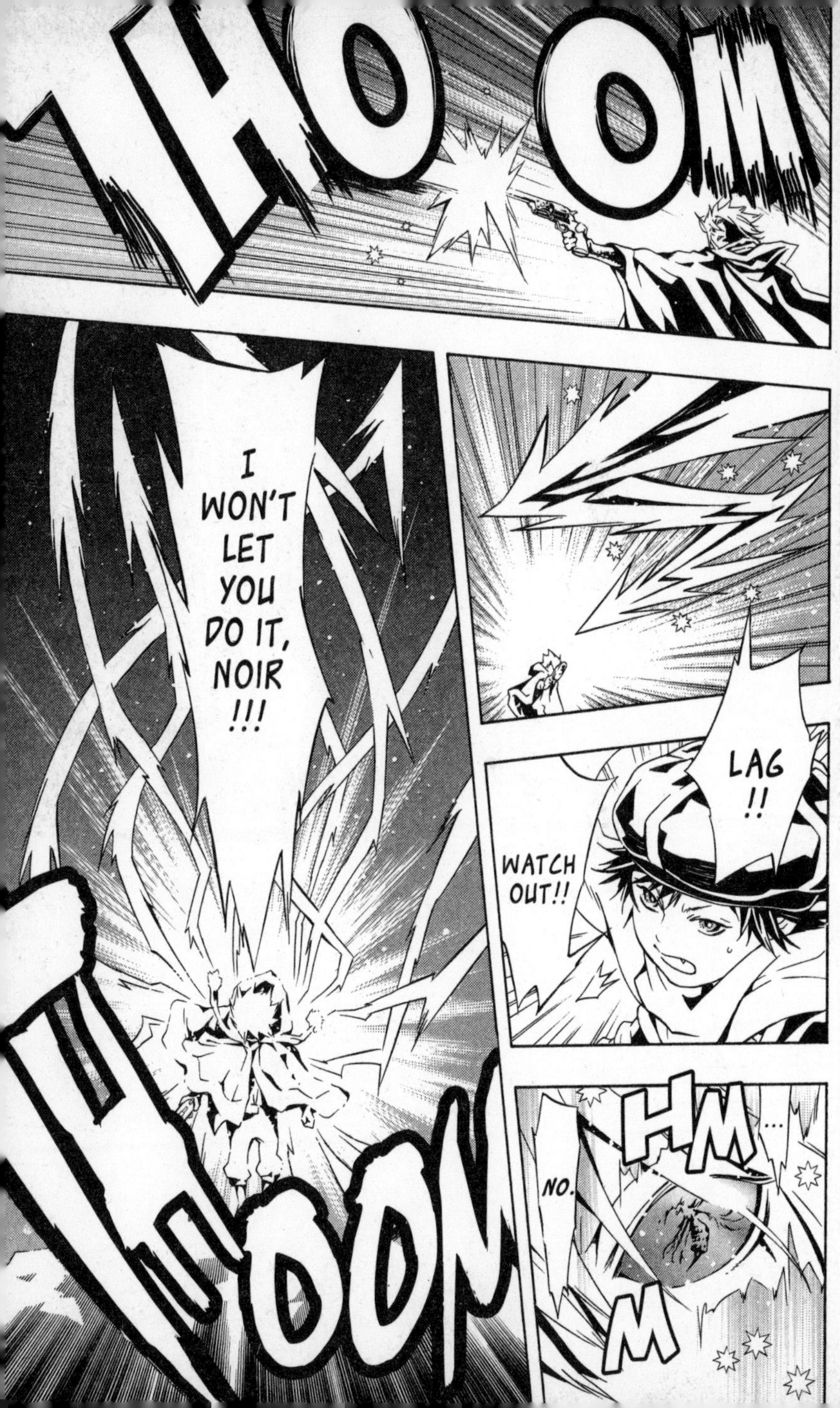
THOOM
LAG!!
WATCH OUT!!
HMM...
NO.
I WON'T LET YOU DO IT, NOIR!!!

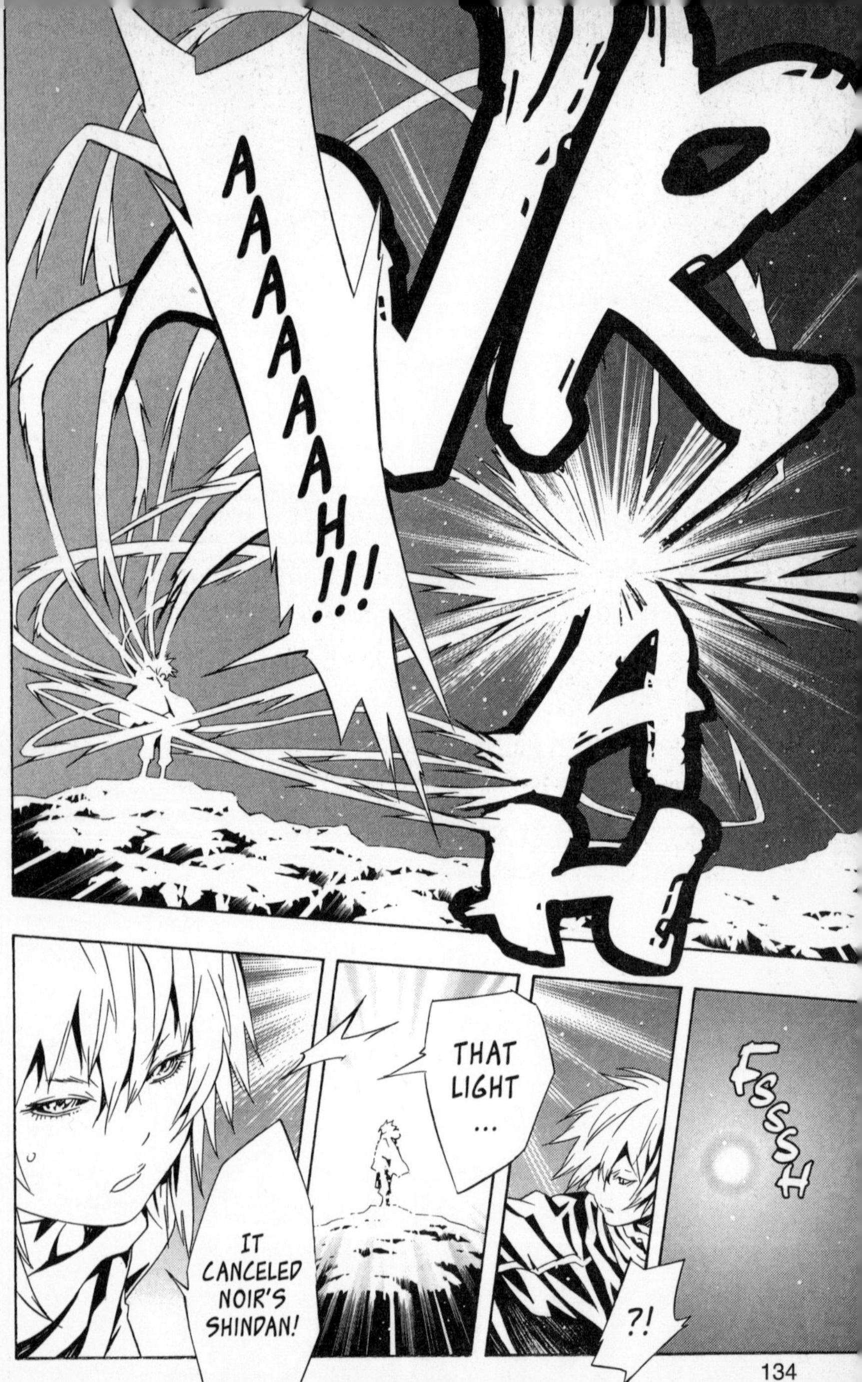
AAAAAAAH!!!
FSSSH
?!
THAT LIGHT...
IT CANCELED NOIR'S SHINDAN!

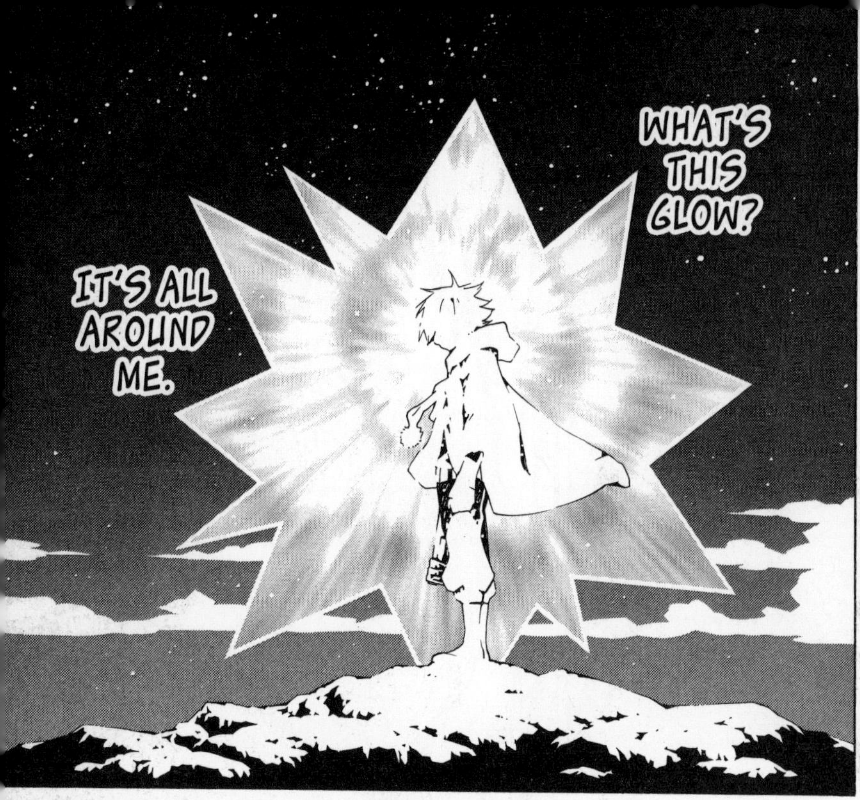
WHAT'S THIS GLOW?
IT'S ALL AROUND ME.
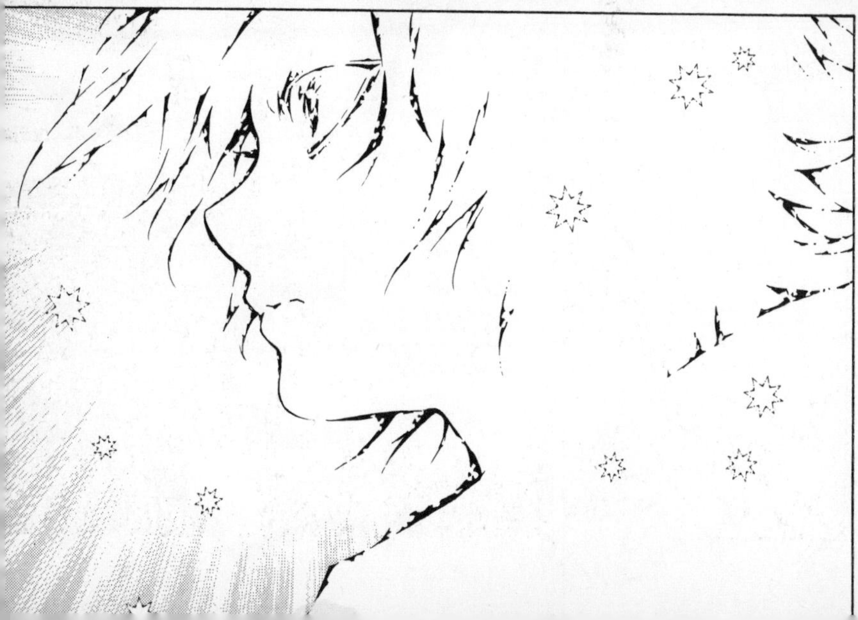

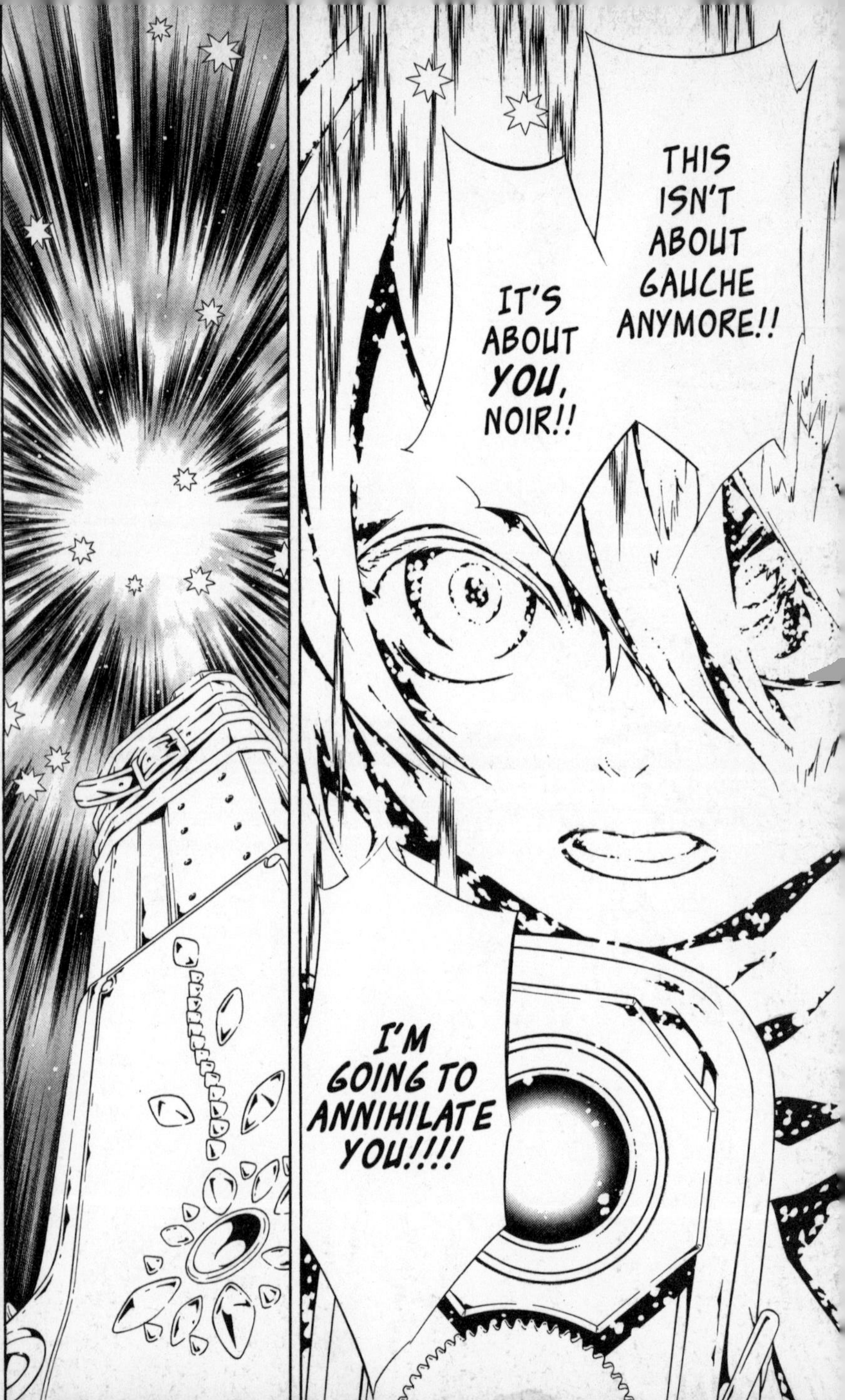
THIS ISN'T ABOUT GAUCHE ANYMORE!!
IT'S ABOUT *YOU*, NOIR!!
I'M GOING TO ANNIHILATE YOU!!!!

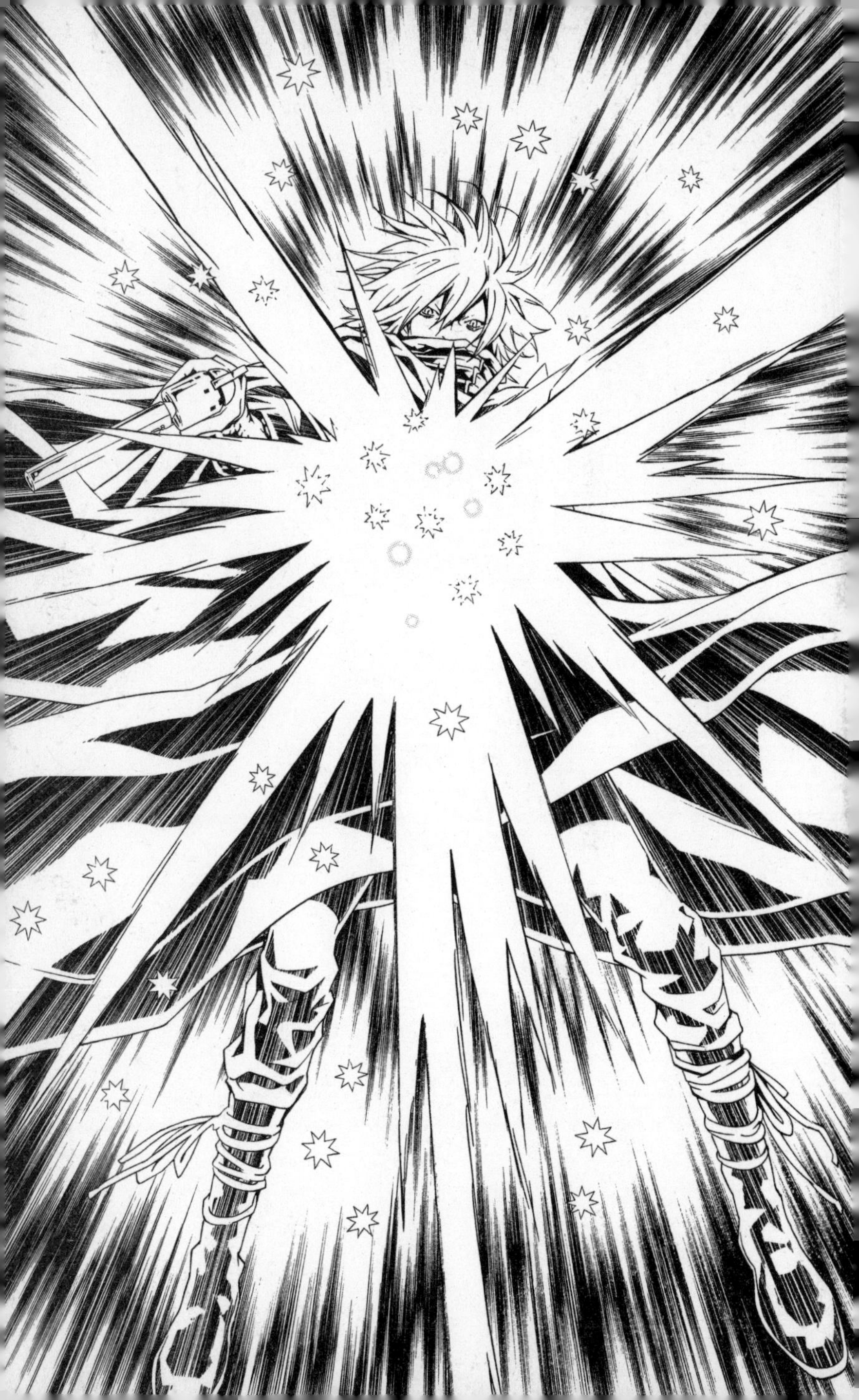

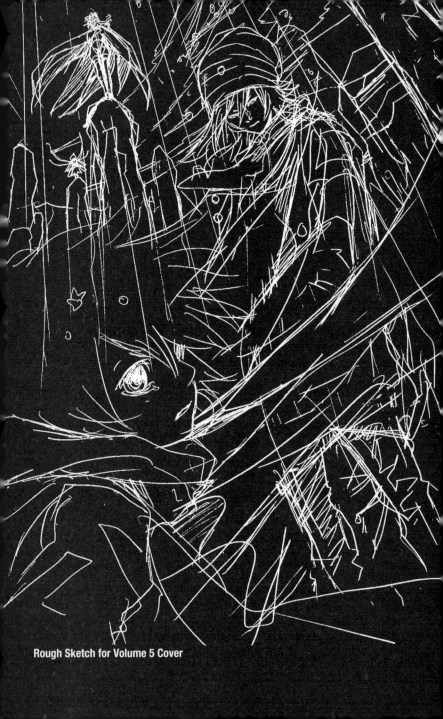

Rough Sketch for Volume 5 Cover

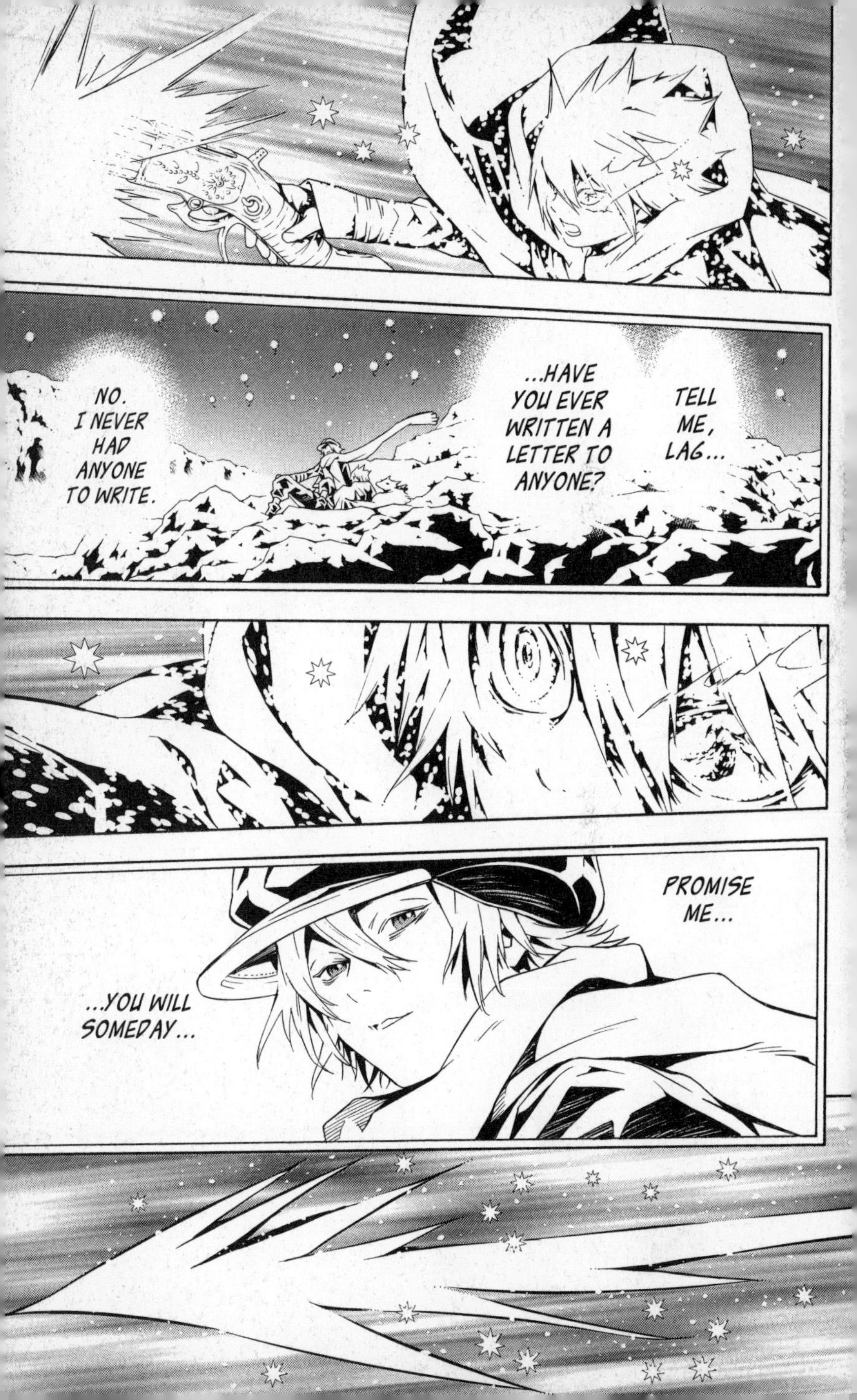
TELL ME, LAG...
...HAVE YOU EVER WRITTEN A LETTER TO ANYONE?
NO. I NEVER HAD ANYONE TO WRITE.
PROMISE ME...
...YOU WILL SOMEDAY...

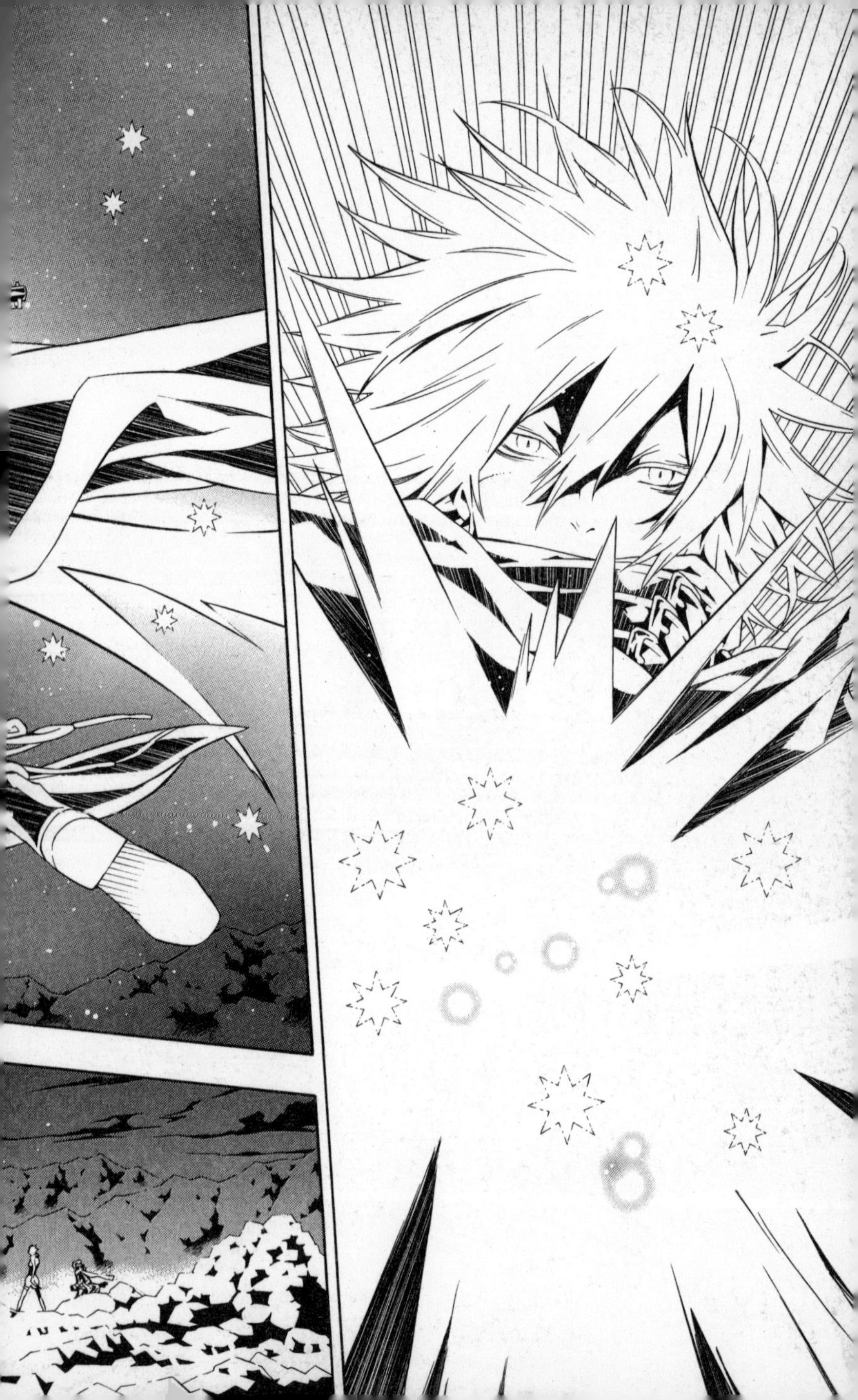

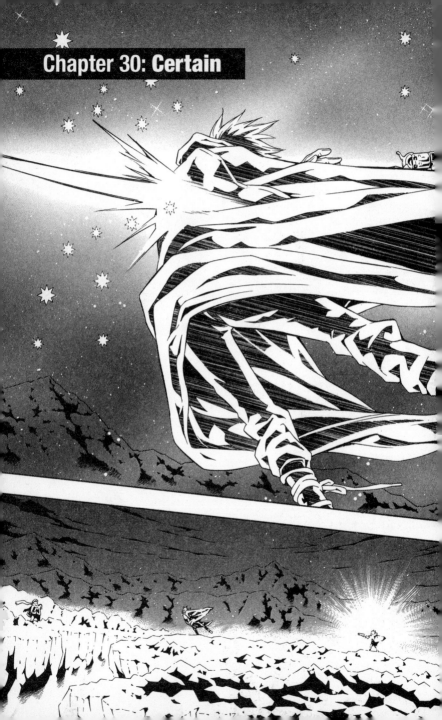

Chapter 30: Certain

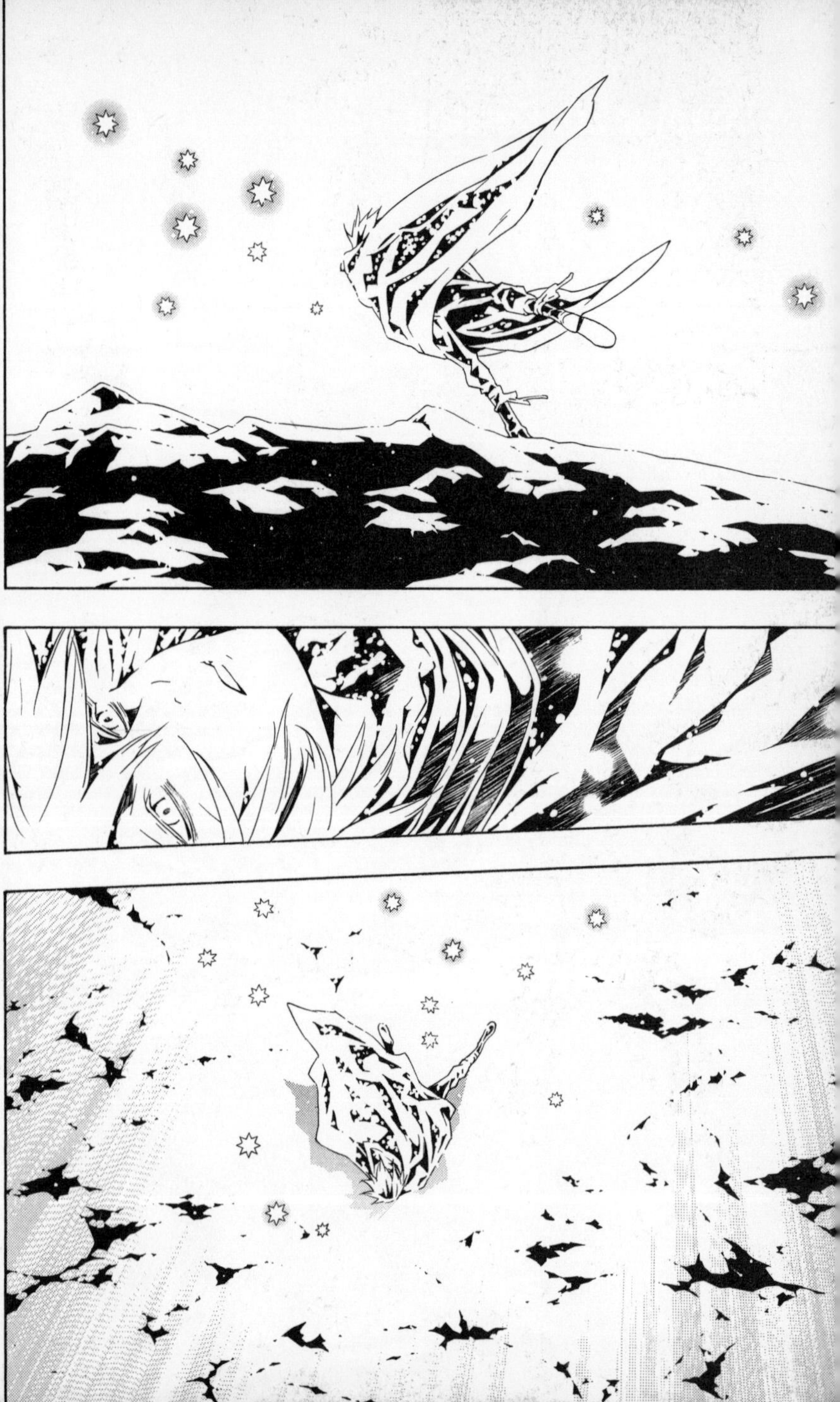

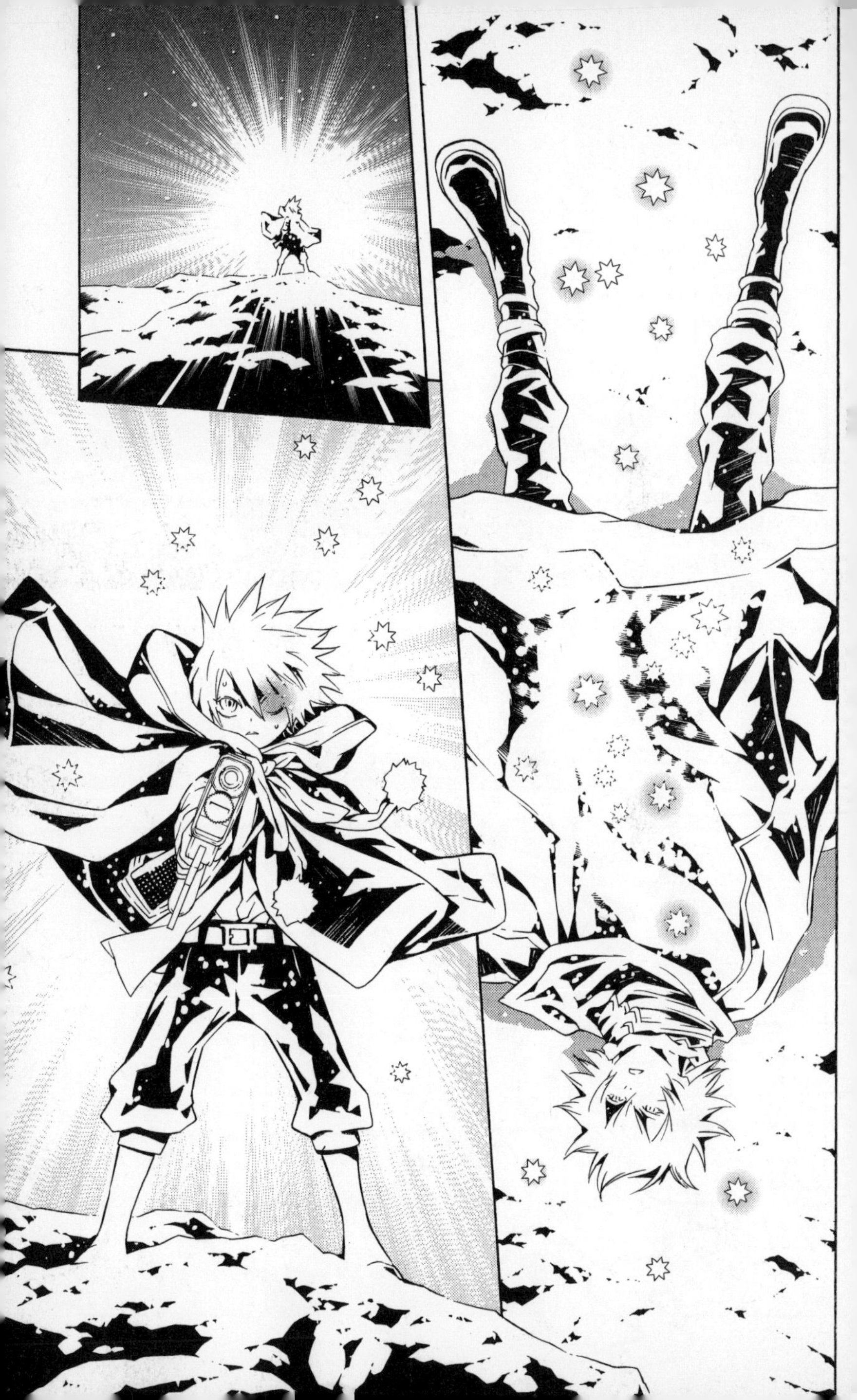

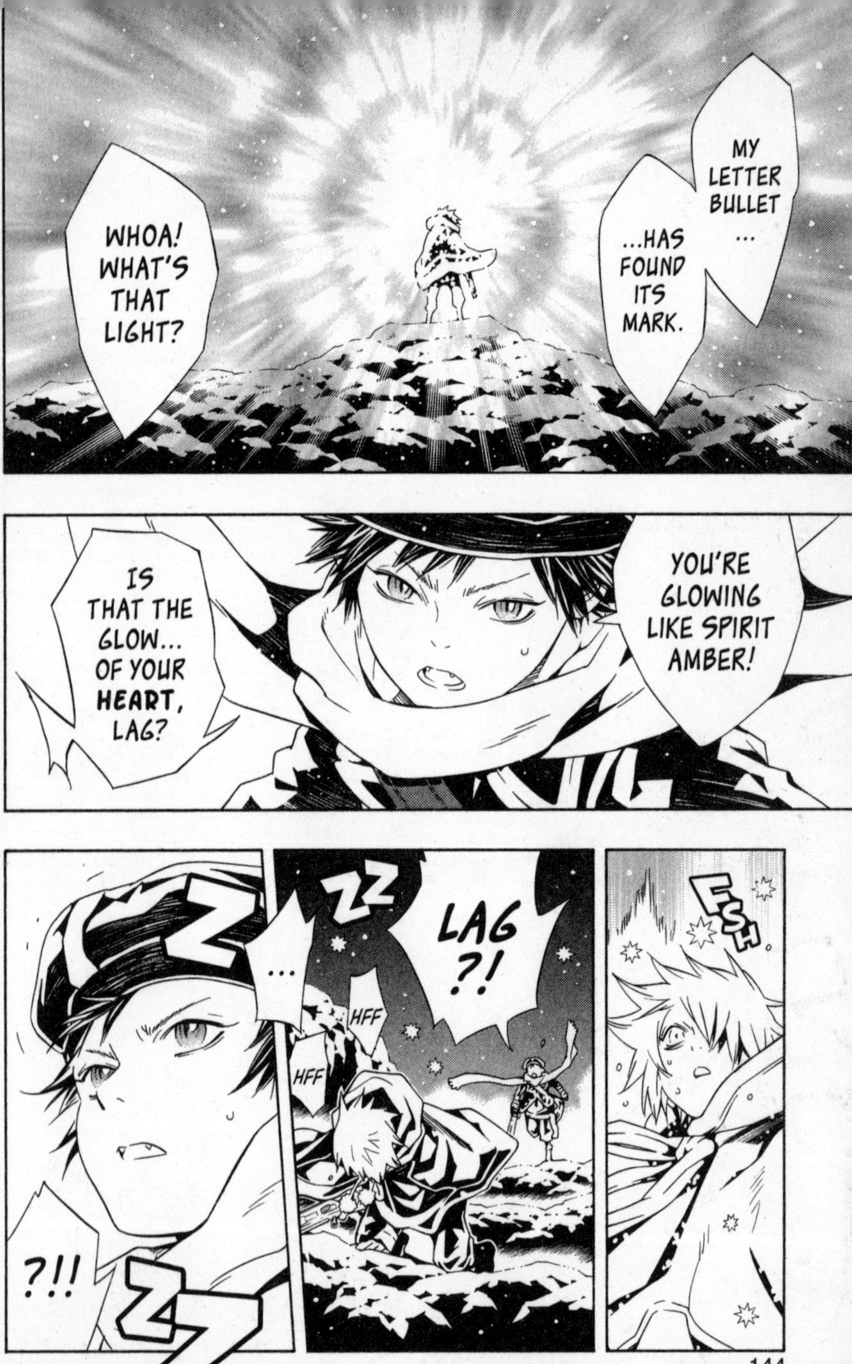
MY LETTER BULLET ...
...HAS FOUND ITS MARK.
WHOA! WHAT'S THAT LIGHT?
YOU'RE GLOWING LIKE SPIRIT AMBER!
IS THAT THE GLOW... OF YOUR **HEART**, LAG?
FSH
LAG?!
HFF
HFF
...
?!!

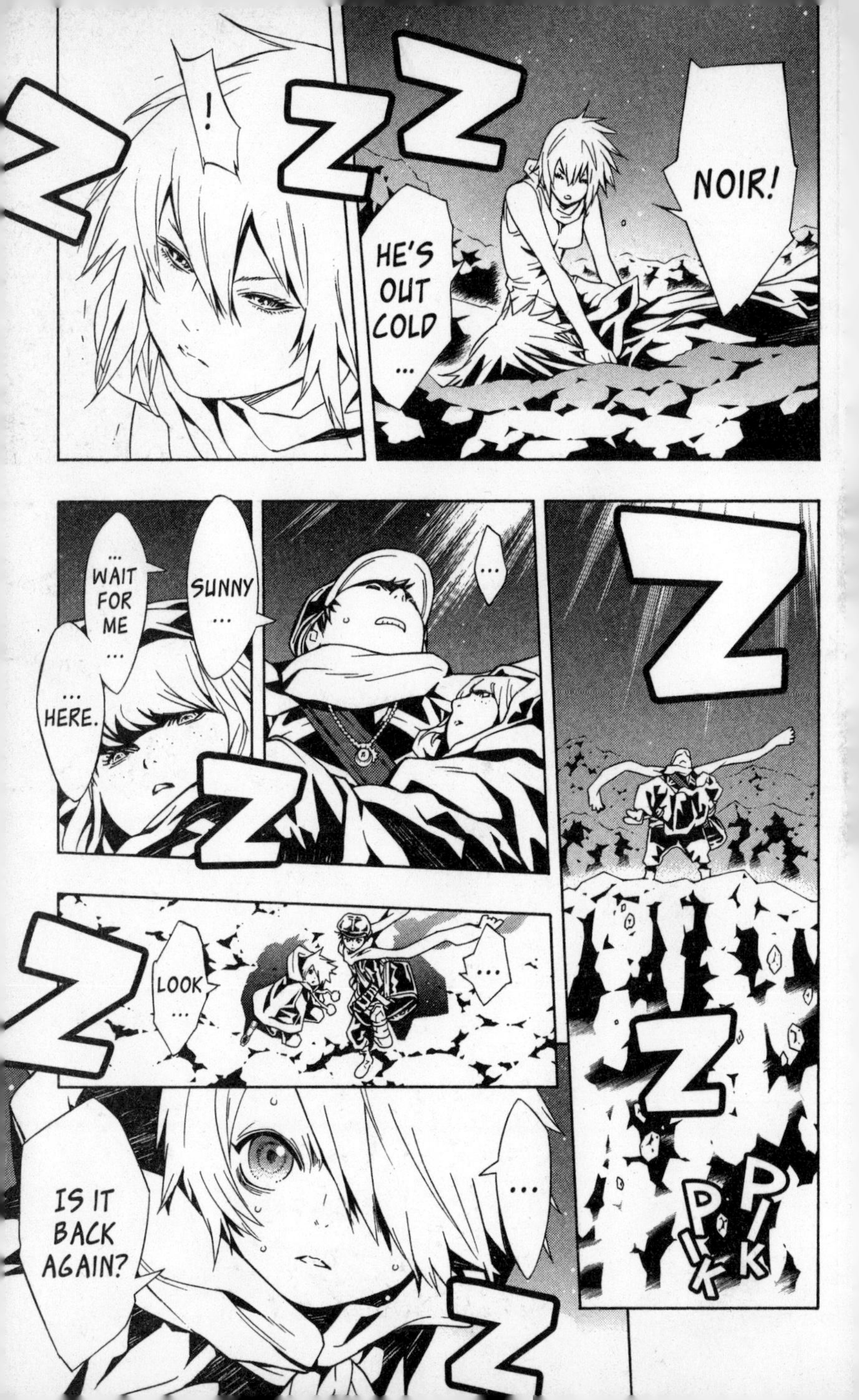
NOIR!
HE'S OUT COLD ...
Z Z Z
!
Z
Z
Z
PIK PIK
...
SUNNY ...
... WAIT FOR ME ...
... HERE.
Z
...
LOOK ...
Z
...
IS IT BACK AGAIN?
Z

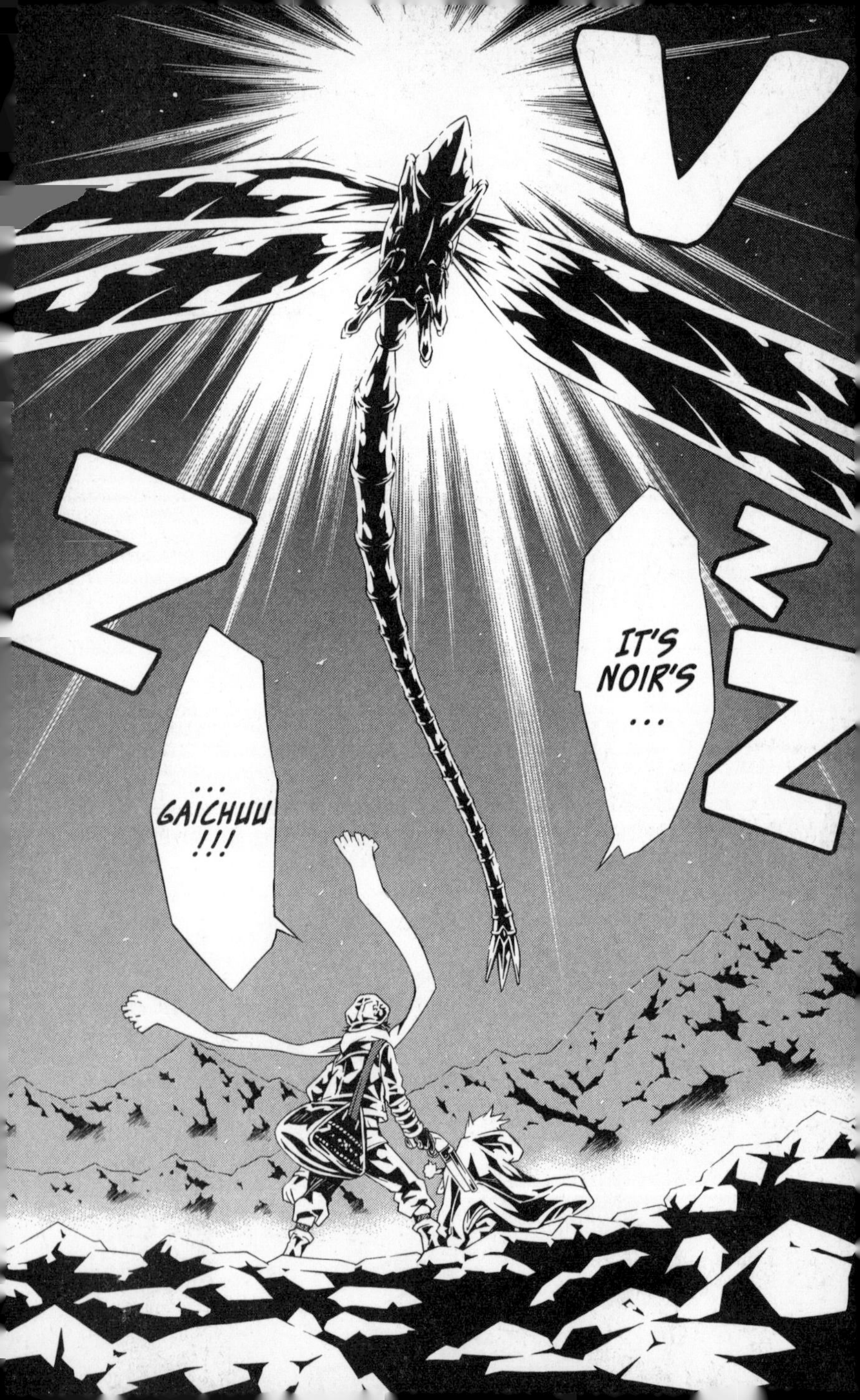
VZZZ
IT'S NOIR'S ...
... GAİCHUU !!!

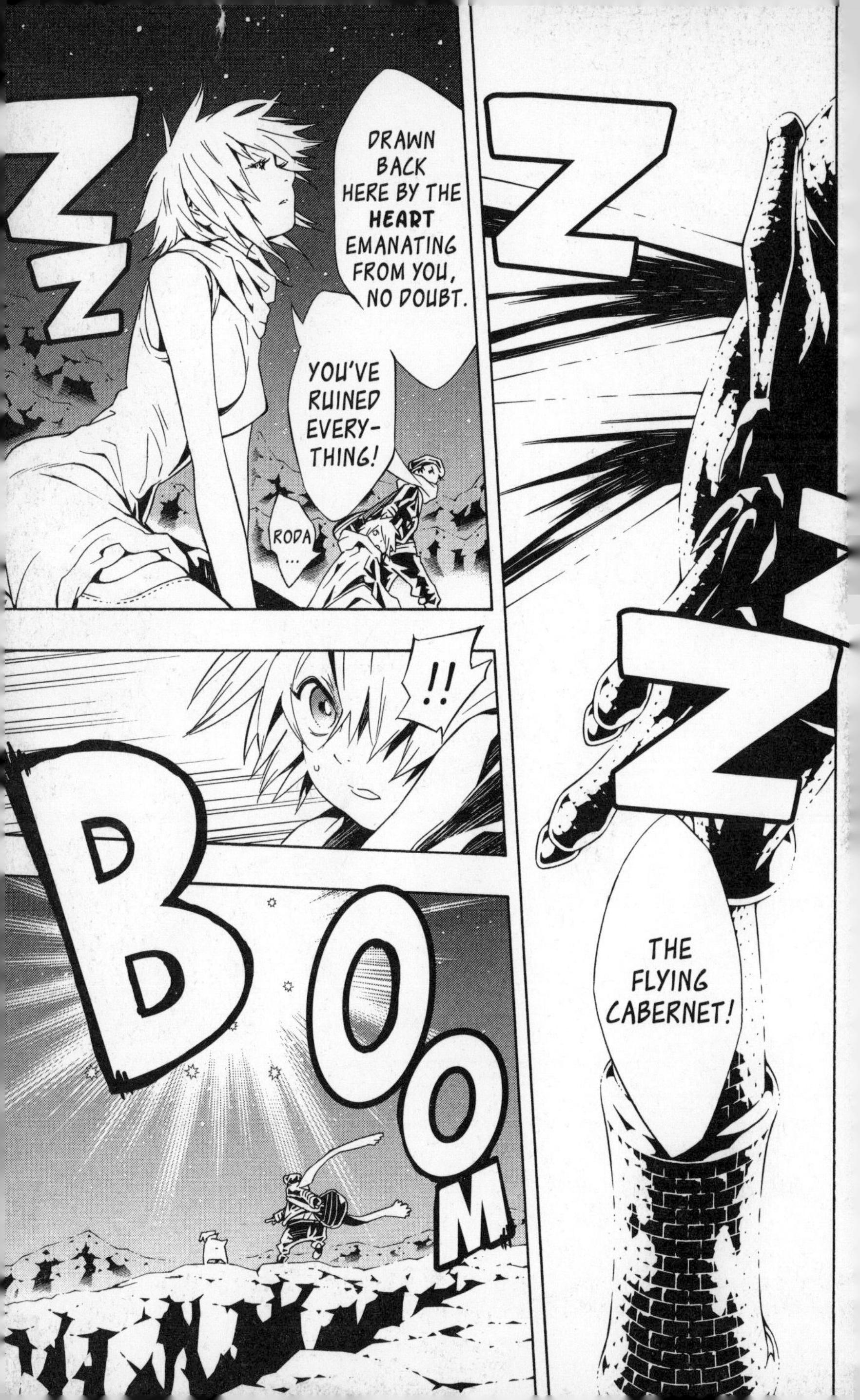

ZZ
Z
THE FLYING CABERNET!
ZZZ
DRAWN BACK HERE BY THE **HEART** EMANATING FROM YOU, NO DOUBT.
YOU'VE RUINED EVERY-THING!
RODA...
!!
BOOOM

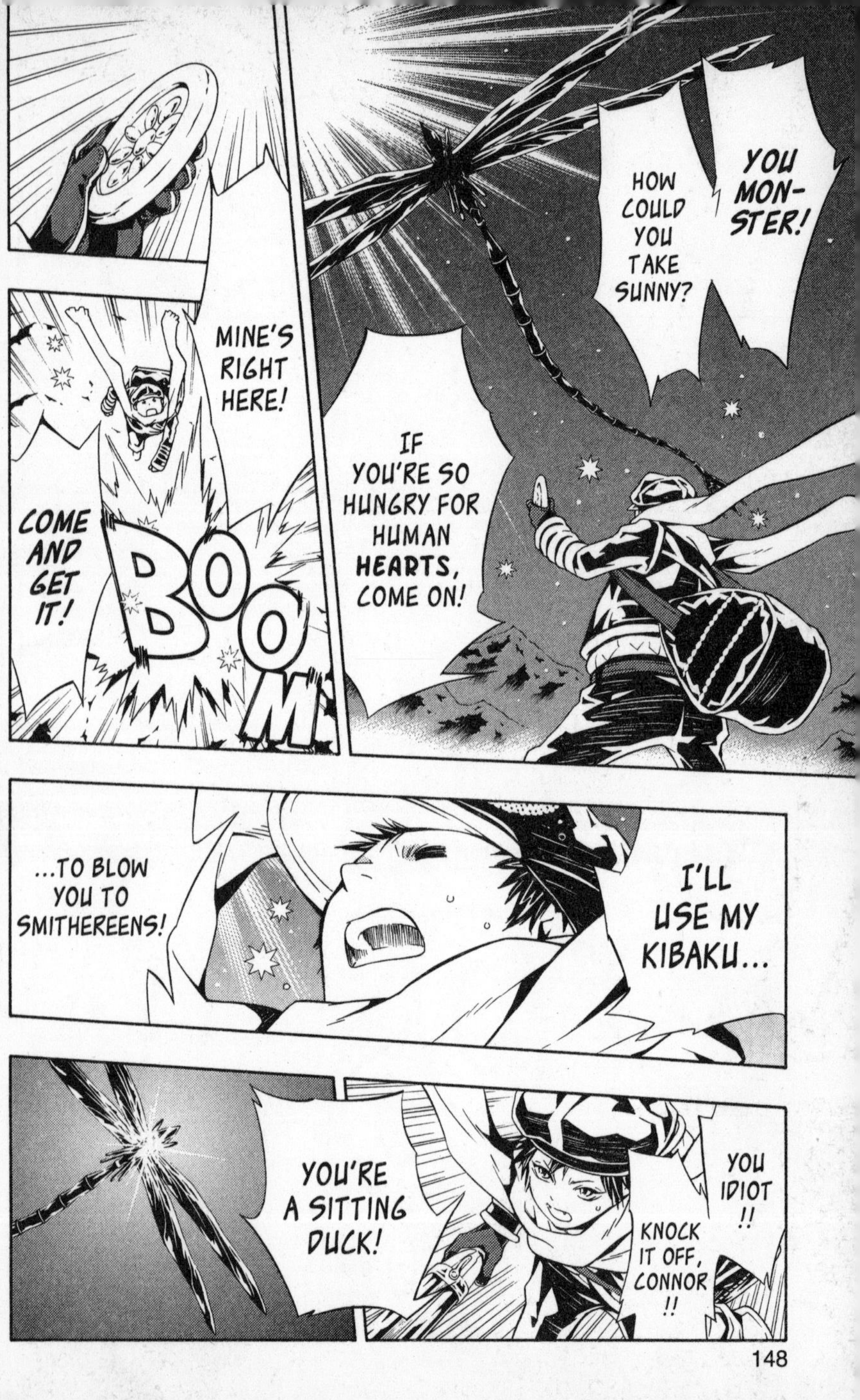
YOU MON-STER!
HOW COULD YOU TAKE SUNNY?
IF YOU'RE SO HUNGRY FOR HUMAN HEARTS, COME ON!
MINE'S RIGHT HERE!
COME AND GET IT!
BOOM
I'LL USE MY KIBAKU...
...TO BLOW YOU TO SMITHEREENS!
YOU IDIOT!!
KNOCK IT OFF, CONNOR!!
YOU'RE A SITTING DUCK!

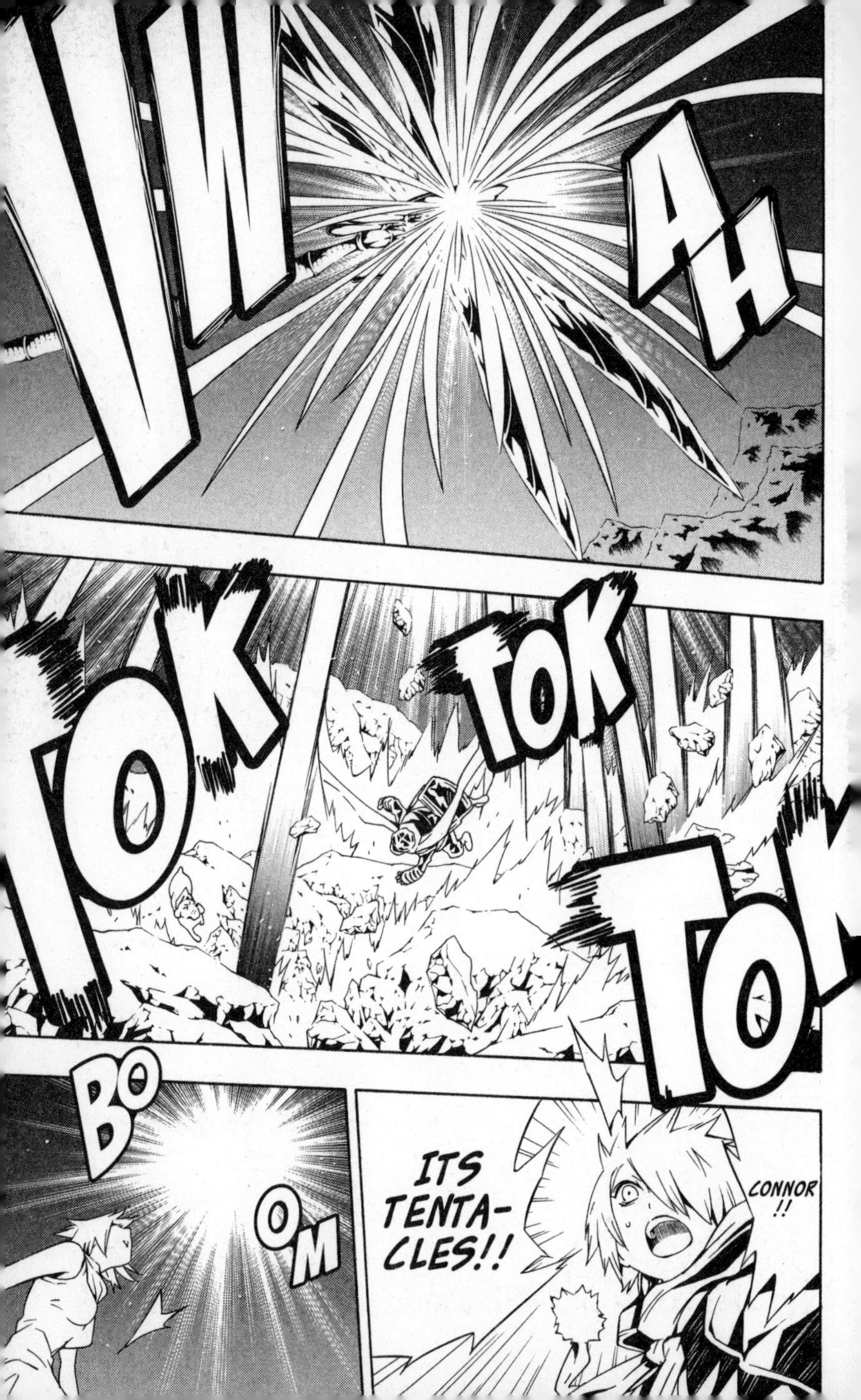

WAH
TOK
TOK
TOK
CONNOR!!
ITS TENTA-CLES!!
BOOM

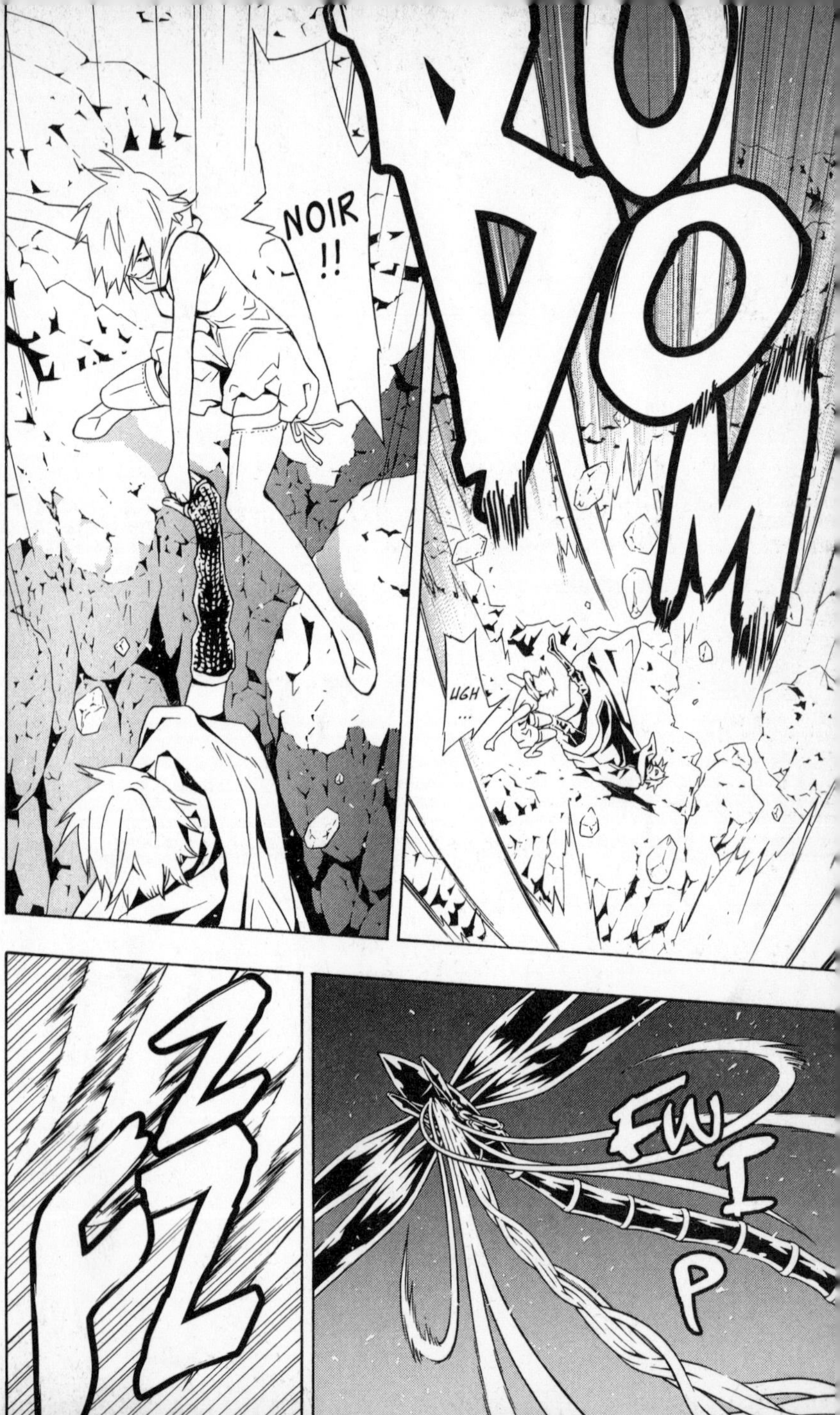
VOOM
UGH...
NOIR !!
FWIP
FZZ

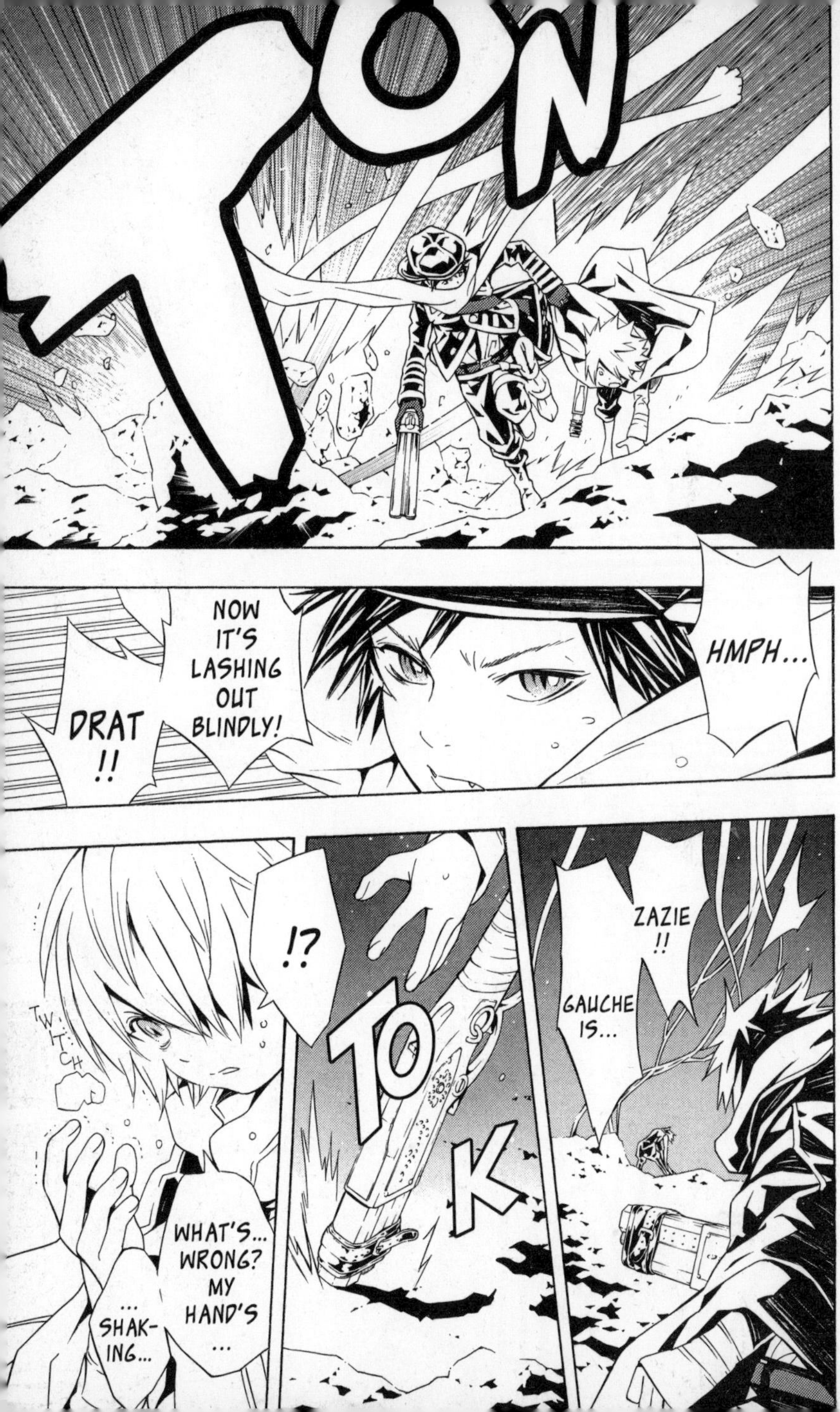
TON
HMPH...
NOW IT'S LASHING OUT BLINDLY!
DRAT!!
ZAZIE!!
GAUCHE IS...
!?
TOK
TWITCH
WHAT'S... WRONG? MY HAND'S ...
...SHAK-ING...

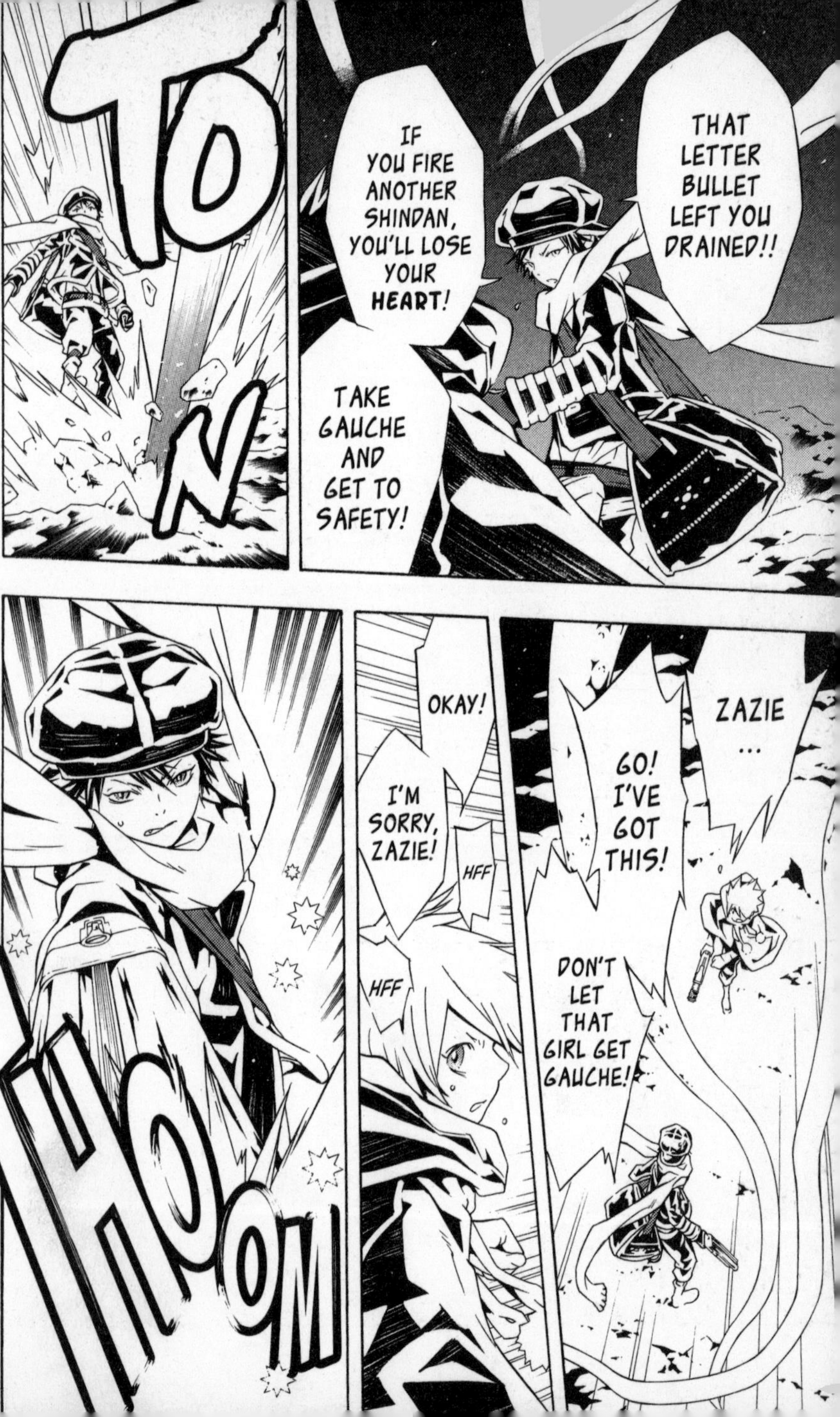
THAT LETTER BULLET LEFT YOU DRAINED!!
IF YOU FIRE ANOTHER SHINDAN, YOU'LL LOSE YOUR HEART!
TAKE GAUCHE AND GET TO SAFETY!
TON
ZAZIE ...
GO! I'VE GOT THIS!
DON'T LET THAT GIRL GET GAUCHE!
OKAY!
I'M SORRY, ZAZIE!
HFF
HFF
THOOM

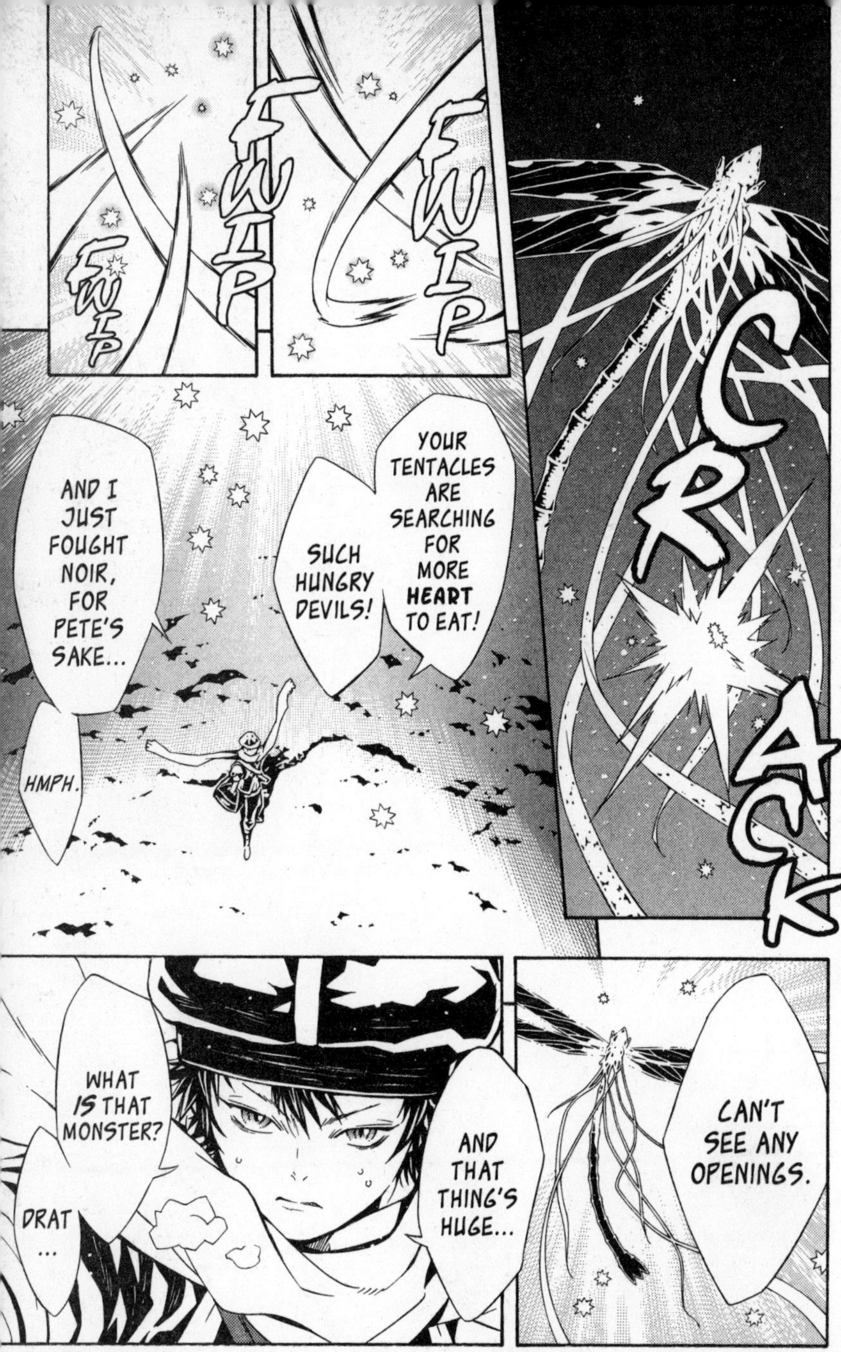
CRACK
FWIP
FWIP
FWIP
YOUR TENTACLES ARE SEARCHING FOR MORE **HEART** TO EAT!
SUCH HUNGRY DEVILS!
AND I JUST FOUGHT NOIR, FOR PETE'S SAKE...
HMPH.
CAN'T SEE ANY OPENINGS.
AND THAT THING'S HUGE...
WHAT *IS* THAT MONSTER?
DRAT...

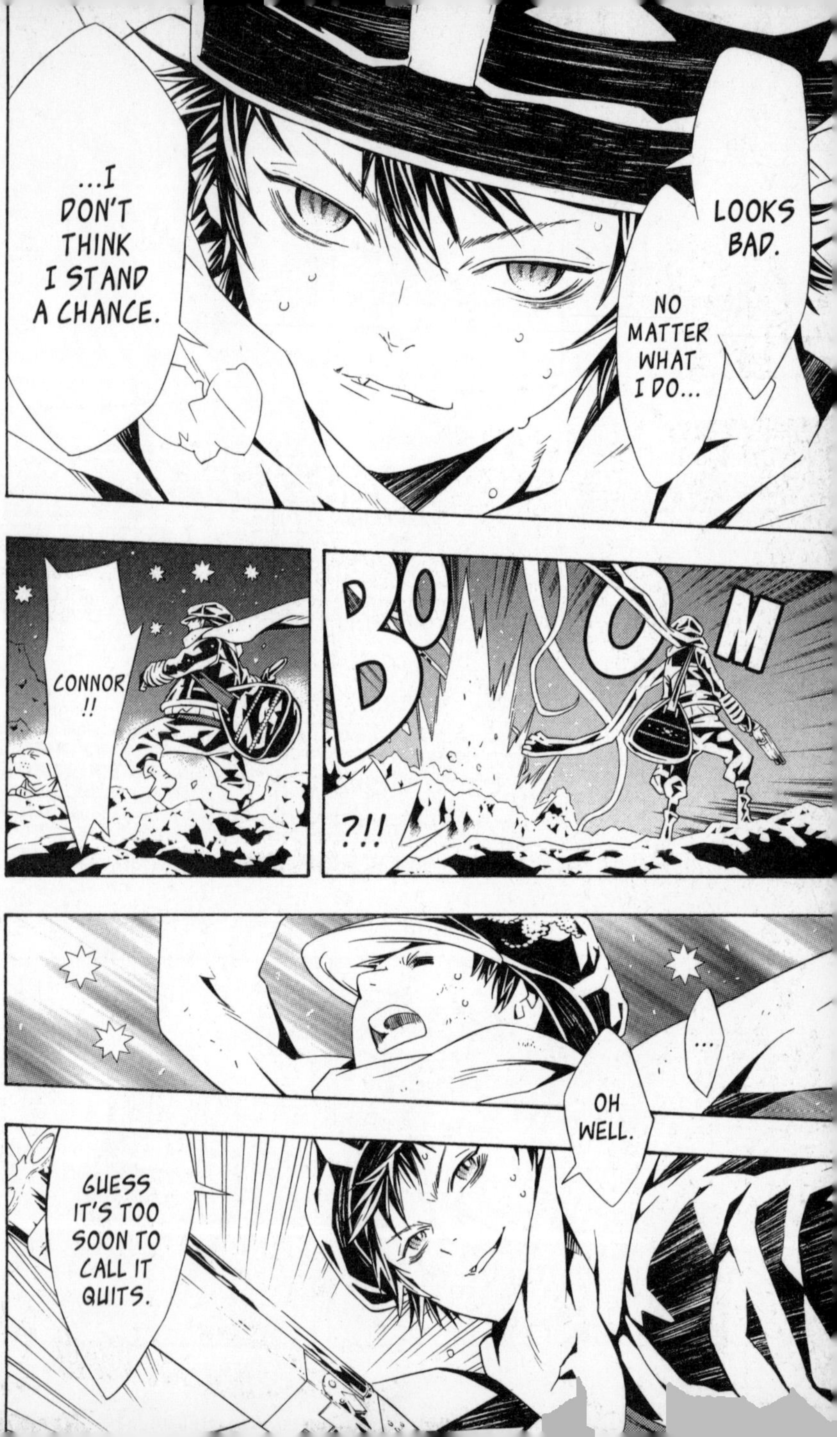
LOOKS BAD.
NO MATTER WHAT I DO...
...I DON'T THINK I STAND A CHANCE.
BOOM
?!!
CONNOR!!
...
OH WELL.
GUESS IT'S TOO SOON TO CALL IT QUITS.

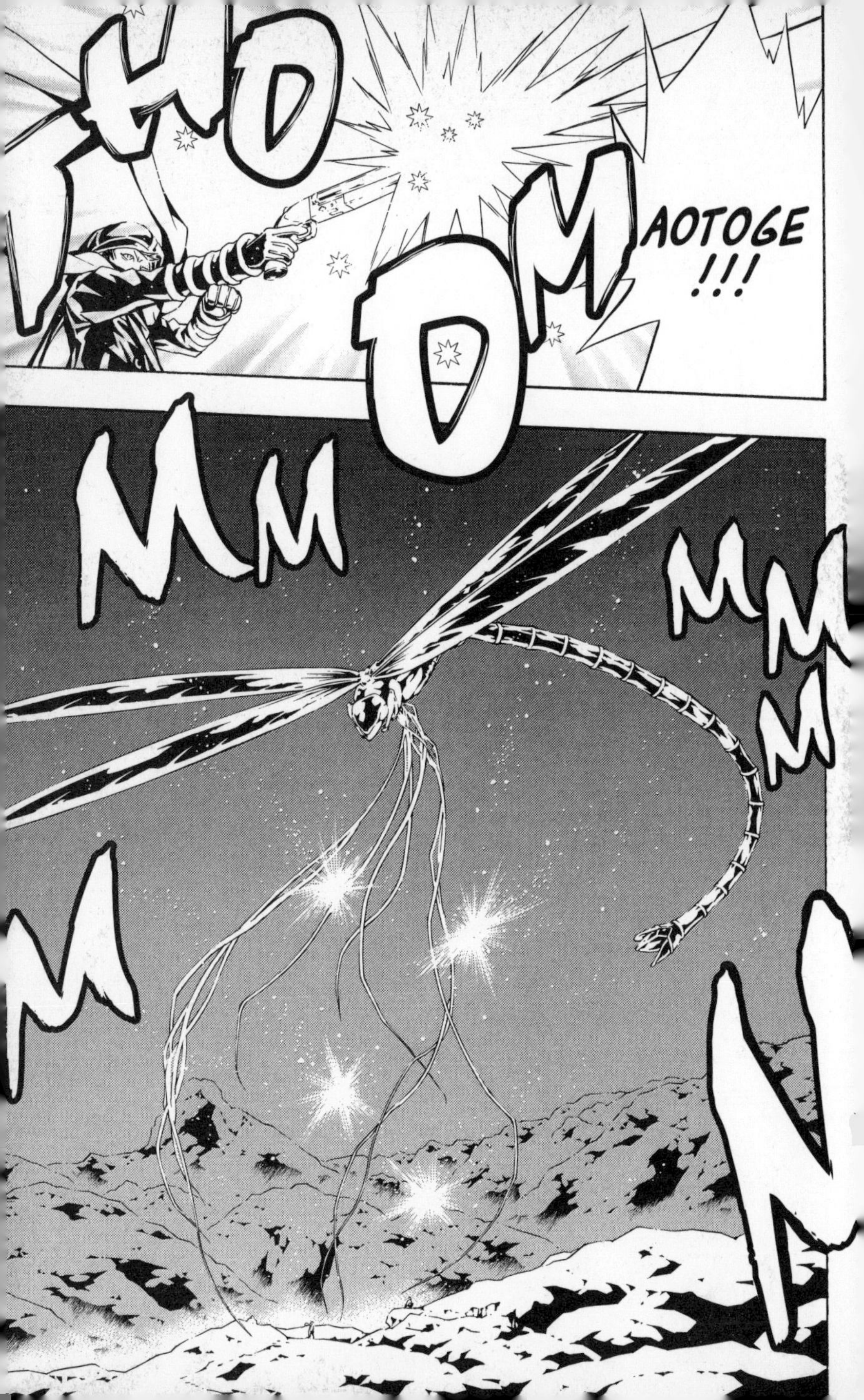
DOM
MAOTOGE !!!
MM
MM
M
M
N

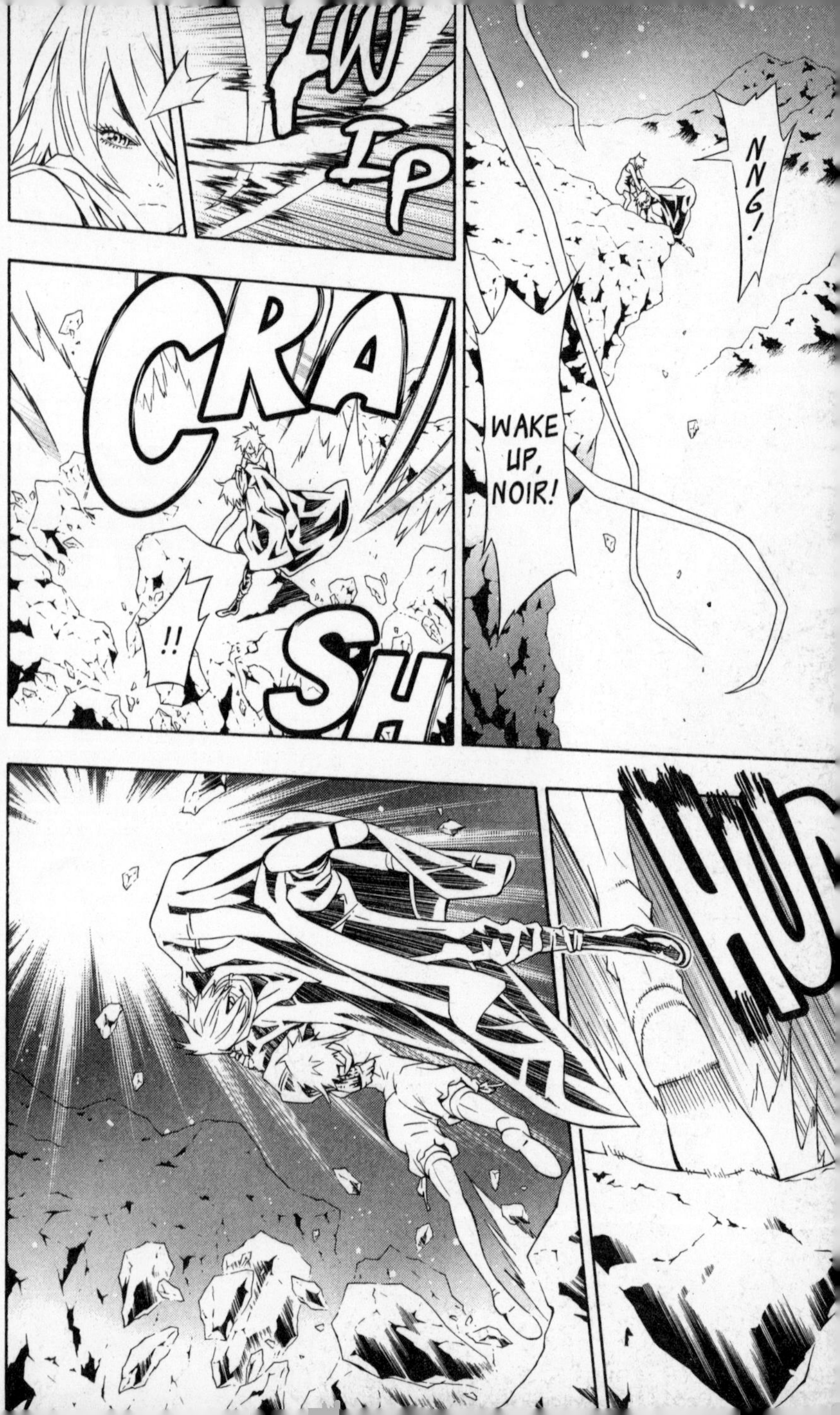
NNG!
WAKE UP, NOIR!
FWIP
CRASH
!!
HU

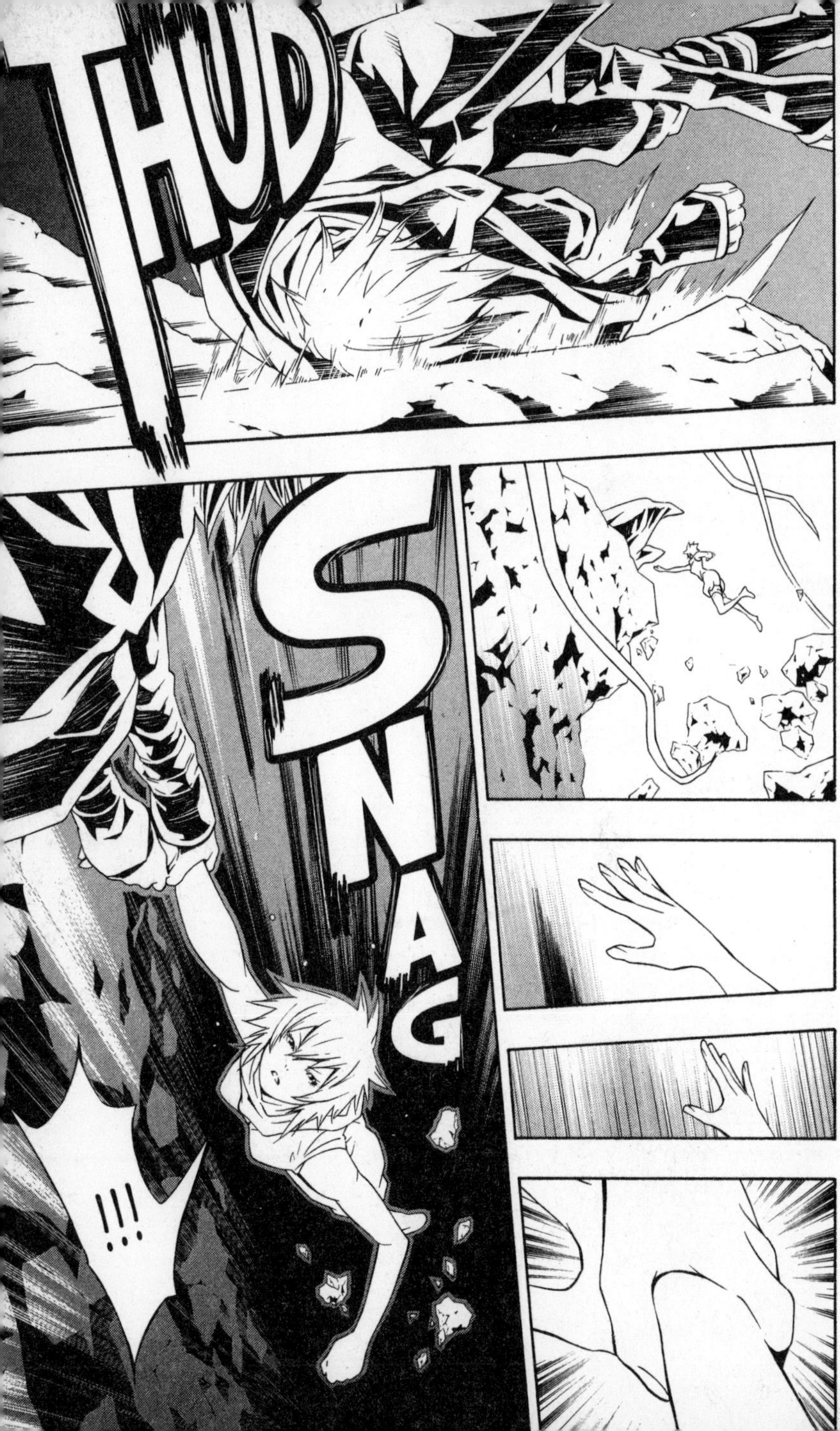
THUD
SNAG
!!!

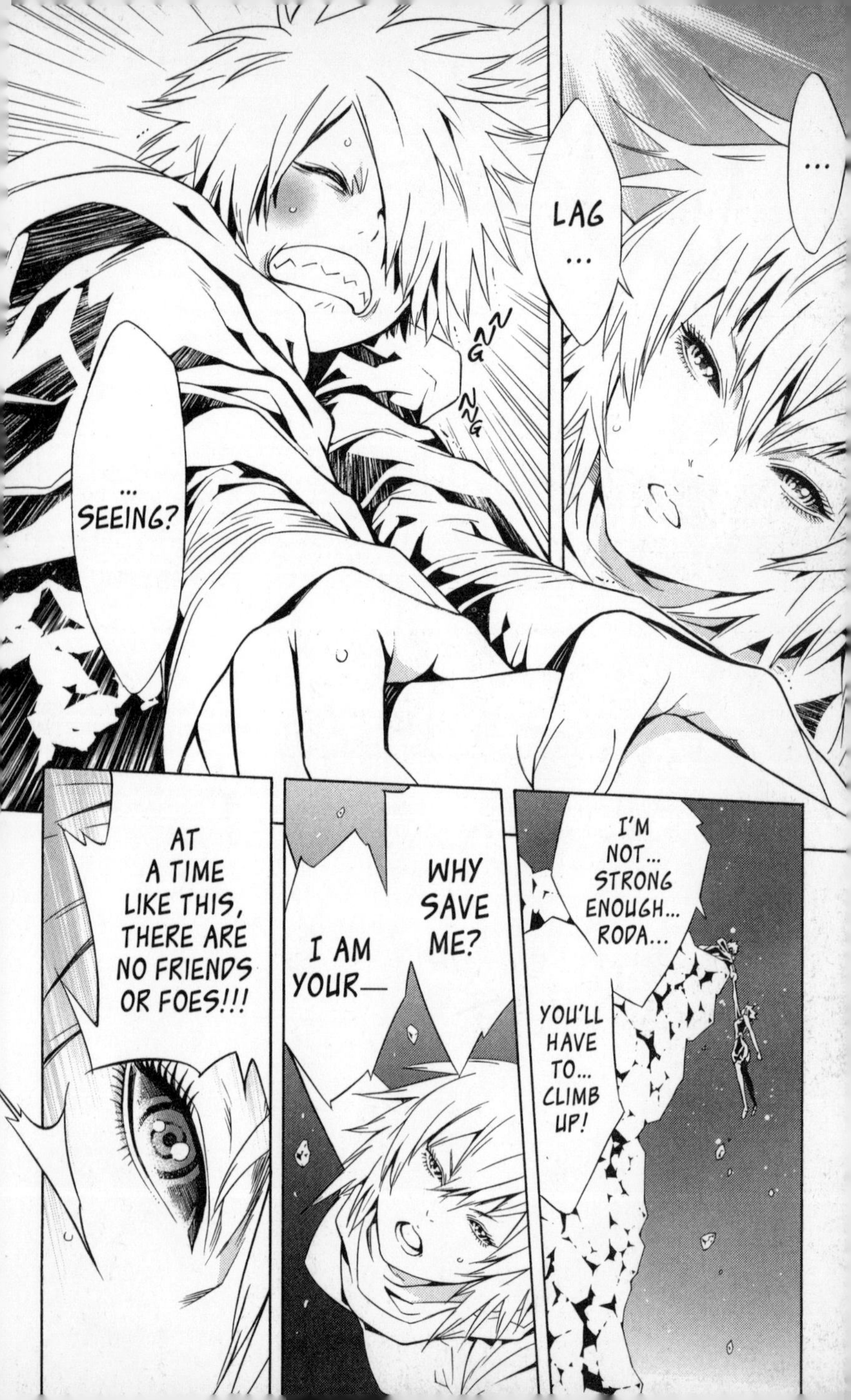
...
LAG ...
...
... SEEING?
I'M NOT... STRONG ENOUGH... RODA...
YOU'LL HAVE TO... CLIMB UP!
WHY SAVE ME?
I AM YOUR—
AT A TIME LIKE THIS, THERE ARE NO FRIENDS OR FOES!!!

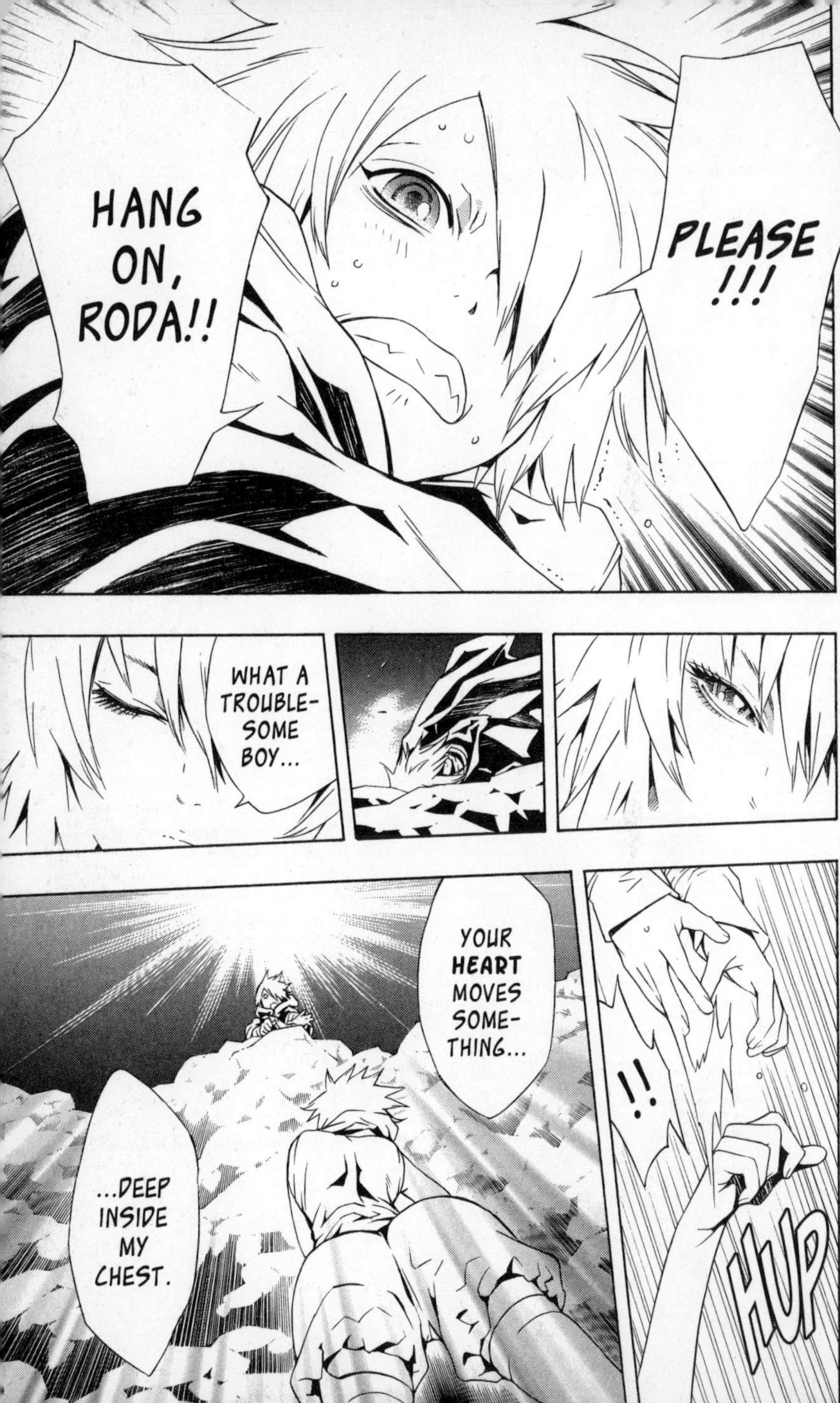
PLEASE!!!
HANG ON, RODA!!
WHAT A TROUBLESOME BOY...
!!
HUP
YOUR HEART MOVES SOMETHING...
...DEEP INSIDE MY CHEST.

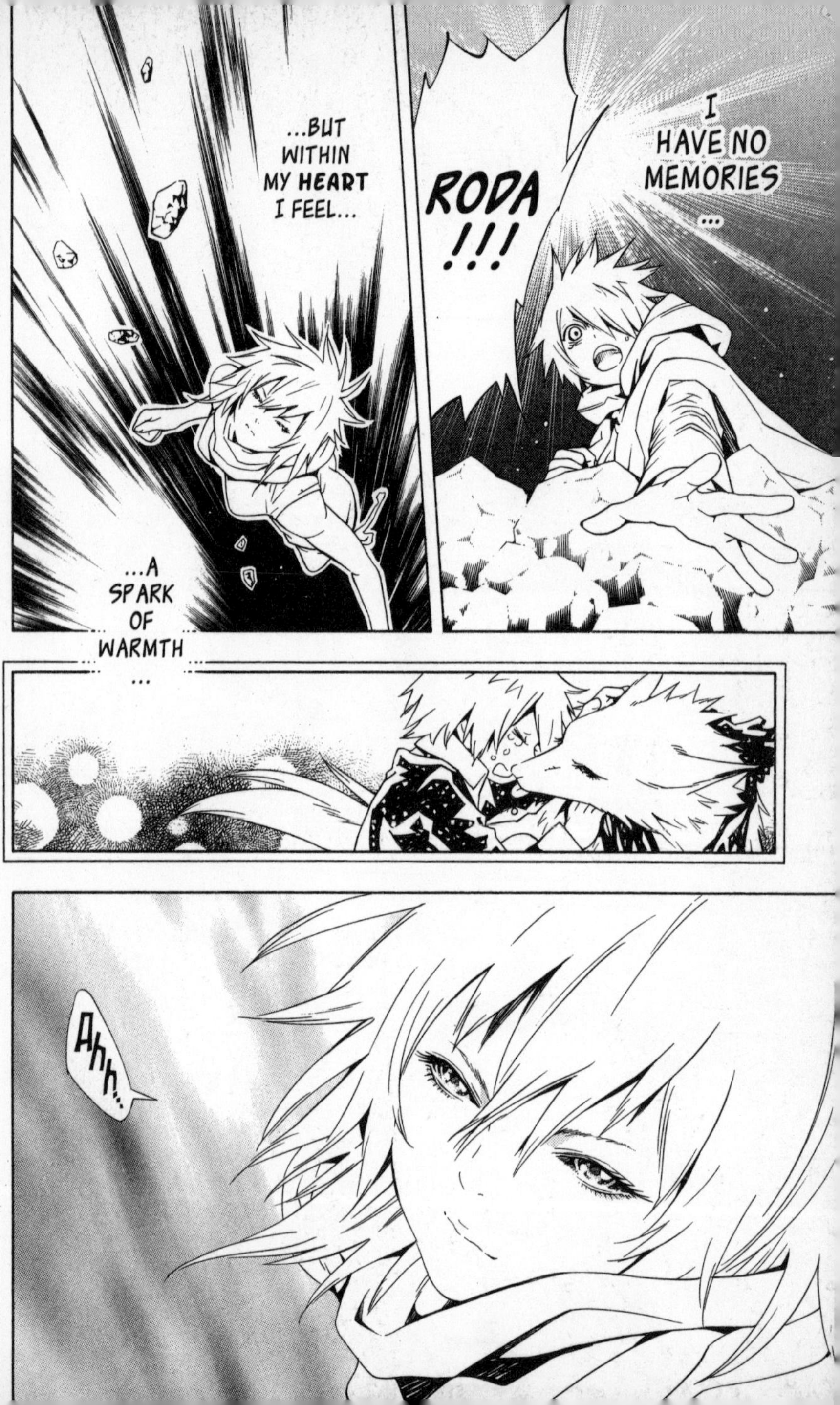
I HAVE NO MEMORIES ...
RODA !!!
...BUT WITHIN MY HEART I FEEL...
...A SPARK OF WARMTH ...
Ahh...

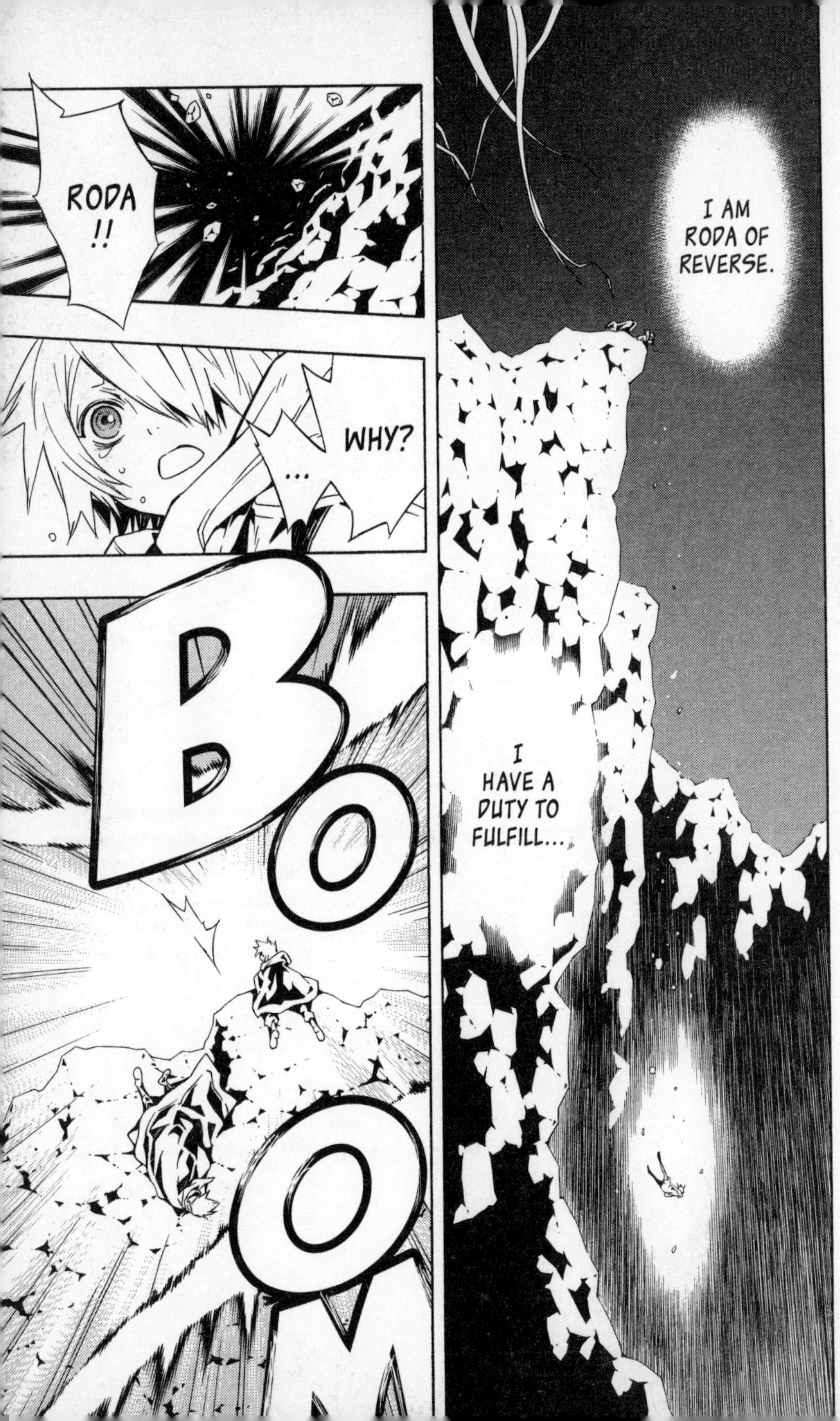
I AM RODA OF REVERSE.
I HAVE A DUTY TO FULFILL...
RODA !!
WHY?
...
BOOM

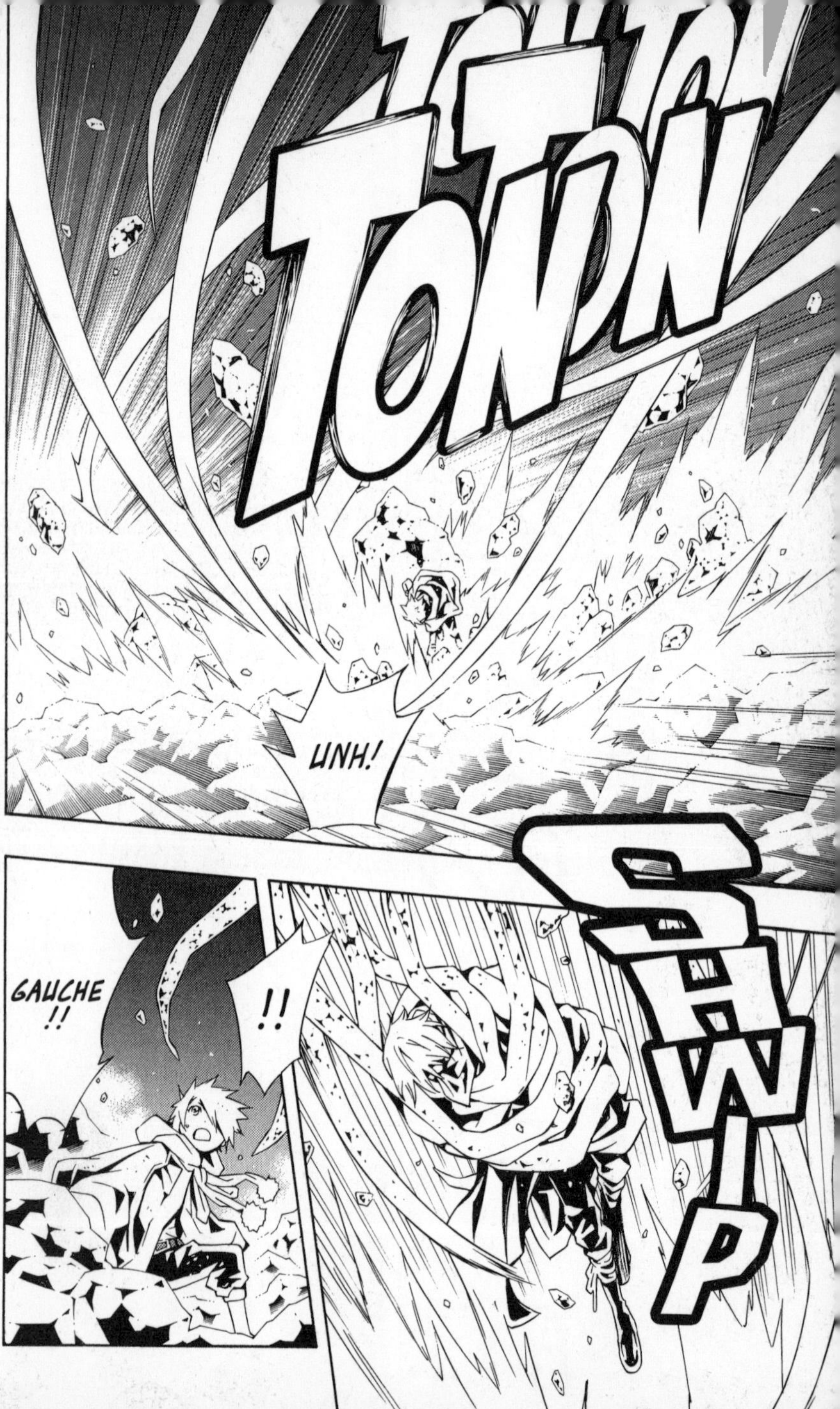
UNH!
SHWIP
!!
GAUCHE !!

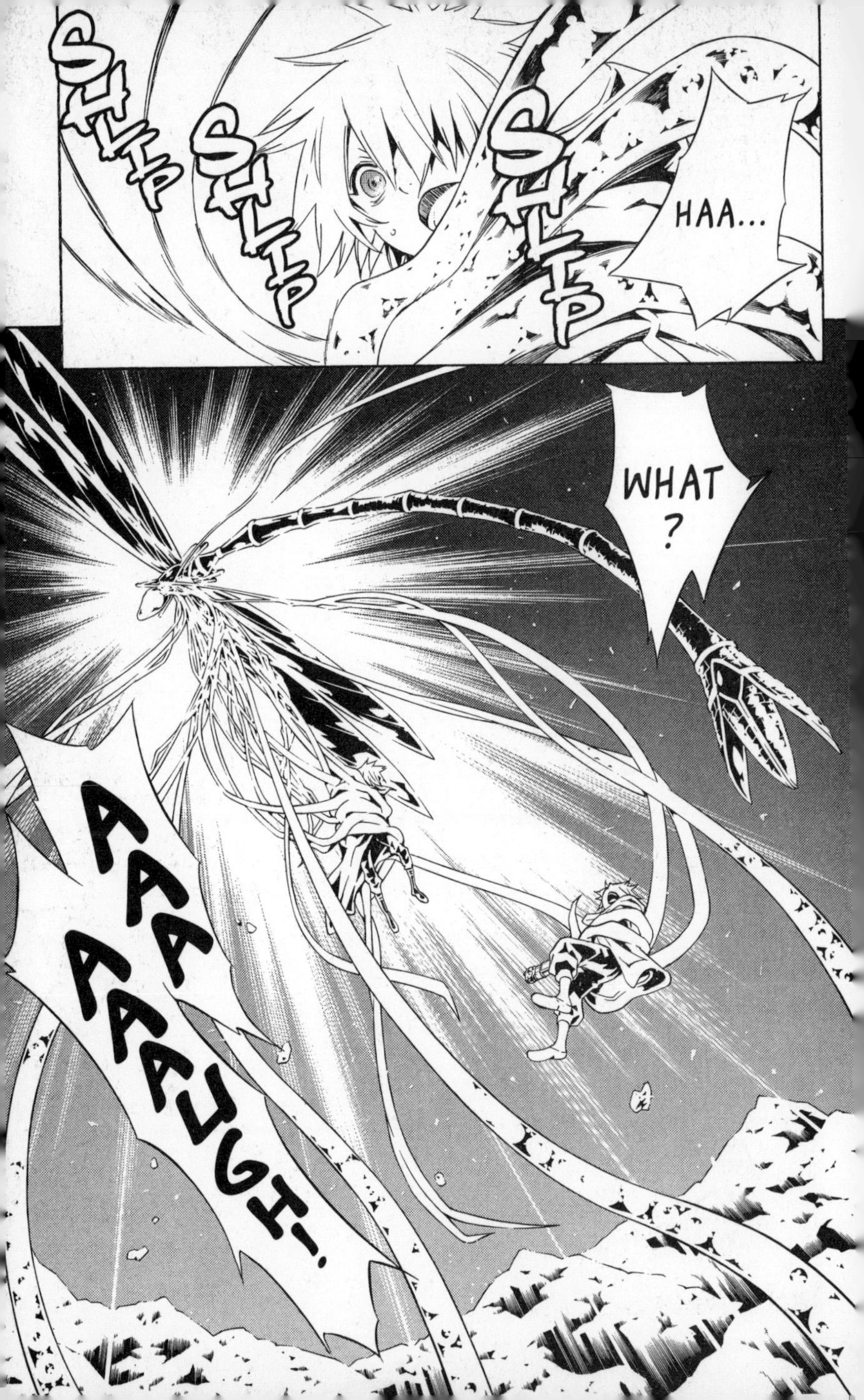
HAA...
SHLIP
SHLIP
SHLIP
WHAT?
AAAAAAUGH!

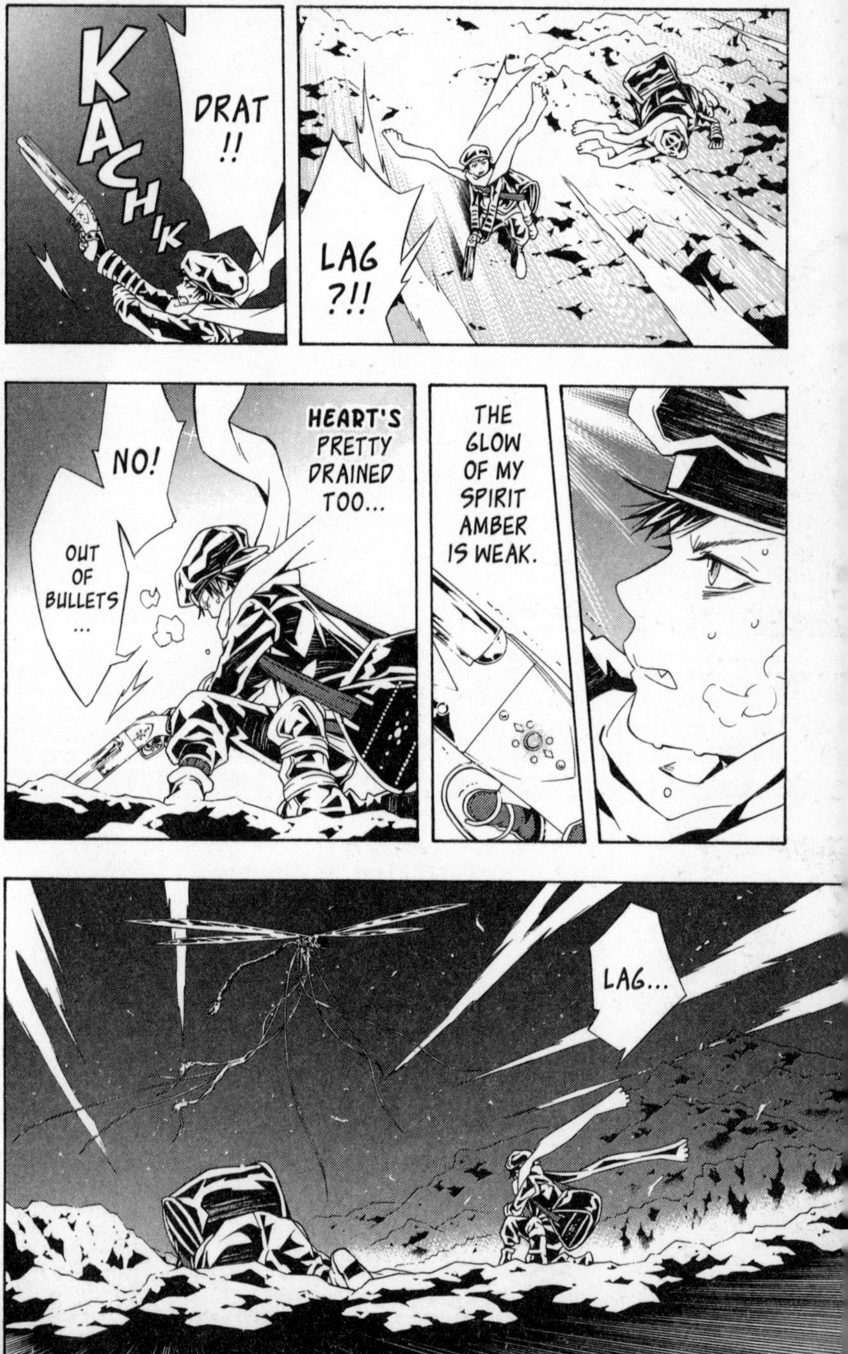
LAG ?!!
DRAT !!
KACHIK
THE GLOW OF MY SPIRIT AMBER IS WEAK.
HEART'S PRETTY DRAINED TOO...
NO!
OUT OF BULLETS ...
LAG...

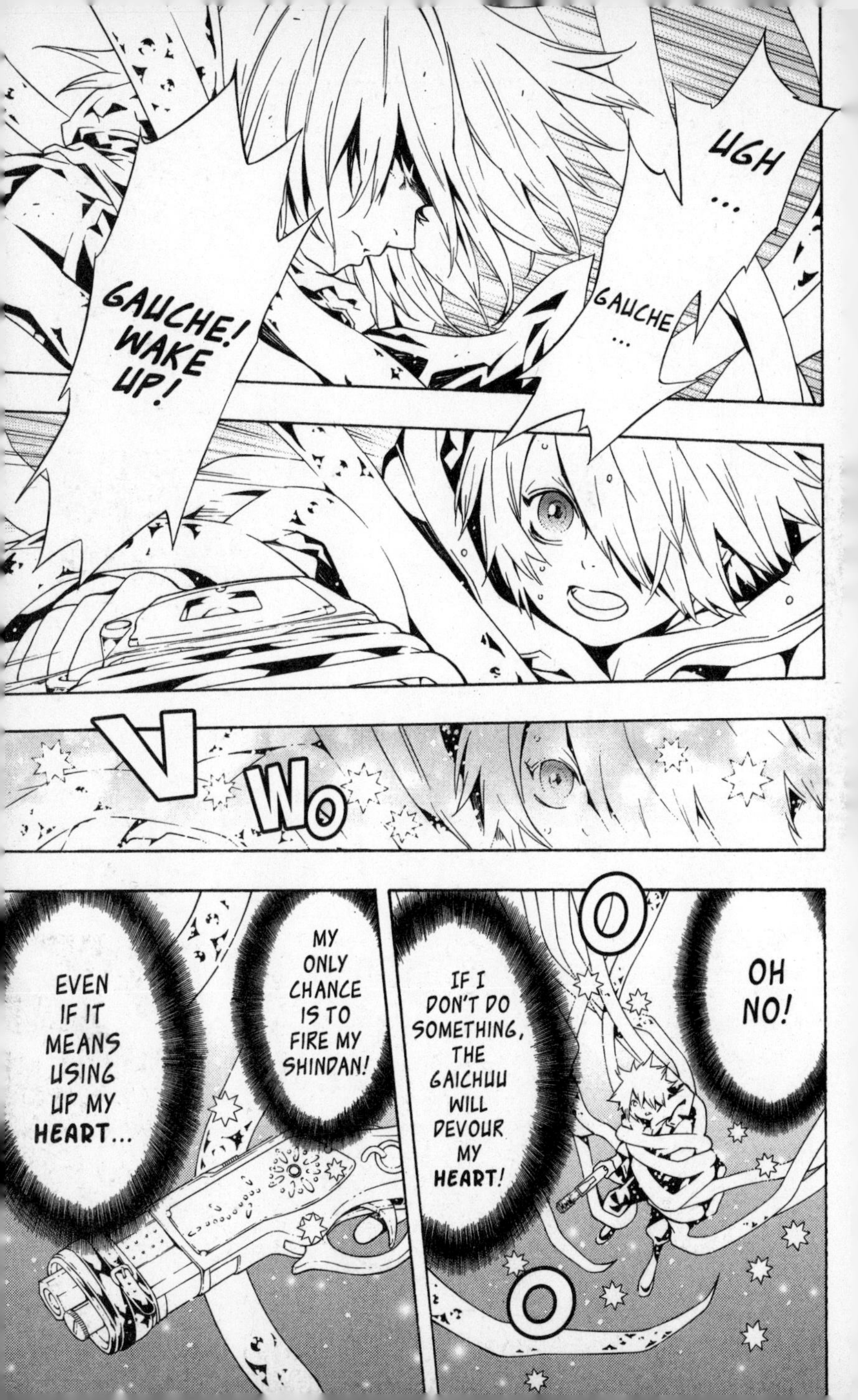
UGH...
GAUCHE...
GAUCHE! WAKE UP!
VWO
OH NO!
IF I DON'T DO SOMETHING, THE GAICHUU WILL DEVOUR MY HEART!
O
O
MY ONLY CHANCE IS TO FIRE MY SHINDAN!
EVEN IF IT MEANS USING UP MY HEART...

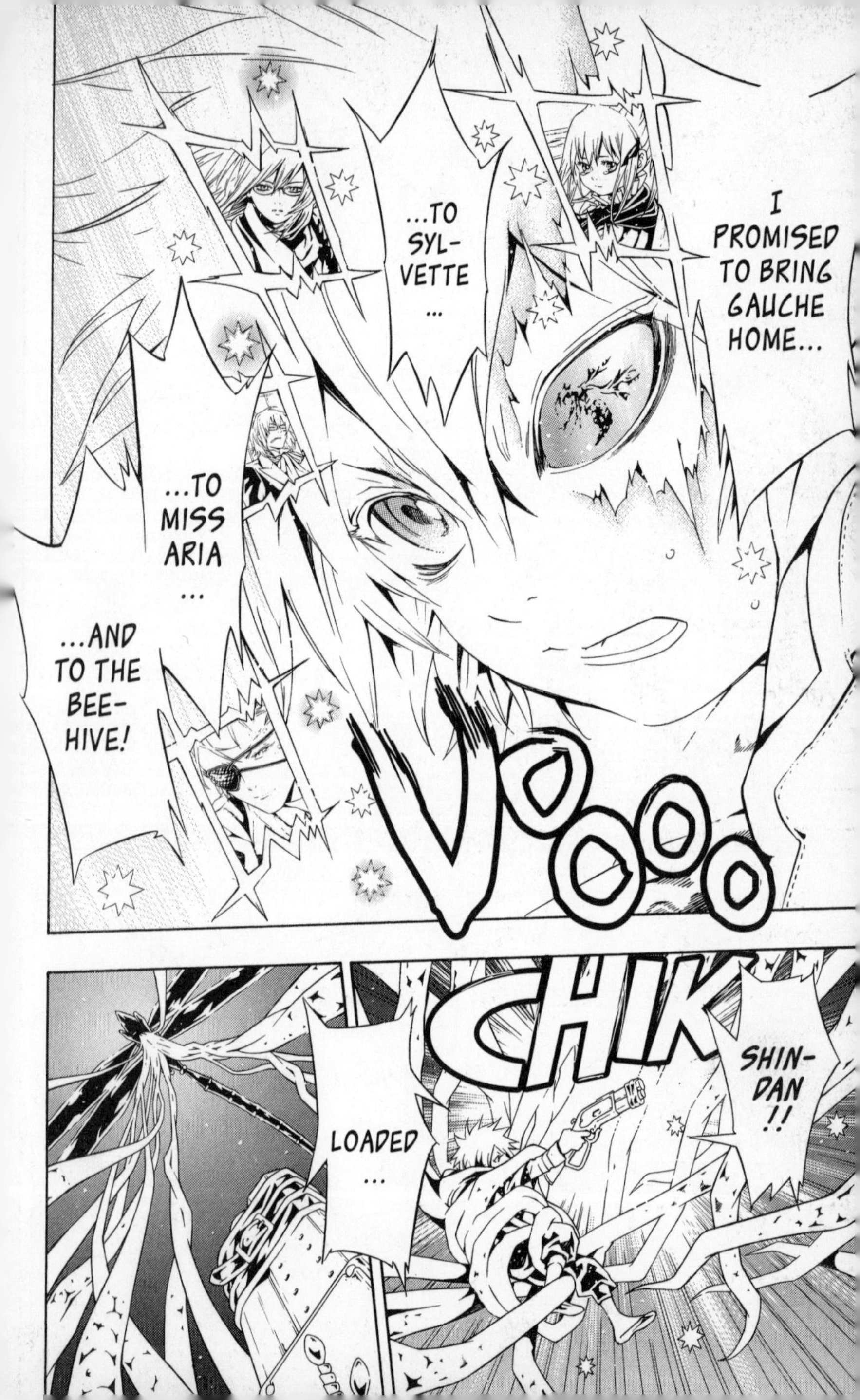
I PROMISED TO BRING GAUCHE HOME...
...TO SYLVETTE...
...TO MISS ARIA...
...AND TO THE BEEHIVE!
VOOOO
CHIK
SHINDAN!!
LOADED...

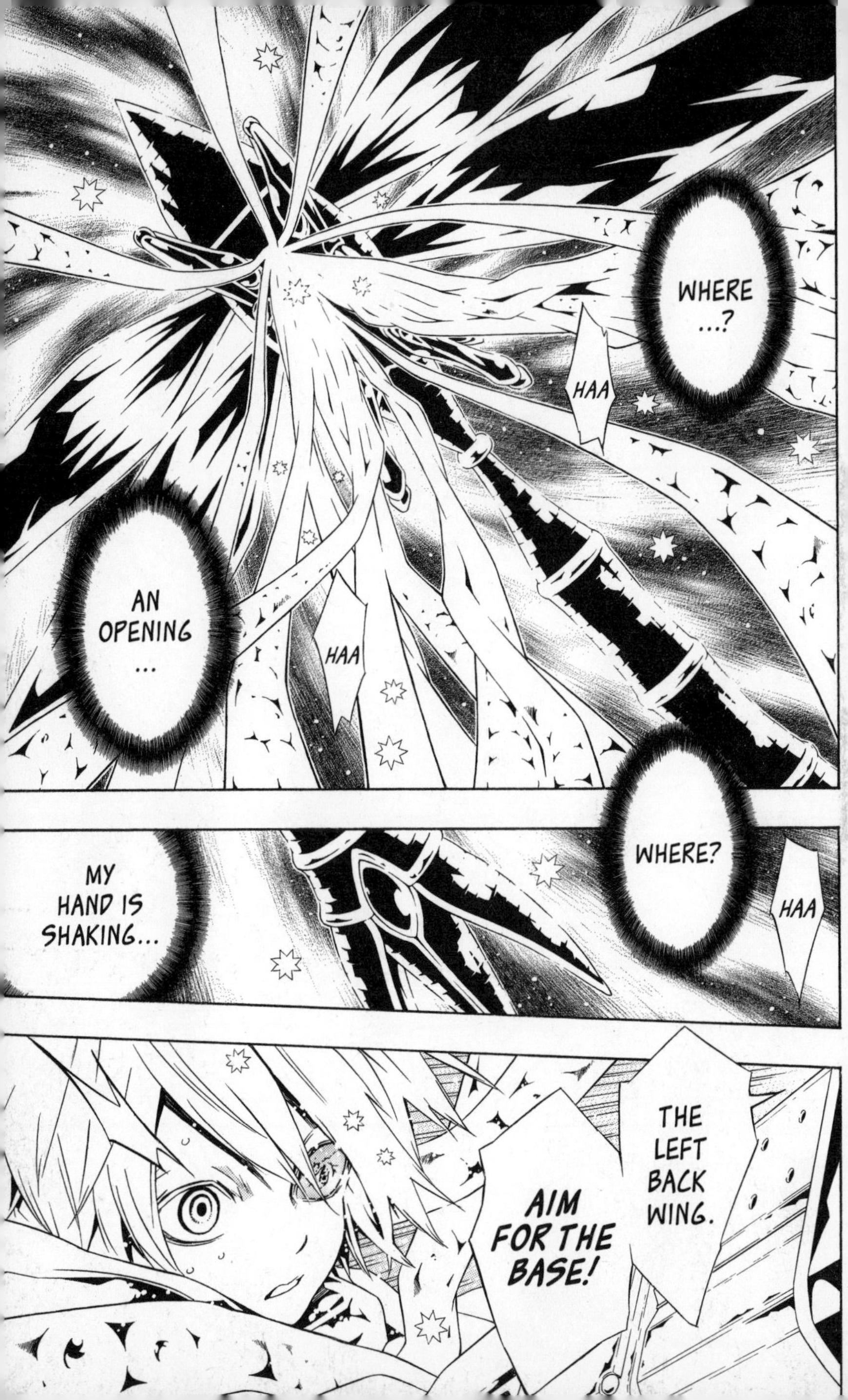
WHERE ...?
HAA
HAA
AN OPENING ...
WHERE?
HAA
MY HAND IS SHAKING...
THE LEFT BACK WING.
AIM FOR THE BASE!

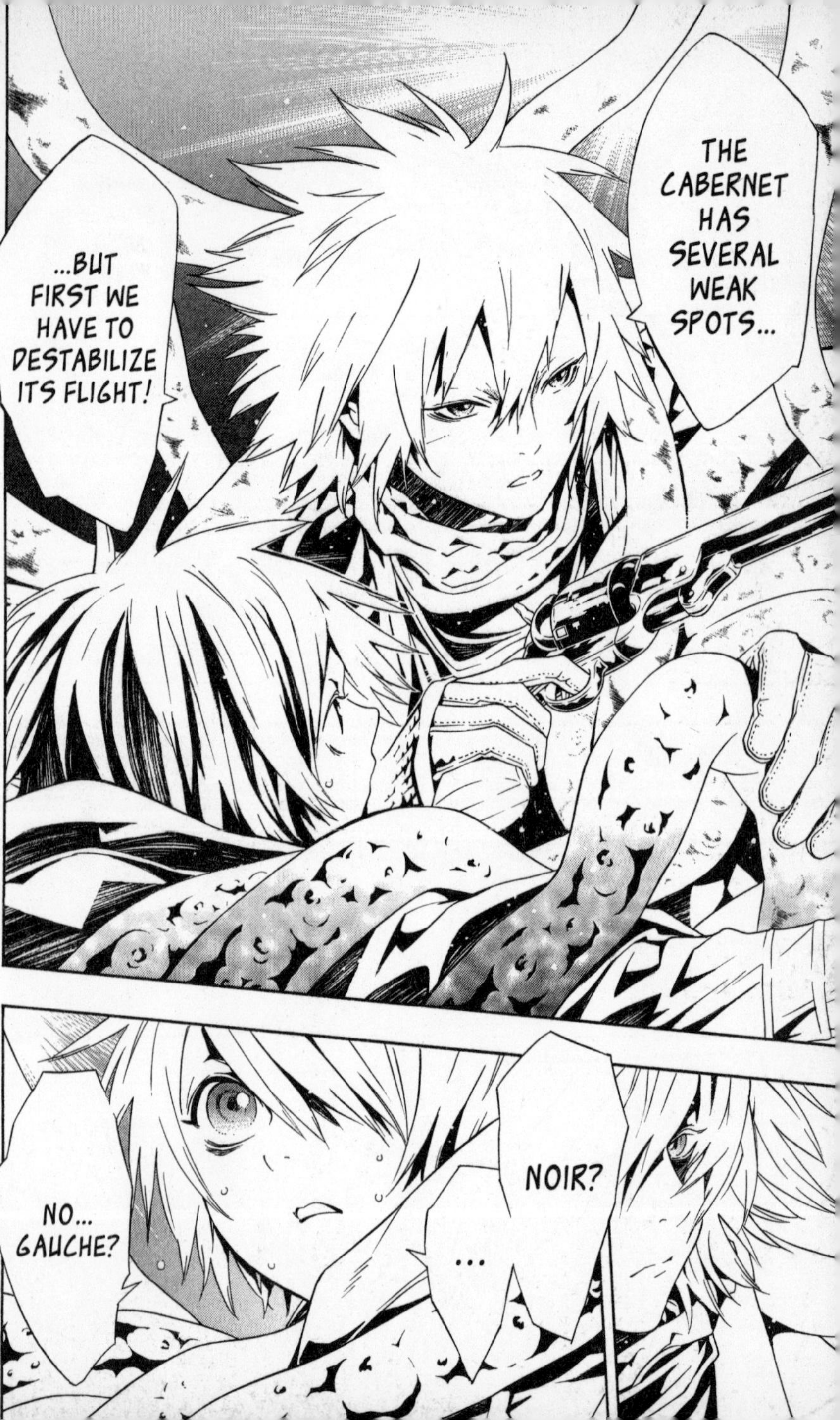
THE CABERNET HAS SEVERAL WEAK SPOTS...
...BUT FIRST WE HAVE TO DESTABILIZE ITS FLIGHT!
NOIR?
...
NO... GAUCHE?

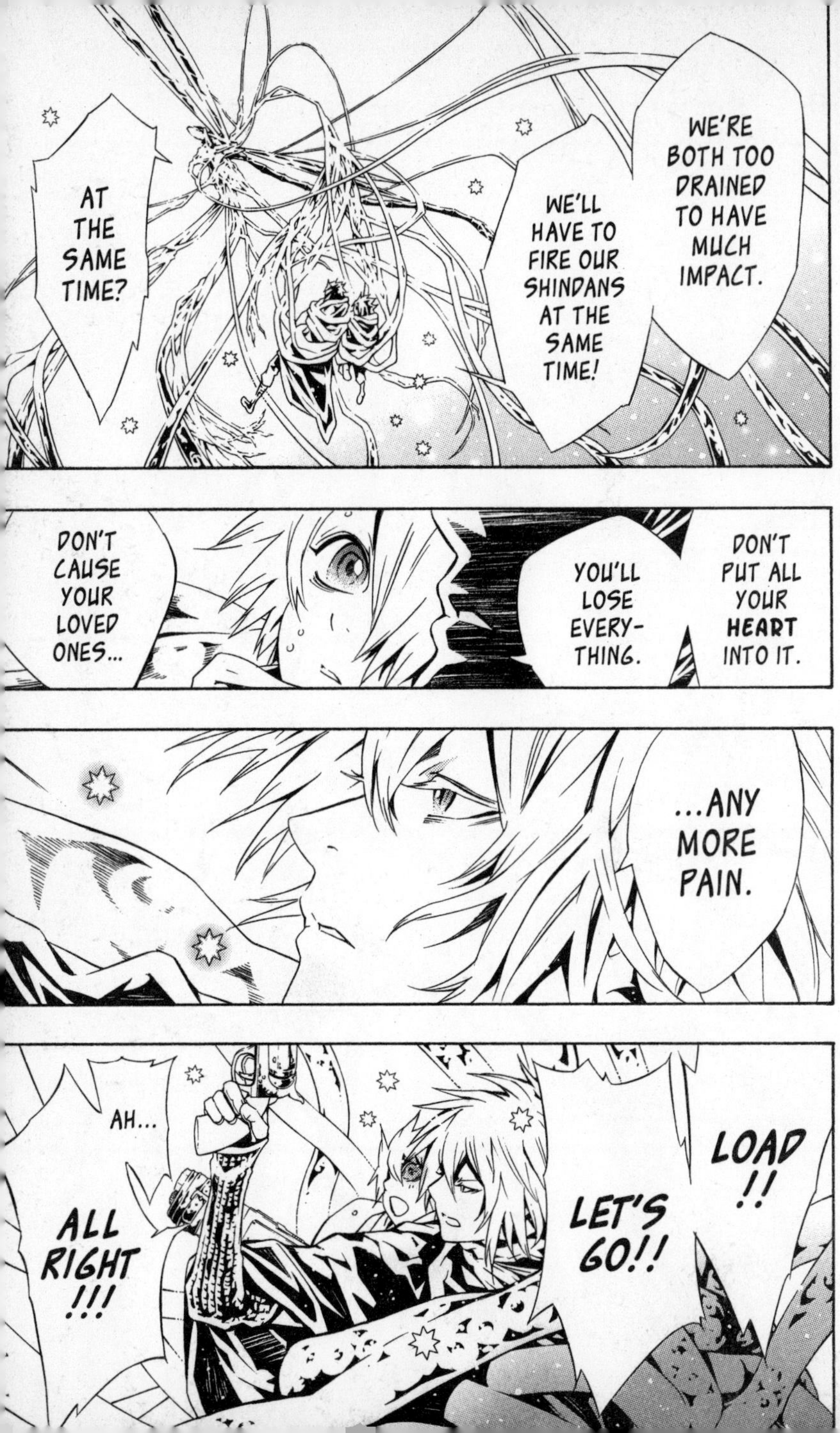
WE'RE BOTH TOO DRAINED TO HAVE MUCH IMPACT.
WE'LL HAVE TO FIRE OUR SHINDANS AT THE SAME TIME!
AT THE SAME TIME?
DON'T PUT ALL YOUR HEART INTO IT.
YOU'LL LOSE EVERY-THING.
DON'T CAUSE YOUR LOVED ONES...
...ANY MORE PAIN.
LOAD!!
LET'S GO!!
AH...
ALL RIGHT!!!

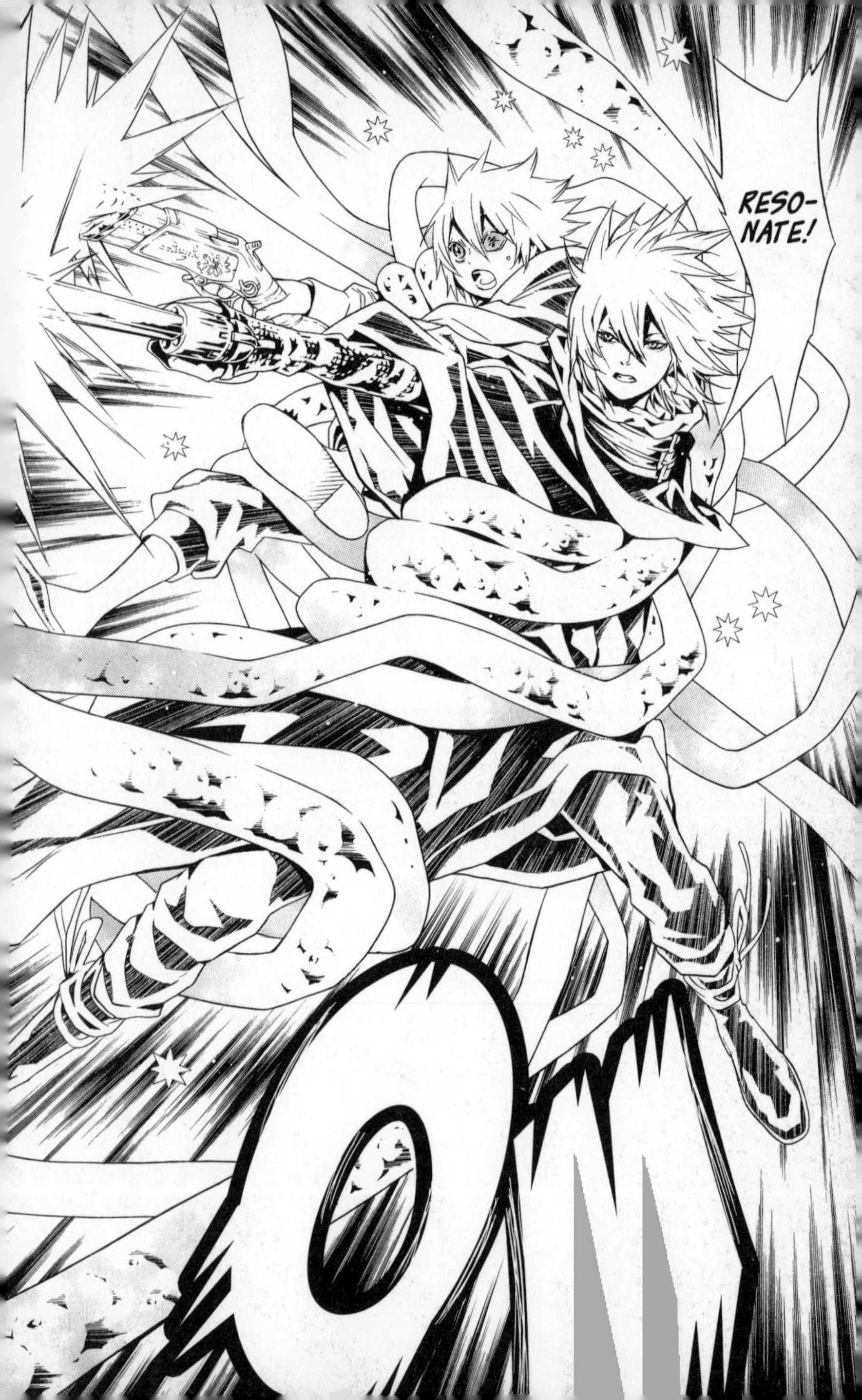
RESO-
NATE!

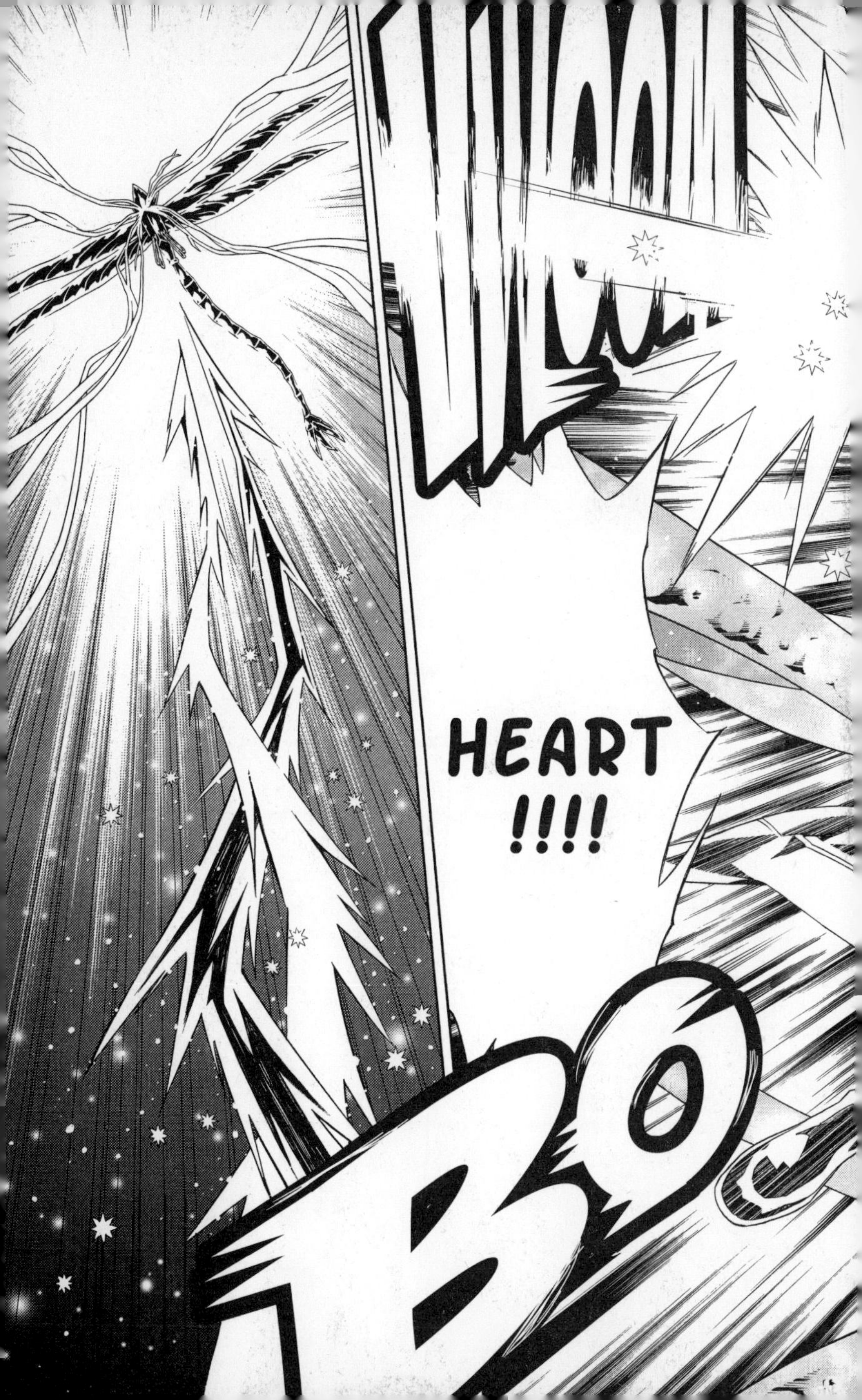
HEART !!!!

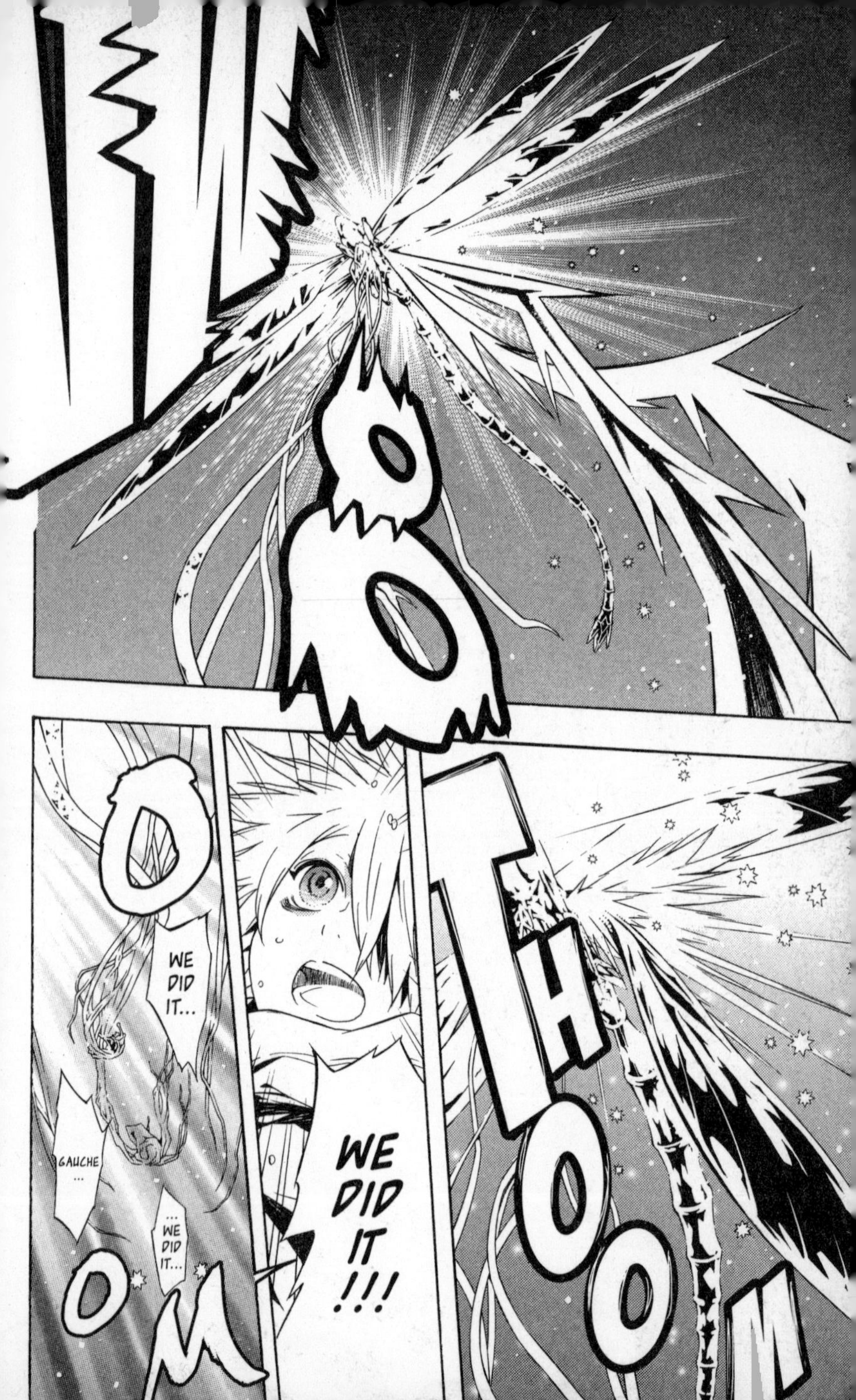
THOOOM
WE DID IT!!!
WE DID IT...
GAUCHE ...
...WE DID IT...

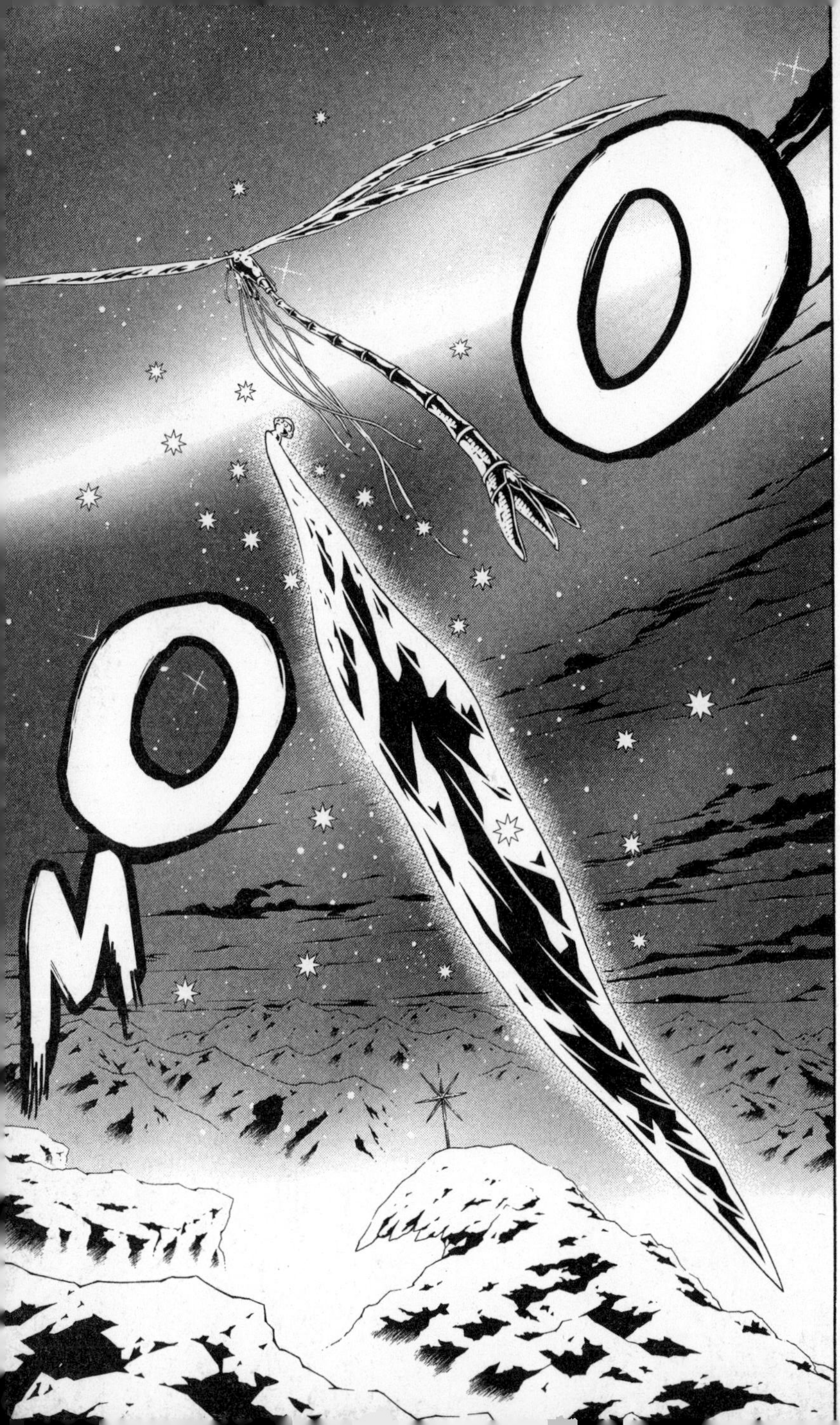
MOO

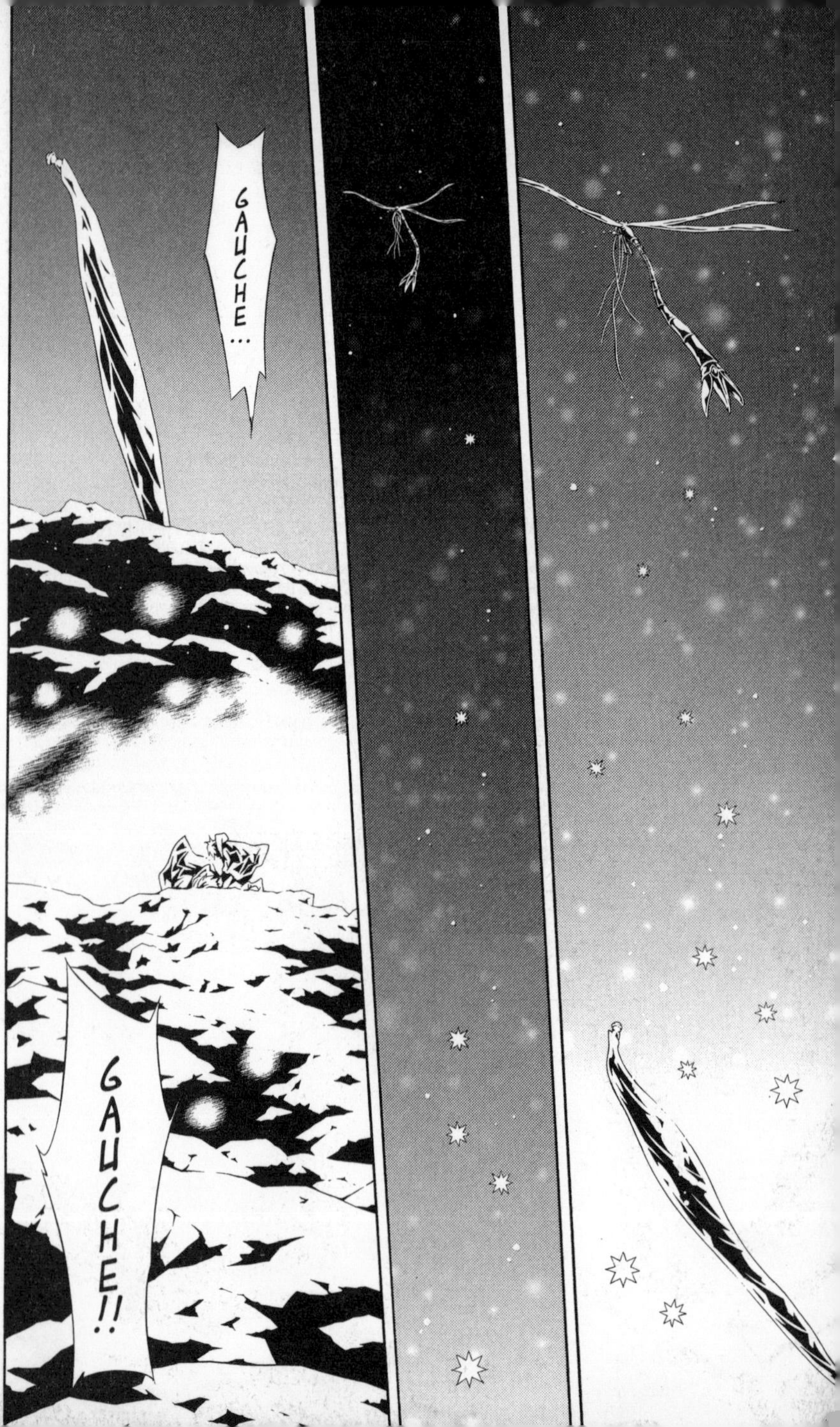
GAUCHE...
GAUCHE!!

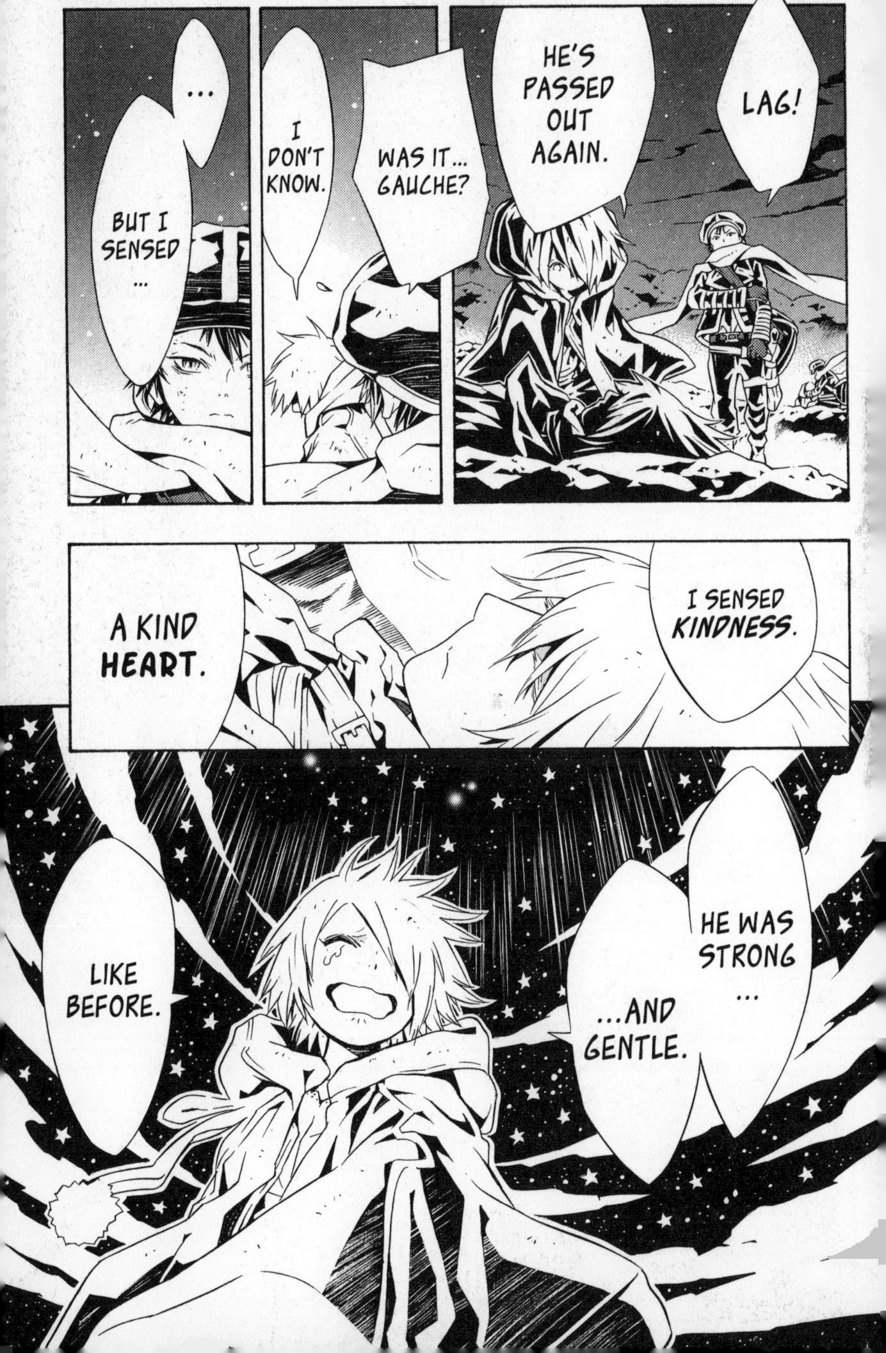
LAG!
HE'S PASSED OUT AGAIN.
WAS IT... GAUCHE?
I DON'T KNOW.
...
BUT I SENSED ...
I SENSED KINDNESS.
A KIND HEART.
HE WAS STRONG ...
...AND GENTLE.
LIKE BEFORE.

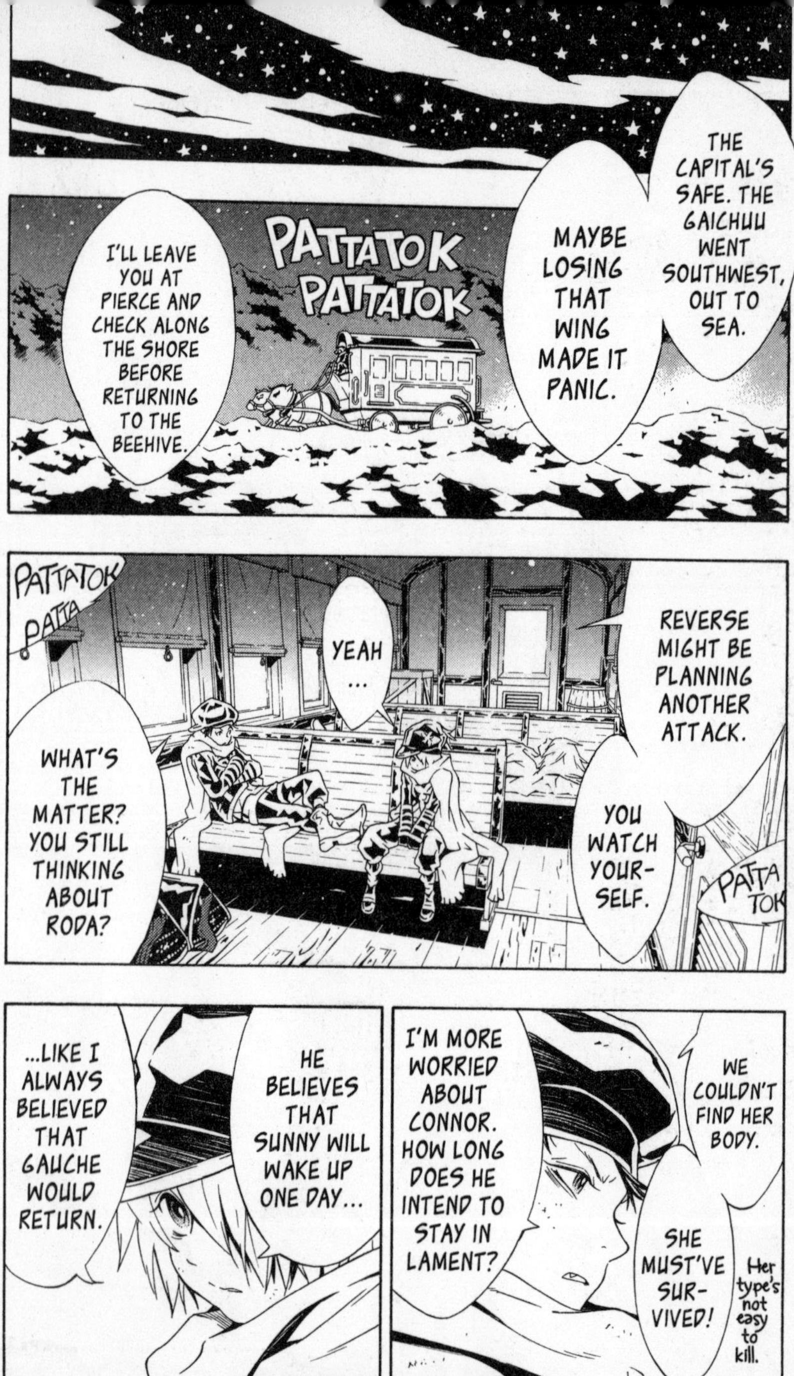
THE CAPITAL'S SAFE. THE GAICHUU WENT SOUTHWEST, OUT TO SEA.
MAYBE LOSING THAT WING MADE IT PANIC.
PATTATOK PATTATOK
I'LL LEAVE YOU AT PIERCE AND CHECK ALONG THE SHORE BEFORE RETURNING TO THE BEEHIVE.
REVERSE MIGHT BE PLANNING ANOTHER ATTACK.
YEAH...
YOU WATCH YOURSELF.
PATTA TOK
WHAT'S THE MATTER? YOU STILL THINKING ABOUT RODA?
PATTATOK PATTA
WE COULDN'T FIND HER BODY.
SHE MUST'VE SURVIVED!
Her type's not easy to kill.
I'M MORE WORRIED ABOUT CONNOR. HOW LONG DOES HE INTEND TO STAY IN LAMENT?
HE BELIEVES THAT SUNNY WILL WAKE UP ONE DAY...
...LIKE I ALWAYS BELIEVED THAT GAUCHE WOULD RETURN.

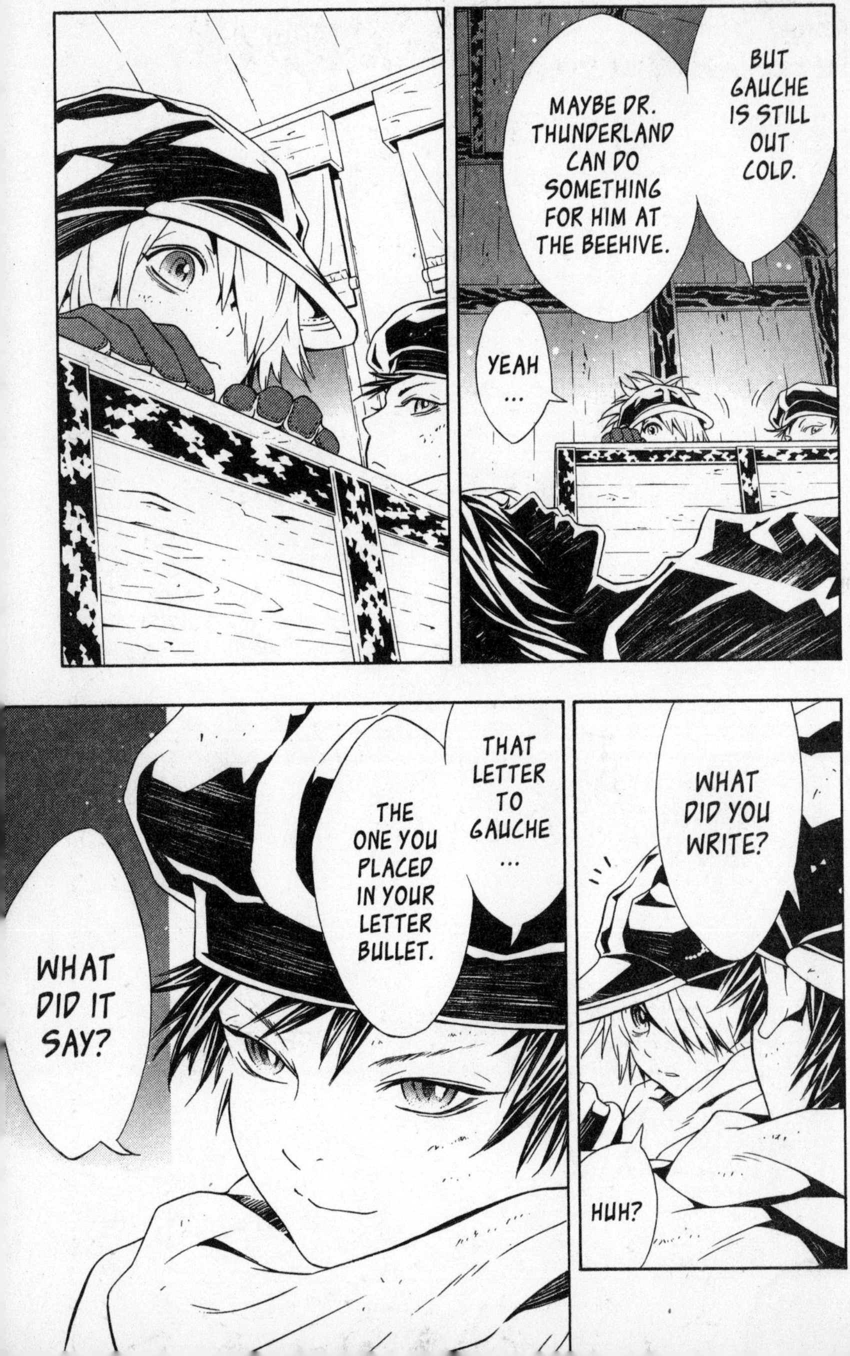
BUT GAUCHE IS STILL OUT COLD.
MAYBE DR. THUNDERLAND CAN DO SOMETHING FOR HIM AT THE BEEHIVE.
YEAH ...
WHAT DID YOU WRITE?
HUH?
THAT LETTER TO GAUCHE ...
THE ONE YOU PLACED IN YOUR LETTER BULLET.
WHAT DID IT SAY?

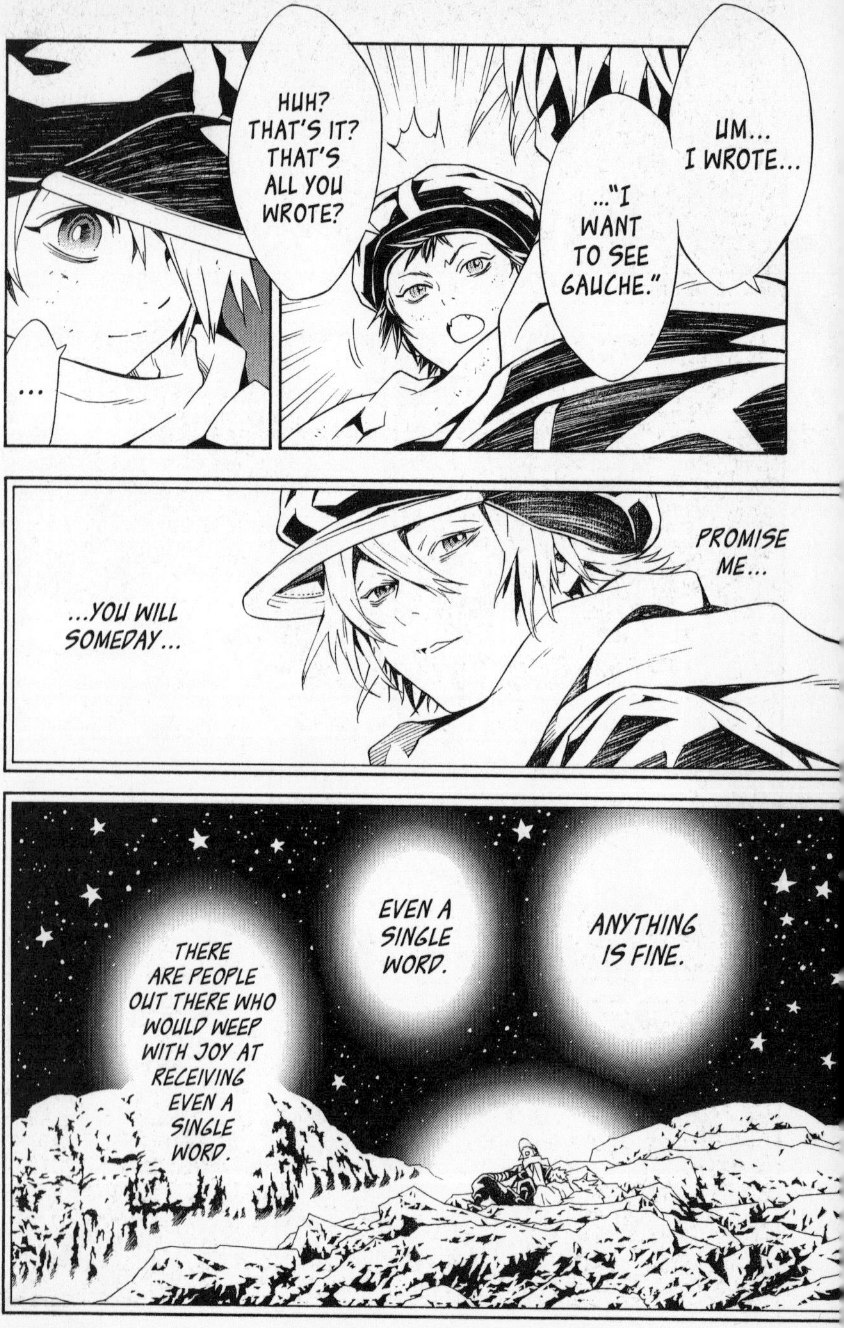
UM... I WROTE...
..."I WANT TO SEE GAUCHE."
HUH? THAT'S IT? THAT'S ALL YOU WROTE?
...
PROMISE ME...
...YOU WILL SOMEDAY...
ANYTHING IS FINE.
EVEN A SINGLE WORD.
THERE ARE PEOPLE OUT THERE WHO WOULD WEEP WITH JOY AT RECEIVING EVEN A SINGLE WORD.

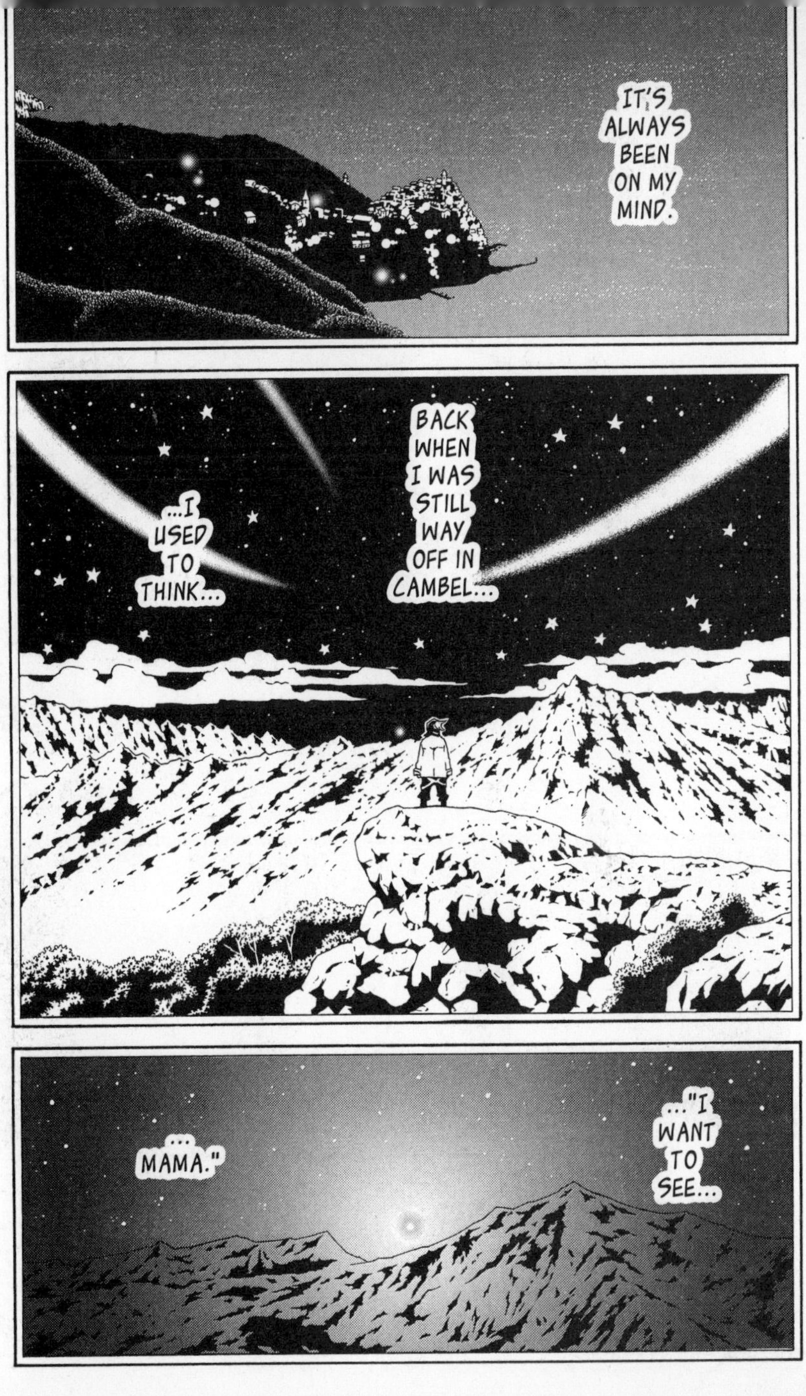
IT'S ALWAYS BEEN ON MY MIND.
BACK WHEN I WAS STILL WAY OFF IN CAMBEL...
...I USED TO THINK...
..."I WANT TO SEE...
... MAMA."

NOW I WANT TO SEE GAUCHE.

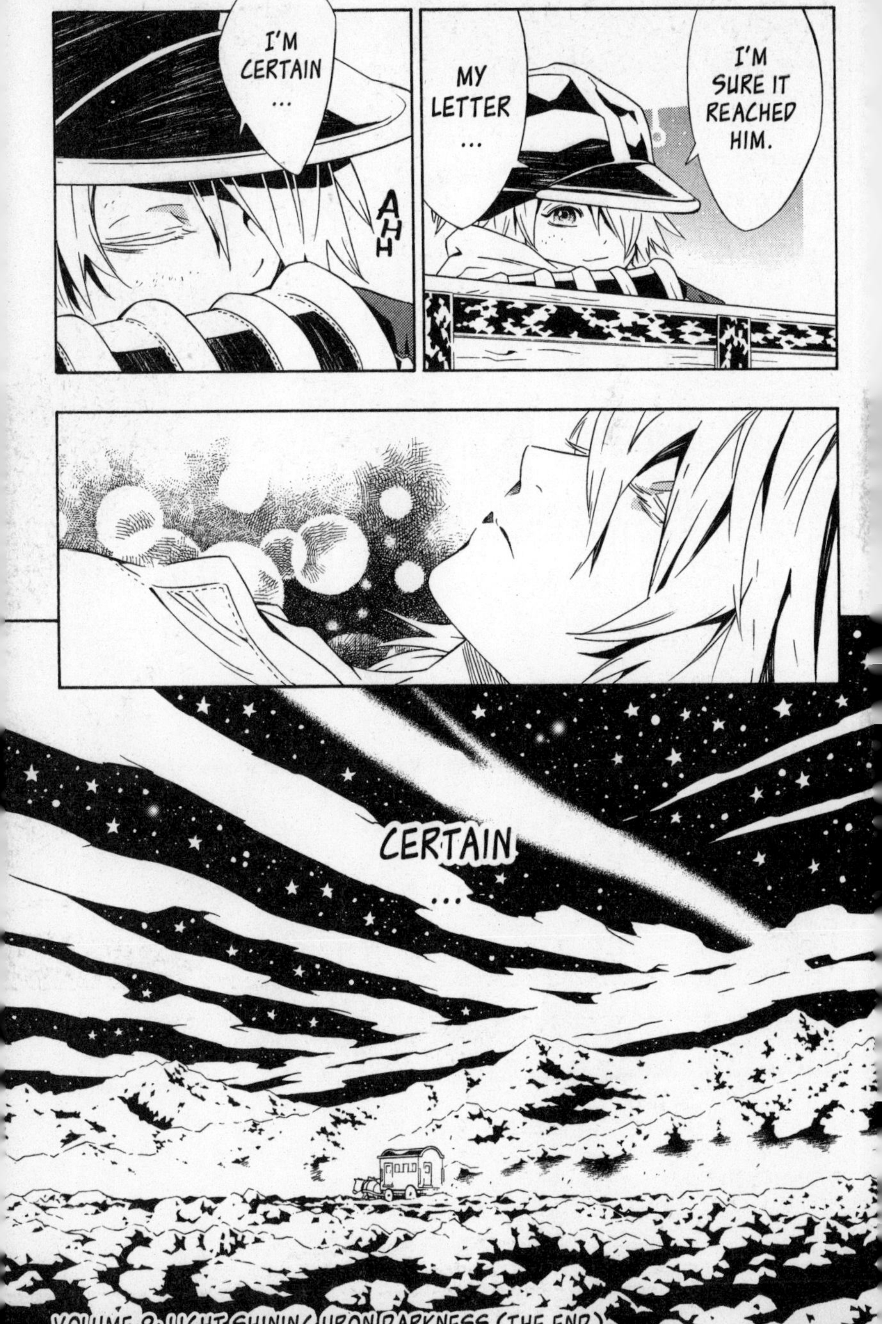
I'M SURE IT REACHED HIM.
MY LETTER ...
I'M CERTAIN ...
AHH
CERTAIN ...
VOLUME 8: LIGHT SHINING UPON DARKNESS (THE END)

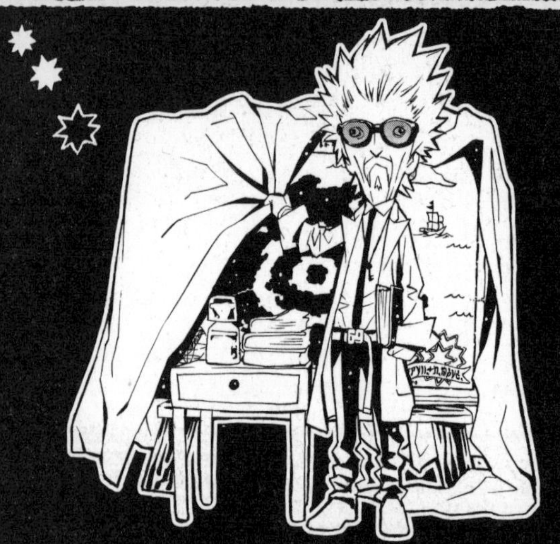
"ΛИ+ŊƏGNɅƐ

Dr. Thunderland's Reference Desk

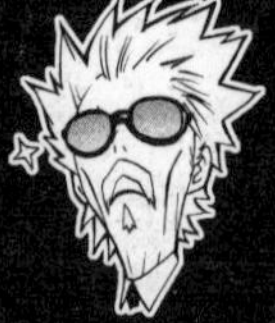

I am Dr. Thunderland.

What a shame! *Such* a shame!! They were so close!!

Lag and his friends didn't return to Hachinosu, where I live! Oh man!! I can't stand it! Quit teasing me!

Volume 9! That'll be my big debut! Forget about volume 8; it's nothing but filler!

For the record, I work at Hachinosu in Yuusari, conducting crucial research every day. Visit me! Come on! I want to review the discoveries about the world that were revealed in this volume! Come on, baby!

Oh…I can't take this waiting much longer.

Hurry up, Lag! Leap into my arms!

■ LAMENT TOWN
nb: lament (English), *lamentazione* (Italian) / Poetry or music expressing grief, sorrow or regret.

■ VERITY CONVENT
I already described this place in the previous volume! Okay, okay. It's a review. Heh... This convent is for those who worship the Empress of Amberground. They believe that "work is prayer," so they live mostly self-sufficiently. They earn their living by selling the wines that they make...and convent cookies. How amusing!

Now it looks like this convent was under the control of Reverse. The nuns of Verity, though poor, took in the abandoned children of Yodaka. By offering financial support and exploiting the faith of the nuns, that darn Reverse turned them into human sacrifices. What scoundrels! I hope I get to show them what for in the next volume! Ooh, I'm looking forward to that. Sunny was such a sweet child; Connor too. But hey, that Lala was almost dangerously cute.

nb: Verity / the truth, unmistakable.

nb: Sunny / Song by Bobby Hebb; became a hit gold record in June 1966. "Sunny" has been covered by over 200 artists, including James Brown, Marvin Gaye and Stevie Wonder. The song was inspired by Hebb's brother, who was killed in a robbery in 1963.

nb: Mil Mascaras / a Mexican *lucha libre* masked wrestler. His name means "A Thousand Masks."

■ FLYING CABERNET
The larva that Noir awakened from the ice pillar in Blue Notes Blues developed into a flying Gaichuu called "Cabernet." Reverse had been stealing letters to lure the Gaichuu to the capital. What scoundrels! (But I repeat myself.)

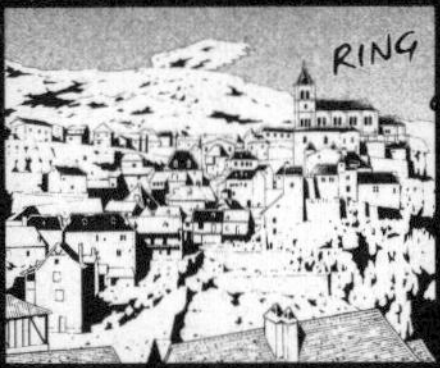
RING

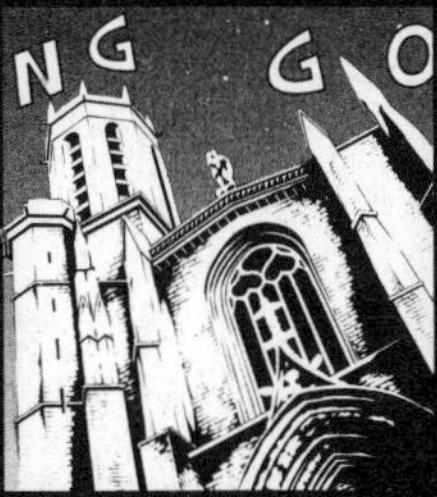

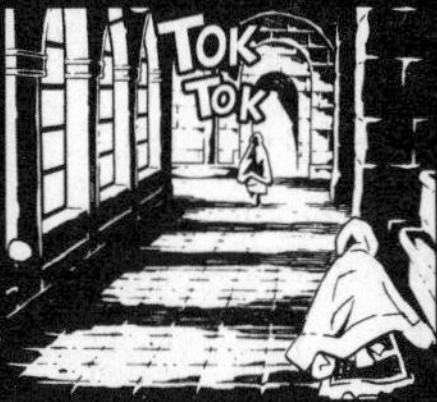
TOK
TOK

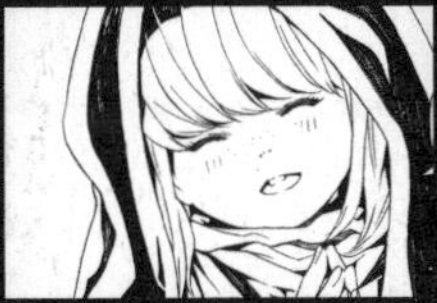

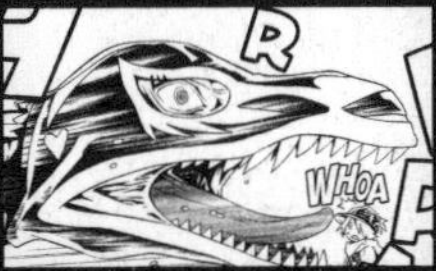
WHOA

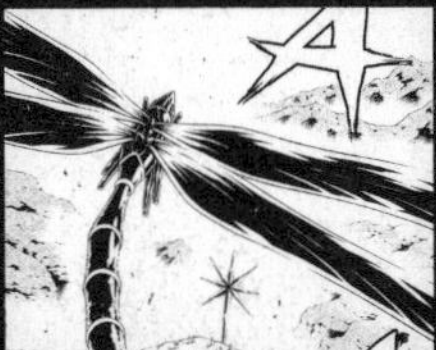

It's amazing that such a gigantic beast can actually fly, but according to Noir (or is it Gauche?), it has a number of weak points. It's still a fearsome foe. Even Zazie seemed to think they couldn't defeat this terrible Gaichuu. Noiche (let's call him Noiche) and Lag managed to drive the Gaichuu away by firing their twin shindan, but where could it have disappeared to? Can its missing wing regenerate? If so, it's probably biding its time somewhere, building up its strength. That could mean trouble... They'd better hurry up and come get advice from me! Right? Right! Come on!

nb: Cabernet Sauvignon / variety of grapes used in the common red wine of the same name.

■ ARTIFICIAL SUN

The capital, Akatsuki, has a small artificial sun that fully lights only the capital. In Yodaka, where it shines like the moon, not only are people less affluent, the light in their *hearts* seems more ephemeral. Perhaps, as Noir says, the artificial sun is the symbol of an unequal society. Reverse intends to destroy the artificial sun and plunge the whole world into darkness. What scoundrels! (Third time...) I will destroy them!! Follow me!! Worship me!! In the next volume, the world will be shaken...because I will shine...

But the Man Who Could Not Become Spirit...I think his name was Lawrence. What could he know about the capital? I worry about that.

■ LIGHT

Lag lit up nice and bright, didn't he? What the heck was that all about? I remember Niche's sister said something about "light" in volume 7. I thought Lag Seeing was just a crybaby, but he sometimes displays tremendous power of *heart*. He's a remarkable boy.

Ignoring Zazie, whose level of *heart* was low, Cabernet attacked the weakened Lag. Even so, Lag shot the Gaichuu and sent it fleeing. Hmm...Yes, Lag must be studied at length. In volume 9! By me, Thunderland! Oh, and Roda too! She must be studied! I theorize that she may have been fused with the first Roda, the dog! I must investigate that! Give me a line like, "Out of the lab, fools! My research is about to begin!" Ah, yes! Hooray!

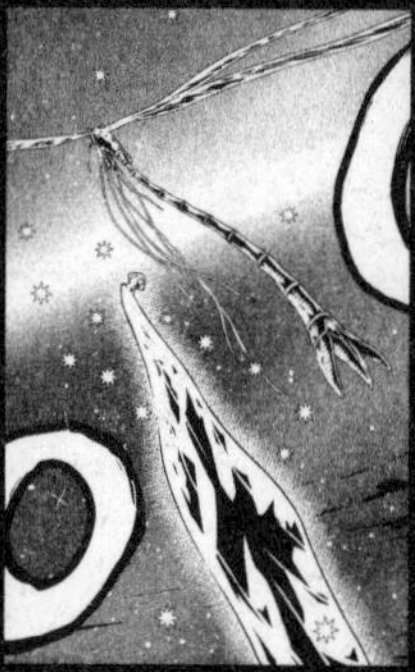

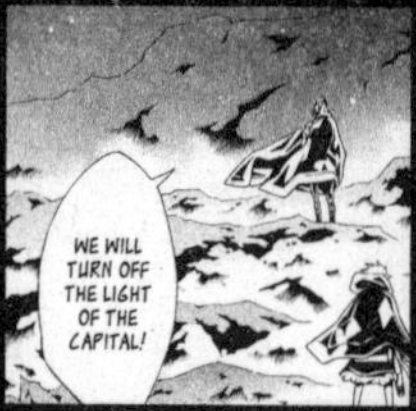
WE WILL TURN OFF THE LIGHT OF THE CAPITAL!

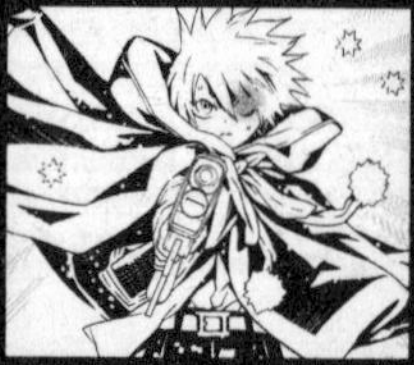

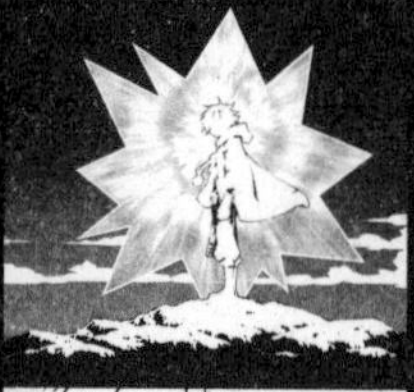

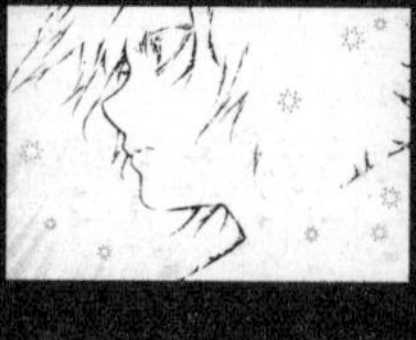

Route Map

Finally, I am including a map indicating the route followed in this volume, created at Lonely Goatherd Map Station of Central Yuusari.

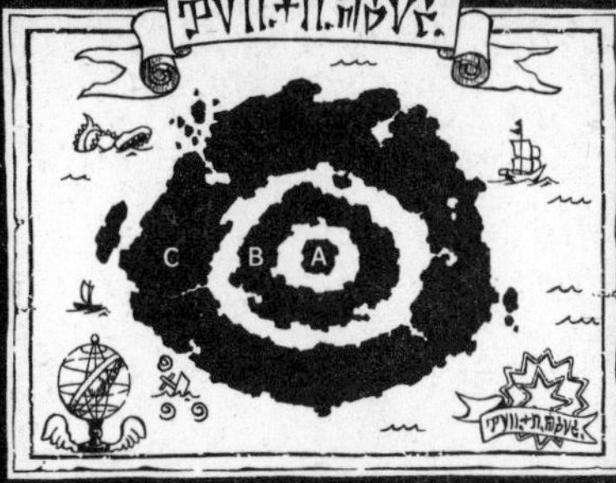

C
B
A

A: Akatsuki B: Yuusari C: Yodaka

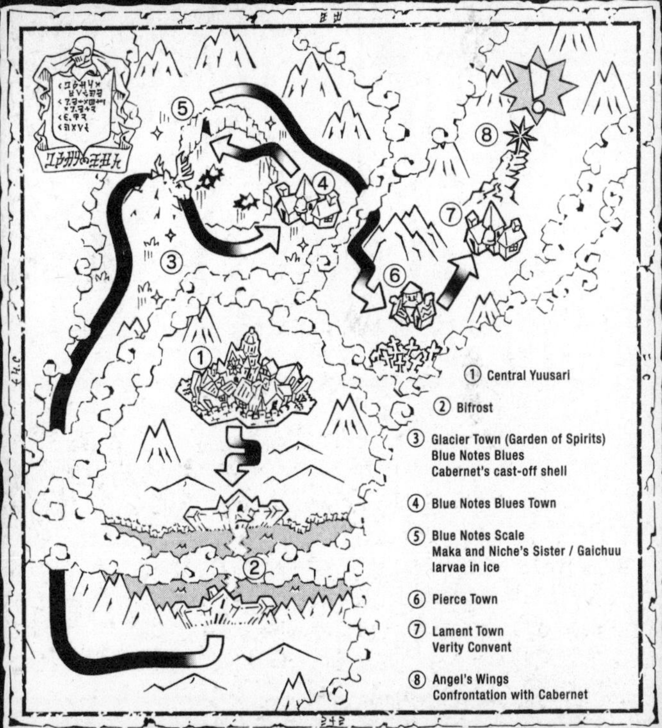

① Central Yuusari
② Bifrost
③ Glacier Town (Garden of Spirits)
Blue Notes Blues
Cabernet's cast-off shell
④ Blue Notes Blues Town
⑤ Blue Notes Scale
Maka and Niche's Sister / Gaichuu larvae in ice
⑥ Pierce Town
⑦ Lament Town
Verity Convent
⑧ Angel's Wings
Confrontation with Cabernet

There? Have I had my revenge? Will you no longer ignore my plight? I'm not asking for much here—just pay attention to me! And maybe put me in the book! And…a cover spread wouldn't hurt either, now that I think about it. Can't you just picture it? Me in full color, leaping into action? Just give me a chance here!

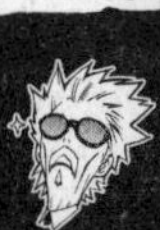

In the next volume...

The Dead Letter Office

Lag has finally found Gauche Suede—but their problems have just begun.
When two agents of the Amberground government show up at the Beehive
to take Gauche away, the Letter Bees realize they've stumbled on a deadly
conspiracy...

Available May 2012!

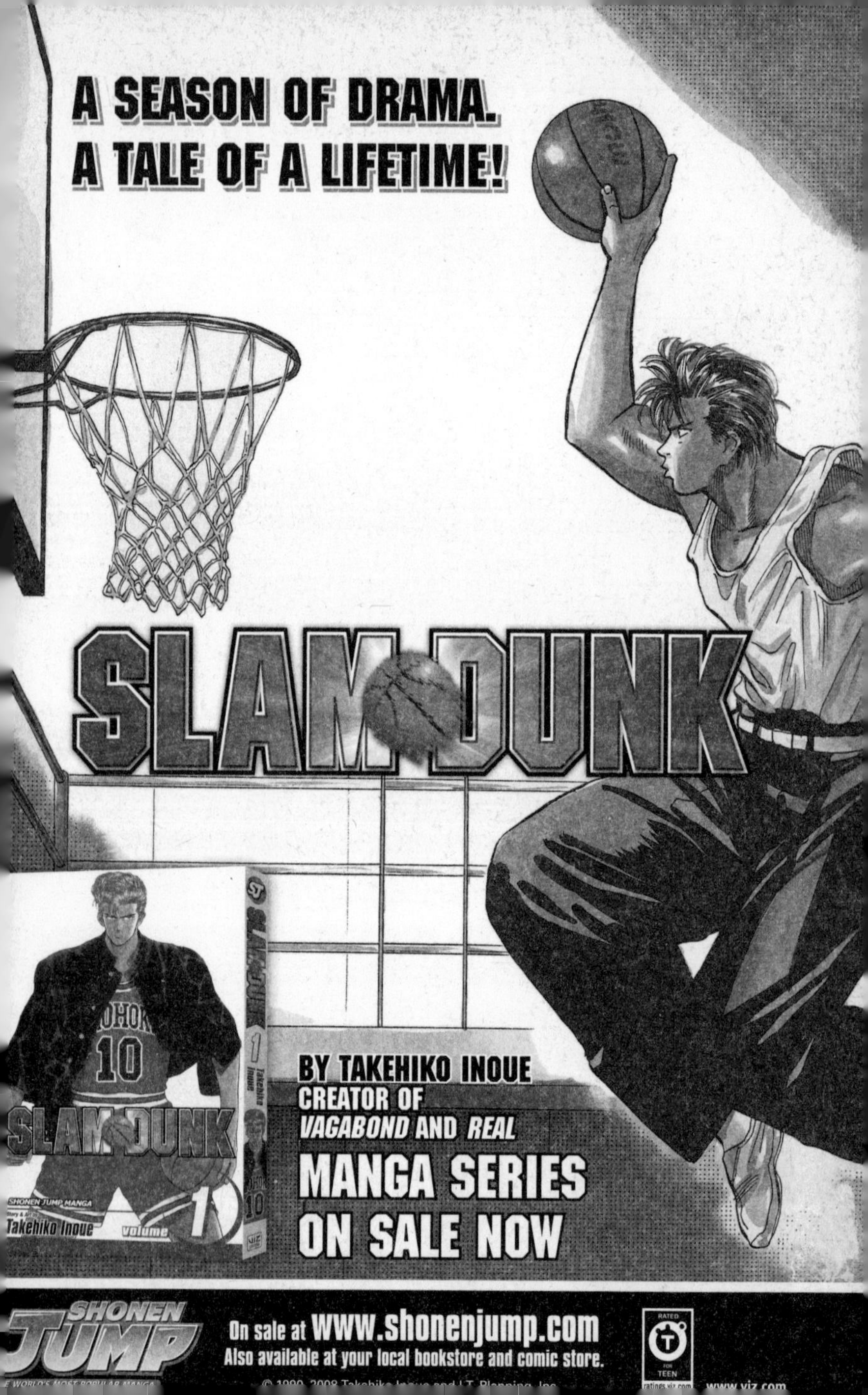

A SEASON OF DRAMA.
A TALE OF A LIFETIME!
SLAM DUNK
SLAM DUNK
SHONEN JUMP MANGA
Takehiko Inoue
volume 1
BY TAKEHIKO INOUE
CREATOR OF
VAGABOND AND REAL
MANGA SERIES
ON SALE NOW
SHONEN JUMP
On sale at WWW.shonenjump.com
Also available at your local bookstore and comic store.
RATED T FOR TEEN
www.viz.com

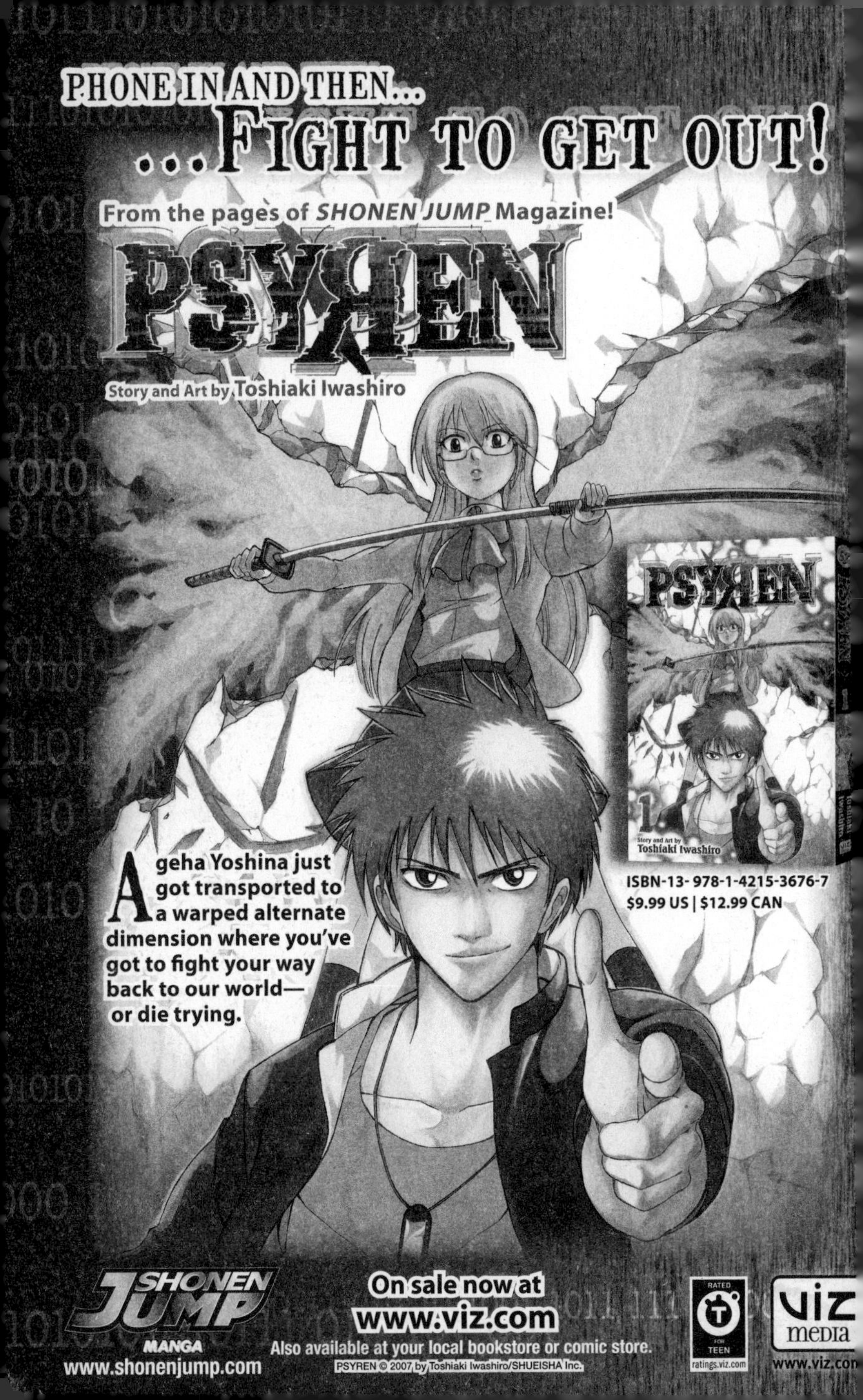
PHONE IN AND THEN...
...FIGHT TO GET OUT!
From the pages of SHONEN JUMP Magazine!
PSYREN
Story and Art by Toshiaki Iwashiro
PSYREN
1
Story and Art by Toshiaki Iwashiro
ISBN-13- 978-1-4215-3676-7
$9.99 US | $12.99 CAN
Ageha Yoshina just got transported to a warped alternate dimension where you've got to fight your way back to our world—or die trying.
SHONEN JUMP
MANGA
www.shonenjump.com
On sale now at
www.viz.com
Also available at your local bookstore or comic store.
PSYREN © 2007 by Toshiaki Iwashiro/SHUEISHA Inc.
RATED
T
FOR
TEEN
ratings.viz.com
viz media
www.viz.com

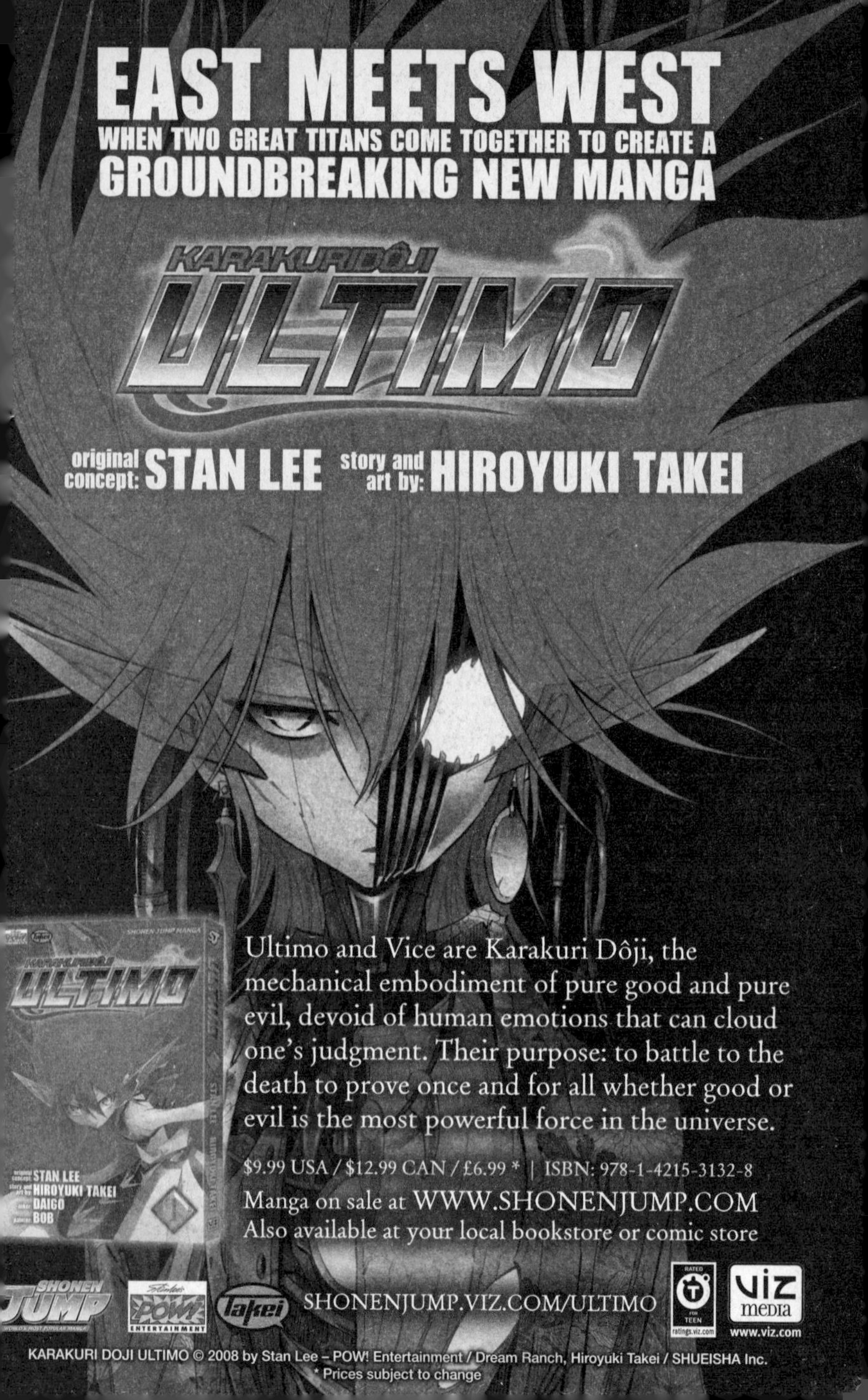
EAST MEETS WEST
WHEN TWO GREAT TITANS COME TOGETHER TO CREATE A
GROUNDBREAKING NEW MANGA
KARAKURIDÔJI
ULTIMO
original concept: STAN LEE
story and art by: HIROYUKI TAKEI
SHONEN JUMP MANGA
KARAKURIDÔJI ULTIMO
STAN LEE
HIROYUKI TAKEI
DAIGO
BOB
Ultimo and Vice are Karakuri Dôji, the mechanical embodiment of pure good and pure evil, devoid of human emotions that can cloud one's judgment. Their purpose: to battle to the death to prove once and for all whether good or evil is the most powerful force in the universe.
$9.99 USA / $12.99 CAN / £6.99 * | ISBN: 978-1-4215-3132-8
Manga on sale at WWW.SHONENJUMP.COM
Also available at your local bookstore or comic store
SHONEN JUMP
WORLD'S MOST POPULAR MANGA
POW! ENTERTAINMENT
Takei
SHONENJUMP.VIZ.COM/ULTIMO
RATED T FOR TEEN
ratings.viz.com
VIZ media
www.viz.com
KARAKURI DOJI ULTIMO © 2008 by Stan Lee – POW! Entertainment / Dream Ranch, Hiroyuki Takei / SHUEISHA Inc.
* Prices subject to change

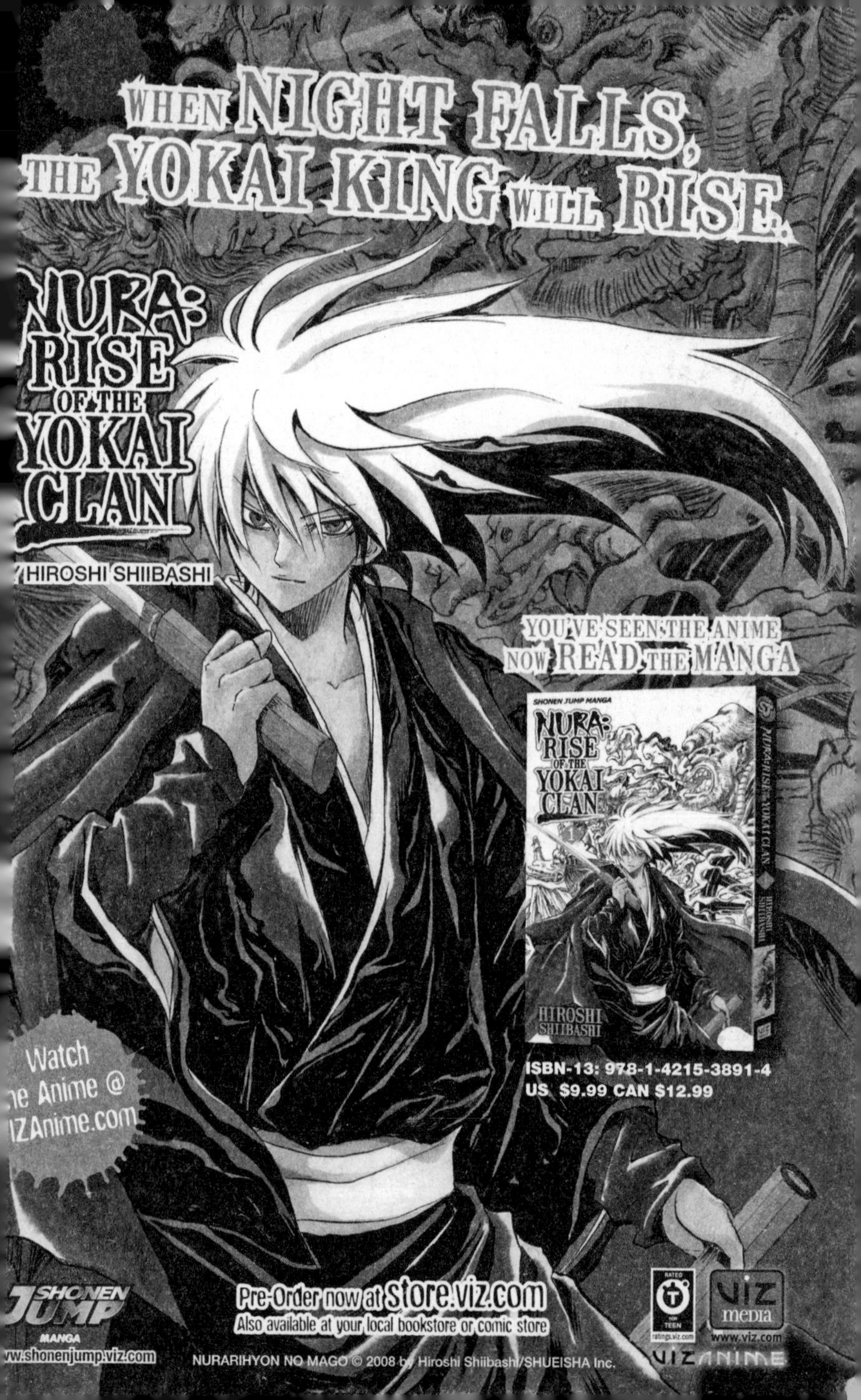